Anthropology, by Comparison

Comparison has long been the backbone of the discipline of anthropology. But recent developments in anthropology, including critical self-reflection and new case studies sited in a globalized world, have pushed comparative work aside. For the most part, comparison as theory and method has been a casualty of the critique of 'grand theory' and of a growing mistrust of objectivist, hard-science methodology in the social sciences.

Today it is time for anthropology to resume its central task of exploring humankind through comparison, using its newfound critical self-awareness under changing global conditions. In *Anthropology, by Comparison* an international group of prominent anthropologists re-visits, re-theorizes and re-invigorates comparison as a legitimate and fruitful enterprise. The authors explore the value of anthropological comparison and encourage an international dialogue about comparative research. While rejecting older, universalist comparative methods, these scholars take a fresh look at various subaltern and neglected approaches to comparison from their own national traditions. They then present new approaches that are especially relevant to the globalized world of the twenty-first century.

Every student and practitioner of anthropology and the social sciences will find this thought-provoking volume essential reading. *Anthropology, by Comparison* is a call to creative reflection on the past and productive action in the present, a challenge to anthropologists to revitalize their unique contribution to human understanding. *Anthropology, by Comparison* is an indispensable overview of anthropology's roots – and its future – with regard to the comparative study of humankind.

Andre Gingrich is Professor and Chair at the Institute for Social and Cultural Anthropology, University of Vienna. **Richard G. Fox** is President of the Wenner-Gren Foundation for Anthropological Research.

Anthropology, by Comparison

Edited by Andre Gingrich
and Richard G. Fox

Foreword by Marilyn Strathern

Key Multiplier Dissemination Copy,
with the Compliments of Andre Gingrich
Wittgenstein Prize
Austrian Science Fund FWF

London and New York

First published 2002
by Routledge
11 New Fetter Lane, London EC4P 4EE

Simultaneously published in the USA and Canada
by Routledge
29 West 35th Street, New York, NY 10001

Routledge is an imprint of the Taylor & Francis Group

Typeset in Goudy by Taylor & Francis Books Ltd
Printed and bound in Great Britain by The University Press,
Cambridge

British Library Cataloguing in Publication Data
A catalogue record for this book is available from the British
Library

Library of Congress Cataloging in Publication Data
Anthropology, by comparison/edited by Andre Gingrich and
Richard G. Fox.
Includes bibliographical references and index.
1. Ethnology–Methodology. 2. Cross-cultural studies. I. Gingrich,
Andre. II. Fox, Richard Gabriel.

GN345 .A579   2002
306–dc21   2001048452

ISBN 0–415–26053–1 (hbk)
ISBN 0–415–26054–X (pbk)

Contents

Contributors

Emmanuel Désveaux is *maître de conférences* at the École des Hautes Études en Sciences Sociales (EHESS) in Paris. He did extensive fieldwork among the Northern Ojibwa in Canada, working on myth, ritual and social organization. In 1999 he received his Habilitation degree from the Department of Anthropology at the University of Paris X Nanterre, submitting a thesis titled *Quadratura Americana: Essai d'anthropologie lévi-straussienne*, which was published in 2001. One of his latest works in English is 'Dravidian nomenclature as an expression of ego-centred dualism', in the 1988 volume *Transformations of Kinship*, co-edited by M. Godelier, T. Trautmann and F.E. Tjon Sie Fat. He was recently appointed scientific director of the Musée du Quai Branly, the new Museum of Mankind in Paris.

Thomas Fillitz is Director of the Institute for Social and Cultural Anthropology of the University of Vienna. His major research topics are theoretical anthropology and the anthropology of art. He has conducted field research in northern Nigeria on political movements and in Côte d'Ivoire and Benin on contemporary art. He recently concluded project direction on 'The practice of intercultural teaching and learning: a case study of eighteen schools in Vienna and Upper Austria'. His most recent publication is the 1999 article 'Globalisierung, Welt der Kunst und zeitgenössische Kunst afrikanischer Künstler' ('Globalization, the art world and the contemporary art of African artists') in the *Mitteilungen der Anthropologischen Gesellschaft Wien*.

Richard G. Fox is President of the Wenner-Gren Foundation for Anthropological Research in New York City. A fellow of the Institute for Advanced Study, Princeton, in 1971 and a Guggenheim Fellow in 1987, Fox is the author of numerous books and articles, among them *Gandhian Utopia: Experiments with Culture* (1989). He is the co-editor (with Orin Starn) of *Between Resistance and Revolution: Dissent and Cultural Protest*, published in 1997.

Andre Gingrich is Professor at the Institute for Social and Cultural Anthropology at the University of Vienna and a member of the Austrian Academy of Sciences. He has conducted research and published extensively on local societies, social hierarchies and cosmologies in southwestern Arabia. His other fields of empirical research include territory and polity in Tibet and immigration in Europe. Gingrich's current interests pursue questions of methodology and conceptualization in anthropology. His recent publications include 'Inside an "exhausted community"', in *The Ethnography of Moralities* (Signe Howell, ed. 1997) and his 1999 book *Erkundungen: Themen der ethnologischen Forschung (Explorations: Themes of Anthropological Research)*. He is co-editing, with Alan Swedlund and Elinor Ochs, a special issue of *Current Anthropology* (2002) on inventories of time in anthropological subdisciplines.

Kirsten Hastrup is Professor of Anthropology at the University of Copenhagen and former Research Director at the Danish Centre for Human Rights. She has worked and published extensively on the culture and history of Iceland and on theatre anthropology; her current main interests are theoretical and philosophical. Among her publications of general theoretical interest are *A Passage to Anthropology: Between Experience and Theory* (1995) and 'The dynamics of anthropological theory' (*Cultural Dynamics*, 1997). Hastrup's most recent monograph in English is *A Place Apart: An Anthropological Study of the Icelandic World* (1998). She has edited two volumes related to the present topic: *Human Rights on Common Grounds: The Quest for Universality* (2001) and *Legal Cultures and Human Rights: The Challenge of Diversity* (2001).

Adam Kuper is Professor of Social Anthropology in the Department of Human Sciences at Brunel University in the United Kingdom. His primary areas of research are the history of anthropology, and kinship and the family. He has conducted extensive field research in Southern Africa. Kuper's latest book is *Culture: The Anthropologists' Account*, published in 1999.

Marit Melhuus is Professor at the Institute of Social Anthropology at the University of Oslo and serves as Dean of the Faculty of Social Sciences. She has done fieldwork in Argentina, Norway and Mexico, where she works on issues of economy, morality, kinship and gender. Melhuus is presently collaborating on a research project on the transnational flow of concepts and substances, where her focus is on the flow of genetic substances. Her publications include *Machos, Mistresses, Madonnas: Contesting the Power of Latin American Gender Imagery* (1996), co-edited with K.A. Stølen, and a volume on kinship in Norway entitled *Blod – tykkere enn vann? Betydninger av slektskap i Norge (Blood – Thicker than Water? Meanings of Kinship in Contemporary Norway)* (2001), co-edited with Signe Howell.

James Peacock is Kenan Professor of Anthropology at the University of North Carolina, Chapel Hill, as well as Director of the University Center for International Studies. His fieldwork has been conducted primarily in Indonesia and Appalachia. In 1993–95 he served as President of the American Anthropological Association. Among his major publications is the book *The Anthropological Lens: Harsh Light, Soft Focus* (1987).

Marilyn Strathern is William Wyse Professor of Social Anthropology at the University of Cambridge. Her interests are divided between Melanesian ethnography (*Women in Between*, 1972) and British ethnography (*Kinship at the Core*, 1981). *The Gender of the Gift* (1988) is a critique of anthropological theories of society and gender relations as they have been applied to Melanesia, and *After Nature* (1992) comments on the cultural revolution at home; both are attempts at synthesis. In 1991 Strathern published *Partial Connections*, an exploration of the comparative method. Her more recent publications include the co-authored *Technologies of Procreation* (1993) and the collection *Property, Substance and Effect: Anthropological Essays on Persons and Things* (1999).

Christina Toren is Reader in Social Anthropology and Psychology in the Human Sciences Department and Director of the Centre for Child-Focused Anthropological Research (C-FAR) at Brunel University. She has conducted extensive fieldwork in Fiji, where her primary interests are ritual, exchange processes, kinship and marriage and Christianity. Toren is the author of 'Compassion for one another: constituting kinship as intentionality in Fiji' (*Journal of the Royal Anthropological Institute* (n.s.) 5, 1999), *Making Sense of Hierarchy: Cognition as Social Process in Fiji* (1990) and *Mind, Materiality and History: Explorations in Fijian Ethnography* (1999).

Jan J. de Wolf is Associate Professor in the Department of Cultural Anthropology, Utrecht University, the Netherlands. He did fieldwork among the Bukusu of western Kenya. His main interests are the history of anthropology, religion, folk-tales and rural development. He is the author of *Eigenheid en samenwerking: 100 jaar antropologisch vereniginglevent in Nederland* (*Identity and Interdisciplinarity: 100 Years of Anthropological Organizational Activities in the Netherlands*), which appeared on the occasion of the centennial celebrations of the Dutch Anthropological Association in 1998. He also contributed 'Right values and good fortune: Bukusu responses to ecological opportunity' to the 1997 book *African Families and the Crisis of Social Change*, edited by T.S. Weisner *et al.*

Foreword
Not giving the game away

Marilyn Strathern

It is unusual for social (or cultural) anthropologists to be quite so forthright about the kind of programme that this work urges. *Anthropology, by Comparison* invites us to think in three dimensions simultaneously, and thus offers something of an internal comparison between different parts of the anthropological enterprise. The first and third sections of the volume, on anthropology's public responsibility and on new approaches to the comparative method, afford, perhaps, not so unpredictable a combination. What is fascinating, however, is that sandwiched between these two parts you will find a set of chapters unashamedly called 'Reinvigorating past comparative methods'. Too often, anthropologists slink away from their own past as though it were not quite proper or were best passed over. But one of the towering strengths of this book is its simultaneous rejection of some parts of the past and retention of others. It is this call to action that knits the sections together.

I refer to these parts as CM1 (Comparative Methods 1) and CM2 (Comparative Methods 2), respectively. The authors reject CM1 *in toto*, while wishing to retain many elements of CM2 – or perhaps not so much retain as recall. One of the aims of this collection is to inform those who do not know, or have forgotten, what the 'comparative method' has been about at various junctures in anthropology's history. Throughout much of that history, CM1 overshadowed a veritable multiplicity of such methods (CM2), a heterogeneous spectrum of middle-range strategies, mainstream and subaltern, that sustained the discipline along numerous lifelines (to use Richard Fox's phrase). Individual cases aside, the book claims it is precisely that pluralism which anthropology needs to carry forward.

And what is so emphatically rejected here? I am not going to give the game away, but I do just note that it was the most heavily programmed twentieth-century methods (CM1) that seem, in the end, to have had the shortest lifespan. Andre Gingrich and Richard Fox will be throwing out other dinosaurs as well, including certain claims to theoretical synthesis, although I would not chuck them into quite the same swamp myself. Let me remain with CM1, however, and especially with the comparative methods the editors refer to as 'scientific' and 'objectivist'. I wonder if we should not be rewriting this vocabulary. For the overall effect of this book is so liberating that it invites recasting some of the terms of its own critique – and widening the horizons of comparison.

Take the charge of the 'hard-core scientific' nature of CM1, for instance. The move from CM1 to CM2 is nothing if not reminiscent of the move from the Mode 1 to Mode 2 type of knowledge production that Gibbons and his colleagues (1994) have identified from *within* science. Scientific practice now faces new pressures to take social contexts into account. Of course, Gibbons *et al.* are talking about knowledge production rather than about methods or models, and thus about practices (heterogeneity of institutional support, multi-sited locations, social accountability and reflexive engagement with non-scientists) that change not the procedures but the environment of scientific work. Nonetheless, the 'growth of uncertainty' to which they subsequently refer (Nowotny *et al.* 2001) is also one of the contemporary contexts for the approach we shall see advocated by Gingrich and Fox. But if the social context of Mode 2 science is in tune with the newly invigorated anthropological methods advocated here (CM2), this raises interesting – and comparative – questions about antecedents. One might ask of scientific practices of knowledge production what might be recovered from past practices there. A distinctive challenge laid out in this anthropological collection is how to pace oneself for a future that is not ashamed of finding 'old' as well as 'new' resources.

Perhaps this volume could encourage a way of thinking that goes beyond the pejoratives of 'objectivism', too. Several chapters are going to suggest – although not in so many words – that what was at fault in CM1 was not objectification as such (do we not want to make new objects of ethnographic knowledge?), but something about the way comparison was being programmed. That is, it is not so much that items of information were decontextualized, or treated as descriptively unproblematic entities, but rather that the operations done on them have turned out to be *uninteresting*. Let me expand the observation.

Critics have tended to focus on the limitations of the initial categories, and Adam Kuper will show us that the boundary problem is not confined to anthropological comparativists, either. Deep in the ethnographic and regional comfort zones of the anthropological enterprise are other actors doing similar things; one has only to look, for example, at the way the political map of Southern Africa has been drawn and redrawn around its diverse populations. It cannot be, however, that decontextualization or reification are errors in themselves, any more than the capacity for connection is a virtue in itself. They are essential, if partial, staging posts in the way knowledge is created, and part, in turn, of what knowledge creates: unique objects for reflection. (The other side of the same coin is that knowledge creates relations between things: anthropologists would be the first to acknowledge that epistemological objects at once contain relations within themselves and are intrinsically relatable to others.)

Now, when a programme goes wrong, it must be because it fails to produce anything. What we need to know is what works – *what does or what does not produce more knowledge.* For some reason, the knowledge that CM1 produced was like an invention that no one – in today's patenting parlance – could 'invent around'. That is, it did not invite further invention; it was hard to see how it could be added to, qualified, introduced into other contexts or travel, like Latour's mutable mobiles – in short, how it could become interesting. It only produced knowledge like itself.[1] The explanations CM1 offered seemed non-generative. One would need to look at – to compare – the CM2 methods that are being advocated here to pinpoint precisely the difference between generative and non-generative information. This is where I would make an exception for some of the theoretical synthesizing that the editors of this collection would also reject; much of it was highly productive. After all, as Gingrich and Fox themselves imply, the real test lies less in the adequacy of the claims (the biggest claim can be done in by the smallest semantic shift) than in the potential of the further work the methods generate.

If one were to adapt James Peacock's slogans, one might have a rubric for proceeding with what this volume so strongly advocates: Think relationally, act uniquely.

Think relationally. It might seem that this is already being done for us. In a globalized world – the second major rationale for this collection – aren't we all already connected? But think relationally, indeed. For a start, what is meant by the global monolith, 'connection'? Are we talking of something like affinity (common circumstances) or consanguinity (common destinies)? Emmanuel Désveaux's penetrating kinship analysis is going to dismantle 'affinity' as a taken-for-granted category, not through today's conventional wisdom of cultural diversity but through a systematic exploration of the logic of relationship within a single set of terms. And if 'affinity' goes, so does any received sense of 'consanguinity', and any assumptions we might make about relations 'between' them.

This warns us to look again at the assumptions of global communication. A problem that jumps out of twenty-first-century imaginings of a connected-up ('globalized') world is the connecting work that the language of connection seems to do. Its epistemological effect (making connections) makes thinkers lazy. Connection also lulls. Like 'network', the very term seems intrinsically benign, desirable; also like network, it gobbles up all the spaces between – a continentalizing empire, leaving nothing that is not potentially connectable to everything else. Yet since this has always been the case (everything has always been connected, give or take new orders of space–time compression), the anthropologist should be interested in 'why now?' Why do we now suddenly start telling ourselves we are all connected? What global–social processes is this language sweetening? Like the human rights discourse with which Kirsten Hastrup opens this volume, what is indisputable as a programme for action may turn out to be less than helpful as a starting point for social analysis.

I take my cue from Andre Gingrich's comments on globalism and nationalism. What does this benign term, *connection*, conceal – especially when it seems to endorse globalism as a kind of super-sociability? On the one hand, we might point to the personalization of communications, as Hart (2000) has projected for money. There are new orders of social spacing here, and the kind of long-distance intimacy afforded by communication systems abuts interestingly onto what Thomas Fillitz will be making of distance comparison. On the other hand, however, we might raise eyebrows at the expectations that seem to accompany new imaginings of intimacy. To think across epochs, as Richard Fox will invite the reader to do, could be a sobering exercise. At the very least, what lies ahead in Andre Gingrich's hypothesis about decaying empires should alert the observer: examining earlier exemplars of globalization, he demonstrates how pan-ideological constructions become manipulated by sectarian appeals. In the case of global connection, one suspects that the more talk there is about connection, the more divisions become visible; that the closer interests in access to resources converge, the more barriers will go up; and that the deeper the rhetoric about sharing common futures, the more things will seemingly require rights protection, proprietorial or otherwise.

Here I would emphatically affirm the editors' intentions. It seems to me that we need the oldest tool kit of all: the kind of critical wariness to which Kirsten Hastrup refers. And that can only come from exercising the most primitive relational faculty: the hesitation that makes one pause (the thought that is already an act), in order to allow a second thought. After all, experience tells us that the character of a thing changes when one places it next to others. Since Thomas Fillitz is to raise the issue, and to anticipate Marit Melhuus's questions: what about art? Art for whom, and whose art is it anyway, and relevant for what? Comparison is fundamental to the critical moment.

But what is true of all human experience, and Christina Toren will underline the point, becomes a unique exercise for anthropology. A comparative mentality becomes a set of disciplinary methods. What we find, however, is that these methods have worked only for short stretches of time. Drawing on two distinctive Dutch traditions of comparative analysis, de Wolf will pose the question of why some traditions have considerable international impact during some parts of their career, whereas other phases of the *same* traditions are neglected or fall into oblivion. More broadly, the book will invite us to think of the difference between the big, futile failures (CM1) and the little, fertile ones (CM2). Each enactment of comparison, and several authors lay out schema for anthropology's century of approaches, often falls short of, is often less than, the intellectual promise of comparison itself.

Now, if we consider that 'falling-short' relationally, if we put it alongside other shortfalls, it begins to look interesting. Think of the ways in which cultures and societies are recognizable entities – up to a point, that is; the anthropologist is the first to admit that they are not (i.e. from other perspectives) 'really' bounded. Or consider the artifice of imagining one could divide social realities into separate domains of action (political, economic and so forth) – denied in the instant they are promulgated. Or the effort to 'translate' meanings – constantly accompanied by disclaimers that no such thing is possible. Translation is impossible in the sense of Evans-Pritchard's aphorism, which both Marit Melhuus and James Peacock invoke, that anthropology's only method is the comparative method, and that it is an impossible one. For in imagining 'method', we see only half of what we do.

Quite apart from the fact that most people probably want to take something more, or different, out of their programmes than what they put into them, is this insight: things never work out according to plan, because operations (the plan enacted as a programme for action) inevitably entail effects that could never be anticipated in the planning.[2] The reason, because of the dovetailing of different orders of knowledge and action, is too obvious to linger on. As most of the contributors to this volume say, one way or another, through this case or that: to speak of generalities is to speak through specificities. And vice versa.

It becomes redundant to turn the coin over. We already know what is on the other side: act uniquely. You can only see with your own eyes, to turn a dictum of Fortes's, and to echo what both Christina Toren and Thomas Fillitz will say in their own specific contexts. As Fillitz spells out, we are not bound to the alleged passivity of Euro-American eyes – elsewhere, the art of seeing can be an explicit activity, and there have even been moments within the Euro-American tradition of high art when 'seeing' has been an invitation to active reflection.

This volume speaks to the uniqueness of anthropological reflection. Comparison is its game in at once the most serious and the most playful sense – not to be given away, but to be played. And with whom does one play but with this or that other side? Adam Kuper's admonition from the past will continue to have its impact: Begin with the problems.

Girton College
Cambridge
June 2001

Notes

1   This is a point at which the analogy with scientific Mode 1 knowledge production ceases to work, for that mode was highly productive of inventions that led to more inventions.
2   Richard Fox offers a case from Sahlins's Hawaii, where the more people acted to sustain their cultural values, the more they put their values at risk.

Bibliography

Gibbons, M., Limoges, C., Nowotny, H., Schwartzman, S., Scott, P. and Trow, M. (1994) *The New Production of Knowledge: The Dynamics of Science and Research in Contemporary Societies*, London: Sage.

Hart, K. (2000) *The Memory Bank: Money in an Unequal World*, London: Profile Books.

Nowotny, H., Scott, P. and Gibbons, M. (2001) *Re-Thinking Science: Knowledge and the Public in an Age of Uncertainty*, Oxford: Polity Press.

Acknowledgements

The present volume is based on contributions prepared for the conference 'Comparative Dimensions in Social and Cultural Anthropology'. The conference took place at the University of Vienna, 12–21 September 1998, under the aegis of the European Union's Sokrates Intensive Programme. The scholars listed here participated in various forms and functions in the conference.

As contributors or conference chairs, in addition to the contributors to the present volume: Maurice Bloch, London School of Economics; Gérald Gaillard, University of Lille; Jean-Claude Galey, École des Hautes Études en Sciences Sociales, Paris; Peter Gow, London School of Economics; Jürg Helbling, University of Zürich; Wim Hoogbergen, University of Utrecht; Joanna Pfaff-Czarnecka, University of Zürich; the late Thomas Schweitzer, University of Cologne; and Ruth Wodak, University of Vienna.

As University of Vienna faculty and alumni discussants: Ulrike Davis-Sulikowski, Richard Gippelhauser, Ernst Halbmayer, Christine Hochsteiner, Wolfgang Kraus, Manfred Kremser, Erika Neuber, Gabriele Rasuly-Paleczek, Elisabeth Reif, Gertraud Seiser, Martina Steiner, Sabine Strasser, Estella Weiss-Krejci and Werner Zips.

As International Sokrates student contributors, from Brunel University of West London: Gillian Evans, Anil Sakya, Aaron Turner; from l'École des Hautes Études en Sciences Sociales, Paris: Alexandra de Mersan, Bibiane Ramersdorfer, Vincent Hirtzel; from the London School of Economics: Alice Forbess, Konstanze M. Frischen, Alpa Shah; from the University of Oslo: Karianne Mörch; from the University of Utrecht: Sonja Leferink, Yvonne van der Pijl, Gerard van Bruinhorst; from the University of Zürich: Sabine Lichtensteiger, Claudia Rossini, Ulises Rozas; from the University of Vienna: Barbara Birkhahn, Barbara Bohle, Jasmine Böhm, Gabriele Brandhuber, Undine Dellisch, Helga Dragosits, Miriam Anne Frank, Claudia Freitag, Florian Gruber, Barbara Grubner, Andrea Hiller, Michael Kimmel, Fernand Kreff, Margot Krismer, Manuela Leopold, Michael Lidauer, Lucia Mennel, Carmen Nardelli, Herta Nöbauer, Heidi Pichler, Sergio Pines, Peter Rohrbacher, Waltraud Schlögl, Olga Sicilia, Angelika Stadlmann, Andreas Stasta, Elisabeth Strasser, Anna Streissler, Jelena Tosic and Clemens Zobel.

The EU Sokrates Intensive Programme conference was organized and hosted by the Institute for Social and Cultural Anthropology of the University of Vienna in cooperation with its partner institutions from Brunel University of West London, l'École des Hautes Études en Sciences Sociales, Paris, the London School of Economics, the University of Utrecht and the University of Zürich. The conference organizers gratefully acknowledge generous support from the Sokrates Programme of the European Commission, Brussels, the Wenner-Gren Foundation for Anthropological Research, Inc., New York, the Austrian Federal Ministry of Science and Transport, the University of Vienna, the Bureau of Cultural Affairs of the City of Vienna and the Institut Français de Vienne.

On behalf of the Vienna Institute for Social and Cultural Anthropology, Andre Gingrich and Thomas Fillitz initiated and designed the conference, for which Thomas Fillitz acted as principal coordinator. Maria Schmidt-Dengler of the University of Vienna's Bureau of International Affairs provided her experience and enthusiasm, without which the realization of the Intensive Programme would not have been possible. Anna Streissler, Helga Dragosits and Jasmine Böhm acted as invaluable assistants to the conference coordinator.

Finally, the conference organizers extend their gratitude to the Board of the University of Vienna for providing financial backing, to Karl R. Wernhart and Walter Dostal, current and former directors of the Vienna Institute for Social and Cultural Anthropology, for their support, and to Dietrich Schüller, director of the Phonogramme Archive of the Austrian Academy of Sciences, for providing the sound equipment. Most importantly, the organizers express their appreciation for the active scholarly, administrative and social involvement of the students, both hosts and guests – after all, the EU's Intensive Programmes are designed for you.

As editors, we have been fortunate in the amount and quality of support we have received from many individuals and organizations. We wish to thank, first of all, the editorial staff of Routledge, UK. The insightful comments of four anonymous reviewers helped to make this a better book; we appreciate their careful readings. We are particulary indebted to Julene Barnes, our editor at Routledge. We thank her for her enthusiastic support of this project, her useful comments on the Introduction, and her skill and patience in guiding the book through review and production.

The editors also thank the School of American Research in Santa Fe, New Mexico, and its then-president, Douglas W. Schwartz, for generously hosting us during a summer 1999 residence that allowed us to finalize the editing of this volume. Additional thanks go to SAR's academic programs coordinator, Nancy Owen Lewis, for arranging our office and living accommodations.

The editors and authors also extend their gratitude to our editor, Joan O'Donnell, whose literary and anthropological expertise contributed not only to the style but also to the form and content of the chapters published here. Many of the manuscripts were given to her in challenging variants of peripheral

English, and their current polished form is due in large part to her sensitivity to nuances of meaning and skill at reading between the lines. In these ways, her contribution was decisive in making this international conversation on comparison accessible to a wider readership.

Funds for the editing and preparation of the volume were made available through a conference follow-up grant from the Austrian Federal Ministry of Science and Transport (BMWV). These and all other funds from the Federal Republic of Austria and any of its subdivisions were received prior to the January 2000 change of government in Vienna.

Every effort has been made to obtain permission for the use of copyright items. Authors and publisher would be glad to hear from any copyright holders not so acknowledged.

Andre Gingrich
Richard G. Fox

Introduction

Richard G. Fox and Andre Gingrich

A familiar paradox currently haunts attitudes towards comparison throughout the social sciences and the humanities in general, and in anthropology in particular. If considered from afar, comparison seems to be the fundamental research tool it always has been, so self-evident that some scholars may not regard it as worthy of closer examination. But when comparison is exposed to close examination, a contradictory intellectual reaction often comes into play, and comparison appears not simple and self-evident but rather as a topic and a method impossible to think about, dissolving into dozens of other issues, pieces and fragments. Paraphrasing what the theologian Augustine (fourth/fifth century AD) said about time (Gingrich 1994), we may fairly characterize this attitude among anthropologists today towards comparative methods: 'When I do not think about [comparison], I know what it is about; but the more I think about it, the more I lose any understanding of it.'

In our view, this intellectual uncertainty with regard to comparison, which ranges from hesitant curiosity to reluctant scepticism, is not completely accidental, and nor is it detrimental. If we recognize that it is not accidental, we must then uncover the reasons for recent scepticism. When we allow that it is not detrimental, we acknowledge that our uncertainty provides a useful starting point for a fresh consideration of the topic.

At first glance, the concept of comparison appears to have been out of fashion for quite some time. As an anthropological practice, however, comparison is in use everywhere – from migration and gender studies to research on ethnicity or elites. A second glance reveals this contradiction between concept and practice to reflect a widespread intellectual impasse: whereas the majority of anthropologists tend to regard comparison as an outmoded methodology loosely associated with obsolete 'grand theories', a small minority still considers comparison the only valid, truly scientific procedure. Ironically, both perspectives share a tacit understanding of comparison that we find to be fundamentally flawed – that of comparison in the narrow, if well-established, sense of a 'hard-science' methodology employed to support some universal theory or meta-narrative.

This volume represents a concerted analytical attack on the validity of such an understanding of comparison in anthropology, and in the social sciences and humanities in general. We believe that this (implicit or explicit) perception of comparison as a quasi-monolithic, coherent, hard-science methodology lies at the core of the prevailing scepticism. In order to break out of this intellectual impasse and make a fresh consideration of comparison fruitful, it is essential to challenge the prevailing paradigm through an alternative conception of a rich *plurality of comparative methods*. These methods may or may not support major theories, but they are not by any necessity tied up with 'grand theory' elaboration.

Such is the programmatic challenge to which this volume is committed, a challenge that stems from a situation of intellectual uncertainty. A number of factors may be identified that both influence such uncertainty and simultaneously indicate the rationale for a new and closer examination. First among them is the general state of anthropology at the beginning of the twenty-first century. By now the postmodern debates of the late 1980s and early 1990s have passed their peak, but their impact on what is and is not taken for granted by most anthropologists has been profound. Much of the established wisdom in international anthropology – in its dominant, mainstream forms between the end of World War II and the end of the Cold War – was seriously criticized, challenged and questioned in these debates, if it had not been already in the late 1960s.

The critical self-inspection begun in the 1960s and 1970s indicted the field of anthropology for its political naïveté, at best, or, at worse, its complicity with European imperialism (Asad 1973; Hymes 1969). The established methodologies of cross-cultural comparison came to be viewed as especially suspicious because they compared what were assumed to be self-contained, stable and highly integrated cultures, when the reality was that all local cultures existed within a single world system integrated by capitalist expansion and absorption. The cultures that anthropologists treated as isolated modules were often, in fact, varieties of social life that had been generated by such expansion and absorption.

In the 1980s this disciplinary self-inspection shifted its focus to the power of anthropologists, through their writings, to inscribe and fix other cultures, to the exclusion of indigenous representations (Clifford 1983; Clifford and Marcus 1986). Again, this critique regarded comparative methodologies as an especially dubious undertaking. For if anthropology's presumed objectivity – the objectivity that had validated cross-cultural comparison up until then – was in fact merely 'science fiction', that is, merely the anthropologist's assertion of authority, then the legitimacy of comparison was undermined.

These various waves of criticism during the late twentieth century cast serious doubt on what previously had seemed a self-evident cornerstone of anthropology. In the 1920s and 1930s many anthropologists accepted cross-cultural comparison as a public responsibility. They not only believed that comparison should be done and could address public issues in significant ways, but also were confident that anthropology could carry out such comparison. Ruth Benedict, for example, set out in *Patterns of Culture* (1934) to compare several markedly different societies. In addition to her direct comparison of three 'primitive' cultures – Zuñi, Dobu and Kwakiutl – Benedict made critical comparisons of their cultural configurations with those of her own contemporaneous US-American culture.[1] Similarly, by use of the comparative method, Margaret Mead expected her work in Samoa and New Guinea (1928, 1930, 1935) to lead to improved social policies in the United States. Before Benedict and Mead, Bronislaw Malinowski had pursued equivalent cross-cultural comparisons on issues of public interest when he questioned the universality of the Oedipus complex (1926, 1927) or when he implicitly contrasted sexual practices in the Trobriand Islands with European norms (1929). These early practitioners were secure in their claim that anthropology could comprehend all varieties of social life, and they accepted without hesitation a public responsibility to make cross-cultural comparisons for the public good.

In retrospect, 'comparison' in anthropology's history is often seen too narrowly as being closely associated with one particular comparative register of the past, the so-called holocultural approach, which gained currency in the 1950s. Holocultural studies pursued functional correlations between culture traits based on statistical manipulation of the Human Relations Area Files (HRAF) data (see Levinson and Malone 1980; Naroll et al. 1976). In their time, these holocultural and statistical sampling methods of comparison appeared to be living up to all accepted standards of a 'truly scientific' methodology – to an extent that had implications for major research funding institutions in North America and (to a lesser degree) Western Europe. Explicitly committed to quantitative procedures and to an objectivist epistemology for elaborating generalizations held to be universally valid, 'holocultural comparison' became almost synonymous with comparative methodology after the mid-twentieth century.

As we pointed out in the first paragraphs of this Introduction, even today there are many who tend to associate any general 'comparison' exclusively with George P. Murdock and this particular intellectual tradition. An only slightly closer look at the discipline's past, however, reveals such a perspective as one-sided and quite useless in understanding anthropology's comparative legacy, let alone in envisioning its comparative potential in the future. Even in their heyday, HRAF-based comparative procedures represented just one (explicitly universalist and objectivist) methodology among several others. This limited number of competing, dominant comparative methodologies of the post-1945 decades varied from universalist to medium-range and regional forms of comparison.

Another form of universalism widely used from the years after World War II through the early 1970s was neo-evolutionist comparison, which proposed stages or typologies of cultural development as having wide validity (Sahlins and Service 1960). Structural analysis, too, in so far as it assumed that cultural diversity was superficial and aimed to discover by comparison of these superficial differences an underlying and shared human cognitive structure, represented still another version of a universalist methodology (Lévi-Strauss 1949, 1958). Medium-range comparative approaches in use in the mid-twentieth century included the investigation of regional variation and of culture areas, and the 'area studies' to which these gave rise. Regional and local-level comparison was prominent in studies of cultural ecology, ethnoscience and certain functionalist approaches. Until the late 1960s and into the 1970s, then, comparative methods were an accepted and secure scholarly resource for anthropologists.

In one way or another, of course, it is true that the dominant and competing comparative traditions of the past (neo-evolutionist, structuralist and holocultural) were closely associated with the grand theories of their time. The critical and differentiated perspective we take here on anthropology's comparative legacy does away with the fictitious 'HRAF monopoly', but it requires two additional qualifications. First, it is important to recognize that a variety of 'subaltern' comparative approaches coexisted, now and in the past, with the dominant traditions outlined so far. Several of these subaltern traditions deserve critical re-examination. This volume intends to stimulate further research along these lines by outlining a number of subaltern examples in past comparison (e.g., Lesser in Fox's paper; Eggan in Gingrich's). A second qualification is our emphasis that comparative approaches in anthropology's history were not exclusively theory-oriented. Most anthropologists today would, in fact, agree that the majority of earlier attempts at elaborating such 'grand theories' by means of comparative analyses were dubious, insignificant or entirely futile. The comparative legacy looks quite different, however, if we inspect not the theoretical, but rather the empirical and conceptual side of the record, particularly within the subaltern spectrum.

One such set of examples is represented by the Manchester school of British anthropology and their work in Southern Africa. Max Gluckman, for instance, was among the first to challenge dominant assumptions about discrete, self-evident empirical units as starting points for comparative analyses. Through his own analysis of 'Zululand' (Gluckman 1958) as a product of colonial and capitalist expansion, Gluckman demonstrated that these units of comparison emerge, within fuzzy and volatile boundaries, at the intersection of wider and more encompassing processes. The point is brilliantly taken up, modified and elaborated by Adam Kuper in this volume. But these critical insights, it must be emphasized, by no means persuaded the anthropologists working in Southern Africa to refrain from comparison. On the contrary, such insights helped them to refine their comparative endeavours in such fields as migration, racism, household organization, indigenous minorities, and so forth.

Another, more recent, case that shows how advances have been made through comparative studies is Melanesia. Indeed, fruitful comparative analyses with an empirical emphasis have been abundant in Melanesianist studies. One need mention only the well-known 'Big Man' debates, in which a broad range of scholars – from different parts of the world and of very different theoretical orientations – participated. In fact, one may justly wonder where anthropology would stand today, if researchers such as Marshall Sahlins, Marilyn Strathern and Maurice Godelier, to name only the most prominent, had not examined regional variation and similarities in local political, social and gender relations over several decades. By developing, applying, re-assessing and differentiating key concepts throughout these comparative processes and debates, these anthropologists not only enriched the discipline's regional knowledge but also produced decisive, bottom-up contributions to anthropological conceptualization and reasoning.

Of course, today many of the grand theories which once inspired comparative analyses in Southern Africa, Melanesia, the Amazon, or, for that matter, in Europe and in urban studies are obsolete. Nevertheless, on the level of conceptual and empirical knowledge, through their errors as much as through their insights, some of these earlier comparative endeavours decisively advanced the discipline.

This implicit use of comparison in anthropology – often not in the service of grand theory but in opposition to it – continues today and provides the rationale for our renewed inspection of comparison in anthropology. Indeed, anthropology, by comparison, required major revision of two recent grand theories: Wallerstein's analysis of the capitalist world system and Said's notion of Orientalism. Wallerstein's theory presumed that capitalism, as it spread out from Europe, transformed the rest of the world to its liking. By use of comparison, anthropologists showed that indigenous resistance to the capitalist juggernaut took many different forms across the globe and frequently forced local outcomes that were less than optimal (Kahn 1980; Mintz 1977; Smith 1976; Wolf 1982). Said's Orientalism and the postcolonial analysis it generated (for example, Jameson 1986) also conflated vast regions of the world as subject to Orientalism and as 'colonial' in an undifferentiated way; anthropologists insisted that Orientalism and colonialism had quite distinctive outcomes as they were put in place around the world (Fox 1985, 1995; Sahlins 1985; Thomas 1994).

To make a fresh start in considering comparison, it is essential to emphasize the heterogeneity of dominant and subaltern traditions in anthropology's comparative legacy and to contrast this analytical and conceptual richness with the many theoretical ambiguities. Today, such a take on the past implies (1) a clear refutation of any alleged monopoly by comparative 'hard-science' methodology; (2) an interest in investigating further the contextually embedded, subaltern traditions in anthropology's comparative legacy; and (3) an unambiguous dissociation from any necessary link between a variety of comparative methods, including their conceptual and theory-oriented elements, on the one hand, and grand theory construction, on the other. The monopolistic, universalist and objectivist claims made in the name of comparison in anthropology today are not necessary. No more necessary is the allegedly essential connection of comparison to grand theory construction.

At the turn of the third millennium, none of these previously well-established comparative methods has escaped the broad critique pervading the social sciences and the humanities since the late 1960s. Some of these methodologies were quickly abandoned by most anthropologists, along with their accompanying theories and epistemologies – often quite rightly so, as we shall shortly argue for holocultural analysis. Others were left at least partially discredited – and sometimes regrettably so, as the chapters in our section on certain earlier methodologies will assert. Still other comparative methods that had already dropped out of the mainstream were buried even deeper under anthropology's critical self-inspection of the 1960s through 1990s.

Cognitive science informs us that humans always compare, whether we intend to or not (Strauss and Quinn 1997). If this is true for everyday life, it is even more likely to prevail in academic labour. Accepting the inevitability of comparison, we might want to rethink where we stand on the issue of comparative anthropology. We might, for example, want to consider which elements from earlier methodologies are still useful, if reinvigorated for present-day research. We might also want to investigate a more innovative approach to comparison by exploring new methodologies that are less rooted in the past. Because these are among the issues that underlie many anthropologists' uncertainty with regard to comparison, they represent key questions to be addressed in this volume.

The contributors to *Anthropology, by Comparison* share a conviction that the time has come to move ahead seriously with these questions. A growing number of indicators currently signal critical re-assessments, fresh re-orientations and new initiatives in theoretical debates in anthropology and related fields. One indicator may be read in the titles of various publications that 'assess', 'examine', 'recapture', 'rethink' or 're-assess' anthropology and anthropological theory in the present.[2] Another indicator is the reinvigorated interest in theory that pervades professional organizations such as the European Association of Social Anthropologists (EASA) and the American Anthropological Association (AAA). Still another indicator, for better or for worse, is the vogue for anthropological topics in such fields as cultural studies, history, political science (Bowen and Petersen 1999) and comparative literature. Finally, the hotly contested theoretical debates inside anthropology over such concepts as culture, society, nationalism, agency, gender and sexuality also reflect a quickening interest in developing an appropriate anthropology for the present.[3] If these indicators betoken a renewed theoretical impetus in international anthropology, as we believe they do, then it is high time to combine this reinvigorated interest in theory with a re-assessment of comparative methods. Against this background, the present volume offers a plurality of theoretical approaches that are situated in the present and that assess the use of comparative methods for specific contexts and problems.

Anthropology's uncertainty regarding comparative methodologies is undoubtedly related to the state of the world at present. In fact, this final factor amounts to a significant theoretical dilemma. On the one hand, globalization in all its aspects – from transnational media flows to mass migrations – connects more and more human beings and makes them experience similar conditions. Individuals may respond to these new interconnections in varying ways: sometimes, converging on their cultural similarities; at other times, conserving or even emphasizing their cultural differences. These global connections and the heterogeneous local responses to them legitimate a renewed comparative agenda for anthropology and related fields. If people all around the globe are increasingly reacting to comparable conditions, it becomes a more obvious challenge for scholars to compare how people react and what results culturally from their reactions.

On the other hand, anthropologists are often confronted with two serious difficulties when they actually set out to meet this obvious challenge of the present and for the future. One difficulty pertains to the myopia imposed on our scholarship by past national traditions of comparative methodology. The second difficulty develops out of the necessity, voluntary or imposed, for anthropologists to meet public responsibility through their comparative anthropological research and, as a consequence, to develop shared standards for doing so. Outlining these two difficulties will introduce our readers to the ways in which this volume, in its overall format and throughout its three parts, sets out to deal with them.

The first difficulty is linguistic, cultural and institutional, rather than intellectual. Even after the critical debates of the 1980s and 1990s, most anthropological approaches in use today are still deeply entrenched in their respective linguistic or national boundaries, and this holds as true for comparative methodology as for general anthropology. To somewhat stretch this point: when anthropologists from the United States discuss early methods of comparison, they will refer to Julian Steward or George P. Murdock (1949); their French colleagues, by contrast, will primarily refer to Claude Lévi-Strauss; and their fellow anthropologists from Germany will most likely refer to diffusionism. 'Retrospective provincialism' might be the appropriate label for this inability to disentangle oneself from anthropology's compartmentalized pasts, in the plural. In a global world, however, referring to only one anthropological tradition is a serious – and dangerous – impediment to moving ahead.

With this issue in mind, the contributions to this volume were invited along two dimensions. First, we wanted to encourage an international dialogue and conversation about comparative research in anthropology today by bringing together scholars from twelve different countries in the meetings that generated these chapters. Although it is true that these scholars come primarily from western Europe and the USA, we see this enterprise as only a first step in breaking down parochial anthropological traditions. Second, we hoped that such an international forum would encourage each contributor to move beyond his or her own 'retrospective provincialism'. As a result, most of the authors represented here share an interest in explaining to a wider, international readership certain valuable (and some retrogressive) elements from their divergent legacies in anthropological comparison. After critically re-assessing such elements from their diverse national pasts, most authors then move on to exemplify, through case studies from their own research, how they combine them with present problems in comparative analyses.

This means of overcoming retrospective provincialism – that is, by introducing valuable elements from divergent national anthropologies and by expediting an international conversation for an anthropology 'of the present' – is best represented in Parts II ('Reinvigorating past comparative methods') and III ('New methods of comparison') of this volume. The contributors achieve the goal in somewhat different ways, some arguing for conserving certain existing methodologies and others insisting on introducing new ones. Our discussion of each of the three sections of this collection will make clear these different approaches. At this point, it is enough to say that the goal of Parts II and III is for anthropologists to overcome this first difficulty, namely, to rise above the different national traditions of scholarship in order to meet the challenge of putting comparative methodologies to work in today's world.

The challenge of putting comparison to work in the world leads us to the second difficulty mentioned earlier: that anthropology must meet its public responsibility. This is the key topic of Part I of this volume ('Comparison and anthropology's public responsibility'), to which we now turn.

Comparison and anthropology's public responsibility

In addition to being a fundamental human cognitive activity, comparison in a more specific sense is basic to all anthropological activities that involve cultural translation. Translation, in this sense, implies analysing and representing human activities and relations in one sociocultural context for audiences (readers, spectators) in another sociocultural setting, which may intersect only to an extent with the first. Such public mediation and representation between sociocultural contexts involve, a priori, some basic comparative assessment of these contexts, carried out by an anthropological author moving between them.

Feminist, postcolonial and other critics inside and outside of anthropology have quite rightly pointed out that such cultural translation and accompanying anthropological comparison usually involve the negotiation of unequal power relations; the entire enterprise, after all, implies intellectual and academic hierarchies that are themselves situated in the wider world. The socio-political preconditions and contexts of such comparative activities therefore must be addressed. The present volume itself, for instance, is unmistakably based on collaborative academic networks related to the European Association of Social Anthropologists and the Wenner-Gren Foundation for Anthropological Research. As such, it brings together (particular groups of) North American and European, female and male, junior and senior voices from anthropology in an initial dialogue at a specific historical juncture. Despite their (encouraging) breadth, these networks do not yet succeed in bringing into the dialogue sufficient numbers of anthropologists from minority groups within Europe and the USA, or scholars from Africa, Latin America and Asia.

The need to clarify responsibly the power-related preconditions for comparative activities, however, is merely one side of the coin. The other side to negotiating unequal power relations concerns how we convey the topics and the results of these comparative activities to the public – and to its hierarchies of power. Anthropologists who pursue comparison encounter all kinds of public demands, ranging from 'accountability' to 'social awareness'. And public responsibility is by no means simply an external moral factor imposed upon anthropologists from the outside; rather, it is inherent in any such comparative project from the outset. We must, therefore, ask ourselves, what are the uses and purposes and the shared standards of comparative endeavours in anthropology?

It should be evident by now that the present comparative project takes very seriously most of the substantial criticism from anthropology's recent past. From the beginning, then, this attempt at a fresh, pluralistic consideration of comparison in today's anthropology includes reflections on our own public responsibility. But these reflections do not represent an attempt at formulating some universal 'code of conduct'; instead, they open up discussion of new ways for assessing comparison and public responsibility for anthropology today.

The authors of the three chapters that make up Part I of this collection argue in different ways that anthropology has a public responsibility to be comparative. They also suggest some of the issues that such a comparative anthropology would have to consider, as well as some of the benefits that anthropology could offer through a comparative focus.

Kirsten Hastrup in Chapter 1 takes up the question of what anthropology has to offer on the troubling issue of universal human rights. Can anthropology, which has invested so heavily in studying cultural difference, now fulfil a public responsibility to speak about human commonalities? Can comparison across societies, the methodology that grew out of anthropology's concern with cultural difference, now argue for cultural unanimity on human rights? Hastrup believes that anthropology is in a position to advance current public debate about human rights precisely because it emphasizes cultural differences and uses the methodology of cultural comparison. She finds that the legal language in which human rights has usually been promulgated and the philosophical discourse in which human rights has often been defended both project essentialized notions of humanity on which to base their universalist claims. Hastrup argues that anthropology's public responsibility is to reinvigorate these 'skeletal' universalist assertions about what humanity is and what laws it must follow with humanity's actual cultural diversity – especially, she maintains, with the 'complex human experiences of undignified behaviour, of violence and of outright evil'.

For Hastrup, anthropology will meet its public responsibility when it translates the violence and evil that people suffer in certain societies in a way that allows this suffering to be understood widely and compared with the plight of individuals in other societies. By such comparisons, anthropology will help to develop an existential appreciation of universal human rights, an appreciation that goes far beyond the bare-bones legalisms and essentialist philosophical speculations about humanity that now undergird our understanding. Hastrup has an abiding faith that humans, cultural differences notwithstanding, are 'imaginable to each other', and she recalls anthropology to its public responsibility to activate this panhuman imagination through a methodology of comparison.

How would an anthropologist, in practice, combine comparative scholarship with public responsibility? Hastrup leaves the question open – no doubt because she feels there are many ways to achieve this end – but the next two chapters in our collection provide case studies of how individual anthropologists have worked to answer public issues by means of comparative scholarship.

James Peacock in Chapter 2 chronicles his own scholarly lifeline – from his early work on modernization in Indonesia to his recent service in higher education – as a continuous effort at what he calls 'action comparison' or 'active anthropology'. What he means is that the comparisons made by an anthropologist do not lead only to external cultural translations presented to audiences. There is also an interior and personal aspect: as anthropologists convert, through comparison, their personal experiences in the field into a professional anthropological identity at home, they develop particular insights and talents for public service. This capacity is Peacock's answer to the question of how to combine the anthropologist's comparative approach with public responsibility. Moreover, it details the particular strengths the comparative tradition gives anthropologists in such service. Peacock's anthropology recognizes itself as competent to take understandings developed from studying Muslims in Indonesia and Primitive Baptists in North Carolina and activate them in service to academic institutions, international scholarly organizations, and the like.

Like Hastrup, Peacock argues for the value, even necessity, of a comparative anthropology that collates these several endeavours. Peacock might have taken up his public responsibility as chair of his university's faculty or as director of a programme to study the American South less readily, and performed his duties less insightfully, had he not had the global perspective gained from his comparative anthropology. Comparison has permitted him to link ethnographic experience in several very different places with global social issues. His answer to the question of anthropology's public responsibility is both more personal and more activist than Hastrup's. Whereas Hastrup reaffirms anthropology's scholarly comparison of cultural difference as an important resource for instructing humanity, Peacock takes it as a resource for the personal instruction of the individual anthropologist – and asserts, moreover, that this instruction must energize the anthropologist into taking public action. Act locally *and* act globally, Peacock advises us. Study locally, think globally is Hastrup's quite different (but not necessarily contradictory) recommendation.

In Chapter 3 Marit Melhuus looks critically at this same issue of the anthropologist's public responsibility, but she approaches it in terms of anthropology's 'relevance'. In using this term, Melhuus highlights the fact that anthropologists are not always, or even often, able to exercise control over whether their scholarship is considered relevant or not. She reminds us that anthropologists' comparative studies of violence and evil may go unheeded by the public, and that activist anthropologists, attempting to act responsibly on public issues, may be thwarted and even rejected by the powerful institutions they hope to serve. Against the very attractive heroic images of the anthropologist as engaged scholar and informed activist that Hastrup and Peacock project (and who would not willingly embrace these images?), Melhuus reminds us that serving public institutions can often subject anthropology to bureaucratic 'quality control' (which is anything but) and can reduce the anthropologist's comparative consciousness to utilitarian and even irrelevant 'training' to qualify students for degrees.

Although Melhuus is wary of anthropology's claim to have control over its ability to speak responsibly in public, she is not pessimistic or dismissive of the anthropologist's need to try to do so. Recognizing the external constraints on anthropology's ability to say whatever it wants, Melhuus then asks the prior question: what exactly *would* we say if we had complete freedom of speech? She thereby begins to move towards a consideration of the canons or standards of scholarship (or personal action) by which anthropology could meet its public responsibility.

Setting such standards for comparative scholarship is essential, and the remaining chapters in this collection work towards this goal by carefully scrutinizing existing comparative methodologies. But setting standards is not purely a scholastic undertaking; it has real significance for the anthropologist's exercise of public responsibility. At a minimum, to set standards allows us to judge the issue of relevance that Melhuus introduces. If anthropology cannot meet its public obligations, is it the fault of anthropology's theory and comparative methodology? Or is it the result of external pressures to be 'relevant' in a bankrupt, bureaucratic way? How will we know, Melhuus asks, unless we set some standards for comparison, unless we are clear about our own methodologies? Melhuus goes on to argue for a seemingly contradictory and certainly very high standard for comparative anthropology: we must, at the same time that we make comparisons across place and time, conserve some of the ethnographic richness, the *context*, as she calls it, of the cultural beliefs and behaviours we study. Underlying her argument is the conviction that in order to make a contribution towards human understanding, anthropologists must engage in 'theory building', and she suggests that it is only by creating what she terms a 'theory of context' that anthropology will be able to proceed comparatively. Melhuus thereby puts forward the important point that 'context' is by no means an argument *against* anthropological comparison, as some have claimed. Rather, a proper conceptualization and theorizing of 'context' (perhaps similar to

Bourdieu's approach to 'practice') seems to be emerging, out of Melhuus's work, as a central asset of comparative methodologies for the present.

This theme of maintaining cultural context while making comparisons is repeated in many of the chapters in Parts II and III of this collection, which make specific recommendations about how this can be done. In this way they begin to bring into open scholarly discussion the characteristics defining comparative methods. The authors suggest that such an anthropology can be accomplished either by reinvigorating earlier methodologies or by inspiring new ones. But before we discuss their specific recommendations, we must recognize what the authors do *not* recommend: all the contributors reject, explicitly or implicitly, certain dominant comparative methodologies that were well established at some point in the past. In keeping with their concern for context, they particularly dismiss the universalist methodologies that promised to find laws, regularities or stages of development that would be applicable to all cultures or to humanity at large. For example, neo-evolutionist typologies – such as the sequencing of human evolution into 'bands', 'tribes', 'chiefdoms' and 'states' – are abandoned in this collection, even when some of the contributors speak of patterns of cultural development. Similarly, the holocultural methodology of comparison, dating back to Murdock's work and building upon the HRAF, pursues what often appear to be superficial or trite correlations at the expense of contextual ethnographic richness. No contributor suggests that there are underlying basic structures – of cognition, of kinship reckoning, or the like – that can be discovered independent of their expression in particular social contexts.

This volume therefore explicitly leaves behind some of the most prominent comparative methods of the past. Ethnoscience, neo-evolutionism and holocultural methodology – each of these sought what we regard as untenable general laws of human behaviour or cognition through methodologies that sacrificed too much ethnographic context for dubious intellectual gains.

The methodological focus of this volume, then, is non-universalist and non-quantitative. Qualitative comparisons clearly prevail here, carried out along various regional, historical, transnational and distant or macro dimensions. Together, they add up to our notion of what comparative methods in anthropology mean today.

To speak of 'the' comparative method in anthropology today seems to us just as myopic as we have indicated it was in the past. This position elaborates a point made by Ladislav Holy (1987) even before the appearance of the postmodern and postcolonial critiques, although it went largely unnoticed at the time. Today, it is possible to move beyond the ruins of a monopolistic claim to one kind of comparison and beyond the stifling of intellectual competition it visited upon anthropology. Now, a rich *plurality of qualitative comparative methodologies* has emerged – none claiming exclusive rights, each offering its insights and evidence – as the next two parts of the volume set out to demonstrate.

Désveaux uses the comparative structural method in a masterful analysis of the kinship sphere, but the results lead him to question basic premises of structuralist theory. He notes, first, that the local system clearly contradicts structuralism's universalist claim about kinship as a system of exchange. Second, his case study challenges the dichotomy of affinity and consanguinity that underlies most comparative studies of kinship. Third, a central element of the local system – an oblique form of 'bifurcate merging' that Désveaux has termed 'skewedness' – cannot be understood independently of the local speaker's gender, which therefore must be introduced from the outset as an analytical category. Désveaux concludes that kinship studies need to be incorporated into overall analyses of local societies and of their wider neighbourhoods. His study thus moves courageously right through the paradox: by pragmatically and creatively applying a comparative *structural method* of analysis, he offers a solution to an old puzzle of classic Native American kinship ethnography. At the same time, he uses his results to dissociate himself critically from certain central, universalist assumptions of *structuralist theory*. In this way, he shifts the problematic away from universalist claims and towards the more open research question of how underlying principles are realized in context and over time.

In the third contribution to this section, Adam Kuper explores regional comparison as a particularly significant legacy within British anthropology. He points out that some of that legacy was established – by Meyer Fortes and Edward E. Evans-Pritchard (1940), for example – by dissociating general 'types' from evolutionist and other theoretical frameworks and by relocating these types, without their prior frames, within a regional scale. Of course, Kuper points out, this did not solve any epistemological or methodological problems of comparison, but rather prolonged them. Kuper argues that regional comparison must actively confront methodological problems similar to those involved in any other comparative procedure in anthropology, including such topics as commensurability, the units of comparison and the question of boundaries.

Presenting examples from his own investigations in Southern Africa, Kuper demonstrates how conceptions about local groups, their sizes and boundaries are the complex outcome of historical processes, local power relations, state politics and other factors. As methodological starting points for regional comparison, such group designations, boundaries and intergroup relations therefore have to be explicitly examined and contextualized, instead of being taken for granted. Kuper proceeds to elaborate how through such work a *longue durée* model of local settlement patterns and their variation has provided a useful tool for historians and archaeologists in parts of Southern Africa. By means of his examples, Kuper is able to show that epistemological and methodological problems pervade any kind of ethnographic analysis. No matter how small or vast the undertaking, comparison is inherent to them all. In conclusion, Kuper makes two additional, and vital, points: first, that regional comparison can in fact be reinvigorated, if subjected to such epistemological and methodological scrutiny and contextualization; and second, that the renewal of comparative anthropology must emerge from engagement with research problems, rather than from elaborating methodologies. This latter judgement is shared by every contributor to this volume, and the injunction is put into practice in each chapter.

Out of their quite different French and British research traditions, Désveaux and Kuper thus both arrive at critical arguments for a new type of regional comparison that is conscious of the limits of its sources, the relativity of its scope and the significance of its connection to theory and context. In a certain sense, both authors represent variants of 'soft' (post- or neo-structural) comparative methods that are interested in identifying local relations with a *longue durée* continuity in time. These *longue durée* relations are not taken as a given, however, but are considered as open research hypotheses and are pursued through regional variations that are themselves embedded within wider local and interregional interactions.

It would be interesting to examine how these two authors confront their different national legacies in comparison while striving towards similar goals. The British anthropological tradition has, by and large, remained somewhat more sceptical than others of grand theory, and this scepticism could manifest in a marked preference for empiricism. But even these periodic swings towards empiricism always met with domestic criticism. In the early 1960s, Edmund Leach (1961), himself a key figure in emphasizing the significance of comparison, issued his famous warning: anthropological inquiries would amount to little more than 'collecting butterflies' if they were not able to move beyond empirical documentation (or, in today's jargon, if they restricted themselves to 'finely grained contexts').

Perhaps priorities similar to those addressed by Leach's warning were also responsible for the initial disinterest on the part of fellow anthropologists in the comparative results of Kuper's work, as has been noted by Kuper himself in Chapter 6. Emmanuel Désveaux, on the other hand, comes from a French anthropological tradition that for most of its history has held grand theory in particularly high esteem. Against this background, it is especially noteworthy to see how Désveaux downsizes elements from the meta-narrative into useful research tools for regional comparison.

In Chapter 7, Richard Fox also attempts to recover a methodology from the past, as he traces out the study of 'historical transformation' in American anthropology from Franz Boas (1896) to Alex Lesser (1933) and on to Sidney Mintz (1985) and Eric Wolf (1959, 1982). Fox's scrutiny of the past differs from Désveaux's and Kuper's, however. The methodology of historical transformation has been until recently (and is perhaps even now) a subaltern tradition in anthropology from the United States. At no time in the past was it ascendant, but Fox is able to trace its history throughout the entire time-span of the national discipline. Lesser's methodology of studying the 'careers in time' of culture traits, though always subordinate in reputation and influence, coexisted with Alfred Kroeber's historical configurations and with Benedict's and Mead's later studies of cultural patterns and key symbols. Wolf's methodology of studying cultural 'lifelines' was less neglected, but it too played a secondary role to dominant approaches in US anthropology, including, at various points, ethnoscience, cultural materialism and interpretive anthropology.

Fox suggests that the methodology of historical transformation is particularly well suited for making comparisons in a world of increasing cultural interconnection rather than cultural distinctiveness. Historical transformation, he asserts, is a very particular kind of comparative methodology, which compares by examining the development of cultural variation over time. It is especially useful, therefore, in studying the outcomes of a single historical process, such as the spread of capitalism beyond Europe or today's course of globalization. Fox demonstrates in his own work on the impact of Indian culture upon transnational flows that the methodology of historical transformation, by focusing on the variations produced by such processes as they materialize or manifest themselves under particular historical and cultural conditions, represents an innovative approach by which anthropology can incorporate history and process into comparative studies today. The pursuit of a comparative methodology through the study of variation over time need not examine only large-scale historical processes, as our discussion of Christina Toren's chapter will indicate.

New methods of comparison

Whereas the chapters in Part II identified and conserved valuable methodologies from the past, the contributions in Part III advance new forms of comparison. The authors of these three chapters pursue innovative methodologies not for the sake of novelty, however, but because the questions they ask require new approaches. Andre Gingrich, for example, queries the effects of recent globalization on the authority of states and on the treatment of national minorities. Christina Toren and Thomas Fillitz argue, each somewhat differently, that existing theories and methodologies cannot effectively analyse the social phenomena they wish to understand, even though these phenomena – enculturation and art, respectively – have long been studied by anthropologists. At issue in all three chapters is the invention of more enlightening comparative methods in anthropology.

Like Fox, Toren in Chapter 8 favours a comparative methodology that analyses the varieties or transformations of a phenomenon that arise over time. For example, whereas Wolf's study of variation led him to ask macro-questions about the varieties of capitalism that were produced as that economic system engulfed new territory, Toren's study of variation is at the micro-level. She concentrates on variation in the attributes of individuals that can arise as a culture is reproduced and transformed from one generation to the next. Her focus is on the developmental process by which children constitute themselves as they grow up – in other words, the process of what anthropologists call 'enculturation', although Toren alters the meaning of this term. Individuals constitute themselves through their intersubjective histories, she argues – that is, through the interactions they have with others, from infancy on.

Calling her perspective 'radically phenomenological', Toren emphasizes a concept of 'intentionality' that she takes from Merleau-Ponty ([1945] 1962). Intentionality means that individuals construct a social consciousness – what could also be termed their cultural beliefs and behaviours – out of their lived experience and the way they try to understand it. Toren calls for a comparative methodology that studies the 'microhistories' of how individuals come into being, which also means how cultural patterns are reproduced or transformed from generation to generation. The term 'microhistory' nicely links Toren's comparison of variations in the development of individuals with the macrohistorical study of variation done by Lesser, Wolf and the other American anthropologists noted in Fox's chapter.

Toren's perspective leads her to make a radical break with three other approaches to enculturation (or 'socialization') and child development. Going against the old enculturation literature, Toren takes the reproduction of cultural patterns as problematic, rather than automatic: if children come to follow the culture of their parents, it is the result of microhistories that have to be studied, rather than of automatic responses to upbringing. Toren also breaks away from Piagetian theory, which supposes that children go through developmental stages unmediated by their lived experiences with others. Toren's emphasis on cognitive development as a (micro-)historical process also dissents from evolutionary psychology's assumption that cognitive development is 'hard-wired' into people. By insisting that individual development is an historical process, Toren recoups enculturation as a fitting subject for comparative analysis in microhistorical transformations.

In a similar fashion, in Chapter 9 Thomas Fillitz examines selected comparative methods of the past and critiques them as inappropriate for his own research focus, namely, African themes in the anthropology of art. In the process, he demonstrates the very limited uses of certain types of regional comparison, in the established context of 'studies of styles' (or 'stylistic provinces'). Fillitz also ranks among the most critical of our volume's contributors regarding holocultural sampling methods. In a detailed examination of various holocultural contributions to art studies, he outlines the clear epistemological and empirical limitations of this method; by tracing Euro-African interactions in the field of art, he moves on to demonstrate that global flows are nothing new in this sphere. An anthropology of art, Fillitz argues, therefore has to be comparative from the outset: it must pursue a 'distant comparison' of the processes and results that are involved from all sides in these cultural flows – within Africa itself, and between Africa and Europe – while simultaneously studying the variations of meaning attributed by the artists to their work. Thus transcending what art historians usually study, such an anthropology of art also has to include aesthetic dimensions relating to the individual artists as well as to the art worlds they inhabit. The cases of two African artists, Youssouf Bath and

Georges Adéagbo, exemplify Fillitz's arguments. In conclusion, Fillitz argues that such anthropological studies of local art, its flows and its variations, also have to include clients' perceptions, which in today's world always bring in a global market factor.

Like Fillitz, Andre Gingrich takes the global condition as his starting point in the final contribution to this volume. Gingrich argues that the present phase of globalization implies a shift away from states to a stronger emphasis on transnational and local factors. This shift gives a renewed impetus for comparative endeavours in an anthropology for today because state violence may represent a reaction to precisely these local and transnational developments. Gingrich, in fact, identifies a whole series of recent anthropological studies in what he terms 'distant' or 'macro-' comparison, such as those of Eric Wolf (1998), Margaret Lock (1995), Bruce Kapferer (1989) and Ulf Hannerz (1992). Drawing on these works and selected elements from among anthropology's methodological legacies, he outlines a methodology of 'controlled, self-reflexive macrocomparison', which he then sets out to apply.

Gingrich's case study concerns the decay processes of the Ottoman and Habsburg empires at the end of World War I and in its aftermath. After identifying the similarities linking these cases, Gingrich posits an explanation for the decay of such multi-ethnic, semi-agrarian empires: if no alternative gains an early hold on mass opinion, the 'dethroned majorities' may easily be seduced by radical pan-nationalism once they face defeat, poverty and secession. Such a rise in pan-nationalism may lead to an ideological 'primordialization', through mass appeals for revenge against alleged humiliation by 'external and internal enemies'. Too frequently, the terrible result of such processes is mass violence against local minorities. After considering this hypothesis for the 1999 Kosovo crisis as well, Gingrich draws a methodological conclusion: self-reflexive, controlled macrocomparison is a qualitative, open research process that can shed additional light on individual local cases and at the same time has the potential to enrich anthropological theories – in this case, those that address nationalism across time and place.

By now, it must be clear that we use the term 'comparative methods in anthropology' in a radically new way. In our usage, it does not refer to the HRAF-style holocultural studies with which it was once commonly identified, nor does it invoke other universalist methodologies such as the stage theories of neo-evolutionism or Piagetian development. We intend, with this unconventional usage, to reclaim a variety of comparative qualitative methodologies, and, even more, to bring these methodologies up again for an open and measured scholarly consideration. We had initially subsumed these methodologies under a single label of 'cross-cultural comparison', but astute readers pointed out the limited methodologies implied by the term. Many anthropologists today, even while employing comparative methodologies, are critical of the isolationist and static understanding of 'culture' implied in 'cross-cultural comparison', and other anthropologists who make comparisons come from scholarly traditions that never used the culture concept. Rather than restrict our inspection of comparative methodologies to those of the 'cross-cultural' variety, we have chosen to address the full spectrum of anthropologists who do their work by comparison.

Anthropology, by Comparison argues the case for a new, pluralistic comparative agenda in anthropology and related fields, an agenda lent a special urgency by the current phase of advanced globalization. Recent criticisms of older anthropological paradigms make it possible to abandon any exclusively objectivist, universalist and quantitative understanding of comparison. The new, pluralistic and primarily qualitative conception of comparative methods in anthropology recognizes from the outset that asking fundamental questions about human commonalities and differences – now as well as in the past – always involves the negotiation of unequal power relations between and among the networks and processes of social actors under study, the author(s), and the audience or readership. This is why the new pluralism in comparative anthropology strives to address shared standards and public responsibility, instead of taking the status quo for self-evident and for granted.

Such a basic shift of perspective also allows new approaches to anthropology's legacy in comparison. We have pointed out that along with a limited number of competing, dominant methods of comparison linked to the construction of grand theory, there often coexisted subaltern procedures of anthropological comparison. Some of them may be regarded, in a transformed and recontextualized manner, as helpful precursors of present tasks. This is particularly important today, when global anthropological networks of scholars need to overcome 'retrospective provincialism' in order to meet common intellectual and practical challenges.

Anthropology's comparative legacy therefore cannot be reduced to a timeless stalemate between confirmed relativists and confirmed universalists, emanating from a founding fathers' conflict (e.g. Boas vs. Morgan). Such a sharp dichotomy was relevant only for very specific periods in anthropology's history, and even then only within certain academic contexts. In a global historical perspective, the middle ground and the subaltern traditions are at least as significant as the dominant extremes of the past. Furthermore, the record of regional and historical comparison shows that, in practice, comparative projects often were able to contribute productive empirical and conceptual advances in anthropological knowledge, whereas the uses and abuses of comparison for elaborating grand theories remained ambiguous and doubtful.

We believe this volume demonstrates how such a broader, more nuanced and more differentiated approach to anthropology's comparative legacy will be useful and inspiring for a new comparative agenda. As has been shown, the 'units of comparison' need not be accepted as discrete, homogeneous and stable entities at all. Indeed, understanding them as the differentiated, changing results of wider developments, within their fuzzy boundaries, is essential for the new pluralism in anthropological comparison. It was likewise indicated that

medium-scale theory may – and indeed should – inspire the pluralistic comparative endeavours of the future. As Edmund Leach pointed out half a century ago,
scepticism about 'grand theory' is no reason to adopt a false empiricist alternative. The public responsibility and intellectual challenges of the present
demand wider answers from anthropologists, answers that move beyond the
empirical and particular context to search for underlying forces, factors or principles as open research questions. This kind of search must be problem-oriented
and theory-inspired at the same time. Problem-oriented, theory-inspired
approaches to pluralist methods of comparison that take fluid, historical, differentiated 'units' as their starting point – these are some of the results for an
anthropology of the future from our alternative excursion into anthropology's
comparative past.

To recap the key points made here, we believe that anthropology today is
facing three dimensions of comparison. First are the basic, or cognitive dimensions of comparison. Humans always compare; comparison is an essential
element of human life and cognition. Since anthropologists study humans and
are themselves human, the question can no longer be whether or not anthropologists should pursue comparison. Rather, the question is *what kind of
recognition* scholars give to this basic human activity. The cognitive dimension
of comparison is, in fact, relevant for scholars of all fields, and particularly for
those working with human beings.

Second are the implicit (what in a philosophical sense might be termed
'weak') or methodological dimensions of comparison. This second dimension of
comparison is more specific to anthropology and related fields. Wherever they
work, anthropologists are always involved in the active pursuit of methodological comparison, at least to a minimum extent. In our writing, speaking or
filming about local or historical contexts, as anthropologists we always address
others who come, for the most part, from different contexts. Even a confirmed
relativist is involved in such elementary sociocultural translation, which usually
involves the use of terminologies from both contexts; of necessity, such 'translation' involves a minimum amount of systematic comparison between them. The
false 'us and them' dichotomy is no more than a bad caricature of these hierarchical, power-laden and partially intersecting double contexts of analysis and
publication.

Third are the explicit ('strong', in the philosophical sense) or epistemological dimensions of comparison. We hold that, whether or not they acknowledge
it, all anthropologists pursue the first two dimensions. By contrast, this third
dimension designates a more specific interest in certain anthropological
research procedures. This is the domain of explicit comparative inventories – a
domain in which a previously dominant, narrow (objectivist and universalist)
paradigm has dissolved and become peripheral, while a broad new pluralism of
qualitative methods is emerging. This volume begins the exploration of this
new comparative pluralism by identifying three main registers within it. One
register is the study of *regional variations* within fuzzy, historically shaped bound-

aries. A second, related set of procedures is the study of *temporal variation and diffusion* that can move along two lines: (1) processes of generational transmission, or (2) historical processes. Finally, *distant or macro- comparison* of a limited number of selected topics represents a third register proposed here.

Differing in this regard from the implicit ('weak', or methodological) dimension, the plurality of explicit ('strong') variants is openly interested in the results of comparative analysis itself. Explicit comparison wants to know if any of these pluralistic comparative procedures might contribute wider (or additional) results and deeper insights than have already been delivered by individual analyses in specific contexts. Implicit comparison therefore leaves the task of explicit comparison either for a later time or for others – but it is not intrinsically opposed to explicit comparison. Likewise, explicit comparison is by no means dismissive of 'weak' comparison, but rather relies on it, requires it and tries to build on it. Without assuming to represent a superior or better path, explicit comparison, if successfully carried out, arrives at results that may yield additional, more extensive, yet complementary insights.

Nevertheless, some tensions between implicit and explicit comparative procedures are inherent and bound to persist, due primarily to the different degrees of abstraction employed in the two approaches. Although, by necessity, any implicit comparison must commit to some unavoidable amount of abstraction, it nevertheless tends to emphasize the specificity of concrete contexts. Explicit comparison, by contrast, inevitably is directed towards some more pronounced (and, at best, careful) abstraction than its 'weak' variant.

A greater or lesser degree of abstraction, then, is part and parcel of the differential in procedures between explicit and implicit (strong and weak) comparison in anthropology. The greater degree of abstraction, however, if carried out in a careful and balanced way through explicit procedures, need not entail radical de-contextualization. On the contrary, this process of more extensive abstraction must go hand in hand with a corresponding self-reflexive theorizing of the very contexts out of which the abstraction is elaborated. This is why we suggest, in this volume, that 'theorizing contexts' is indispensable for any explicit comparison.

The basic, the implicit and the explicit – these three dimensions of comparison make up the core of our argument in *Anthropology, by Comparison*. If anthropologists are simply aware of the comparative element inherent in human cognition; if they appreciate the implicit 'weak' comparative aspect of any kind of anthropological method and practice; or if they explicitly pursue the 'strong', epistemological paths of new, pluralistic procedures: It is *by comparison*, and not without it, that anthropologists will find answers to the questions they ask.

Notes

1   The editors and authors of this volume are sensitive to the use of the terms 'America' and 'American', which we understand to refer broadly to the states and peoples of *all* the Americas – North, Central and South. In keeping with common

practice, however, individual authors sometimes use 'American' to refer specifically to the 'US-American' or 'US' case, and 'America' in reference to the United States of America.
2   Examples of this trend are volumes edited by Robert Borofsky (1994), Daniel de Coppet (1992), Michaela di Leonardo (1998), Richard G. Fox (1991), Adam Kuper (1996) and George E. Marcus (1999).
3   See, for example, the recent debates about the term 'culture' published in *Current Anthropology* (1999) and recent feminist publications such as di Leonardo's *Gender at the Crossroads of Knowledge: Feminist Anthropology in the Postmodern Era* (1991).

Bibliography

Asad, T. (ed.) (1973) *Anthropology and the Colonial Encounter*, London and Ithaca, New York: Cornell University Press.
Benedict, R. (1934) *Patterns of Culture*, New York: Houghton Mifflin.
Boas, F. ([1896] 1940) 'The limitations of the comparative method of anthropology', in F. Boas (ed.), *Race, Language and Culture*, New York: Macmillan, pp. 270–80.
Borofsky, R. (ed.) (1994) *Assessing Cultural Anthropology*, New York: McGraw-Hill.
Bowen, J.R. and Petersen, R. (eds) (1999) *Critical Comparisons in Politics and Culture*, Cambridge and New York: Cambridge University Press.
Clifford, J. (1983) 'On ethnographic authority', *Representations*, 1: 118–46.
Clifford, J. and Marcus, G.E. (eds) (1986) *Writing Culture: The Poetics and Politics of Ethnography*, Berkeley, CA: University of California Press.
Current Anthropology (1999) 'Culture: a second chance?', 4: Supplement.
de Coppet, D. (1992) *Understanding Rituals*, EASA Series, London and New York: Routledge.
di Leonardo, M. (ed.) (1991) *Gender at the Crossroads of Knowledge: Feminist Anthropology in the Postmodern Era*, Berkeley, CA: University of California Press.
—— (1998) *Exotics at Home: Anthropologies, Others, American Modernity*, Chicago: University of Chicago Press.
Durkheim, E. (1912) *Les formes élélmentaires de la vie religieuse*, Paris: Alcan.
Fortes, M. and Evans-Pritchard, E.E. (1940) *African Political Systems*, London: Oxford University Press.
Fox, R.G. (1985) *Lions of the Punjab: Culture in the Making*, Berkeley and Los Angeles: University of California Press.
—— (ed.) (1991) *Recapturing Anthropology: Working in the Present*, Santa Fe: School of American Research Press.
—— (1992) 'East of Said', in M. Sprinker (ed.), *Edward Said: A Critical Reader*, London: Basil Blackwell, pp. 144–56.
—— (1995) 'Dis-integrating culture and the invention of new peace-fares', in R. Rapp and J. Schneider (eds), *Articulating Hidden Histories*, Berkeley, CA: University of California Press, pp. 275–87.
Gingrich, A. (1994) 'Time, ritual, and social experience', in K. Hastrup and P. Hervik (eds), *Social Experience and Anthropological Knowledge*, London and New York: Routledge, pp. 166–79.
Gluckman, M. (1958) *Analysis of a Social Situation in Modern Zululand*, Manchester: Manchester University Press.
Hannerz, U. (1992) *Cultural Complexity: Studies in the Social Organization of Meaning*, New York: Columbia University Press.

Holy, L. (ed.) (1987) *Comparative Anthropology*, Oxford and New York: Blackwell.

Hymes, D. (ed.) (1969) *Reinventing Anthropology*, New York: Pantheon.

Jameson, F. (1986) 'Third-World literature in the era of multinational capitalism', *Social Text* 15(Fall): 65–88.

Josselin de Jong, J.P.B. de (1913) *De waardeeringsonderscheiding van 'levend' en l'levenloos' in het Indogermaansch vergeleken met hetzelfde verschijnsel in enkele Algonkin-talen. Ethno-psychologische studie*, Leiden: Van der Hoek.

—— (1952) *Lévi-Strauss's Theory on Kinship and Marriage*, Leiden: Brill.

Kahn, J. (1980) *Minangabau Social Formations*, Cambridge: Cambridge University Press.

Kapferer, B. (1989) 'Nationalist ideology and a comparative anthropology', *Ethnos* 54, III–IV: 161–89.

Köbben, A.J.F. (1952) 'New ways of presenting an old idea: the statistical method in social anthropology', *Journal of the Royal Anthropological Institute* 82: 129–46.

——(1966) 'Structuralism versus comparative functionalism; some comments', *Bijdragen tot de Taal-, Land- en Volkenkunde* 122: 145–50.

Kuper, A. (1996) *Anthropology and Anthropologists: The Modern British School*, 3rd rev. edn, London: Routledge.

Leach, E.R. (1961) *Rethinking Anthropology*, London School of Economics Monographs on Social Anthropology 22, London and New York: Athlone.

Lesser, A. (1933) *The Pawnee Ghost Dance Hand Game*, Madison, WI: University of Wisconsin Press.

Levinson, D. and Malone, M.J. (1980) *Toward Explaining Human Culture*, New Haven, CT: HRAF Press.

Lévi-Strauss, C. (1949) *Les Structures élémentaires de la parenté*, Paris: Presses Universitaires de France.

—— (1958) *Anthropologie structurale*, Paris: Librairie Plon.

Lock, M. (1995) *Encounters with Aging: Mythologies of Menopause in Japan and North America*, Berkeley, CA: University of California Press.

Lowie, R.H. (1912) 'Social life of the Crow Indians', *Anthropological Papers of the American Museum of Natural History* IX: 179–248.

—— (1917) 'Notes on the social organization and customs of the Mandan, Hidatsa, and Crow Indians', *Anthropological Papers of the American Museum of Natural History* XXI: 53–99.

—— (1935) *The Crow Indians*, New York: Rinehart.

Malinowski, B. (1922) *Argonauts of the Western Pacific*, London: Routledge.

—— (1926) *Sex and Repression in Savage Society*, London: Routledge.

—— (1927) *The Father in Primitive Psychology*, London: Norton.

—— (1929) *The Sexual Life of Savages*, London: Routledge.

Marcus, G.E. (ed.) (1999) *Critical Anthropology Now: Unexpected Contexts, Shifting Constituencies, Changing Agendas*, Santa Fe: School of American Research Press.

Mead, M. (1928) *Coming of Age in Samoa*, New York: Morrow.

—— (1930) *Growing Up in New Guinea: A Comparative Study of Primitive Education*, New York: Morrow.

—— (1935) *Sex and Temperament*, New York: Morrow.

Merleau-Ponty, M. ([1945] 1962) *Phenomenology of Perception*, London: Routledge and Kegan Paul.

Mintz, S.W. (1977) 'The so-called world system: local initiative and local response', *Dialectical Anthropology* 1(4): 253–70.

—— (1985) *Sweetness and Power*, New York: Penguin.

Morgan, L.H. (1871) *Systems of Consanguinity and Affinity of the Human Family*, Washington, DC: Smithsonian Contributions to Knowledge 17.

Murdock, G.P. (1949) *Social Structure*, New York: Macmillan.

Naroll, R., *et al.* (1976) *Worldwide Theory Testing*, New Haven, CT: HRAF Press.

Nieboer, H.J. (1900) *Slavery as an Industrial System: Ethnological Researches.* 's Gravenhage: Nijhoff.

—— (1910) *Slavery as an Industrial System: Ethnological Researches*, 2nd rev. edn, 's Gravenhage: Nijhoff.

Sahlins, M. (1985) *Islands of History*, Chicago: University of Chicago Press.

Sahlins, M. and Service, E. (1960) *Evolution and Culture*, Ann Arbor, MI: University of Michigan Press.

Smith, C.A. (1976) 'Exchange systems and the spatial distribution of elites: the organization of stratification in agrarian societies', in C.A. Smith (ed.), *Regional Analysis*, vol. 2, New York: Academic Press, pp. 309–74.

Steinmetz, S.R. (1894) *Ethnologische Studien zur ersten Entwicklung der Strafe, nebst einer psychologischen Abhandlung über Grausamkeit und Rachsucht*, two volumes, Leiden: Van Doesburgh and Leipzig: Harrassowitz.

Steward, J.H. (1950) *Area Research: Theory and Practice*, New York: Social Science Research Council Bulletin 63.

Strauss, C. and Quinn, N. (1997) *A Cognitive Theory of Culture*, Cambridge: Cambridge University Press.

Thomas, N. (1994) *Colonialism's Culture*, Princeton, NJ: Princeton University Press.

Tylor, E.B. (1871) *Primitive Culture*, London: Murray.

Wolf, E.R. (1959) *Sons of the Shaking Earth*, Chicago: University of Chicago Press.

—— (1982) *Europe and the People without History*, Berkeley, CA: University of California Press.

—— (1998) *Envisioning Power: Ideologies of Dominance and Crisis*, Berkeley, CA: University of California Press.

Part I

Comparison and anthropology's public responsibility

Chapter 1

Anthropology's comparative consciousness

The case of human rights

Kirsten Hastrup

> All human beings are born free and equal in dignity and rights. They are
> endowed with reason and conscience and should act towards one another in
> the spirit of brotherhood.
>
> (Universal Declaration of Human Rights, 1948, Article 1)

This first article of the Universal Declaration of Human Rights (UDHR),
whose fiftieth anniversary was celebrated in 1998, is a pertinent preamble to a
reconsideration of anthropology's comparative consciousness. Few anthropologists would fail to note serious practical and theoretical problems in the
universal achievement of the standard set by the declaration, but fewer still
would denounce it. The first reaction would be spurred by the extensive,
detailed ethnographic knowledge of local differences; the last would be inspired
by an intimate experience of a shared humanity across these differences. Both
scepticism and endorsement, therefore, hinge on a comparative spirit.

For generations of anthropologists, comparison has been at the core of the
discipline. It has been envisaged differently at different points in time, as a
comparison either of parts or wholes, or of past or present cultural patterns, but
it was there – the implicit yardstick of the scholarly endeavour. The yardstick
could be used for measuring differences in time, comparing stages of evolution,
growth or mentality, or more often, differences in space, comparing different
societies, institutions or concepts in the ethnographic present. In the twentieth
century, the comparative mode was invariably fuelled by the tradition of fieldwork and its holistic implications.

Of late, the notion of whole cultures or integrated societies has been questioned, and new ideas of globalization, cultural flows, fragmentation and fluid
signs have been touted as definitive blows to anthropology's traditional object
of study: local communities of some order. Arguably, the notion of a comparative science had to go down the drain together with the sense of distinct
cultures or other commonalities – if it had not already been swept away by a
constructionist outlook that claimed that social wholes were fictions created in
anthropological writing.

It is my contention that for anthropology to be meaningful at all, in its own right and not simply as another branch of cultural studies, it has to retain a comparative consciousness. This notion, which has been relaunched recently by Laura Nader (1995), implies a sense of both global unity and local distinction, like the dual reactions we are faced with when dealing with human rights. As a subject of no small anthropological significance, the study of human rights leaves us squarely in a loaded political, moral and theoretical problem of how simultaneously to claim universality and respect cultural diversity.

Although human rights as such were not on the international agenda until 1948, the concept has been latent for centuries, especially as far as civil rights have been concerned. In the nineteenth century, when a wave of humanism swept over Europe, one result was a new idea of an essential 'humanity'; this idea derived more from seventeenth- and eighteenth-century treatises in political philosophy than from the 'renaissance humanism' that was invoked at the time (Davies 1997: 25 et passim). Political philosophy in many respects was a forerunner of anthropology, and the idea of universalized humanity was a precondition of the nascent discipline, which was destined to give the proposition empirical substance. In the early years of anthropology the conjunction of the two concerns of equal rights and local difference was passionately attested to by Franz Boas, who, in his letter-diary from Baffin Island (1883–84), wrote about his sincere wish to live in America:

> I should much prefer to live in America in order to be able to further those ideas for which I live. But how to do this, I do not know. Well, I cannot do anything about it now and I shall have to wait patiently and see how matters develop when I return ... What I want to live and die for, is equal rights for all, equal possibilities to learn and work for poor and rich alike! Don't you believe that to have done even the smallest bit for this, is more than all of science taken together? I do not think I would be allowed to do this in Germany.
>
> (Boas, in Stocking 1983: 37)

Whatever happened subsequently in America – and in Germany – we know that Boas was to fight fervently against racism in his adopted homeland. On the whole, I believe that most anthropologists since Boas have seen their discipline as genuinely respectful of all peoples. In a branch of scholarship that insisted on fieldwork and intimate interlocution as the route to knowledge, no doubts could be harboured about all people being equally endowed with reason and conscience. This collective sentiment, and its empirical corroboration, make no simple entry into the discussion of a universal standard of human rights, however, as this is conceptualized and articulated in the declarations, conventions, charters and protocols that have been passed in the half-decade following 1948.

This is not the place to review the relationship between anthropology and human rights standards, which has been done elsewhere (e.g. Downing and

Kushner 1988; Messer 1993; Wilson 1997a). We should note a few salient points, however. Until recently, anthropology has more or less routinely taken a sceptical position in relation to any notion of universal standards (Wilson 1997a: 1). This dates back to the statement made by Melville Herskovits (1947) in the name of the American Anthropological Association, when he was questioned in 1947 about the organization's view of the prospect of a United Nations charter of universal human rights. In his reply, Herskovits stressed that culture is the sole legitimate source of moral values:

> Even where political systems exist that deny citizens the right of participation in their government, or seek to conquer weaker peoples, underlying cultural values may be called on to bring peoples of such states to a realization of the consequences of the acts of governments, and thus to enforce a brake upon discrimination and conquest.
>
> (Herskovits 1947: 543)

As pointed out by Wilson (1997a: 2), this is an attempt to play anthropology's trump card, its unique ability to elicit and assert any culture's underlying values. We might like to add that it also features the comparative knowledge inherent in anthropology, a knowledge both of cultural difference and of its translatability into valid, and more or less shared, human standards of good governance and respectable political action. In spite of the disclaimer, which was militantly underscored by Julian Steward (1948: 251) when he said, 'We are prepared to take a stand against the values in our own culture which underlie ... such imperialism', a Universal Declaration of Human Rights was passed in 1948, the first article of which I quoted above.

Together, the two attitudes exemplified by Boas and Herskovits, both of which are understandable and laudable, take us right to the core of anthropology's comparative consciousness and its ambiguous implications. They also indicate that it is not the concept of cultural particularity itself that defies the utopia of human rights; if ever there were a particularist in anthropology it was Boas, who founded the school of 'historical particularism'.

Since 1948, the discussion of human rights in anthropology has centred on the unsolved question of universalism or relativism, on the one hand, and on the cultural translation of human rights concepts – allegedly deriving from a Western liberal tradition – into 'like' cultural concepts within other moral and political systems, on the other (Hastrup 2001a). Neither of these debates is central to my argument in the following, even if I cannot entirely avoid touching on them both in my quest for the comparative wisdom of anthropology in matters of human rights.

According to some anthropologists, globalization and human rights conjoin in a social transformation of unprecedented magnitude in the present day. Ellen Messer, for one, writes that:

Since the close of World War II, the United Nations has been assembling declarations, legislation, and enforcement mechanisms to promote human rights. Both the ongoing efforts to establish a global community and to base membership on a universal, but evolving standard of values constitute perhaps the greatest social transformation of this century.

(Messer 1996: 1)

This transformation is part of a larger trend that has often been seen as the end of modernity, implying also, according to Anthony Giddens (1991), an end to traditional ontological security as anchored in trusted cultural knowledge. This could be one of the reasons why human rights have become the new standard of hope to many; they certainly provide an opportune democratic counterpoint to those fundamentalisms that others seek refuge in to temper their existential anxiety. The historical changes are matched by new scholarly efforts. We have witnessed important changes in the conception of the anthropological object, which can be summed up under the rubric of a de-essentialization of the object (culture, society) and a humanization of the subject, seen now as an active agent of history and not its passive victim.

Intellectually, one of the greatest advances in this century, according to Richard Rorty (1993: 115), is a willingness to learn from history and anthropology that humans are extremely malleable. Instead of asking, 'What is our nature?', people across the world have substituted the question, 'What can we make of ourselves?'. Thanks to comparative knowledge in time and space we have realized the flexibility and the self-shaping character of humans, and have abandoned the idea of a given human nature.

This development provides an historical and intellectual climate in favour of a 'human rights culture' (Hastrup 2001b). Although the dominant trends in present-day anthropology – the stress on globalization, on process and on agency, among other things – make a new approach to universal human rights possible and seem to favour an idea of a global culture of human rights, there is no theoretical reason why we should not at the same time maintain a distinct, more or less bounded object of ethnographic analysis: the local worlds of people. In spite of the declared universal culture, which in many ways is mainly a feature of language and procedural practice, the local world is still where this culture must be lived and trusted. Meanwhile, let us start unfolding the comparative problem of human rights, suspended between – and connecting – the global and the local dimensions of social life.

Language: law and the levelling of difference

In the half-decade succeeding this first declaration, the language of rights has become ever more subtle. If human rights exist mainly by virtue of their being talked about (Dembour 1996: 22), with each 'generation' of rights, or with each expansion of the area of their validity, this 'talk' has had to express increasingly complex ideas (cf. Bobbio 1996: xi). From the civil and political rights, over social, economic and cultural rights, and on to the solidarity rights (such as the right to development and the right to a clean environment), the inherent notions of both the subject and the object of these rights and responsibilities have changed dramatically. Across these changes, the language of rights displays a remarkable and fairly consistent modernist legacy, a legacy that accounts, among other things, for the implicit ideas of moral progress (Hastrup 2001c). It is also a language that in spite of its changing subject is distinctly legalist, and as such it is all too often neglectful of social and cultural context (Wilson 1997b). There is sufficient reason, then, for starting these reflections with a consideration of the language of rights in general, not least because we may use this investigation in a broader understanding of the comparative anthropological contribution to the human rights discourse.

It has often been noted that most human rights cases are presented in a legalistic language that decontextualizes events; this is what Clifford Geertz (1983: 170), in his work on law in a comparative perspective, has referred to as the 'skeletonization of fact'. It is a cutting to the bone of a complex reality. 'Law', in the view of Geertz, and a view that I would endorse here, is a distinct way of imagining the 'real'; as such, it is much more than a simple statement of rules and norms. Each society would imagine the real in terms of a particular code, and the role of the anthropologist would be to sort out both the code's legal representation and its transformation into a language of decision and justice. With the universal standard of human rights, this concern would expand to the global community.

Geertz, and many of his contemporaries, are protagonists of a variegated trend in anthropology that has been summed up under the label of 'the linguistic turn'. This implies a broad range of approaches to matters social and cultural in terms of language and a 'reading' of culture as text. It comprises large parts of the early cognitive anthropology (mainly) in the United States, semantic or symbolic anthropology (mainly) in Britain, and a structural anthropology (mainly) in France. 'The linguistic turn' has affected almost all human and social sciences, implying not only a concern with language as such and as an entry into psyche, law, religion and culture, but also a partial hegemony on the part of linguistics over other disciplines. Thus, from the early efforts of Ferdinand de Saussure ([1916] 1974) and others who sought to 'rationalize' the study of language, a whole array of structuralisms, of which Lévi-Strauss was one of the leaders, developed and grew into theories of culture, literature, myth, kinship, fashion, perception and the unconscious that were modelled on theories of language. One of the significant consequences was the idea of culture being 'like' a language, distinct and with its own grammar. In the same vein, people were seen as more or less culturally 'competent'.

Within anthropology, the linguistic turn in many ways followed from and continued earlier studies of classification, like those of Durkheim and Mauss ([1903] 1963). The basic idea of their work was one of language arising out of the need to classify the world, in terms of a particular social and moral order. The first classes were social, and the linguistic categories that arise in individual societies are designed to order life, to distinguish between things forbidden and things allowed. What is clear, at least from the work of Lévi-Strauss, is that the theoretical intent is objectivist, 'scientific'. This is part of the Enlightenment heritage, and certainly also a function of the linguistic turn of the human sciences itself, in which a correspondence between language and thought was never far away, either in substance (as for Boas) or in structure (as for Lévi-Strauss). The roots of this particular vision in fact go back to Plato, whose *logos* implied both language and thought. In this view of language, words have been seen as more or less transparent entries into the life-worlds and thoughts of people.

With reference to the problems posed by the human rights debate, clearly the comparative study of concepts, such as the concept of person, the concept of dignity, the concept of evil, and so forth, are of prime relevance. In a recent article, Talal Asad (1997) has shown how the notions of torture, cruelty and so forth – as invoked for instance in Article 5 of the UDHR ('No one shall be subjected to torture or to cruel, inhuman and degrading treatment or punishment') – are, if not untenable, then at least unstable. Asad reminds us of Elaine Scarry's claim that war is an obvious analogue to torture (1985: 61) and makes us party to his consternation that 'normal' (!) warfare is not condemned by the international community, only war that does not follow the rules of the game – this, quite irrespective of the fact that modern war always involves 'cruel, inhuman and degrading treatment' of people on behalf of governments. This example is one good reason to be sceptical of a universal rights standard.

Even the overarching definition of what we (and who are 'we'?) should mean by humanity in the first place is an open question, raised by Bourdieu, for instance: 'To confer "humanity" upon everyone in a purely formal way is, under the appearance of humanism, to exclude from it all those who are deprived of the means of attaining it' (Bourdieu 1997: 80, quoted by Dwyer 1997: 17). The idea of a universal category of humans, 'born free and equal in dignity and rights', is not simply a theoretical problem, however. It is also a cruelly practical issue for people who find themselves dehumanized by the perpetrators of violence. We might think of those sixteen Cuiva Indians who were killed in 1967 by settlers in the Colombian rainforest – settlers who were since acquitted because they claimed to believe that the Cuivas were apes (Arcand 1972: 9–10) – or of the Serbs who have often portrayed the Muslims as animals without whom the world would a better place (cf. Rorty 1993: 112–13).

The language of rights and the language of defilement have one feature in common: they generalize or objectify what they are talking about. As Edward Bruner (1986: 7) has it, language is better suited for measuring and classifying than for changing the world. It achieves this measuring capacity at the cost of disregarding time and, to a large extent, particular experiences. In this way, language is one of the main devices of 'impersonalization' (Rapport 1997: 12ff.).

Much social science, including large parts of anthropology, hinges precisely on this very capacity. There is no way to 'tell' the world as the sum of individual stories.

The language of human rights, certainly, by being a 'legal' language in the first place, is also totally dependent on this objectifying capacity; it has some serious consequences of leaving out those personal experiences that would have granted the discourse life and pertinence beyond the rights talk itself. As 'talk', however, it cannot but externalize and level different personal experiences and replace them with an objective, and largely timeless, account of a universal standard. Similarly, in anthropology we are trapped in an insurmountable methodological problem of how to analyse, for instance, human suffering without dehumanizing the subject, the sufferer (Kleinman and Kleinman 1991).

In contrast to most criticisms of a universal standard, the (comparative) problem of human rights language is not that it imposes a particular, Western, view of the world upon others at the expense of their legitimate right to cultural distinction, as implied, for instance, by Talal Asad (1997: 128), as a late echo of Steward, when he argues against the 'attempt by Euro-Americans to impose their standards by force on others'. In a thorough analysis of the minutes of the meetings of the UN work group that drafted the first declaration, Tore Lindholm (1992) has shown how different cultural perspectives gradually filtered into the formulation of Article 1. The Article, therefore, is not immediately 'Western', and nor is it necessarily in conflict with other value systems. The overarching problem, if any, is that any universal standard must be rendered in some language, and any language refracts reality by generalizing those diverse actualities it seeks to comprise, not to speak of the different conventions of (legal) representation that have to be fused into one.

The objectification inherent in the appeal to language is a corollary of what Carol Feldman (1987) has called 'ontic dumping', a notion that has recently been recycled by Nigel Rapport (1997: 14ff.). Language presents us with more or less ready-made concepts, categories, images and symbols that are used for objectifying the world. What we are really objectifying is the epistemic – our way of understanding the world – but cognitive economy allegedly urges us to 'ontically dump' our conceptualizations onto the world, in order to free some of our thinking capacity to think new thoughts. The 'ontic dumping' resembles what I have discussed in another work (Hastrup 1995b) in terms of a process of sedimentation, referring to Bateson's view of habit formation:

> The phenomenon of habit formation sorts out the ideas which survive repeated use and puts them in a more or less separate category. These trusted ideas then become available for immediate use without thoughtful inspection, while the more flexible parts of the mind can be served for use in newer matters.
>
> (Bateson 1972: 501)

Human rights are not yet among the 'trusted ideas' on a global scale. Rather, they belong to those 'newer matters' for which a more flexible and thoughtful mind is needed. Trusted ideas, or ontically dumped concepts (including values, of course), are generally local, and one of the major problems of achieving a truly universal standard of human life in practice is the discrepancy of scale between the local and the global. Even where the universal standard seems most 'obvious', politically and morally, to 'us' (whoever 'we' are, again), it may conflict radically with cultural concepts or values. One example is provided by the oft-invoked debate on 'female genital mutilation' (cf. Dembour, in press). The phrase is not neutral, of course, and it covers diverse practices that are actually more or less mutilating. Again, it is *language* that allows for the generalization. Whatever we call it, it does seem to conflict dramatically with, for instance, Article 18 of the Vienna Declaration of Human Rights (1993), which is the latest global declaration:

> The human rights of women and of the girl-child are an inalienable, integral and indivisible part of universal human rights. The full and equal participation of women in political, civil, economic, social and cultural life, at the national, regional and international levels, and the eradication of all forms of discrimination on grounds of sex are priority objectives of the international community.
>
> Gender-based violence and all forms of sexual harassment and exploitation, including those resulting from cultural prejudice and international trafficking, are incompatible with the dignity and worth of the human person, and must be eliminated. This can be achieved by legal measures and through national action and international cooperation in such fields as economic and social development, education, safe maternity and health care, and social support.
>
> (Vienna Declaration of Human Rights, 1993, Article 18)

Clearly, this article refers back to the opening article of the 1948 Declaration, and on both scales there is little doubt that the most radical mutilations (and I for one do not hesitate to use this word) are violations of a woman's bodily integrity. Nevertheless, as we know, it is a practice endorsed by hundreds of thousands of women, striving for normality and dignity. Which legal measures can effectively abolish 'the natural', ontically dumped concepts of the culturally given?

To sum up what we have so far learned about language, including the language of human rights: language seems to engender an objectified view of the world, on the one hand, and a conceptual relativism, on the other. In both respects, and partly as a consequence of the linguistic turn in anthropology and elsewhere, language has been treated as broadly 'instrumental' with regard to obtaining our goals and with regard to understanding the world. Language, in this view, is a 'tool' of action as well as thought.

These features are partly responsible for the fact that language cannot fully capture human experience, which is subjective and cannot be abstracted from the experiencing subject. There is an ontological distance between language and experience, partly due to the fact that experience takes place in time, a dimension that tends to disappear from language. This distancing effect also applies to the language of human rights, which levels and objectifies human suffering on a global scale.

Experience: individuality and moral horizons

The language of rights possibly remains better suited to classify the world than to change it. Classifying hinges on the instrumental use of language, and from there theories of the social tend towards designation. There is another dimension to language, and to theory, however, namely the 'expressive' (Taylor 1985a: 215ff.). This view of language, including theoretical language, stresses that what is expressed is thereby (and only thereby) also made manifest (Hastrup 1995a). Language in this sense reflects a particular mode of being in the world (Taylor 1985a: 234).

Expressive language is therefore closer to experience than is designative language. It does not purport to represent or to mirror reality, because after all most of the real is not linguistic, and evidently language portrays speech more faithfully than other events. In anthropology, what followed the linguistic turn was a 'literary turn'. One could argue that this development reflects a change from a designative to an expressive perspective of language. Thinking about culture and cultural difference in terms of 'concepts' was in a sense turned inwards and transformed into a concern about writing: the way in which we shaped cultures in the anthropological texts. Nigel Rapport (1997: 45) suggests that 'writing' is a kind of meta-experience, in the sense that it is a considered ordering of experience in symbolic form and a conscious production of meaning. With ethnographies based on fieldwork, this makes immediate sense.

Another feature of this literary turn was an increasing attention to the ways in which people in general 'authored' their life stories; anthropology began studying how experience, expression and identity became woven together (Bruner 1986). From Paul Ricoeur (1984), the notion of narrative, involving a distinct sense of time, fuelled the feeling of getting closer to lived experience in writings that were not simply considered 'representational' and conceptually transparent. Thus, the literary turn in general coincided with a renewed interest in human experience. This led either to an extreme constructionist position ('the world only exists in narrative'), which discarded conceptual relativity as ontological relativism, or to a renewed theoretical concern about the shared human experience beyond the conceptual and discursive differences. The former is not only a caricature of comparative anthropology, it is also essentially self-refuting; the latter makes way for a reconciliation of universal claims, on the one hand, and cultural diversity, on the other. From this position we can see that conceptual and ontological relativity is not one and the same thing.

Language is 'not just the medium in virtue of which we can describe the world, but also by virtue of which we are capable of the human emotions and of standing in specifically human relations to each other' (Taylor 1985a: 235). Language is expressive of human emotion; it is through language that we come to know what we feel. Emotional language is a particularly apt example of a subject-referring language, a language that cannot objectify but only express. When we move from the designative to the expressive dimension, the phenomenon of language broadens from the instrument of clear-cut classification to an approximate articulation of what is at base nonlinguistic; such articulations are always open to challenge from our inarticulate sense of what is important (ibid.: 75). With Taylor, we can highlight the qualities of language by posing the question:

> [W]hat is the characteristic excellence of expression[?] On the designative view, this was clear. Language was an instrument. It was at its best when it best served its purpose, when its terms designated clearly distinct ideas, and we maintained their definitions clearly before us in our reasoning. On this understanding language was an all-purpose tool of thought. But for the expressivist, it is an activity which constitutes a specific way of being in the world.
>
> (Taylor 1985a: 236)

Giving up on an exclusively designative view of language (and theory) means leaving behind the instrumentalist view, together with the view of referential transparency. The inscrutability of reference does not entail ontological relativity, however (Davidson 1984: 235); an insight that actually leads to a renewed understanding of the statement made by Herskovits against the idea of a universal standard. It may not be Herskovits's understanding, but we can actually see how it simply implied that all cultures possess resources for dealing with violations of human integrity. The local moral world rarely is articulated in terms of human rights, but certainly there are other ways of expressing concern with order and dignity. Beyond conceptual relativities, there is a shared human experience. The anthropological contribution to the study of human rights, then, could be a recontextualization of rights and violations within a comparative framework of local discourses and political contexts (Wilson 1997b).

One of the experiences we share is the experience of difference, and of understanding each other across such difference. The distance between our outlooks may be smaller or greater, but in principle we are capable of understanding others – possibly not as they understand themselves, but certainly as they make sense to both themselves and to others. This observation simply confirms the collective experience of ethnographic fieldwork, noted for instance by Ernest Gellner in his discussion of relativism in the social sciences:

[P]artial incomprehensions are common, but they have not, to my knowledge, prevented the drawing-up of an account of at least large parts of the social life, language and so on of the community in question. I have heard an anthropologist who had come back from a but recently discovered group in New Guinea say that they really were 'very very distant' in their way of thinking, implying that the strenuousness of his effort had had to be much greater than on his other field experiences with 'closer' cultural communities; but he did not report *failure*.

(Gellner 1985: 87)

We can still understand other worlds, in spite of their being constituted differently in language. The whole notion of a comparative anthropology rests on this assumption. Fieldwork is a practising of comparison in this sense. It is also a way of incorporating ethnographic knowledge by taking part in local experience (Hastrup 1994).

All the evidence we have in anthropology is experience (cf. Gellner 1985: 15); of course we speak and elicit vocabularies and local semantics, but it takes more than a lexicon to understand people, and only experience can confirm the understanding. If fieldwork never exhausts what there is to know about other people, still the comparative wisdom of anthropology allows us to make precisely such generalizations – as on the relationship between language and experience, for instance. It also helps to substantiate the claim that ontologically, the reality of social phenomena is not in the phenomena themselves or in their representations in language, but in our experience of them (cf. Taylor 1985a: 47). There is, then, all the more reason to look at the individual subject as the locus of human experience.

The relationship between the individual and the community has always been on the anthropological agenda, and with the literary turn and the expressive perspective on language a new possibility for understanding this relationship became possible. Clearly, in the designative view of language and the 'linguistic' perspective on the world, there was no individual creativity. There were speakers and inhabitants of a universe that was given, prefabricated and directly mirrored in the language spoken. With the literary turn, individuality came back as an important feature of the 'cultural'. This again has some repercussions both in the social sciences and in the debate about human rights.

In the social sciences today, there is a dominance of *methodological* individualism, according to which the study of society must commence from the study of the experiences and actions of individuals. Anthropology, too, has become 'self-conscious' in this sense (Cohen 1994). But, as pointed out by Norberto Bobbio:

[There are] at least two other forms of individualism without which the human rights point of view would become incomprehensible: *ontological* individualism which starts from the premise that each individual is autonomous in relation to all the others and is of equal dignity (it is difficult to say whether this premise is more metaphysical or theological); and *ethical* individualism according to which each individual is a moral agent.

(Bobbio 1996: 42)

The three individualisms combine in a positive connotation of individualism that is the foundation of democracy and human rights. So far so good, but when Bobbio goes on to claim that 'as such it has and will always oppose holistic concepts of society and history, wherever they originate' (ibid.), I strongly disagree. My dissent is not a simple defence of anthropology, but a conviction, based on both practical and theoretical considerations, that there is no 'self' without society, no character without a stage on which to play (cf. Hastrup 1998). Even the subject of speech can be seen as a community (Taylor 1985a: 237).

After having been ostracized by much Durkheimian social science, which claims the ontological primacy of 'society' over individuals, methodological individualism has resurfaced in anthropology, facilitated not least by the literary turn. Its return provides a new basis for a 'social science which recognizes individuals as universal human agents above whom there is no greater good, without whom there is no wider society, and in contradistinction to whom there is no cultural tradition' (Rapport 1997: 181). Now, this is not akin to claiming that individual empowerment, as envisaged by the human rights discourse, concerns only the individual person. Acknowledging the autonomy and integrity of selves, by contrast, implies a thorough concern with the ways in which individual lives are implicated in a whole series of other lives, of power structures, of habits and of discourses. Individuality itself, logically, presupposes an 'other'. We only learn to talk because other people are talking to us, and we learn to distinguish ourselves partly through the fact that these other people give us a name: 'In being given a name we are made into beings that one addresses, and we are inducted into the community whose speaking continually remakes the language' (Taylor 1985a: 237). It is only as interlocutors that we learn to say 'I' of ourselves.

In approaching the world through the individual, rather than the other way round, one need not endorse narcissism on the personal level or cultural fragmentation at the societal; rather, such an approach allows us to see how, in a comparative perspective, agency is shaped partly by moral horizons of different scales; there would be no 'selves' without moral spaces of orientation (cf. Taylor 1989). In short, it allows for a new kind of holism, one that is neither deterministic nor simply designative, but rather an expression of those life-worlds of people that are not otherwise manifest (cf. Hastrup 1995a). It is, in other words, a theoretical holism that will take care of naturalism (cf. Rorty 1991: 109). As such, it has immense implications for our view of human rights.

Human rights need not entail a levelling of cultural or substantial differences between people, but simply a subscription to basic ideas of individuality (not *individualism*, which is a culture-specific ideology of autonomy, built upon the general idea of individuality and connoting the singularity and subjectivity of any individual) as transformed into a shared standard of procedural justice. This shift in perspective is facilitated by the realization that people are not simply incarnated vocabularies, eternally trapped in particular languages and self-contained conceptual universes. As Richard Rorty has put it:

> The idea that we all have an obligation to diminish cruelty, to make human beings equal in respect to their liability to suffering, seems to take for granted that there is something within human beings that deserves respect and protection quite independently of the language they speak. It suggests that a nonlinguistic ability, the ability to feel pain, is what is important, and that difference in vocabulary is much less important.
>
> (Rorty 1992: 88)

This shift in perspective paves the way for a new sense of solidarity, even when solidarity with all possible vocabularies, conceptual worlds and their embedded values seems impossible. A universal ethics derives from the recognition of the shared human liability to suffering, and from an acknowledgement of the shared human experience of living among others. Although verbal appeals may induce the more fortunate of peoples to donate aid to the less fortunate,

> it is quite a different thing to be moved to action by a strong sense that human beings are eminently *worth* helping or treating with justice, a sense of their dignity and value. Here we have to come into contact with the moral sources that originally underpin these standards.
>
> (Taylor 1989: 515)

Anthropology still has an important contribution to make to this universal ethics by providing ethnographic substance to both the shared and the unique dimensions of lived experiences. Anthropologists of today have inherited a field where 'a comparative consciousness illuminates connections, between local and global, between past and present, between anthropologists and those they study, between uses of comparison and implications of their uses' (Nader 1995: 86).

By means of an invigorated comparative consciousness, and an insistence on the possibility of a unified theoretical comprehension of different ways of living in the world, anthropology might now begin to fulfil the promise made by Boas, to work for equal rights amidst different cultures.

Conclusion: theory and comparative conscience

I have argued in this chapter that legal language, including the language of human rights, in many ways functions as a leveller of qualitative difference, not only transculturally but also within cultures or political systems. Beyond the words, and only partly representable in words, are complex human experiences of undignified behaviour, of violence and of outright evil that not only disrupt individual and communal life-courses, but also erupt as silences into social discourse. Such silences may be as salient as the narratives that we are used to listening to; they are not empty or meaningless.

Ethnographies of violence and suffering are needed, not to satisfy the vultures of disaster but to add a dimension of experience to the language of rights and thus contribute to a shared understanding of those sufferings that a universally accepted standard of human rights may help alleviate – if it can be truly shared, that is. Not only ethnography, but also our regained confidence in anthropological theory may contribute to such a shared understanding. Anthropology's theoretical language can embrace both local expression and experience; it is a language of contrast that can, furthermore, span cultural differences within a single (scholarly) discourse. Theory expresses what is not otherwise said; as such, it is a social practice and contributes to the making of the world (Taylor 1985b). One of the things that anthropology has helped realize is the imaginability of 'others' as being somehow like 'us', in spite of diversity. This imaginative contribution takes us away from basing human rights on a notion of an essence of humanity, and allows us to base it precisely on the fact that we are imaginable to each other and that we may conjoin in a shared standard of justice from diverse rationales; in short, that we are equally human beyond our diverse vocabularies.

Returning to Article 1 of the original Universal Declaration of Human Rights with which we started, it seems to me to be sufficiently open-ended to be sensitive both to shifting historical contexts and to intellectual debate. Like all language, it is inherently generalizing, but this of course is a precondition for its being able to comprehend diverse actualities, while still referring to a shared humanity. Even if our ambition is to fuse horizons, we still do not want to escape them (cf. Taylor 1995: 151).

By this, I do not mean that we should lay the debate on human rights to rest. I, for one, will continue to take the stand of the critical intellectual rather than the expert – to invoke the distinction made by Edward Said (1994) – and I would like to see this stand taken by anthropology as a whole. Through critical comparative investigation and solid ethnographies of experience we may add life to the language of rights, which by itself guides our perception in particular directions. Theory shares with legal language, if at another level of abstraction, the inclusiveness of diversity.

In respect for the venue of our conference, let me conclude with an article from the 1993 Vienna Declaration of Human Rights that surely must inspire anthropologists to further reflection:

> All human rights are universal, indivisible and interdependent and interre-lated. The international community must treat human rights globally in a fair and equal manner, on the same footing, and with the same emphasis. While the significance of national and regional particularities and various

historical, cultural and religious backgrounds must be borne in mind, it is the duty of States, regardless of political, economic and cultural systems, to promote and protect all human rights and fundamental freedoms.

(Vienna Declaration of Human Rights, 1993, Article 5)

The comparative conscience of anthropology, building on the discipline's long tradition of comparison and contextualization, could start from here and generate work that might contribute to transforming human rights from being primarily a linguistic phenomenon to being also lived experience and trusted ideas, cross-culturally.

Bibliography

Arcand, B. (1972) *The Urgent Situation of the Cuiva Indians of Colombia*, Copenhagen: IWGIA Document 7.

Asad, T. (1997) 'On torture, or cruel, inhuman and degrading treatment', in R.A. Wilson (ed.) *Human Rights, Culture and Context: Anthropological Perspectives*, London: Pluto Press.

Bateson, G. (1972) *Steps to an Ecology of Mind*, New York: Basic Books.

Bobbio, N. (1996) *The Age of Rights*, Cambridge: Polity Press.

Bourdieu, P. (1997) *Méditations pascaliennes*, Paris: Seuil.

Bruner, E.M. (1986) 'Experience and its expressions', in V. Turner and E.M. Bruner (eds) *The Anthropology of Experience*, Urbana, IL: University of Illinois Press.

Cohen, A. (1994) *Self Consciousness*, London: Routledge.

Davidson, D. (1984) *Inquiries into Truth and Interpretation*, Oxford: Clarendon Press.

Davies, T. (1997) *Humanism*, London: Routledge.

Dembour, M.-B. (1996) 'Human rights talk and anthropological ambivalence: the particular contexts of universal claims', in O. Harris (ed.) *Inside and Outside the Law*, London: Routledge.

—— (in press) 'The pendulum of the human rights debate exemplified in the FGM debate', in J. Cowan, M.-B. Dembour and R. Wilson (eds) *Culture and Rights: Anthropological Investigations*, Cambridge: Cambridge University Press.

Downing, T.E. and Kushner, G. (eds) (1988) *Human Rights and Anthropology*, Cultural Survival Report 24, Cambridge, MA: Cultural Survival.

Durkheim, É. and Mauss, M. ([1903] 1963) *Primitive Classification*, transl. R. Needham, London: Cohen and West.

Dwyer, K. (1997) 'Beyond a boundary? "Universal Human Rights" and the Middle East', *Anthropology Today* 13: 13–18.

Feldman, C. (1987) 'Thought from language: the linguistic construction of cognitive representations', in J. Bruner and H. Haste (eds) *Making Sense: The Child's Construction of the World*, London: Methuen.

Geertz, C. (1983) 'Local knowledge: fact and law in comparative perspective', in C. Geertz, *Local Knowledge*, New York: Basic Books.

Gellner, E. (1985) *Relativism and the Social Sciences*, Cambridge: Cambridge University Press.

Giddens, A. (1991) *Modernity and Self-Identity*, Cambridge: Polity Press.

Hastrup, K. (1994) 'Anthropological knowledge incorporated', in K. Hastrup and P. Hervik (eds) *Social Experience and Anthropological Knowledge*, London: Routledge.

—— (1995a) *A Passage to Anthropology: Between Experience and Theory*, London: Routledge.

—— (1995b) 'The inarticulate mind: the place of awareness in social action', in A. Cohen and N. Rapport (eds) *Questions of Consciousness*, London: Routledge.

—— (1998) 'Theatre as a site of passage: some reflections on the magic of acting', in F. Hughes-Freeland (ed.) *Ritual, Performance, Media*, London: Routledge.

—— (2001a) 'The quest for universality: an introduction', in K. Hastrup (ed.) *Human Rights on Common Grounds: The Quest for Universality*, The Hague: Kluwer Law International.

—— (2001b) 'Accommodating diversity in a global culture of rights: an introduction', in K. Hastrup (ed.) *Legal Cultures and Human Rights: The Challenge of Diversity*, The Hague: Kluwer Law International.

—— (2001c) 'Representing the common good: the limits of legal language', paper presented to the ASA conference on 'Rights, Claims and Entitlements', University of Sussex, April 2001.

Herskovits, M. (1947) 'AAA Statement on Human Rights', *American Anthropologist* 49: 539–43.

Kleinman, A. and Kleinman, J. (1991) 'Suffering and its professional transformation', *Culture, Medicine and Psychiatry* 15: 275–301.

Lindholm, T. (1992) 'Article 1: a new beginning', in A. Eide, G. Alfredsson, G. Melander, L.A. Rehof, A. Rosas and T. Swinehart (eds) *The Universal Declaration of Human Rights: A Commentary*, Oslo: Scandinavian University Press.

Messer, E. (1993) 'Anthropology and human rights', *Annual Review of Anthropology* 22: 221–49.

—— (1996) 'Anthropology, human rights, and social transformation', in E.F. Moran (ed.) *Transforming Societies, Transforming Anthropology*, Ann Arbor, MI: University of Michigan Press.

Nader, L. (1995) 'Comparative consciousness', in R. Borofsky (ed.) *Assessing Cultural Anthropology*, New York: McGraw-Hill.

Rapport, N. (1997) *Transcendent Individual: Towards a Literary and Liberal Anthropology*, London: Routledge.

Ricoeur, P. (1984) *Time and Narrative*, Chicago: University of Chicago Press.

Rorty, R. (1991) *Objectivity, Relativism and Truth*, Philosophical Papers I, Cambridge: Cambridge University Press.

—— (1992) *Contingency, Irony and Solidarity*, Cambridge: Cambridge University Press.

—— (1993) 'Human rights, rationality, and sentimentality', in S. Shute and S. Hurley (eds) *On Human Rights: The Oxford Amnesty Lectures 1993*, New York: Basic Books.

Said, E. (1994) *Representations of the Intellectual*, London: Vintage.

Saussure, F. de ([1916] 1974) *Course in General Linguistics*, Eng. transl., Glasgow: Collins.

Scarry, E. (1985) *The Body in Pain*, Oxford: Oxford University Press.

Steward, J. (1948) 'Comments on the Statement of Human Rights', *American Anthropologist* 50: 351–2.

Stocking, G.W. (ed.) (1983) *Observers Observed: Essays on Ethnographic Fieldwork*, Madison, WI: University of Wisconsin Press.

Taylor, C. (1985a) *Human Agency and Language*, Philosophical Papers I, Cambridge: Cambridge University Press.

—— (1985b) *Philosophy and the Human Sciences*, Philosophical Papers II, Cambridge: Cambridge University Press.

—— (1989) *Sources of the Self: The Making of the Modern Identity*, Cambridge: Cambridge University Press.

—— (1995) *Philosophical Arguments*, Cambridge, MA: Harvard University Press.

Wilson, R.A. (1997a) 'Human rights, culture and context: an introduction', in R.A. Wilson (ed.) *Human Rights, Culture and Context: Anthropological Perspectives*, London: Pluto Press.

—— (1997b) 'Representing human rights violations: social contexts and subjectivities', in R.A. Wilson (ed.) *Human Rights, Culture and Context: Anthropological Perspectives*, London: Pluto Press.

Chapter 2

Action comparison
Efforts towards a global and comparative yet local and active anthropology

James Peacock

There is only one method in social anthropology, the comparative method – and that is impossible!

(Evans-Pritchard, as recalled by Rodney Needham, 1973)

In comparison a magic dwells.

(Jonathan Z. Smith, 1982)

Im Anfang war die Tat.
In the beginning was the Deed.

(Johann Wolfgang Goethe, *Faust* I)

I was a sojourner in a strange land.

(Walter Evans, Primitive Baptist elder)

In this chapter I argue the following: first, that the global world ushering in the new millennium creates a distinctive opportunity for comparison (by which is meant in this chapter the comparative method, especially as used in anthropology); second, that anthropology faces an appropriate moment in its history to seize this opportunity; and third, that, in so doing, comparison can be usefully engaged with issues in the world. Pursuant to this three-step strategy, I explore and propose a deeper immersion in the cultural milieu that constitutes the anthropologist's own life-world, especially his or her regional or local milieu. My illustrations of ways to enter this life-world range from outreach and activism to regionalism and *Volkskunde*. I call this approach *action comparison*.

The phrase 'sojourner in a strange land' is biblical, a favourite phrase of some of the people among whom I have done fieldwork, the Primitive Baptists of the Blue Ridge Mountains of North Carolina and Virginia. I use it here to allude to the anthropological journey, not only for each of us as anthropologists but also for our discipline, during what I call our 'hundred years of solitude' – a century featuring solitary fieldwork and the position of outsider as key elements in the role 'anthropologist'. We are all sojourners in a strange land. I refer also to my own sojourn or *Bildung* in recent years, and attempt to draw together elements not often combined in anthropology: regionalism, globalism and engagement.

I take note of *Volkskunde*, also, as a distinctively German or continental European concept that may have special resonances for the comparative method and that remains mysterious, though intriguing, to many of us outside Europe. Although the context of my 'action comparison' is American, the heritage on which it draws includes such concepts as *Volkskunde*, and the European context of this conference on comparison has provided an opportunity to acknowledge and explore this background as a continued source of inspiration and insight for a renewal of comparison.

To assess and (re)build the comparative method, we must address several questions:

1   What is the relation between the comparative method as classically conceived (e.g. by Galton), on the one hand, which saw each culture as an independent variation, and globalism, on the other hand, which sees all cultures as interconnected?
2   What does globalism imply for classic definitions of fieldwork?
3   What is the relevance of the postmodernist question of reflexivity? In other words, What is the source (gender, race, class, etc., or – more profoundly – what Gadamer (1982) termed one's 'prejudices' derived from tradition) of one's questions that generate one's comparisons? How prominently should this source and the resulting relativistic 'view from below', from one's own situation, be acknowledged, as compared to pursuing a universalist 'view from above', which has been the classic objective of the comparative method?
4   What are the implications of comparison for practice? Can anthropology contribute to policy? To leadership? Should it remain oppositional, marginal, outside the centre of society? If the oppositional stance derives, in part, from our nay-saying ethnographic particularism, might a more constructive stance derive from a generalizing comparative method?

I will comment briefly on these questions before reviewing some of anthropology's European heritage and developing my approach of action comparison.

To answer the first question, globalistic perspectives, such as those of Appadurai (1990) or Hannerz (1992) in anthropology and Harvey (1996) or Massey (1991) in geography, emphasize what we used to call diffusionism and now term globalization: the 'coca-cola-nization' of the world, the orientalization of the West, the periphery entering the centre and the centre swamping the periphery. While globalization is driven by capitalism (dollars make the world go 'round, and dollars go 'round the world, quipped Massey – before the advent of the euro, to be sure), its profound effect is the interconnecting and merging of cultures. In this regard, globalization poses a challenge for the comparative method, in so far as that method is premised on the assumption that one can define cultures as distinct and independent units. The comparative method (whether one employs it in Weberian terms, using ideal types, or in statistical modes as with Köbben [1952] or Murdock [1949], Swanson [1960] and other Human Relations Area Files approaches) emphasizes a certain integrity and distinctiveness of each unit's pattern. This is true whether that unit is a 'tribe' or 'society' (as in HRAF) or a pan-national cultural-historical 'type' (as in Weber's Protestant ethic v. Asian type, whether Chinese or Indian; an approach elaborated in an ethnographic version by Geertz, with his Moroccan or Indonesian Islamic types and his *santri/abangan/prijaji* types within Indonesia). Structuralist comparison, *à la* Lévi-Strauss, Leach, Needham and Douglas, still emphasizes the logic and integrity of a pattern, while the unit in which that pattern is manifest may range from humanity as a whole to particular variations in the universal pattern. (Examples are Needham's left/right logic as a universal pattern [1973], Leach's mirror-imaged patrilineal/matrilineal formulae elucidated in *Rethinking Anthropology* [1961], Douglas's combinations of group and grid [1970], Lévi-Strauss's sacrifice v. totemistic societies [1966].) In all of these, comparison serves to elucidate a logic of patterning, either universal – common to all – or in regularities of covariation.

Globalism, on the other hand, emphasizes not such logic of patterning but rather interaction – the continuous interaction of elements (capital, labour or cultural commodities) in the world. To inject, perhaps prematurely, a critical question: might not the globalist approach be rather mindless? Instead of discerning pattern and logic, distilling principles from particulars, some globalists simply trace interconnections: diffusions. Others, perhaps, seek some simple functional pattern in those interconnections, for example, exploitation of the third world by the first, as in Greider's *One World, Ready or Not* (1997). Journalists, geographers, politicians, and businesses embrace globalism in this conceptually simple (though empirically complex) paradigm of functional interaction; in a word, this is the approach of political economy. Anthropologists and other social scientists who have classically pursued the comparative method face a conceptual task at once more challenging and more debatable because it entails analysis through abstraction to selectively highlight types or principles. Thus, Weber strove to lay bare the deep logic of the Protestant ethic compared to Asian ethics. Somewhat combining the two approaches – simplistically and dangerously, some would argue – are works such as Samuel Huntington's *The Clash of Civilizations: Remaking of World Order* (1996). Huntington's thesis, that the post–Cold War is a clash of Western, Islamic and other cultural/political entities, combines ideal-typical constructions with political-economic analysis, envisioning the ideal types as at war with each other.

Second, what are the implications for fieldwork? The comparative method and ethnographic fieldwork in the classic structural–functional Malinowskian sense are traditionally seen as opposed to each other because fieldwork emphasizes context. An aspect of a group or a culture can be understood only in its localized context, ethnographers argue, hence comparison is suspect ('impossible', says Evans-Pritchard) because it abstracts aspect A from context A in order to compare it with aspect B from context B. Globalism challenges both approaches by denying the boundary between context A and context B; both A and B are part of a world system. Accordingly, A can only be understood as interacting with that world system, and if one pursues the point, one ceases to locate one's fieldwork in place A or any particular place but instead tries to grasp the movement of things and people and ideas from A to Z. An example is studies of migration – of refugees from third to first world, of factories and of tourists from first to third world. How does one do globalistic fieldwork, tracing movement around the world, while retaining in-depth immersion in a localized culture? And without such in-depth studies, how is valid comparison to be made? On the other hand, how does one avoid defining artificial boundaries that may enhance scholarly and scientific clarity and depth but distort realities of world movement?

Third, the postmodernist question is to a degree rendered moot by globalism. Postmodernism denies the comparative method any claim of a universalistic perspective because the comparativist always looks out from below – as a Westerner, as a white male, etc. – rather than from above, as an omniscient god, a cosmic intelligence, an objective scientist. While this critique is obviously true, in a globalistic world the particular stance of anyone is presumably merged with the stance of everyone. With multicultural globalism, many voices sing together, and even if particular ones – e.g. the subaltern or suppressed voices – sing special songs, the resulting polyphonic chorus creates commonality. The Western white male and the majority of human beings, who are not white males, share more under globalism than under isolationism. Hence, one could argue, globalism can reaffirm comparison through leading towards a common framework.

This is not to deny that diversity remains, of course. Diversity remains even within the discipline of anthropology. An example: at the International Congress of Anthropological and Ethnological Sciences held in July 1998 at Williamsburg, Virginia, two sessions were held simultaneously in neighbouring rooms. One involved Asian anthropologists who expressed frustration at being persistently misunderstood by Western anthropologists and therefore are launching their own journal. The other was a session by Romanian anthropologists on the concept of the beauty of the human being, which elucidated a perspective, including a comparative perspective, quite distinct from anything I have heard in Anglo-American anthropology – which may describe ideals of beauty but rarely if ever prescribes such an ideal, as did the Romanians. A third example, to be elaborated later, is the concept of *Volkskunde* and its distinctive perspective, which was discussed at the hundred-year meetings of the Polish Ethnological Society in 1996.

To answer the fourth question; what about action, about anthropology making a difference in the world? The comparative method is potentially one of our weapons, as I noted in a presidential address to the American Anthropological Association, where I listed the comparative method as one of ten key contributions anthropology can make to wider concerns (Peacock 1997). This is standard lore. Anthropologists have long touted their comparative scope as holding a special wisdom for humankind. But exactly how can the comparative method contribute? And how has it already done so?

Thus far, anthropology's comparative contribution has been of two kinds: formal and informal. Formal comparative analyses, e.g. of kinship, political or economic organization, have made some impact on thinking, policy and action in fields such as international development or legislation (examples are comparative studies of law or kinship that guided tribal administration by colonial governments). Perhaps greater impact has been made, however, by more informal comparisons – the telling anecdote, or perhaps the telling ethnographic anecdote made into a parable to illustrate a principle. As examples, consider the impact on psychiatry of Gregory Bateson's double-bind hypothesis about schizophrenia (Bateson *et al.* 1963) or Margaret Mead's *Sturm-und-Drang* argument about maturation (Mead 1928) – Bateson's comparison based partly on Bali, partly on a few cases in an asylum in Palo Alto, California; Mead's based on the contested ethnography of Samoa. Perhaps comparatively based psychological insights such as Bateson's and Mead's could impact on psychology and psychiatry because one can sense intuitively that a common human mind is shared globally, i.e. that there is a 'psychic unity of humankind'. Hence, one can draw on the ethnographic parable as a path to *Verstehen*, an intuitive and empathetic insight into a human experience such as schizophrenia. For a more localized example, consider Wade Smith, a trial lawyer in the state of North Carolina, who had Colin Turnbull testify, on the basis of his ethnography of the Ik, about the 'law of the jungle'. Through Turnbull's testimony, Smith secured the acquittal of his client, a Lumbie Indian who had killed a fellow prison inmate, on the ground that prison life, like life among the Ik, followed not civilian law but 'the law of the jungle' (Turnbull 1972; Wade Smith, personal communication). In this example (as in those of Bateson and Mead), rhetoric was important in influencing the audience, which may advantage the exotic narration as a means of influencing outcomes in emotional arenas such as court trials and psychiatry.

Though the ethnographic anecdote or parable will continue, no doubt, to be key to the anthropological soapbox, globalism has reduced or certainly changed its impact. As the world grows smaller and more interrelated, the exotic becomes less intriguing, and arguing difference and relativism becomes both less informative and less compelling. What about alternative ethnographic narrations that would demonstrate globalism – the interpenetration of cultures? These may be more accurate but are perhaps less interesting, since everyone has anecdotes about globalism, many of them just as telling as the anthropologist's. As for the postmodernist twist – inserting relativistic and personalistic narration ('This is how I, as an X, from background Y, came to see and understand Z') – these would seem tediously narcissistic and uninteresting to an audience that mainly wants to learn about Z, not X and Y (i.e. what the anthropologist might say about Bosnia or Rwanda or Indonesia or Eritrea, not about him- or herself and his/her methodological perspectives).

So if ethnographic tale telling in its old (and slightly newer) form ('I come from afar to tell about being there') is losing its impact, has the time come to regain comparison and mobilize it to illuminate global and local issues? And if so, how? My several suggestions, based partly on efforts illustrated below, are these:

1   Broaden the universe of discussion. For example, when historians or lay persons or policy-makers in my region, the southern USA, obsessively take as their point of reference the northern USA, it is helpful to suggest comparisons beyond the USA (comparisons that show, for example, that in global perspective the North is rather exceptional, whereas the South is closer to many other places in the world and can both inform and be informed by them).

2   Make pointed comparisons. Comparing whatever locale or life-world is the focus of discussion or practice and even a single relevant case, including one's own field site, can shift perspectives usefully, emotionally as well as intellectually, and aid in the ability to perceive patterns. (This is not the same as an ethnographic tale to show how exotic the other is, but a combination of mirroring and contrasting the other and one's own culture.)

3   Use mid-level theorizing (à la Merton). Such theorizing draws together strategically varying instances to address such questions as, What will happen to A, if we do B? Anthropologists have long used this technique, based on standard anthropological knowledge, to broach methodological issues in a way at once prudent and not cripplingly convoluted.

None of these measures aspires to formulate formal comparative theories, which have their place, too, but are often unavailable for issues at hand. Later, I explore some contemporary cases that raise questions entailed in these three main points. Before looking at these current efforts, however, I wish to explore some aspects of anthropology's heritage, focusing especially on European ideas.

Globalism, *Bildung*, *Volkskunde*, ethnography: comparison in historical perspective

In his opening remarks at the July 1998 International Congress of Anthropological and Ethnological Sciences, President Vincent Sutliffe evoked an image of the comparative method in 1898 that both resonated and contrasted with the globalistic focus of the 1998 Congress. Sutliffe showed a film taken by the Torres Straits Expedition of 1898 for the Cambridge University archive. It depicted dancing natives, captured and preserved as an exhibit of an isolated, documented 'specimen'.

This expeditionary phase of anthropology, leading towards museum exhibits and ethnological collections and archives, was, as we know, followed by a fieldwork phase, which led to ethnographies that strove to capture the functioning societies studied by the method of participant observation.[1] The fieldwork phase, which has dominated the twentieth century, now confronts the globalistic phase that is ushering in the twenty-first century.

Andre Gingrich and Sylvia Haas trace a parallel history in their account 'Vom Orientalismus zur Sozialanthropologie: Ein Überblick zu österreichischen Beiträgen für die Ethnologie der Islamischen Welt' ('From orientalism to social anthropology: an overview of Austrian contributions to the ethnology of the Islamic world') (1995/96). In microcosm, the 110 years of Islamic studies at the Wiener Institut für Völkerkunde exhibit a movement from a philological and expedition phase of research to a fieldwork phase which has led in turn to encounters with issues of gender, refugees and the forces of globalism.

On the surface, these two vignettes depict commonly recognized parallel histories: from expedition to fieldwork to globalism. One question to pose, however, in comparing such histories, is how much difference the Anglo-American and continental European philosophical backgrounds make. Consider the simple question of comparison v. particularism, often denoted as ethnology v. ethnography in the Anglo-American tradition and *Völkerkunde* v. *Volkskunde* in the German/Continental. *Völkerkunde* and *Volkskunde* are similar to but not identical to ethnology and ethnography, as Vermeulen (1995) and Jasiewicz and Slattery (1995) point out; but the former comes more from a Herderian and Humboldtian perspective, the latter from a Baconian empirical science perspective. To oversimplify, the first is Continental, especially German in the larger cultural sense, the second Anglo. The US anthropological and, more broadly, academic and cultural context, however, combines aspects from both the German and British perspectives.

Gingrich, in his 1998 review of Dumont's *German Ideology* (1994), traces the German emphasis on holism that associates culture with the idea of *Bildung*. *Bildung* unites cultural understanding with personal development and is basic to German philosophies of education as well as to meaningful existence generally. *Bildung*, for example, is key in Gadamer's recasting of philosophy in a postmodernist reflective mode (1982); that is, reflexivity is part of self/cultural learning. Dumont's and Gingrich's evocation of *Bildung* leads to many ruminations and questions about the effect of this heritage on anthropology. Recall the key literary origin of *Bildung*, Goethe's *Wilhelm Meister's Lehrjahre*. That *Bildungsroman* recounts Wilhelm's coming of age through travelling (with a theatre troupe – an experience ironically part of my own first fieldwork), a story linked to the tradition of *Wanderung* or *Wandervogel* that is still romanticized in German culture in a way that is absent in Anglo-American stories of maturation, even after the 1960s instituted a somewhat parallel habit. The story also evokes, in the person of Wilhelm's exotic (Italian) consort, Mignon, nostalgic yearning for homeland. This is the other side of wandering, as exemplified in

Hugo Wolf's, Beethoven's, Liszt's, Schubert's and Schumann's Mignon song 'Kennst Du das Land', in which Mignon remembers the idyllic Mediterranean scene of her childhood. *Bildung*, then, foreshadows both anthropology and psychoanalysis, combining the 'far away' with the 'deep within', and travel with nostalgic introspective remembering of past, childhood (notably that of an exotic female – a Jungian *anima*) and homeland. This is a potent emotional package to combine with a humanistic perspective on learning and maturation. An intellectual tradition that entails *Bildung* will shape a *comparative* or generalizing thrust different from that of the ahistorical, impersonal, objective, empirical, laboratory model of the Baconian/Anglo scientific heritage.

Exactly how would this heritage shape Germanic anthropology? Consider several examples: the search for particulars that manifest the universal, as in Weber's ideal types; the search for the original – the *Ur*-language or *Ur*-culture – that lies behind current variations, as in Grimm's Law, perhaps the most successful of comparative formulations in cultural anthropology. Returning to Vienna, we find yet another variation in the *Kulturkreislehre*, which formulates an *Ur*-type that diffuses globally.[2]

What, then, do these three examples (Weber, Grimm, *Kulturkreislehre*) exhibit? First, a sense of particularism embodying universals (an ideal – *Ur* – type or a regional but diffusing *Ur*-pattern); second, a sense of history and existence intersecting, so that a pattern is part of process and history, rather than an abstracted laboratory-based law; third, perhaps less apparent but hovering around the edges, an awareness of concepts as part of a larger cultural existence and spirit, of which one's own journey is an aspect. Jungian notions of archetype as key to individuation elaborate this perspective. The reason Jung has impacted anthropology so little, compared to Freud, is, in part, I suspect, due to the Anglo-American discomfort with the *Bildung*-like organicism of Jung's Germanic view.

Volkskunde is, like *Bildung*, a tradition stemming from a Germanic or Continental scholarly and philosophical world view but with an objective (e.g. artefactual, or museum) manifestation, as contrasted to the subjective dimension of *Bildung*. *Volkskunde* is complementary to the comparative method (which is grounded in *Völkerkunde*) in that it focuses on the scholar's 'home' culture, especially its folk roots, whereas *Völkerkunde* and the comparative method treat the rest of the world.

Although Anglo-American and German/Continental perspectives, including museology, interact and overlap, they do seem somewhat distinctive, as may be suggested by a few examples. This distinctiveness seems stronger in regard to *Volkskunde* than to *Völkerkunde*: the Museum für Völkerkunde in the New Hofburg in Vienna, for example, is broadly similar to the Museum of Man in London, the Pitt-Rivers Museum in Oxford, the ethnological sections of the Museum of Natural History in Washington, DC, and the Peabody Museum in Cambridge, Massachusetts, in this regard. Each of these (*Völkerkunde*) institutions exhibits major culture areas of the world, with an emphasis on material culture. Museums of *Volkskunde*, on the other hand, including open-air museums in eastern Europe and Scandinavia, do the same thing but with respect to local rather than 'exotic' or 'foreign' cultures. This sort of *Volkskunde* tradition is less prevalent in the Anglo-American context. In the Smithsonian Institution complex, for example, one finds the Museum of American History, which differs from the Museum of Natural History in that it focuses on local, as opposed to exotic, peoples. However, material folk culture distinguished or categorized by region or ethnic group is not a major organizing principle in the Museum of American History, as it would be in a *Volkskunde* museum. Instead, particular ethnic, regional or religious groups are woven into the overall flow of 'American history', which is often seen as a march of technological progress – from the horse-drawn buggy to the diesel locomotive, for example. In this organizational system, American Indians are not considered an *Ursprung* of majority group national culture in the United States in the same sense that peasant cultures in Central and Eastern Europe are seen as *Volkskunde* at the root of the majority culture; instead, American Indians are distinguished as ethnically different from, rather than as roots of, 'American' culture as a majority historical tradition.

What about *folklore* as opposed to *anthropology*? Is this not equivalent to *Volkskunde* in an Anglo-American context? In some senses, yes. For example, such tales as those of John Henry, Johnny Appleseed and Jack are equivalent to the Siegfried, Brunnhilde and Baron Münchhausen stories, and Appalachian ballads are equivalent to *Volkslieder*; in both instances, a 'folk' root is identified for a majority culture, Germanic or Anglo-American. The difference lies in two features, however, one material and the other less tangible. The material feature is that folklore in Anglo-America is not so explicitly linked to museums – the material manifestation of folk culture – as is *Volkskunde*. The intangible feature is suggested by the word *Geist*. Owing to philosophical and cultural influences from Herder to Hegel, the German/Continental notion of folk culture has been seen as a manifestation of an overarching *Geist* or 'spirit', something akin to Kroeber's 'superorganic' culture: an organic, integrative configuration of ideas and symbols that unites folk custom and majority civilization and history. But the Anglo-American empirical perspective undermines a concept such as *Geist* and indeed is sceptical and reticent about it, in part for political reasons. Therefore, folklore has not played so strong a role in Anglo-American majority history as *Volkskunde* has in continental Europe.[3]

Volkskunde, then, looms as a dimension that informs a study of comparison by building on an 'inner' focus on one's own cultural roots. In this sense, it complements the introspective aspect of *Bildung* and has provided a distinctive path – one fraught with its own excesses and dangers, of course, as the Nazis, Afrikaners and Serbs demonstrate – through which cultural scholars connect to the life-world in which they reside.

Dumont's important 1994 work (cf. Gingrich 1998) notes two dominant themes in German thought since the time of Goethe: a sense of (1) an objective, organic cultural framework, in dialogue with (2) a subjective path of individual development. The concept of *Volk*, including *Volkskunde*, *Völkerkunde* and museums to express and display these, could be taken to illustrate the objective, organic theme, while *Bildung*, as Dumont elaborates, expresses the subjective, individual one. Out of both themes, Humboldt developed the concept of the university as distinct from the *Gymnasium*-type of school; both served *Bildung*, but the school taught received knowledge, whereas the university sought new knowledge (*Wissenschaft*) through original research.

In the United States, we have merged the German concept of the university with the British. Stated briefly, prior to the late nineteenth century the USA had colleges, which taught received humanistic knowledge. The German university model added the research component in the late nineteenth century, and the land-grant state university model – home-grown American, to a degree – added the concept of public service. The result is the conglomerate university in the United States today, which includes a liberal arts (teaching) component, often identified as a College of Arts and Sciences, a graduate research component, and a service component, sometimes located in extension and professional units.

Anthropology in the United States exists within this mixed framework, selectively emphasizing varied heritages and missions: British, German, global, teaching, research and service, or 'practice'. Several of these emphases can be seen in the efforts I characterize here as 'action comparison'. These examples, however, are only one set within a broader spectrum. Before focusing on my own background and endeavours, it is worth noting briefly other ways to mobilize our disciplinary heritages in ways that impact society and culture. Particular note should be taken of the *Volkskunde*/folklore approach, since it is one de-emphasized by most US anthropologists, including myself. Consider two examples, one in Poland and one in the United States. In the Polish parliament, the Silesian representative is a folklorist/anthropologist who joins a *Volkskunde* approach to celebrating Silesian heritage with a political position representing Silesia. In the United States, both the current heads of the National Endowment for the Humanities and the National Endowment for the Arts are folklorists. Why folklore, why *Volkskunde* in these positions of political and cultural power? Folklore and *Volkskunde* honour forms and identities that are celebrated by the 'folk' themselves (as well as tourists, preservationists, politicians and others who 'construct' identities). Therefore, folklorists, especially public folklorists, achieve something that social and cultural anthropologists rarely do (as explained below), namely, identify simultaneously with a studied tradition and with a life-world in which one resides and operates as a citizen and participant. This kind of activism could be termed 'action particularism', as compared to the approach that I illustrate below, 'action comparison'. The distinction is worth noting, even as the two approaches sometimes merge in practice.

As I move, now, to consider how comparison can become 'activated', I shall also keep in mind the *Volkskunde*/*Bildung* stream as one both complementary to and informative of comparison.

Towards action comparison

Critical theoretical critiques aside, the heroic (heroinic) contribution of field-work is the great achievement of a century of anthropology. But anthropology's century is tragically heroic in having been one hundred years of solitude, so to speak, as anthropology became, after the early years of evolutionary synthesis, an oppositional discipline, a nay-sayer to generalization (such 'nays' being derived from the experience of lonely individual fieldworkers who contest conventional wisdoms). Periodically, even continuously if erratically, we try to harvest the fruits of this ethnographic labour. We work under siege. Our enemies vary. Some are excessively critical, others excessively scientific, still others excessively bureaucratic and pragmatic. Certainly the grand visions of synthesis – whether Viennese *Kulturkreislehre*, structuralism, Marxism, Weberian/Parsonsian-ism and neo-Parsonsian-ism – have suffered assault, and we have wandered in the wilderness. Yet globalism, if it does nothing else, forces us at the beginning of this century and this millennium to seek additional ways to harvest the fruits of fieldwork: to generalize, to compare and to apply our insights cogently so as to make a difference in a world whose shrinkage threatens to trivialize – if not obliterate – those differences we have worked so heroically to document.

What I report here is an effort, not entirely successful, to apply anthropology comparatively: to work within a tradition of regional scholarship and localized practice while drawing on the comparative framework and on fieldwork of an evolving type. This work has entailed the following contexts, which I will elaborate below:

1   Fieldwork in Southeast Asia and the south-eastern USA, and other kinds of international and local immersions/exposures.
2   Administrative work directing a centre for international studies and a centre for the study of the American South.
3   Theoretical reflection derived from a mixture of Weber, Freud and an anthropology struggling to encounter critical theory and other newer trends.
4   Envisioning directions of our discipline and others while carrying out elected leadership tasks in an era when academia is confronting significant challenges.

Ethnographic grounding

None of my fieldwork was undertaken with specifically applied intentions, nor did I have a comparative project in mind in most instances. In 1962–3, I lived with a family in an Indonesian slum and studied working-class theatre (Peacock 1968). In 1969–70, I did fieldwork among Singapore Muslims, then lived among the Muhammadiyans, a Muslim movement in Indonesia (Peacock 1978). In 1979, I worked briefly with Sumarah, a mystical sect in Indonesia.

Since the 1970s, I have done fieldwork among so-called Christian fundamentalists, including Pentecostals and the Primitive Baptists, in the upper South of the United States, with a brief stint in California (Peacock and Tyson 1989). Some of this work has been published in monographs, reporting and analysing findings. It is known mostly by academics, but some of it is even better known among the fieldwork peoples themselves, notably Muhammadiyans and Primitive Baptists. The Muhammadiyans, who now number 28 million, translated and distributed a short book I wrote about them, and Primitive Baptists have shared copies of our 1989 book among relatives and members of the Mountain District Association, the group we studied. Thus the fieldwork has begun to reach out to the organizations on which it was based. Beyond that, further unanticipated spin-offs have occurred.

On Thursday, 6 May 1999, I visited Williamston, North Carolina, a town some two and a half hours east of Chapel Hill. A legislator, Congressman Gene Rogers, who was hosting a meeting of alumni and other constituents of the University of North Carolina (UNC) at Chapel Hill as an outreach of the Board of Visitors, had asked me to discuss what is currently going on at the university. I was invited because of previous work as Chair of the Faculty, but my relationship to Congressman Rogers was based on fieldwork, as he pointed out to the assembled group. He told how we had met at a football game and talked about the Hassell family of Williamston and the book Sylvester and Cushing Hassell had written about the history of the Primitive Baptists. He recounted that I, and other researchers, had lived among Primitive Baptists up in the mountains and had written a book about them (*Pilgrims of Paradox*, 1989), which he had read because his own forebears were Primitive Baptists and he himself was raised as one.

I carried forward this ethnographic theme by reading a passage from the Hassells' book, which truly is remarkable, and then went on to discuss the university. After the talk, a lawyer, Mr. Manning, and the local Chief District Court Judge, James W. Hardison, approached me to ask about the Primitive Baptists. They wanted to know how to get copies of our book (Peacock and Tyson 1989), which is out of print, so I left a copy with Manning. He has since sent me a copy of the Hassells' will and has initiated a correspondence; Hardison, who that night described a document on the 'Rules of Church Decorum', which he sent me the next day, also told a story about his grandfather and the issue of predestination. Finally, Congressman Rogers and his wife took my wife and me to the Hassells' graves and to their house, where the current owner gave us something he had written about the Hassells' history.

This experience exemplifies how fieldwork can connect to life. Rogers happens to be a co-chair of the appropriation committee for education in our state legislature's House of Representatives. He is among those who decide the shape of education in the state, including our public university. Our mutual interest in Primitive Baptists, based on my fieldwork and Rogers' life history, have no direct link to our mutual interest in education, but the two interweave in a fabric of relationship.

Action, outreach and application, in company with comparison, have thus begun to flow out of my fieldwork. The interweaving of the Primitive Baptist research with legislative relations is but one example. Another is the coincidence that a son of the family with whom my wife and I lived while doing fieldwork in 1962 now lives just a few minutes away, in Durham, North Carolina, and our lives intertwine. A third is the Muhammadiyah connection, reactivated during a stay in Indonesia in 1996 and reciprocated by a visit with us from a brother of Amien Rais, then the head of Muhammadiyah. (I had participated with Amien Rais in training camps in 1970.) As I write in 1999, Amien is one of three candidates for the presidency of Indonesia – although he could have been a candidate for prison after leading the revolt against then-President Suharto a year earlier. Such relationships, familiar to any fieldworker today, entail unanticipated and informal 'engagements'. Such informal engagements, evolving from friendships forged through fieldwork, can connect to more formal administrative applications, such as a mutual exchange with the University of Gaja Mada in Indonesia that has been set up through our University Center for International Studies, or, of potentially much deeper local significance, some deep changes in the administrative structure of our entire state university system generated by some of the UNC faculty in company with certain legislators.

Comparison, too, is a familiar and natural – indeed, almost inevitable – outcome of reflection over time on multiple fieldworks and multiple engagements. Some of my comparisons are specific; for example, a comparative analysis of Muhammadiyah, Pentecostal, Primitive Baptist and Sumarah as part of a volume dedicated to the comparative study of fundamentalism (Peacock 1995). Another kind of comparison is a restudy, for an undergraduate thesis, of a Pentecostal congregation by a student of mine, Kim Diehl, whose black and female perspective brought new questions that interestingly connect to changes in the church itself over a quarter century. Although I have not followed up comparatively my study of Indonesian theatre, many of its ethnographic points foreshadowed theoretical perspectives others have developed subsequently, emphasizing performance and narration. More broadly and less directly, these fieldworks enter into discussions of key issues such as the relationship between globalism and more particularistic forces – regionalism, fundamentalism and ethnicity. These discussions, which are necessarily comparative, are entailed in some of the projects noted above, such as the 'Reading Regions Globally' Mellon Foundation seminar sponsored by our Center for International Studies.

If there is a message in all this, it is the following: at the same time that, here and elsewhere, I am pressing anthropologists to address issues that *matter*, and to do so by broadening their scope through comparison and by sharpening their work toward practice, I would also advocate and confirm what may seem a detour – the importance of doing fieldwork, and fieldwork that is not too narrowly circumscribed by an applied focus. Such fieldwork has proved repeatedly, in the work of many anthropologists, to be the indispensable ground for significant understanding that can lead to action. Lévi-Strauss (1966) once proclaimed that 'History, like many careers, can lead anywhere provided you get out of it'. The same can be said of fieldwork, except that you never really get out it. The ten cases described below, by continuing efforts initially derived from fieldwork, illustrate action comparison.

Cases in action comparison

1   The Nike case

In its summer 1998 issue, a *Cultural Survival Quarterly* (1998, 22, 2: 8) headline reads, 'Nike wins spot in top 10 worst corporations'. As author Julia Dickinson explains, 'Nike has been chosen by human rights activists as the company that "best represents the worst of global economy"'. The article cites labour abuse as the reason for the criticism of Nike and states that negative press resulted in Nike experiencing a 30 per cent stock drop. Under the heading 'Action you can take', Dickinson proposes, 'Write a letter to Nike CEO Phil Knight' or e-mail the 'Boycott Nike Homepage'.

An additional/alternative proactive effort was taking place just prior to this *Cultural Survival* item, during the spring of 1998. At the University of North Carolina, Chapel Hill, students had protested against a multimillion dollar contract between Nike and the university's athletic department, partly on grounds of alleged labour abuses. Believing that the issues deserved informed discussion, three faculty members and one student (myself; current Chair of Faculty Richard Andrews, a Professor of Environmental Engineering; Nicholas Didow, Associate Professor of Business; and Carla Jones, a PhD candidate in anthropology) organized a course that considered the labour issue and others entailed in the Nike case. Our purpose was to explore with concerned students issues and data concerning Nike and its various contexts: Asia, labour relations, athletics and academics. Guest lecturers ranged from critics of Nike, such as Nguyen, a Vietnamese labour analyst, to representatives of Nike, and included scholars of Asia, economists, historians, anthropologists and William Friday, the Chancellor and former President of the university, who chaired the Knight Commission on collegiate athletics, a major national group. The course received a good deal of publicity, including a spot on ESPN, the US cable sports channel, which resulted in Nike CEO Phil Knight paying a surprise visit to the class. The students presented Knight with their critique of Nike, based on our studies. A few days later, Knight gave a National Press Club speech in Washington, DC, that was widely covered in national and international news. In it, he proposed reforms in Nike-linked manufacturing plants. Knight attributed the reforms, in part, to this UNC–Chapel Hill course. Other, perhaps more enduring, results of the course include a code this university, in company with many others, has drafted to govern relations with corporate sponsors; that code, now backed by a coalition of universities and corporations, is having a strong impact on corporate practice.

Certainly appropriate scepticism is in order, and protest and critical stance remain crucial components in promoting change (in fact, the disclosure clause added to the code was spurred by sit-ins in spring 1999 led by a student from our course). Still, the course and its follow-up, including a licensing committee that I co-chair, illustrate an effort to combine the types of critical and constructive actions that characterize proactive anthropology.

2   The Center for the Study of the American South (CSAS)

In 1990, in company with a Norwegian–Charlestonian historian, David Moltke-Hansen, and a regionalist sociologist, John Reed, I helped create this centre, which includes faculty, students and citizens. I was chair of the board of CSAS until 1998.

Among the centre's notable features are its focus on the region, the sponsorship of celebratory events (e.g. the North Carolina literary festival in spring 1998) and critical or policy-oriented events (e.g. fora concerning race relations and entitled 'Unfinished Business' were held in twenty-two Southern cities during 1998), and scholarly publications such as the journal *Southern Cultures*, published by UNC Press. The CSAS has succeeded in drawing support and participation from local and regional donors, corporations and community groups; in our spring 1998 literary festival there were 4,000 participants. The Unfinished Business meeting in Birmingham, Alabama, included Congressman John Lewis, later an important spokesperson in the Clinton impeachment trials, and former Mississippi Governor Winter, a member of President Clinton's Commission on Race. The centre's focus is local and regional, but also somewhat comparative. As part of the literary festival, for example, I chaired a panel entitled 'Deep Within and Far Away', which featured readings by Greek, Chinese and Viennese authors who are migrants to North Carolina. Assuming that changing cultures motivates introspection, we asked a psychoanalyst to serve as discussant. Although cultural anthropologists have not participated much in CSAS activities, archaeologists and folklorists have, and there is wide participation from other academic disciplines and the laity. I suspect the lack of participation by anthropologists reflects the attitudes about regionalism and local elites that I note below.

3   Comparative fieldwork

As I have mentioned, I did participant observation among the Muhammadiyah of Indonesia in 1970 and visited them again in 1996, participating in discussions of social issues. In 1975 I did fieldwork among Pentecostals and in 1980–1 among Primitive Baptists in the Blue Ridge Mountains. Because the Muslim and Christian groups are both 'fundamentalist', I have attempted comparative analysis of fundamentalism based on this fieldwork, e.g. in the Stewart lectures at Princeton University and the volume on fundamentalism edited by Martin Marty and Scott Appleby (Peacock 1995). The Muhammadiyah case also entered global comparative projects such as that of Huntington, who references it in his depiction of Islamic movements (1996, Chapter 12, n. 21). While 'symbolic' or 'interpretive' anthropology is entailed in my work, the clearest framework is the Weberian comparative study of religious traditions and movements, illustrated by my collaboration with religious studies scholar Ruel Tyson (Peacock and Tyson 1989). A strong part was also folklore or *Volkskunde*, working with folklorist Daniel Patterson and ethnomusicologist Beverly Patterson in recording and archiving Primitive Baptists' music and sermons. An activist aspect was also involved: fieldwork led to my contact with Rais, a leader in Indonesian politics, and the comparative project addressed fundamentalism as a global issue.

4   The American Anthropological Association

As has been the case with other presidents of the American Anthropological Association, my stint as president was marked by a pull between three often conflicting forces: (1) prestigious scholarly commentators who seek intellectual currency, largely in critical theory arenas divorced from anthropology's four-field and comparative method tradition; (2) equally prestigious scholarly commentators who sustain that four-field tradition and/or press for 'scientific' and 'positivistic' approaches; and (3) practitioners of applied work, who are both removed from anthropology's classic centre and impatient with critical theory. As president, and as chair of the long-range planning committee, I helped formulate a vision and plan to link these elements and push towards a unified set of goals, including action or outreach mobilizing comparative perspectives.

5   The University Center for International Studies (UCIS)

The University Center for International Studies, of which I am currently director, parallels the Kenan Institute for Free Enterprise at the University of North Carolina at Chapel Hill, but differs in its focus: the Kenan Institute fuels globalism in the capitalist creation of business (e.g. by creating partnerships between US and Asian businessmen), while the UCIS addresses the humanistic dimension of globalism as a transition from localism. The Institute, in other words, stimulates globalism, whereas the Center both stimulates it and copes with it, analysing it critically and exposing local cultures to it selectively – while also exposing global visitors to local cultures. The UCIS organizes seminars on migration (a phenomenon that results not only in diversity in the state and region but also in tensions between regionalism and globalism) and introduces global concerns locally (by sponsoring outreach to schools and other local groups) and local concerns globally (by hosting state and regional orientation programmes for international students). A comparative perspective is brought to these endeavours implicitly and sometimes explicitly. A grant from the Rockefeller Foundation funded, over a four-year period, a seminar entitled 'The South in comparative perspective', which involved faculty and students (including international postdoctoral scholars) with a research interest in the South. The seminar culminated in a conference for the wider community and region that emphasized questions of identity and memory in the South, but also took an explicitly comparative perspective (which was doubtless swamped by the participants' sometimes nostalgic focus on local identities, on what it means to be 'Southern'). Anthropologists were involved, but they tended to take a critical stance; the greatest impact was made by regional literary figures who appealed to the heart more than the head.

Growing out of this project and the Center for the Study of the American South are several comparative projects by the UCIS. One is being conducted in cooperation with the American Studies programme at the Rheinische Universität in Bonn and is headed by Lothar Honighaussen, a specialist in William Faulkner. This project is a comparative study of the place of 'space' in globalism, especially regionalism; it focuses on Europe and America, particularly Germany and the Southern United States. Somewhat similar projects include faculty/student/citizen seminars, funded by the Mellon and Rockefeller Foundations, which treat the South and regionalism within a comparative and global perspective.

The ambivalence anthropologists express about this regionalist focus is notable, and is answered by the regionalists' ambivalence towards an anthropological focus, including globalist and comparativist views. Such ambivalence – about globalist v. regionalist, critical v. 'identity' perspectives – is, of course, shared by many. The University Center for International Studies therefore attempts to negotiate between these, as expressed in our concept of 'Globgro' – denoting 'global' and 'grounding' – which links global and localized milieux and the transitions between them. The global-to-local spectrum lends itself to comparison as well as to action, such as the outreach programmes Worldmobile, Worldteach and Worldview, which are geared to elementary, middle and high school students and deal with the interplay between the global and the local. This comparative perspective, I have found, offers a sort of cultural therapy and pedagogy in a *Bildung* sense; that is, it helps people to work through, emotionally as well as intellectually, the disorientations entailed in transitions from local to global and vice versa.

6   Faculty Council

From 1993 to 1995 I chaired the Faculty Council, the governing body of our university's 2,300-member faculty. My challenge was to sustain a global vision

and implicit comparative perspective while dealing with nuts-and-bolts legislative or administrative measures. One issue that involved both aspects was the
proposed creation of what was to be called a Black Culture Center. Thousands
of students participated in protests sparked by a perception that the centre
would claim an exclusivist ethnic identity. I helped to add a comparativist
perspective that envisioned the centre as inclusive rather than exclusive, a
springboard for probing broader issues of identity. While heated debate (but no
actual violence, despite threats and protests) surrounded the Black Culture
Center's beginnings, the result so far is promising. The centre currently is
explicitly comparative in exploring questions of African-American identity, e.g.
by hosting conferences that include Japanese and German scholars of African-
American culture.

7   Ethnic cleansing and human rights

Globalism may lead to the destruction of one group by another. Cultural relativism and the comparative method, classically conceived, are akin in that each
assumes the independence of cultural units. Human rights, on the other hand,
postulates universal rights shared by persons of all cultures. The American
Anthropological Association's Human Rights Committee, of which I am a
member, attempts both to formulate an anthropological concept of human
rights in relation to such issues as ethnic cleansing, and actively to deal with
cases of abuse. Human rights is an issue that challenges anthropologists to be
comparative in assessing both local contexts and universal ideals and abuses.

8   The future of universities

In 1993 the Wirtschafts Universität Wien was the site of a conference on the
future of European and American universities, at which I represented my university. The general focus of the meetings was the challenge posed by
business-based models of education, which emphasize downsizing, accountability
and vocational-training, in opposition to the classical liberal arts ideal, which in
some ways is captured by the notion of *Bildung* (or American variants thereof, as
in *The Education of Henry Adams* [Adams 1918]). In 1996 the German-
American Foundation held a conference in Washington, DC, which compared
the future of German and American universities and included explicit consideration of the demise of *Bildung*. And *Transforming Academia*, a recent American
Ethnological Society volume, focuses on the question of the future of anthropology as a discipline (Basch *et al.* 1999). Implicit in the volume is this question:
Will anthropology as a humanistic, '*Bildung*-based' mode of learning (as exemplified by the fieldwork experience, both as training mode for students and
educational/conversion parable for teachers) endure?
    All three of these projects direct attention to questions of higher education.
Can the kind of learning and insight that comes with fieldwork and comparison

be pursued through distance learning? Can changing conditions of employment, such as replacing the professorate with temporary instructors viewed as wage labour, sustain the *Bildung* ideal?

Commentators have blamed both capitalist society and the self-absorbed professorate for the decline of public support for universities. Recommended anti-dotes include (1) reform of society, and (2) reform of universities, which are urged to re-engage with society – either in the general-education mode of the college prior to the influence of the German university or in the applied-education or public-intellectual modes. One could argue that the comparative method is crucial for anthropology's role in either mode, but also that an overly particular-istic and ideological oppositional or 'critical' stance endangers as well as properly tempers this potential contribution.

How does the role of the anthropologist as both particularizing critic (e.g. of universalist issues such as the Human Genome project or human rights) and generalizing comparativist (e.g. temporizing advocacy of human rights) play out in emerging global conditions? Let us take an example. In reviewing anthro-pology terms included in the *Oxford Dictionary of Social Sciences* and the *International Encyclopedia of Social Sciences*, I note the following: prior to the 1980s, many specifically anthropological terminologies were coined (e.g. in kinship and linguistics). In more recent and present times, cultural anthro-pology has coined few new terms and instead uses terms derived from other disciplines and from intellectual movements such as feminism or postmod-ernism (e.g. identity, hegemony, subaltern, etc.). Does this trend reflect a demise of anthropology as a positivistic scientific discipline? A maturation of anthropology as an interdisciplinary comrade? Does it bode well or ill for the future of anthropology in the academy? In the public arena? As a comparative discipline?

Will anthropology seize its opportunity as a generalizing (albeit critically conceived) comparative discipline? If not anthropologists, then who will offset other powerful generalizing forces such as the global multinational capitalistic vision? Can the creaky machinery of the older anthropology, including the comparative method, be re-engineered to meet these new challenges? Can the newer anthropologies be distilled into a force for change, as opposed to a monkey wrench thrown into the machine?

9   Bildung *tutorial*

A UNC alumnus and lawyer, Edgar Love, is undertaking with me and Dr Marilyn Grunkemyer, a former student, a project of life-long learning in a comparative, international, intercultural context. I term this tutorial (which involves discussions about classical literary works) an experiment in *Bildung* because it follows Wilhelm Meister's model of uniting exploration of the 'deep within' and the 'far away', of the domestic self and the international other.

10 Carolina in a global world

In a recent outreach opportunity, I gave the commencement address for our university's December 1999 commencement, at which some 2,600 graduates received degrees (Peacock 1999). Graduates, alumni and parents were present, and local newspapers covered the talk, which was also posted on the worldwide web (a colleague in Germany e-mailed me that she had read it there). I argued that the university, its graduates and all of us must internationalize while also honouring localized groundings. While mentioning sociological and anthropological ideas such as Weber's *Verstehen* (and acknowledging Weber's kinfolk who reside in North Carolina), I attempted to translate these into experiences of alumni, locally and globally. Comparison was implicit, for example, in chastising ethnocentrism, whether expressed towards 'foreigners' or 'natives' (whom newcomers often treat rather as 'foreigners' – as being odd and inferior) and in addressing the possibility that regionalism might one day merge with globalism. To judge from reactions in local newspapers, the general impact of the talk was strong, but journalists emphasized either the 'preserving local' or the 'globalizing' message, rarely both, and thus lost the comparative framework.

Issues for anthropology's action comparison

How does one form these steps in a personal and professional sojourn into the warp threads that can support a coherent fabric for anthropology? As a start, I propose to consider the slogan, 'Think globally, act locally', which equates thinking (theory) with the global, and action (practice) with the local. Admittedly simplistic, it nonetheless provides a shorthand vision against which we may project and evaluate the anthropological endeavour, extending ideally from theory (think globally, including the comparative method) to action (act locally).

Four terms: think / act, global / local

Anthropology is inherently local, but it focuses on thought: local knowledge is what we seek; we honour learning in local contexts. Anthropology thus enriches the intellectualist paradigm by refusing to confine thought to the global realm, which too often privileges intellectuals and planners at the centres of power and detached from local struggles. As anthropology proclaims, locals think too! Yet anthropology is contradictory, as well. Anthropologists honour the local knowledge of certain groups, but not of others. We tend to respect the disempowered and peoples far away from where we reside; we are likely to deny or contest the knowledge of empowered groups, especially when they are part of power structures local to our own residences and life-worlds or if they are suspect in terms of intellectual fashion. By contrast, historians, cultural preservationists, archaeologists, economists, sociologists, political scientists, even some folklorists and writers tend to be less aloof from local groups with power and status. Like the practitioners of *Volkskunde*, such scholars acknowledge and document local knowledge in the very areas where they reside.

What is the consequence for anthropology if anthropologists are less likely than other scholars to focus on their own regions? By removing themselves from engagement with the areas within which anthropologists themselves are located institutionally – and which may be endowed or financially supported by local governmental bodies (e.g. the Committee of Regions of the EEC) – anthropologists become alienated from their home regions. At the same time, anthropologists tend to alienate themselves from certain global perspectives as well. We often challenge the global knowledge of certain groups (e.g. the World Bank, the UN) and critique comparative generalizing perspectives, including science and policy planning. Planners, administrators, economists, and others, by contrast, become involved in and leaders of local and global affairs.

Is this removed and critical anthropological stance necessary for the discipline's intellectual independence and integrity? Does it enhance understanding, or undercut it? And what does it imply for action? This question leads me to the 'act' part of the slogan.

Act locally. Anthropologists affirm the action of certain local groups while denying others: we affirm acts by 'community' and critique acts by 'exploiters'.

Act globally. Anthropologists often affirm the actions of certain causes (e.g. Amnesty International, world congresses on women [Beijing] or ecology [Kyoto]), while denying or opposing global capitalism in the form of multinational corporations (e.g. the World Bank, IMF development projects). There is variation, however, among anthropologists: some practising anthropologists work with multinational development, and some academic anthropologists oppose 'human rights' as a universalizing framework. Other anthropologists deny, critique or bypass world or local action. To the extent that these anthropologists profess relativism, action is difficult, and the most intellectually prestigious theorists and commentators tend to be detached from organized causes, working at a level of critical theory that elucidates more abstract issues. Thus, at the end of its first century, anthropology has created a perspective and a paradigm that are problematical for action: we struggle to find a way to impact and to shape the world that is also ethically, scientifically and humanistically acceptable.

Consider again, in this context of prevailing anthropological perspectives, various approaches to comparative method. Where does comparison fit into this theory-to-action paradigm?

Bildung, as an inner focus and cultural perspective, finds its place as the humanistic and psychological dimension of the quest for identity and understanding. As I have illustrated above, I believe that comparative perspectives can also serve this quest, just as they do the more rigorously scientific objectives that classically guided Galton and his followers. This is the approach I have taken in my 'activist' comparison, with its pedagogical '*Bildung*' tone. *Volkskunde* and folklore both offer ways to deepen the 'local identity' aspect of anthropology and may lead, as suggested above, to a political or cultural activism built on heartfelt regional, ethnic or other local identities. While 'action comparison', as compared to this 'action particularism', may be more quixotic – and also more ambitious, in that it encompasses particularism – it brings into play a wider spectrum of anthropological sensibilities.

Conclusion

What paths are implied by this approach? Let us leave now my own sojourn and trace the steps in the 'think globally, act locally' process, weaving in the issues raised above as they concern the role of anthropology and the comparative method.

1   'Think globally, act locally' implies global planning and local application. If anthropologists refuse to *think globally*, they will be relegated to *applying locally* others' global plans – or critiquing them or sabotaging them in guerrilla actions that may or may not prevail. At the same time, if anthropologists fail to think locally in the sense noted above – that is, to develop interest in the locales where they live and work as well as in their field sites – they will be left out of thought and actions that pertain to their own life-worlds, to use Habermas's term. Anthropologists can enrich the slogan – they can think *and* act globally, think *and* act locally – but only by enriching the paradigm by extending 'local' to their own life-worlds as well as their field sites.

2   Critical theory that emphasizes reflexivity provides little impetus for action and can even paralyse it, but it is necessary and relevant for critically evaluating action.

3   *Volkskunde*, which connects to historical archives, archaeological and material culture museums, antiquities and cultural preservation and tourism, can be a powerful tool for providing identity and inspiration through linkage with the deeper past, memory and tradition (constructed or not). It thus provides a direct pathway to acting locally and globally, as well as a localized base for comparative work.

4   Comparative method is an abstracted – hence, imperfect – but powerful method that suggests implications, critiques and systematic analysis of how global patterns develop, both variously and similarly.

Action comparison

Goethe's 'In the beginning was the deed' (replacing John's 'In the beginning was the word') not only suggests a union of knowledge and action, but reminds us how this union was manifested in his own life and in the concept of *Bildung*. There are parallels for anthropology. *Bildung* grew out of encounters with the other. Wilhelm Meister's study abroad led him to encounter Mignon, the enchanting girl from the South with her nostalgic song, '*Kennst du das Land wo die Zitronen blühn? ... O Vater, laß uns ziehn!*' (Do you know the land where the lemons blossom? ... Oh, Father, let us go!). The encounter resonates with both the German tradition of *Wanderung* and with Goethe's own life, during his student days and his later travels to Italy. As an adult, however, Goethe moved beyond travel and introspection towards work in the world; for several decades he was administrator for Count Augustus. Thus, for Goethe, *Bildung* included fieldwork, reflection and action: truth is in the deed. (Should one seek an American parallel to Goethe, the closest might be Thomas Jefferson. No mean writer himself – witness the Declaration of Independence – Jefferson's deed was to create a new nation, founded on 'truths self-evident'. Like Goethe, he embraced an optimistic scientific rationalism, a bright light shielding a Faustian appetite for shadows, including the provincial locales of Weimar and Charlottesville, and the aesthetic, natural and romantic experiences in those places. Goethe and Jefferson were virtual contemporaries, dying at approximately the same age and only six years apart.)

What about anthropology? The argument here is that comparison lends itself to this Goethian model. Fieldwork necessarily entails comparison, as does any scholarly and scientific work with the 'other', and so do outreach and application. In order to bring home its insights to domestic contexts, anthropology's strongest weapon is comparison within a global context.

Anthropology's insights also run in the opposite direction, as comparison throws 'other' into dialogue and dialectic with 'self'. Anthropological thinking and theory are informed by the experiment of throwing ideas into action and discussion with the wider society. Exactly what implications the experiment carries for anthropological models remains to be discovered, but it is clear already that the process differs from traditional scholarly and scientific 'testing' of comparative theory against 'cases' analysed statistically, or in other ways detached from 'action arenas'. The trick is to challenge ideas with action while not sacrificing clarity, profundity and the integrity of science and scholarship – and especially that hard-won reward of anthropology's hundred years of solitude: fieldwork.

Speculating, if not fantasizing, one can imagine anthropological Goethes and Jeffersons as the leaders/poets/scientists of the twenty-first century.[4] The argument is simple. The emerging global world demands complex understandings of diversity coupled with action models more nimble than the mechanical ones of the industrial age. Rather than hierarchies headed by mono-minded decision makers counselled by mono-minded economists,[5] pollsters and spin-doctors, the new world arguably requires Goethes and Jeffersons who embody within themselves both an understanding of cultural complexity and a capacity for action – in a word, truths and deeds suited for the coming age. Among the disciplines or interdisciplines, anthropology looms strong in its potential for nurturing such a capacity, and perhaps an anthropologist or quasi-anthropologist could even surface as a leader. But this leadership role will happen only if the discipline moves beyond its elements of relativism, alienation and particularism to build on its great strengths and infuse them into a society that has need of them – whether it knows it or not.

Comparative method in some version is essential if anthropology is to effectively address issues in a global age, whether or not my utopian vision comes to pass. Comparative method is the link between field-based ethnography and society-based issues. 'Impossible' it may be, in a strictly scientific or scholarly sense, but magical it can be, in translating truths into deeds.

Notes

1 Interestingly, both phases involved W.H.R. Rivers, connected to the Marrett-led Torres Straits Expedition, who later was a mentor to Malinowski in his Trobriand work.

2 Here I acknowledge the generative contribution to my own area, Southeast Asian studies, of Robert von Heine-Geldern's formulation of the God-King concept. Heine-Geldern's work was an inspiration, hardly acknowledged, of Geertz's *Negara* (1980), Benedict Anderson's 'The idea of power in Javanese culture' (1972) and other regionally grounded comparative generalizations.

3 One could argue that folklore has played a strong role in Anglo-American minority history (i.e. Scots, Welsh and Irish), which would lead, then, to comparison with the role of folklore in United States minority history (i.e. Native American or African-American), but this takes us too far afield – except to note in passing the absence of academic 'scientific' anthropology in these Anglo-American cultural movements as compared to continental Europe.

4 Gingrich (1998) writes, 'Out of this historical context and intellectual climate, *Bildung* emerged as a crystallized constellation of values – with Herder as its inventor, Goethe as its founding hero, and Wilhelm von Humboldt as its main theorist and reformer', and he speculated about comparison with 'early U.S. American ideology', to which these comments about Jefferson are pertinent. To my mind, Gingrich's discussion of Dumont usefully frames the comparison of Goethe and Jefferson as formative figures in German and American ideology and culture, of which two somewhat distinct anthropologies are an expression. Although the comparison of Jefferson and Goethe is in one sense arbitrary, violating prudent comparative method, it is nonetheless instructive. Jefferson was born and died six years before Goethe (Jefferson 1743–1826, Goethe 1749–1832), both men lived 82 years and both sustained creativity from youth to death. Goethe completed *Faust* shortly before he died, and Jefferson was overseeing construction of the University of Virginia in his last years. Jefferson's authorship of the Declaration of Independence is in one sense comparable in significance to *Faust*: both assert a great freedom of the human spirit.

5 An example is a local economist who argues that North Carolina's economy is larger than Indonesia's, so Carolinians needn't worry about Indonesia's crisis. Such comparisons are based on statistics that ignore the actual daily activities of 200 million people. Anthropologist Janine Wedel (1998) has provided a devastating analysis of economists' miscalculations in Eastern Europe; on the other hand, the openness to dialogue of such economists as Dennis Whittle of the World Bank holds greater promise (personal communication, 1999).

Bibliography

Adams, H. (1918) *The Education of Henry Adams*, Boston: Houghton Mifflin.

Anderson, B. (1972) 'The idea of power in Javanese culture', in C. Holt (ed.) *Culture and Politics in Indonesia*, Ithaca, New York: Cornell University Press.

Appadurai, A. (1990) 'Disjuncture and difference in the global cultural economy', *Public Culture* 2, 2: 1–24.

Basch, L., Saunders, L., Scharff, J., Peacock, J.L. and Craven, R.J. (1999) *Transforming Academia: Challenges and Opportunities for an Engaged Anthropology*, Arlington, VA: American Ethnological Society Monograph Series 8.

Bateson, G., Jackson, D.D., Haley, J. and Weakland, J.H. (1963) 'A note on the double bind – 1962', *Family Process* 2: 154–61.

Douglas, M. (1970) *Natural Symbols*, London: Cresset.

Dumont, L. (1994) *German Ideology: From France to Germany and Back*, Chicago: University of Chicago Press.

Gadamer, H.-G. (1982) *Truth and Method*, New York: Crossroad.

Geertz, C. (1960) *Religion of Java*, Glencoe, IL: Free Press.

—— (1968) *Islam Observed*, New Haven, CT: Yale University Press.

—— (1980) *Negara: The Theatre State in Nineteenth-Century Bali*. Princeton, NJ: Princeton University Press.

Gingrich, A. (1998) 'Toward an anthropology of Germany: a culture of moralist self-education?' (Review of Louis Dumont, *German Ideology: From France to Germany and Back*), *Current Anthropology* 39, 4: 567–72.

Gingrich, A. and Haas, S. (1995–96) 'Vom Orientalismus zur Sozialanthropologie: Ein Überblick zu österreichischen Beiträgen für die Ethnologie der Islamischen Welt', *Mitteilungen der Anthropologischen Gesellschaft in Wien* (MAGW) 125/126: 115–34.

Goethe, J.W. (1790, 1808, 1832) *Faust*, Hamburger Ausgabe 3: 44 (10th edn) Munich: Back Verlag.

Greider, W. (1997) *One World, Ready or Not*, New York: Simon and Schuster.

Hannerz, U. (1992) 'The global ecumene', in U. Hannerz (ed.) *Cultural Complexity*, New York: Columbia University Press.

Harvey, D. (1996) *Justice, Nature, and the Geography of Difference*, Oxford: Blackwell.

Heine-Geldern, R. von (1956) *Conceptions of State and Kingship in Southeast Asia*, Southeast Asia Programme, Data Paper 18, Ithaca, NY: Cornell University Press.

Huntington, S. (1996) *The Clash of Civilizations: Remaking of World Order*, New York: Simon and Schuster.

Jasiewicz, Z. and Slattery, D. (1995) 'Ethnography and Anthropology: The Case of Polish Ethnology', in H.F. Vermeulen and A.A. Roldan (eds) *Fieldwork and Footnotes: Studies in the History of European Anthropology*, London and New York: Routledge, pp. 184–201.

Köbben, A.J.F. (1952) 'New ways of presenting an old idea: the statistical method in social anthropology', *Journal of the Royal Anthropological Institute* 82: 129–45.

Leach, E.R. (1961) *Rethinking Anthropology*, London: Athlone Press.

Lévi-Strauss, C. (1966) *The Savage Mind*, Chicago: University of Chicago Press.

Massey, D. (1991) 'The political place of locality studies', *Environment and Planning* A, 23: 267–81.

Mead, M. (1928) *Coming of Age in Samoa*, New York: Morrow.

Murdock, G.P. (1949) *Social Structure*, New York: Macmillan.

Needham, R. (1973) *Right and Left: Essays on Dual Symbolic Classification*, Chicago and London: University of Chicago Press.

—— (1983) *Against the Tranquility of Axioms*, Berkeley, CA: University of California Press.

Peacock, J.L. (1968) *Rites of Modernization*, Chicago: University of Chicago Press.

—— (1978) *Muslim Puritans*, Berkeley, CA: University of California Press.

—— (1995) 'Fundamentalisms narrated: Muslim, Christian, and mystical', in M.E. Marty and R.S. Appleby, *Fundamentalisms Comprehended: The Fundamentalism Project*, vol. 5, Chicago: University of Chicago Press.

—— (1997) 'The future of anthropology', *American Anthropologist* 99, 1: 9–29.

—— (1999) 'Carolina in a global world', University of North Carolina at Chapel Hill Commencement Address, *University Gazette*, 13 January.

Peacock, J.L. and Tyson, R. (1989) *Pilgrims of Paradox*, Washington, DC: Smithsonian Institution Press.

Smith, J.Z. (1982) *Imagining Religion: From Babylon to Jonestown*, Chicago: University of Chicago Press.

Swanson, G.E. (1960) *The Birth of Gods: The Origin of Primitive Beliefs*, Ann Arbor, MI: University of Michigan Press.

Turnbull, C. (1972) *The Mountain People*, New York: Simon and Schuster.

Vermeulen, H.F. (1995) 'Origins and institutionalization of ethnography and ethnology in Europe and the USA: 1771–1845', in H. Vermeulen and A.A. Roldan (eds) *Fieldwork and Footnotes: Studies in the History of European Anthropology*, London and New York: Routledge.

—— (1996) 'Stowarzyszenia Antropologiczne, Etnologiczne i Etnograficzne', *Spojrzenie Porownawcze*, LUD, 99–102.

Weber, M. (1988) *Gesammelte Aufsätze zur Religions-Soziologie*, Tübingen: J.C.B. Mohr (Paul Siebeck).

Wedel, J. (1998) *Collision and Collusion: The Strange Case of Western Aid to Eastern Europe 1989–1998*, New York: St. Martin's Press.

Whittle, D. (1999) Interview, Washington, DC, 10 June 1999.

Chapter 3

Issues of relevance

Anthropology and the challenges of cross-cultural comparison[1]

Marit Melhuus

As the debate between Marshall Sahlins and Gananath Obeyesekere reminds us (cf. for example Borofsky 1997; Geertz 1995; Obeyesekere 1997; Sahlins 1997), there are divergent anthropological perspectives on the interpretation of what I assume is understood to be the same fact: in this case, the death of Captain Cook. Every so often, such controversies surface in anthropological circles, sometimes in the form of restudies such as those by Lewis of Tepoztlán (Lewis 1951; Redfield 1930), by van Beek of the Dogon (van Beek 1991; Calame-Griaule 1991), and the Freeman–Mead 'debate' (Freeman 1983).

For those of us who follow these debates from afar, they may provide instructive readings about the thrusts of ethnographic endeavours, pointing to the intrinsic connections that exist between theory and method and the factors that inform this relationship. For a wider – and perhaps critical – public, however, such controversies serve only to underscore what some view as anthropology's innate weakness: its idiosyncratic nature, based as it is on the practice of fieldwork, and its lack of criteria of truth and validation. The controversies thus disclose fundamental issues in anthropology and highlight questions of interpretation, representation, subjectivity and intersubjectivity with respect to our understandings of the renderings of empirical realities and with respect to the intersubjectivity that exists within an anthropological community. Such tensions, although splitting and fragmenting the anthropological community, serve also to refocus the anthropological agenda and bring to the surface overall concerns about the construction of ethnography and the production of anthropological knowledge. Differences of representation are, as Borofsky claims, 'less part of the problem than part of the solution. In conversing across our differences, we enhance the opportunity to learn from them. We also enhance the discipline of anthropology' (1997: 279). In the current situation, in which questions are being raised about the future of anthropology, such debates, quaint as they may seem to non-anthropologists (and perhaps self-indulgent to some anthropologists), serve to provoke reflections about what anthropology is about. They also remind us of our anthropological heritage, and hence of the continuity that underpins anthropological thinking today.

The echo that reverberates in anthropological circles is that there is a 'crisis' in anthropology. Some argue that it is a crisis of representation, others that it is a problem of relevance and concomitant legitimacy (e.g. Ahmed and Shore 1995a, 1995b; Harries-Jones 1996). The postmodern impasse pushes yet others to reframe anthropological debates in terms of science or objectivity (e.g. D'Andrade 1995; Spiro 1992, 1996; and, in a somewhat different vein, Grimshaw and Hart 1995), while some prefer to flag ethics and advocacy as our *raison d'être* (e.g. Scheper-Hughes 1995; for further discussion see Harries-Jones 1996; Moore 1996b). The camps are many, as are the agendas; it is no easier to create order out of anthropological worlds than it is out of any other world.

At the same time, we see an ever-increasing number of students seeking out the halls and auditoriums where anthropology is taught and spoken, wanting to partake of the anthropological world view, to become party to what has been seen as rather esoteric, but exciting, knowledge. We see a keen interest in anthropology on the part of theologians, historians, medical professionals and the like. Anthropological methods and anthropological knowledge are being incorporated into courses as well as research; anthropological jargon and, perhaps more significantly, anthropological perspectives are being peddled by journalists and media workers more generally (at least in Norway). Anthropological perspectives are being employed by development workers in planning and implementation (and not just at the evaluation end) and by corporations in organizational planning and management strategies. In sum, the reach of what might loosely be termed 'anthropological thinking' has not only gone far beyond academia (and the working situations of professional anthropologists), it has done so unawares, being inscribed in a *Zeitgeist* that has surpassed the imaginings of anthropological communities. While we may well ask what it is anthropology has to offer that is so appealing, this proliferation of anthropology – becoming common property, common knowledge – could be read as a great success story. So why the unease?

There appear to be several different and in part converging trends that may throw light on these misgivings. In what follows I will attempt to frame some of the issues that concern anthropologists. I do so from a particular vantage point: that of an anthropologist trained and working in a Norwegian academic context. This training *cum* context has its own local characteristics and simultaneously is inscribed in more overarching processes both with respect to the development of the discipline and with respect to current educational policies directed at institutions of higher learning. My further considerations hinge on three concerns central to anthropology: the practice of fieldwork, the notion of context and the comparative method. In order to frame my arguments, I focus on different notions of relevance and the implications these have for the practice of anthropology. Ultimately, I am interested in raising a discussion about anthropology – on its own terms. I am also interested in discussing whether anthropology has any terms that might be called its own.

This is a complex matter, and the path I have chosen leaves many stones unturned. Thus it might be apposite to pre-empt the conclusion by positing the following: anthropology's claim to fame has been detailed microsocial studies and cross-cultural analysis. In recent years, the problems related to fieldwork and the making of ethnography have been amply debated, and I will also venture a few remarks here. In these debates, however, comparison seems to be a non-issue, a moot point, impeded, perhaps, by the recurrent stress on particularities and localities, fluidities and processes, subjectivities and positionings. Yet it is my contention that comparison is, at different levels, inherent to anthropology and that to disregard the challenges posed by cross-cultural comparison is to undermine the anthropological enterprise. This position assumes that we have an enterprise (in the positive sense of the term) that we wish to uphold, which I believe we do. In the last instance, the legitimacy of anthropology (as for any other social science) depends not only on its ability to document different life-worlds, but also on its ability to generate theories, thereby contributing towards human understanding. In this effort, the comparative method represents a potential that needs to be explored.

Much current thinking in anthropology has been aimed at unsettling the ground on which our predecessors stood. In that process, some lessons appear to have been overlooked, if not forgotten, and in need of restoration. In other words, the deconstructionist turn begs some form of reconstruction. A step in that direction would be to set the issues of comparison on the anthropological agenda yet again, simultaneously drawing on our own 'cultural heritage' and taking into account the present conditions under which anthropology is being created. This is perhaps not a very radical or novel move, but given the present predicaments it appears to be a timely one, to which this book bears witness.

Positioning the subject

Before I turn to issues of relevance and questions of fieldwork, context and comparison, some comment on my understanding of anthropology – or anthropological thinking – seems appropriate.

In the 1970s, I was taught (at what was then the Ethnographic Institute and is now the Department of Social Anthropology at the University of Oslo) that anthropology is the comparative study of society and culture, that it was mainly concerned with non-Western societies and that fieldwork was the basis for our understandings and our theory building. I was warned of the pitfalls of ethnocentrism and inculcated with the importance of grasping the 'native points of view', of understanding people on their own terms. As a general description, these claims can, perhaps, still be made (and most probably are still told to novices in anthropology), although what is now meant by them is likely to be somewhat different than what was assumed twenty years ago.

Anthropology is created at the interface between us and them, between sameness and difference, between one and many, between is and ought. Hence anthropology implies by definition a relational perspective, one that also forms the premise for grasping and conceptualizing other life-worlds, other sociocultural forms. The underlying assumption is that there are systematic variations in the ways people organize and perceive their life-worlds and, moreover, that recognition is possible across these differences. Anthropological work consists, among other things, of bridging these differences, of translating between one and the other, of cultural interpretation. Thus, anthropology rests on a notion of cultural relativism, which is inscribed in anthropological theory and which is itself a product of the variations that exist in the world. Anthropology can be seen to represent a kind of intervening space – an interstice. Conversely, this imagined space is made visible only by anthropological (or similar) practices.

One of the operating principles that underpins anthropological methods is a practice of distantiation: to make the strange familiar and the familiar strange. This form of distantiation is deliberate. It is an analytic device and a necessary technique to avoid ethnocentrism and to avoid 'going bush' completely; it is not a violation or an act of abuse. It locates the anthropologist in a transient position, neither here nor there, both here *and* there. This positioning of anthropologists necessarily creates tensions – and tensions always create apprehensions. It is easy to be accused of stepping over the line.

The focus of anthropology has traditionally been non-Western societies, and the method of extended fieldwork developed as a consequence of that initial interest. The practice of fieldwork involves precisely that – a field, and a lot of work. Fieldwork in anthropology is learning (by doing, by observing and by talking) the nitty-gritty of daily and public life, from such basic things as hygiene and how to eat to more subtle information about love, anger and honour. It is not empathy and it is not intuition, though both are necessary contributing factors. Fieldwork is a registering of empirical details, and anthropological analysis is the concerted effort to make sense of them by eliciting both explicit and implicit meanings. Anthropology implies an experience – a form of embodied knowledge – and a systematic reflection of that experience. The empirical details and experiences that ground our ethnography also form the basis of anthropological theorizing, and comparison in some form is intrinsic to all these procedures in anthropology.

Issues of relevance: public pressures

The question of the relevance of knowledge – in particular academic knowledge – is becoming critical and is being raised in many fora worldwide. Norway is no exception. In fact, it seems that some notion of 'relevance' is now a criterion by which knowledge is qualitatively assessed. This points not only to the problem of the meanings of relevance, but also to a more general problem: that of the relation that obtains between notions of knowledge and notions of relevance in different contexts. The questions are not only, relevant for whom? and relevant for what?, but also, relevant in what sense?[2] In what follows I only highlight some trends – focusing on various issues related to anthropological knowledge –

within these more general debates as they are being raised both within the discipline and outside it.

At least two opposing (yet also intertwined) positions can be discerned. On the one hand, the relevance of knowledge is framed in terms of utility, production and market mechanisms. Thus, some governments are increasingly demanding value for their money, a value that can only be measured in terms of productivity. Increasing pressure (in Norway and elsewhere) is brought to bear on academic institutions in order to 'demonstrate their relevance according to market principles', prompting 'a major shift in the *context* in which anthropology operates, and particularly the way it is funded' (Ahmed and Shore 1995b: 31; my emphasis). On the other hand, anthropologists who are concerned with the future of the discipline raise issues of relevance, questioning both whether and how anthropology can be relevant to the contemporary world. Thus, two currents of relevance are working at the same time: one pressing from outside the discipline, one from within. The two currents do not necessarily run in the same direction, either; their 'relevant' motives are different, as is the very understanding of the term. Nevertheless, it is worthwhile exploring these two trends, especially if they seem to be mutually reinforcing, stressing the sense of urgency that prevails: the feeling that anthropology is in some way at a turning point. The question is, What are we turning from, and where are we turning to?

In considering the first sense of relevance, that posed by governments and educational policy, I will be brief. It is important to keep in mind, however, that policy issues reflect (although not unilaterally) values that have to do with meanings of knowledge and their place within an overarching sociocultural and moral universe – values that are tied to such fundamental issues as legitimation and good faith. In the case of Norway, somewhat disparate tendencies can be discerned. At a more abstract level, these tendencies have to do with rooted, ambivalent attitudes to knowledge, which directly and indirectly inform the conditions under which knowledges are produced.[3] On the one hand, notions of knowledge are reified, elevated and seem to take on almost mythical dimensions, wherein knowledge (*kunnskap*) represents not only the panacea for securing the future of our society (Norway's comparative advantage in an increasingly competitive world is its knowledgeable labour force) but also equity (a more equal distribution of knowledge will create a more equal population). Thus, knowledge serves both democracy and capital at the same time, and these understandings of knowledge result in increased attention to the overall educational system.[4]

On the other hand, we find that centres of knowledge, such as universities, are somehow defined out of Norwegian notions of reality, as not being of 'any use'. It is *work* (read labour), *professions* (doctors, lawyers, nurses, who can be seen as 'doing something'), and *practice* (here understood as doing something practical) that constitute the real world. Knowledge seems somehow to float outside of all this – being not quite of this world – and this apparent state of knowledge infects the producers of knowledge as well. We are not of the real world. This attitude has obvious implications for the valuation of knowledge producers (be they school teachers or university professors) and their work, as well as their workplaces. Recent trends in educational policy can be seen as a way of rectifying the situation by incorporating 'knowledge producers' into the world by way of the market, the terms set by productivity and utility.

From the position of the policy-makers, we are back to questions of relevance: both criteria for assessing relevance (what type of knowledge for what purposes) and how standards of relevant knowledge are made and met. These questions concern, among other things, how knowledge is made available or made visible, in relevant ways. They also have (literally) to do with accounting. In Norway, *formidling* – that is, popularizing or mediating scientific knowledge to a general public – has been instituted as one of the three obligations, along with teaching and research, which the academic staff at universities must meet, and courses are offered in how to handle the press. Within research institutions such as universities and research foundations, new models of budgeting are important techniques in this scheme. Budgeting models and budgeting procedures serve not only as a means of making knowledge visible, but also as incentives to production, with respect to both teaching and research. The number of students registered, number of hours taught, number of examinations held, number of interviews given, etc. are ways of making the efficiency of the production of knowledge visible. Depending on the ratio between production output and money input, knowledge becomes 'relevant' or 'irrelevant'. Yet some of us, almost anachronistically, keep insisting on quality, not quantity.

This situation is in fact critical. It creates a particular context – and new conditions – for those employed as producers of knowledge, engaged in positions of higher learning whose goal is to contribute to the advancement of their discipline through research and teaching. Not only does there appear to be a fundamental discrepancy in world views between policy-makers and those affected by the policies, there also appears to be a (mutual?) crisis of confidence. And it is frightening that in the face of such governmental forces academics have few counter-strategies. Bogged down as we are in meeting the terms set, we seem to have little time to think about our own conditions for thinking. We are drawn into the process heels first, succumbing to a sense of the inevitable.

This context is powerful in more ways than one. Not only does it set the scene, making some things possible (and others not), it also reveals certain cultural expectations as to what academics should be about, pointing to issues of legitimacy. Moreover, it appears that this very way of thinking (about knowledge) has crept upon us insidiously: the very vocabulary I use to describe the situation is an obvious example. In my opinion, we should be even more concerned with detailing the processes that affect our working lives as anthropologists; they will also affect what becomes of anthropology. There may be something to be learned in comparing different contexts for the production of anthropological knowledge and the effects such contexts may have on the type of knowledge being produced, on the very attitude to knowing and on the conditions for thought. In so far as knowledge is only appreciated (or understood) in terms of a notion of relevance that implies utility, it will be impossible to defend the relevance of knowledge as a value in itself. Many may argue that to hold such a position is to retreat from society and public obligations, but to value knowledge does not imply shirking public responsibilities. On the contrary, recapturing the true sense of the public (as Fox, in the discussions at the conference that led to this volume, has proposed) would imply creating a space in which other criteria of relevance (of knowledge and knowing) are valid.

Issues of relevance: a view from within

It has been argued that the crisis in anthropology

> is not a crisis of *representation* ... but a problem of *relevance*. Social anthropology as we have known it is in danger of becoming marginalized and redundant unless it adapts to the changing world which now threatens to undermine its cherished theories, methods and practices.
>
> (Ahmed and Shore 1995b: 15; emphasis in original)

This notion of relevance is of quite a different order than the one I have discussed above and is one that I assume will more easily engage an academic audience. The premise is that times have changed so much that anthropology must change too, in order to recapture its critical and prominent position and to avoid becoming redundant.

There are several ways of approaching the question of the relevance of anthropology.[5] One criterion that has gained some prominence (and would perhaps match Norwegian policies about academics being more active in the media) is the ability to command public attention. Anthropologists should engage more actively in public debates, draw a much wider readership and on the whole be much more attuned to current affairs.[6] Ahmed and Shore (1995b) argue that the marginalization of anthropology develops from two quarters simultaneously. First, other disciplines – journalism, literature, cultural studies – are encroaching on anthropological terrain. And second, anthropologists themselves are too limited. Not only is their communication restricted to a close circle of academics, cutting off wider audiences and interdisciplinary dialogues, but their professional gaze is also restricted to that which can be studied empirically. Hence, critics claim, it is the failure of anthropologists to engage with current affairs and contemporary social and political interests that itself indicts anthropology, and fieldwork – as it has been handed down as the core of anthropological theory building and method – has been the main impediment to such engagement. As these arguments seem to reflect attitudes towards anthropology that are reiterated in different settings, I will pursue them a bit further.

I think, in fact, that we are hard put to argue that anthropology is being marginalized, at the same time that anthropological perspectives (or what are recognized as such) are being incorporated into an ever-increasing number of fields. That others are succeeding in drawing attention to issues that fall squarely into the field of anthropology does not necessarily make anthropology either irrelevant or redundant. The fact that journalists seem able to give more immediate coverage of social phenomena that anthropologists also have (or should have) access to is *not*, to my mind, cause for lament. On the contrary, the better journalists write, the better informed the public will be and, perhaps, the greater the interest in anthropology. Journalists and anthropologists are not really competing on the same turf, nor should they be. Hence, the suggestion that grant-giving agencies might begin to question the logic of channelling diminishing resources 'to fund leisurely academic ethnographic studies' (Ahmed and Shore 1995b: 23) when 'a good journalist can produce what anthropologists produce, only more cheaply, better and faster', is getting hold of the wrong end of the stick. Surely the goals and ambitions of anthropologists are of a different order than those of journalists. And, surely, the day research-funding agencies equate journalism with anthropology, or any other social science, we will have quite a different problem on our hands, namely, the end of social sciences as it has been envisioned and established.[7] That would be serious indeed. However, the fact that our practices entail some scientific and epistemological grounding that differs from that of journalism does not preclude anthropologists from engaging a wider audience through public debates, nor does it preclude us from putting our knowledge to public use in one form or another. A greater anthropological presence in the public sphere is both warranted and desirable – not just because this would attract more funds but because we have something to contribute. Nevertheless, greater visibility does not necessarily make for better anthropology, and public presence is, in the long run, a dubious criterion for assessing the relevance of anthropology.

The threat posed by cultural studies, however, is of a different order, in that the two disciplines occupy, at least nominally, the same turf. There are those who claim that anthropology is being usurped by cultural studies, which is filling the space (and picking up the fragments) left in the wake of a deconstructed anthropology.[8] Lodged as it is in a contemporary, post colonial vision of the world, cultural studies undoubtedly offers a challenging alternative to anthropology, but it does not render the discipline superfluous.

Juxtaposing the discourses of social anthropology and cultural studies, Signe Howell questions whether anthropology has become redundant, 'the last remnants of colonialism in this postcolonial era' (1999: 103). She recognizes that exciting theory has come out of cultural studies and admits that much of the literature has a 'heady feel; as a reader you feel that you are at the cutting edge of social theory' (ibid.: 104). Even as she acknowledges that the stated theoretical aims and themes of cultural studies and anthropology are much the same, however, Howell argues that there are major differences between the two fields. Her paper is a *tour de force* recognition of anthropology's unique contribution to the study of social and cultural institutions and processes, of ethnography's grounding in sociocultural life-worlds, and of the value of extended fieldwork and the use of empirical data in constructing social theories.

Yet it is precisely the practice of fieldwork, as it has been handed down, that is being contested. There is no doubt that the world today demands anthropologists to ask new questions and seek new domains for research. Moreover, it is imperative that such questions and new areas of study not be hampered by the fact that they do not represent a traditional 'field' and cannot therefore be approached by the traditional methods of 'fieldwork'. Hence, questions that pertain to the relevance of fieldwork for the study of contemporary society are crucial to the development of methods – the generation of data as well as their interpretation – and to theory building in anthropology.

In recent decades, anthropologists have turned their attention to many areas that require a different approach to the subject matter than that of conventional fieldwork. There has been a shift away from local studies to more thematically oriented work. Place no longer holds its privileged position. Not only are anthropologists today more concerned with history and with texts, they are also working on issues of policy and policy-making, governmentality, new reproductive technologies, ideologies, adoption, the international Olympic Games, consumerism, surrogate motherhood, diasporas, world trade exhibitions, the Internet – in fact, there is no limit to what may capture the interest of anthropologists. Although anthropologists study the phenomena in a different way, however, we do not approach these fields *tabula rasa*, nor do we strip them of their sociocultural bearings. Rather, we work to situate carefully these social phenomena in their context, relating them to other social phenomena in order to elicit patterns of meaning that are in some way grounded in sociocultural life-worlds. Such studies, and the resulting ethnographies, come out of a tradition of knowledge rooted in ethnography, based on fieldwork and implying a particular experience. This knowledge is brought to bear on whatever phenomena we choose to examine, whether or not we are engaged in 'proper' fieldwork.

Like any other academic discipline, anthropology has a history of accumulated knowledge. Some may consider this a burden, but to anthropologists who are engaged in the current debates and concerned with the practice of knowing (even 'other knowing', as Sahlins has put it), the history of anthropology, our 'cultural heritage' in all its diversity, represents a creative source of reflection.[9] And so it should. Without it, such central concepts as kinship, marriage, culture and society could not have been deconstructed, and the ethnographic realism and poetics of previous texts would not have been disclosed. We could not have challenged the practice of fieldwork and the very grounds on which our discipline has been built. The point is obvious, but perhaps worthy of consideration.

To do away – completely – with fieldwork would certainly mean doing away with anthropology as we know it; it also would require new methods and new ways of theorizing. The end of fieldwork is often linked with the end of holism, which again relates to the complexities of a contemporary world in which boundaries are dissolved, people are displaced, identities are fragmented, concepts are dislocated and theories forever travel back and forth – a world in which simultaneity, coexistence and co-temporality reign. This vision of the world necessarily compounds the problems of fieldwork not only because appropriate 'field sites' seem to disappear but because their inhabitants do too. Yet in this world people nevertheless live and work and eat and die. People interact with other people, create and maintain relations, create and maintain meaning and moral universes. In this world of women and men, essentialism is often the name of the game, underpinning notions of order as well as of disruption. However, living in the world and trying to grasp what this living is all about are two very different endeavours. As anthropologists, our job is to make another sense of the world, another kind of order. If our notions of fieldwork restrict our possibilities of accessing the social world, and hence our understanding of that world, we must find other ways of doing ethnography while still acknowledging the important influence fieldwork has had on anthropological reasoning. We must also rethink the explanatory value of anthropology and its place within the social sciences. A step in that direction would be to set comparison on the anthropological agenda.

Challenges of cross-cultural comparison

Over the past two decades, anthropologists have been posing a series of challenging questions about the nature of the anthropological endeavour. This has been voiced in relation to problems of *representation* (i.e. the 'orientalism syndrome', the all-encompassing Western discourse that presents the other as so many refractions of ourselves, v. 'the natives speak back'); of *authority* (i.e. who speaks for whom; 'this native can speak for herself'); of *alterity* (radical or not); of *accountability* (advocacy v. science); and of *accessibility* (i.e. globalization processes such as media reach: we all watch the same soaps, more or less at the same time; we all have, theoretically at least, access to the same technology, videos, Internet, etc.). These concerns cover a range of different fields, from the transformation of the objects of anthropological enquiry to a reassessment of its subjects and practices to pleas for affirmative action and for a more ethical anthropology that reflects both momentary, situated views and more reflexive subject positions. In these probing concerns little is said about the comparative aims of anthropology, however. This may be because anthropologists still hold implicitly to that ideal, or it may be because a deconstructed anthropology makes cross-cultural comparison a non-issue. There is nothing to compare.

Both positions create problems, albeit of different kinds. The second position, if it gains ground, will in the end undermine the anthropological enterprise. That is perhaps not the most important point to make in this connection, however. The issue is not, ultimately, the survival of anthropology.

The issue is rather the significance (another reading of the term 'relevance') of the knowledge anthropologists produce, the contribution of anthropological thinking to the body of knowledge of societies and cultures. The first position, which implies an implicit goal of comparison and is probably the most prominent, rests on a tacit understanding that only the initiated share. From this perspective comparison will be part of any anthropological endeavour, and we can only hope for greater awareness of its practices and implications. In my opinion, however, we need more conscious reflection about comparison in order to access the potentials of theory building in anthropology, which has been all but ignored.

In many ways, the above discussion of fieldwork is intimately linked with any discussion of comparison. Fieldwork – whether it is carried out in sites with people or on policies produced by people – implies 'submission to the understanding of [the] other', and that submission, in turn, implies 'integration of what is thus learned in a general anthropological understanding' (Sahlins 1997: 273). To my mind, a general anthropological understanding implies, by definition, comparison. But what does comparison imply?[10]

Evans-Pritchard is reported to have said, 'There is only one method in anthropology, the comparative method – and that is impossible' (Needham 1975: 365). Others following the same path have pointed to the futility of the comparative project (e.g. Needham 1975; Schneider 1984; but see also Boon 1982; Evans-Pritchard 1965; Leach 1971). These critiques are grounded in part in a recognition of the inadequacy of a positivist approach to social facts, but they also derive from an awareness of the difficulty of rephrasing other meaning complexes in unambiguous analytical terms (in so far as anthropologists engage with conceptual and moral universes with gravitational fields different from their own) in such a way that comparison would be accepted as legitimate. There are serious theoretical and methodological problems in performing such comparisons. As we know, questions have to be posed concerning not only translation but also what properties, categories, institutions, practices, etc. may be legitimately compared. It is precisely from such a background that previous central anthropological concepts – kinship, marriage, religion, etc. – have been deconstructed, leaving us without the basic tools with which to perform cross-cultural comparison.

Nevertheless, anthropologists continue to insist on the importance of comparison and a cross-cultural perspective. In recent years, however, it seems that while paying lip service to this ideal, anthropologists have tended to neglect the methodological challenges posed by systematic comparison (but cf. Holy 1987; Kuper 1979, 1980; Spiro 1992; Strathern 1987).

Just as it appears that a focus on the particular has superseded an interest in the whole, so also are any attempts at generalizations viewed with suspicion. This shift can be conceptualized as a more general move from an emphasis on sameness (with a view to generalizations) to one on difference (stressing the unique and particular). These two categories – sameness and/or difference – and the tension inherent between them underpin anthropological thinking and, concomitantly, anthropological debates and positionings. The present mood in anthropology (which is also concurrent with a general mood 'out there', i.e. universalism expressed through human rights; particularism expressed through collective rights) reflects this double pull and is a constant reminder of the different levels of analysis and the different ends that anthropological research seeks to address. Among other things, this tension has to do with the role of description in anthropological analysis.

Description is Ladislav Holy's focus in the introduction to his edited volume *Comparative Anthropology* (1987). His discussion, which centres on the relation between description and generalization, demonstrates the shift in emphasis that has occurred. Holy argues that there is no longer a comparative method in anthropology, but that 'it has been replaced by various styles of comparison' (ibid.: 2) reflecting the different objectives and methods of the comparative project.

Within the positivist paradigm, cross-cultural comparison was seen as the method for generating and testing hypotheses when the methodological issues were related to problems of generalization, not description – a paradigm, according to Holy, 'in direct reversal of the way in which the relation of description and generalization is perceived today' (1987: 5). The constructionist move in anthropology insists that facts do not exist independently of the meanings used to account for them; hence the stress on context as necessary for interpretation. This shift in focus from generalization to description is a shift in methodological emphasis. As anthropologists we are asked *how* we come to know what we claim to know about a particular culture, so that rather than compare *results* of research, we compare *methods* of research. This has in turn spurred the very involved discussions about fieldwork and the process of transforming data into texts. The interpretative turn in anthropology ascribes high value to *non-comparative* analytical description, in which cultural diversity becomes an end itself and difference supplants sameness. The subsequent deconstructionist turn only serves to reinforce the retreat from comparison.

I stated initially that comparison is integral to anthropology, and, moreover, that to neglect the challenges posed by cross-cultural comparison is to undermine the anthropological enterprise. My grounds for these claims are several and of different orders. First, it is generally accepted that implicit comparison is inherent in all cognition. Anthropology, of course, is no exception. This, however, is a trivial point to make. Second, the very effort of translation implies comparison of some sort (see e.g. Overing (1987) for an interesting discussion on the practice of translation; but see also Hobart (1987)). Third, the practice of deliberate distantiation invokes comparison *ipso facto*, in the conscious shifting of positions (as participant and observer) and resultant contrasting of realities. All these may perhaps be subsumed under what Holy labels 'the unselfconscious, commonsensical comparison of everyday judgement', which he claims 'shares with everyday judgement its lack of rigour' (1987: 16). We make such judgements, and we do not think much about them.

The challenges of comparison lie elsewhere, however. They are tied, first and foremost, to accepting comparison as an important issue in contemporary anthropology.[11] It is a question of 'why'. From the 'why' flows the possibility of carrying comparison through. This is a question of 'how'. The why of comparison is grounded in an assumption that there exist different ontologies, epistemologies and cosmologies with little or no reference to Western traditions, and that it is the task of anthropologists to attempt to describe these worlds, as well as our own. In my opinion, such descriptions are valuable as documentations of the fact of cultural variations in the world. However, the question remains whether they are simply interesting in and of themselves or if such descriptions ultimately should – or could – also serve another purpose, address broader issues and contribute to a more general understanding of sociality. To do so, some comparative perspective is necessary.[12]

Obviously, it is paramount to be aware of what is being compared. We are not comparing objects, names of things or essences but meanings, ways of constructing relationships between objects, persons, situations, events. Because similarities or differences are not given in the things themselves but in the ways they are contextualized, i.e. in the relations of which they form a part, we must compare frameworks, processes of meaning construction, structures of discourses. The emphasis is on signification and making distinctions, and how these are perceived (a point also stressed by Goodenough 1970). In other words, what we compare are the *contexts*, or circuits of meanings, which create a certain coherence – or rather, which we deem as relevant for creating a certain coherence – whether it be situated, applicable to only one situation, or systemic, and hence of a more encompassing nature (see Hobart 1987: 34). In either case, we must spell out the arguments that establish the relevant context. This is not as straightforward as it may seem: for one thing, frameworks and processes are not the same; moreover, we may well question what is relevant about a context that makes it an interesting focus for comparison, and how such knowledge will feed into social theories.

Problems of context

Despite a tacit acknowledgement of the significance of context in all anthropological practice, anthropology lacks an adequate theory of context (see e.g. Scharfstein 1989). The term context is in itself problematic, often used in a self-evident way, with no attempt to distinguish between context as a concept and context as a social phenomenon. We need to ask, what type of social phenomenon is a context – beyond what is brought to bear in order to make sense of an event, person or thing? What is it that makes a context? What is it about the context that in a concrete case renders something meaningful and significant? Is there a difference between the context the anthropologist constructs in order to render phenomena meaningful and the context people themselves create? And if it is *contexts* we should compare, how can we go about establishing a framework of comparison? This question pushes the issue of comparison to another analytical level, at which we compare the processes of construction (cf. Holy 1987): in other words, how claims are made and how cultural interpretations are grounded. Such comparison points to the different ways in which contexts are made available, explicitly or implicitly.

The problem of context becomes all the more evident in light of the challenges anthropologists face when addressing contemporary issues, where field 'sites' are of a different order – not localized in terms of place – and which demand an approach other than conventional fieldwork methods. The problem, of course, is not the 'site' itself, but rather establishing the relevant context that makes the site a meaningful field of enquiry. It is through contexts that sense is made, and it is the task of the anthropologist to substantiate that the context established for making sense of particular social phenomena is not only reasonable, but also plausible. The persuasive power of context cannot be overlooked.[13]

Marilyn Strathern has argued that the comparison of contexts as a new framework for the anthropological endeavour comes with the rise of modernist anthropology. It is the postmodern mood that permits a deliberate play with context. As Strathern says:

> It remains up to the reader to pick his or her way through the differing positions and contexts of the speakers. Mere points of view[,] … these contexts have ceased in themselves to provide the organizing frameworks for the ethnographic narrative.
>
> (Strathern 1987: 265)

If I am correct that sense derives from context and that making sense underlies anthropological analysis, then to disregard context would be tantamount to producing nonsense – and that would indeed be shirking public responsibility! Even where the play with context is deliberate, the point is nevertheless to make a different sense and leaving it to the reader to pick his or her way through, willy-nilly, still creates a context, albeit with a different intent.

It is my contention that there are significant differences in the ways contexts are established (in this case by anthropologists) and that these differences depend fundamentally on the ways in which data are generated. In other words, the new sites for fieldwork not only demand new methods, they also require other forms of contextualization in order to make sense. I cannot explicate this postulate in detail here but will briefly illustrate what I am driving at with examples from two of my own 'fieldworks' – one carried out in a village in Mexico (see Melhuus 1997, 1998), the other on new reproductive technologies in Norway, with a special emphasis on the 'involuntary childless' and public policy, with a view to eliciting indigenous meanings of kinship in contemporary society.[14] The very phrasing of the foci of these two projects is indicative of the difference in the nature of the anthropological pursuits. The following exercise, then, is tentative and serves merely as a pointer; it is instructive, and in no way conclusive.

My fieldwork in Mexico involved living in a village, and place was a relevant category for both the anthropologist and the villagers (a condition that does not apply in the Norwegian case in the same way). I was present during most parts of the day and the villagers' daily life became, to an extent, my daily life; I was present over an extended period of time and in very diverse situations. Hence, I was able to corroborate the meanings of a particular cultural statement by tracing its articulations in various settings, with various (and the same) people at different times. In the work I am doing now, however, this is impossible. I see people in very limited and specific settings and with respect to one specific aspect of their lives: their infertility, an aspect that is both extremely intimate and very pervasive. I go to the same meetings that they do, I may read some of the same literature, but I do not participate in – or have any direct access to – their daily lives.

In contrast to the villagers in Mexico, the people I am involved with in Norway do not necessarily know each other, and, equally important, they do not have much chance to get to know me. I see some of them perhaps only once, through formal interviews; others I may meet several times through organized group discussions or formal meetings run by the Association of the Involuntary Childless. These men and women are constituted as a group only through their mutual fate of being involuntarily childless; sharing a state of infertility and a desire to overcome it, their social interaction is also limited to that one issue. The experience of infertility is what brings them together. In the village in Mexico, people are brought together for a variety of reasons: as neighbours, kin, affines, friends, political allies, Protestants, Catholics and so on. In Mexico, I thus have access to a series of relations in a variety of settings, and the resulting ethnographic material is not only rich in detail, but also spans a wide range of topics; it is varied. The reverse holds true in Norway, where my presence as a researcher is legitimated by my interest in a certain issue. People are very much aware of that fact, and the material obtained through interviews and participation in discussion groups is to a certain degree narrow, revolving around the same topics again and again. Repetition is, in fact, a salient characteristic of this material. Although this continual repetition of stories and events is in itself an interesting datum, it is thin stuff for thick descriptions.

Precisely because I do not have access to people's lives outside of clearly defined settings in the Norwegian fieldwork, I have no way of tracing or accounting for the meanings and implications of their infertility in other life situations. Nor do I gain immediate access to other preoccupations and daily concerns, which may or may not have to do with childlessness. This absence of other settings (or being present in the flow of events) poses a problem: how to grasp the relevant contexts for eliciting meanings in regard to the nature of the relationship (in their understandings) between infertility and kinship. In order to be able to contextualize adequately the phenomena under study, I must find ways of compensating for this lack of alternative sources of information. Thus I have turned, for example, to public policies such as legislative processes and the resulting legislation (e.g. child law, family law, biotechnology law), public debates on issues of fertility, as well as tangential issues relevant for the problematics at hand. As there is no end to what might seem relevant, the problem, of course, is where to draw the line. This is a problem in any fieldwork, but it seems to take on a different dimension here, where the constraints are so different from those in the Mexican research. To a much greater extent than in the Mexican case (and also with a somewhat different intent; see Melhuus 1994), I have turned to texts as a source of ethnography. My fieldwork includes collating and systematizing many different types of 'texts', including policy documents, newspaper clippings, books, TV shows, and radio programmes, in order to capture a sense of the public and to be able to juxtapose and relate these to the private, intimate and personal experiences of the people I interview. Not only do these texts constitute data of a different kind, they are also very disparate and in no obvious way interconnected.

Disjunction is what characterizes this field situation, both with respect to time (i.e. the lack of continual presence) and with respect to type of data collected. If I were to stretch the point, I could say that the only connection these people, events and texts have is the one I make: I am the nexus around which a web of significance is spun; in a certain sense *I* am the 'site'. The fact of my subjects' infertility obviously exists without me. That is not the point. The point is that it is primarily their infertility that I have information about, and in order to grasp its more overarching significance I need to inscribe that fact in a wider context, a context that is basically my creation. I have to make a double move involving both decontextualizing and recontextualizing: on the one hand, I extract the data from their original local boundedness; on the other, I then reinscribe these data in a wider universe of meaning.

In the Mexican situation these operations occur very differently. This has to do in part with the fact that my presence as anthropologist takes on a different meaning in the two situations; in part it is related to my different knowledge of these two societies; but most importantly it has to do with the differences in the types/sites of fieldwork. In Mexico I represent a focal point (for my own work, obviously), but my presence is irrelevant for the actualization of social relations and their articulated meanings. Although I certainly facilitate or even provoke a certain flow of information, I do not have to take the same compensatory measures to make sense of it as I do in the Norwegian research. Moreover, in the Norwegian case I am not a stranger in the same sense as in Mexico. Not only do I share a certain cultural background with the various subjects involved, my daily life resembles that of other women. I am recognizable.

The differences in these two situations have implications for how the relevant context is established, both the one I make and the one the people I am working with make. In both cases, I construct a context in order to make sense of what is going on (according to some notion of what it is I wish to depict, of course). However, the context made relevant in the Mexican case and brought to bear on my interpretations is different from the context made relevant in the Norwegian case. One way of phrasing this difference is to say that whereas in Mexico, I tend to let the local contexts define the themes to be pursued (and my place in pursuing these themes), in Norway, it is the theme that defines the context and the place for pursuing the theme. Whereas in Norway, the context is but a construction, in Mexico, it can perhaps best be characterized as a reconstruction. Even though, in both cases, I extract a context that is relevant for the issues at hand (in order to make evident a particular coherence), there is, nevertheless, a difference with respect to the reference that the contexts evoke. In the Mexican case the context (or contexts) should concur with the way people themselves frame their acts; there must be some congruence between my understanding and theirs. However, in the Norwegian study of new reproductive technologies and how various practices/policies/opinions related to them can be inscribed in understandings of kinship (indigenous and anthropological), the context I establish should resonate with indigenous understandings but need not necessarily be congruent with them. My aim is precisely to transcend the disjunctions or discontinuities the data imply in order to delineate a circuit of meaning, a cultural pattern, that may or may not be immediately recognized.[15] I realize that this is a fine line to draw, that the distinction is not an altogether easy one to envision, and that in practice it may be hard to discern. Nevertheless, I am convinced that in order to get a better grasp on what anthropology is about, we need to explicate (and compare) these processes of making sense – ours, as well as theirs.

The very access to cultural specificity should give access to knowledge about how that cultural specificity is constructed. Knowledge of the *how* of construction makes possible not only the acknowledgement that different meanings of, for example, *macho* exist (rather trivial knowledge, in my opinion), but also the various ways in which the different meanings come about, which to my mind is much more interesting and, to return to a previous topic, much more relevant. In this respect, getting the context right implies a particular knowledge, a certain cultural understanding. And conversely, if I am uncertain about what I know, I am also uncertain about how to contextualize (a point raised by Adam Kuper in the general discussion of the papers at the conference). Thus, the significance of context in anthropological (and popular) reasoning cannot be overemphasized. In fact, I would argue that to develop a theory of context is at the same time to develop a comparative method. Cross-cultural comparison may serve then to enhance the understanding of the cultural specific, bringing forth different cultural logics, but it may also serve to enhance our own reflexivity and critical examinations of our own – and other – societies.

We can never truly know if some sort of violation occurs in the processes of transformation that comparison implies. Such is the problem with all anthropological practice: it rests on the available data that we have brought forth and the way those data are interpreted. It is a truism in anthropology that social facts can be – and are – interpreted variously by the people studied and by the anthropologists who study them. For the interpretation to be plausible, attention must be placed on making the context for the interpretation visible and available. That context is doubly constructed, first by the people themselves and then by the anthropologist. However, people *live* a context; contexts (normally) are intuitively assumed. The task of the anthropologist is not only to make that (intuitive) context visible, but also to upset or transcend the very boundaries and discontinuities that particular contexts seem to imply in order to delineate a more encompassing universe of meaning. In this manner, the goal of anthropological practice is (among other things) to recontextualize the various lived contexts with which we are confronted.

The more attention we pay to detail and contradictions, to exceptions as well as the rule, the more attention we pay to grounding our arguments empirically and spelling out the intrinsic connections we make, and the more attention we pay to the relation between observer categories and indigenous ones, the more reliable our interpretations appear. Our strength lies in our ability to convince our audience that although the interpretation presented is only one possible interpretation, it should be the most plausible one. So also with comparison. Accepting the postulate that 'comparison is not between these two societies or even between sets of "raw", "objective" data, but rather between various representations of these societies, or between interpretations of data' (Howe 1997: 150) implies a focus on context, in so far as our interpretations rest on getting the context right.

Whether a comparison results in an emphasis on sameness or on difference is an empirical question. Comparison implies establishing relations of both similarity and difference and, as Fardon (1987) suggests, will in the same instance reify these constructs. Thus, in order to grasp this very reification and to limit its effects, it is necessary that we state clearly the presuppositions we make for our analysis (not the fact that we make presuppositions; we always do). By making them explicit, we may facilitate the readings of our efforts and, moreover, lay them bare for constructive criticism. This is one of the lessons that can be learned from the controversy between Sahlins and Obeyesekere about the 'apotheosis' of Captain Cook.

I think it is paramount for the legitimacy of anthropology that we again inscribe ourselves in a discourse that insists that anthropology has a contribution to make not only to human understanding in all its diversity (and as such is relevant to the contemporary world), but also to theory building in the social sciences. Reinstating the comparative ambition would be a step in that direction. Comparison depends on drawing boundaries, and drawing boundaries is intrinsic to establishing contexts. Ultimately, the relevance of social anthropology will be judged by the empirical knowledge it produces and the theories it generates. Anthropological contributions to social theory – such as exchange, notions of the person, ritual, the relation between individual and society – have all been made on the basis of a cross-cultural comparative perspective. The appeal of social anthropology, I think, can be attributed to the unique contributions anthropology has made to social theory based on a comparative method grounded in local knowledges. This is where anthropology has made – and will continue to make – a difference. It is the upholding of this legacy, which takes us beyond middle-range, localized theories and aims at an understanding of human forms of sociality, which will, in the end, guard us against redundancy. However, such a goal demands that we think and do anew. It also demands that the contexts for our thinking be conducive to radical thought. That context may well come to represent a major hurdle. In order to set new terms of anthropology that we may call our own, we first might well have to overpower the very conditions that currently structure our thoughts. And thus, we are back to square one.

Notes

1 This article is a revised version of a paper entitled 'Back to basics? Anthropology and the challenges of cross-cultural comparison', first presented in Barcelona (1997) at a conference organized by Mercedes Fernández-Martorell and sponsored by U.I.M.P. and the Museo de la Sciencia on the topic *'Pensar desde la antropología'*. The spirit of the conference was one of reflection and critique, and I am grateful to both Fernández-Martorell and Maria Gomís for inviting me to share my thoughts at this event. The Vienna conference (1998) on 'Comparative dimensions in social and cultural anthropology' gave me a further opportunity to rethink – and rework – some of my arguments. My thanks to the organizers, Thomas Fillitz and Andre Gingrich, as well as the co-participants and students for thoughtful and provocative comments. Signe Howell has read an earlier version of this paper, and, as always, her observations are to the point.

2 The discussions after the presentation of my paper revealed interesting differences with respect to what is understood by the term 'relevance'. On the one hand, in the light of present-day trends in Norwegian educational policy, I was arguing for less 'relevance' (for example, in the sense of 'being useful' as a criterion for evaluating research proposals) and more autonomy for the individual researcher. On the other hand, both Richard Fox and James Peacock were arguing for 'more relevance' in the sense that anthropologists should be much more responsible *vis-à-vis* the public, more sensitive to public response. These two positions are not necessarily contradictory. Public awareness does not automatically translate into 'doing what the policy-makers want'. On the contrary, public awareness may imply instilling a critical perspective – a position I would welcome.

3 Norway is undoubtedly an interesting case. Although Norwegian perceptions of knowledge must be understood in the broader European tradition, there lies much potential in tracing local conceptualizations. An interesting comparative example is put forth by Sirnes (1997) in his study of the parliamentary debates on new reproductive technologies in Great Britain and Norway. Sirnes demonstrates the different understandings of science (*vitenskap*) in the two countries and the way these differences influence policy decisions.

4 Recent trends are, for example, internationalizing our university degrees; the transformation of universities to institutions of mass education; increasing the number of obligatory school years from nine to ten; changing the age of school entry from seven to six; implementing a new educational reform for 'life-long learning'; granting people the right to continual education; and constant debating about the quality and direction of Norwegian school curricula and about the 'place' of universities and

centres of higher learning in society. These processes have culminated in a proposal to the Norwegian parliament (June 2001) that represents radical shifts in Norwegian higher education policies.

5 Ahmed and Shore put forth three definitions: relevance equated with the idea of utility (the one favoured by governments, which I have already noted); relevance in terms of anthropology's explanatory power; and relevance in terms of the discipline's moral significance (Ahmed and Shore 1995b: 32–3).

6 This was a point strongly reiterated by Michael Herzfeld at a lecture given in Oslo in November 1998, and it was also a matter of discussion at the Vienna conference. In fact, in Norway anthropologists are quite visible, being variously engaged in public debates and policy elaboration and actively drawn in by media workers (see Melhuus 1999).

7 I do not mean to imply that good journalists do not have academic backgrounds. Many do. Hence, they may uphold the same scholarly values as anthropologists, but apply them differently.

8 Believing that cultural studies poses a threat to anthropology presupposes a position that posits that the traditional fields of anthropological enquiry are *passé* (the primitive has disappeared; the local community no longer exists; culture is out and society is gone; the other is no different from me) and that the complexity of modern societies renders traditional anthropological methods obsolete.

9 This volume is a good example. Asked to reflect on comparison, many of the contributors chose to approach the topic from an historical perspective (see also Fardon 1990).

10 Some of the arguments presented in the following are taken from a research project, 'Kinship – *quo vadis?* Meanings of kinship and procreation in Norway and beyond', jointly formulated by Signe Howell, Marit Melhuus and Olaf Smedal (1996). The project received funding from the Norwegian Research Council. The elaboration of a comparative perspective is a crucial element of the project.

11 This issue is closely tied in with the discussion of whether or not anthropology is to be considered a science, and hence to the explanatory – and not just descriptive – nature of anthropology. The discussion of anthropology as science is an important one, which cannot be pursued in the present context (but see Spiro 1996 for one argument; Grimshaw and Hart 1995 with a different twist; Holy 1987; Morris 1997).

12 It is vital to point out the centrality of good ethnography, which leaves no doubt about the accuracy of the materials presented even when there may be questions about the theoretical understandings through which they are filtered. Such empirically detailed, well-documented descriptions are a prerequisite for any comparative effort. Poor theories will die, but good ethnographies will survive, their empirical data open for reinterpretation (see also Fardon 1990).

13 To me, the best way to visualize simultaneously the ambiguity and the power of context is via the figure/ground motif. In such a configuration, the elements are the same but provide shifting contexts for each other. Depending on the observer's perspective, the total configuration changes, thereby also changing the image conveyed.

14 An important dimension distinguishing the two fieldworks is the fact of doing fieldwork 'at home', which raises a whole series of questions that I cannot pursue here, but which are intrinsically connected to the issues of method and context being discussed.

15 I am *not* implying that village life in Mexico dissolves into a seamless whole. On the contrary, my work in Mexico has been particularly concerned with discontinuities, contradictory moralities, etc. and with finding ways of accounting for these. This has also meant transcending local contexts (recontextualizing) and reinscribing them in a more encompassing universe of meaning. For present purposes, however, I have intentionally stressed the differences in order to illustrate an important methodological point.

Bibliography

Ahmed, A. and Shore, C. (eds) (1995a) *The Future of Anthropology: Its Relevance to the Contemporary World*, London: Athlone.

Ahmed, A. and Shore, C. (1995b) 'Introduction: is anthropology relevant to the contemporary world?', in A. Ahmed and C. Shore (eds) *The Future of Anthropology: Its Relevance to the Contemporary World*, London: Athlone.

Boon, J.A. (1982) *Other Scribes, Other Tribes: Symbolic Anthropology in the Comparative Study of Cultures, Histories, Religions and Texts*, Cambridge: Cambridge University Press.

Borofsky, R. (1997) 'Cook, Lono, Obeyesekere and Sahlins', *Current Anthropology* 38, 2: 255–77.

Calame-Griaule, G. (1991) 'On the Dogon restudied', *Current Anthropology* 32, 5: 557–73.

D'Andrade, R. (1995) 'Moral models in anthropology', *Current Anthropology* 36, 3: 399–408.

Evans-Pritchard, E.E. (1965) 'The comparative method in social anthropology', in E.E. Evans-Pritchard, *The Position of Women in Primitive Societies and Other Essays in Social Anthropology*, London: Faber and Faber, pp. 13–36.

Fardon, R. (1987) ' "African Ethnogenesis": limits to the comparability of ethnic phenomena', in L. Holy (ed.) *Comparative Anthropology*, Oxford: Basil Blackwell.

—— (1990) 'General Introduction', in R. Fardon, *Localizing Strategies: Regional Traditions of Ethnographic Writing*, Edinburgh: Scottish Academic Press.

Fox, R.G. (ed.) (1991) *Recapturing Anthropology: Working in the Present*, Santa Fe, NM: School of American Research Press.

Freeman, D. (1983) *Margaret Mead and Samoa: The Making and the Unmaking of an Anthropological Myth*, Cambridge, MA: Harvard University Press.

Geertz, C. (1995) 'Culture war', *The New York Review of Books* 830, November.

Goodenough, W. (1970) *Description and Comparison in Cultural Anthropology*, Chicago: Aldine Publishing Company.

Grimshaw, A. and Hart, K. (1995) 'The rise and fall of scientific anthropology', in A. Ahmed and C. Shore (eds) *The Future of Anthropology: Its Relevance to the Contemporary World*, London: Athlone.

Harries-Jones, P. (1996) 'Afterword', in H. Moore (ed.) *The Future of Anthropological Knowledge*, London: Routledge.

Hobart, M. (1987) 'The coming of age of anthropology', in L. Holy (ed.) *Comparative Anthropology*, Oxford: Basil Blackwell.

Holy, L. (ed.) (1987) *Comparative Anthropology*, Oxford: Basil Blackwell.

Howe, L. (1997) 'Caste in Bali and India: levels of comparison', in L. Holy (ed.) *Comparative Anthropology*, Oxford: Basil Blackwell.

Howell, S. (1999) 'Cultural studies and social anthropology: contesting or complementary discourses', in C. Shore and S. Nugent (eds) *Anthropology and Cultural Studies*, London: Pluto Press.

Howell, S., Melhuus, M. and Smedal, O. (1996) 'Kinship – *quo vadis*? Meanings of kinship and procreation in Norway and beyond', Research proposal presented to the NFR (project number 115014/530).

Kuper, A. (1979) 'Regional comparison in African anthropology', *African Affairs* 78, 310: 103–13.

—— (1980) 'The man in the study and the man in the field: ethnography, theory and comparison in social anthropology', *Archives Européennes de Sociologie* 21, 1: 14–39.

Leach, E.R. ([1961] 1971) *Rethinking Anthropology*, London School of Economics Monographs on Social Anthropology 22, London: Athlone.

Lewis, O. (1951) *Life in a Mexican Village: Tepotzlán Restudied*, Urbana: University of Illinois Press.

Melhuus, M. (1994) 'The authority of a text: Mexico through the words of others', in E. Archetti (ed.) *Exploring the Written: Anthropology and the Multiplicity of Writing*, Oslo: Scandinavian University Press.

—— (1997) 'The troubles of virtue: values of violence and suffering in a Mexican context', in S. Howell (ed.) *The Ethnography of Moralities*, London: Routledge.

—— (1998) 'Configuring gender: male and female in Mexican heterosexual and homosexual relations', *Ethnos* 63, 3: 353–82.

—— (1999) 'Insisting on culture?', *Social Anthropology* 7, 1: 65–80.

Moore, H. (ed.) (1996a) *The Future of Anthropological Knowledge*, London: Routledge.

—— (1996b) 'Introduction', in H. Moore (ed.) *The Future of Anthropological Knowledge*, London: Routledge.

Morris, B. (1997) 'In defence of realism and truth: critical reflections on the anthropological followers of Heidegger', *Critique of Anthropology* 17, 3: 313–40.

Needham, R. (1975) 'Polythetic classification: convergence and consequences', *Man* 10: 349–69.

Obeyesekere, G. (1997) 'Comment to Borofsky "Cook, Lono, Obeyesekere and Sahlins"', *Current Anthropology* 38, 2: 255–77.

Overing, J. (1987) 'Translation as creative process: the power of the name', in L. Holy (ed.) *Comparative Anthropology*, Oxford: Basil Blackwell.

Redfield, R. (1930) *Tepoztlán: A Mexican Village*, Chicago: University of Chicago Press.

Sahlins, M. (1997) 'Comment to Borofsky "Cook, Lono, Obeyesekere and Sahlins"', *Current Anthropology* 38, 2: 255–77.

Scharfstein, B.-A. (1989) *The Dilemma of Context*, New York: New York University Press.

Scheper-Hughes, N. (1995) 'The primacy of the ethical: propositions for a militant anthropology', *Current Anthropology* 36, 3: 409–20.

Schneider, D.M. ([1984] 1998) *A Critique of the Study of Kinship*, Ann Arbor, MI: University of Michigan Press.

Sirnes, T. (1977) *Risiko og mening: Mentale brot og meiningsdimensjonar i industri og politkk*, Rapport 53, Bergen: University of Bergen, Institutt for administrasjon og organisasjonsvitenskap.

Spiro, M. (1992) *Anthropological Other or Burmese Brother? Studies in Cultural Analysis*, New Brunswick, New Jersey: Transaction Publishers.

—— (1996) 'Postmodernist anthropology, subjectivity and science: a modernist critique', *Comparative Studies in Society and History* 38, 4: 759–80.

Strathern, M. (1987) 'Out of context: the persuasive fictions of anthropology', *Current Anthropology* 28, 3: 251–70.

Van Beek, W. (1991) 'Dogon restudied: a field evaluation of the work of Marcel Griaule', *Current Anthropology* 32, 2: 139–58.

Part II

Reinvigorating p:
comparative met

Chapter 4

Conditions of comparison

A consideration of two anthropological traditions in the Netherlands

Jan J. de Wolf

Cultural comparison has meant different things to different anthropologists. A minimal definition entails the establishment of socially significant cultural *differences* and *similarities* between groups of people. The two aspects presuppose each other: if people were completely different, it would be impossible to register the differences; if people were entirely the same, there would be no point in comparing them (cf. Fay 1996: 72–91). As Howe and Hobart argue, however, 'relations of similarity and difference are not given in the empirical phenomena themselves but are generated by people who act on them and decide, using criteria of their own choosing, to which class, category or concept they conform' (Holy 1987: 16).

In this chapter I shall deal with two Dutch traditions of cultural comparison that pursued very different aims. One sought to establish quantitatively based generalizations on a global scale, the other attempted to validate common structural patterns within one region. Both traditions made original contributions to the development of the anthropological discipline as a whole, but their international impact varied greatly in different times and places. As I hope to show, the reasons for this variation include the general state of theoretical development in anthropology, the amount and kind of empirical evidence available (or at least possible to collect) and institutional factors influenced by the wider social, economic and political contexts of the times. In this respect, it is important to note that, for much of the period considered here, the Netherlands was a colonial power with extensive dominions in Asia. On the one hand, this provided a powerful impetus for the scientific study of this territory and its inhabitants; on the other hand, 'with the rapid development of a number of specializations in Indonesian studies ... anthropology in Indonesia became a "science of leftovers"' (Held 1953a: 868, cited in Koentjaraningrat 1975: 114).

S.R. Steinmetz (1862–1940) founded the tradition of global comparison, characterized by the study of large numbers of different societies of the same 'type' in order to formulate generalizations about the relative prevalence of certain cultural elements. If it were assumed that societies of the same type represented a particular stage in the general evolution of humankind, conclusions could be drawn about the development of specific institutions, such as forms of kinship organization or religious beliefs (cf. Tylor 1889). However, the same comparative method could be used to establish causal connections between social phenomena without recourse to necessary developmental sequences, as was demonstrated brilliantly by Steinmetz's student H.J. Nieboer in his classic work on slavery (1900).

Later studies completed by Steinmetz's students at the University of Amsterdam lacked the relevance of Nieboer's, however, and adhered instead to an already out-dated belief in evolutionary stages. In the 1950s, influenced by the work of Murdock in the United States, A.J.F. Köbben undertook a critical review of the way Steinmetz's ideas on the comparative method had been applied. Köbben proposed his own comparative functional method as an improvement on Murdock (Köbben 1952, 1955b; cf. Murdock 1949) and encouraged his students to follow his example. But at a time when other theoretical orientations were successfully contesting many of the basic premises of the comparative functional method, their work remained very much exercises in what Thomas Kuhn has called 'puzzle-solving' within the limits of an established paradigm.

The founder of the second, or regional, comparative tradition in the Netherlands was J.P.B. de Josselin de Jong (1886–1964). Influenced by Durkheim and Mauss's 1903 study of primitive classification, and particularly by the way in which W.H. Rassers (1922; cf. Ras 1973) had applied their insights to his study of Javanese theatre and ritual, de Josselin de Jong combined the results of Rassers's study with his own analysis of kinship structure along the lines (but in advance) of A.R. Radcliffe-Brown's treatment of Australian kinship (Locher 1988: 60–1). He presented the resulting model of archaic Indonesian culture in his inaugural lecture of 1935 (J.P.B. de Josselin de Jong 1977), the year he was appointed professor of the ethnology of the Dutch East Indies at Leiden University, where he had exercised considerable influence as a part-time professor of general ethnology since 1922. The colonial boundaries of his official brief coincided largely with the Malay Archipelago, which he took as the subject of his regional comparison. In part a synthesis of several studies that had been prepared as dissertations under his guidance, de Josselin de Jong's model was to serve as a guide for his students' future research. The model identified a structural 'core' that could be considered a reconstruction of an ancient cultural pattern, one that located the common origin of observable cultural phenomena from the present as well as the documented past.

The Leiden school was an important source of inspiration for Claude Lévi-Strauss in his *Elementary Structures of Kinship* (1949). Lévi-Strauss likely derived some of his basic ideas from G.J. Held (Héran 1998: 317–19), the only pre-war student of J.P.B. de Josselin de Jong to write his PhD thesis in English (Held 1935). Although M. Granet seems to have had a more significant influence than Held on Lévi-Strauss's kinship research (Héran 1998: 320–2), the Dutch connection to the work is significant: The *Elementary Structures of Kinship* received an early and favourable reception from J.P.B. de Josselin de Jong and his post-war generation of students, and we find references to it in the thesis of P.E. de Josselin de Jong, submitted in English in 1951, and in an extended review essay, also in English, published in 1952 by J.P.B. de Josselin de Jong himself. More important, perhaps, was Rodney Needham's attendance at the Leiden seminar where the *Elementary Structures* was discussed. Needham went on to familiarize the English-speaking world with Lévi-Strauss's kinship theory, and might not have done so if he had not been thoroughly versed in the way Indonesian kinship systems were being analysed at Leiden. In their turn, Lévi-Strauss's publications on mythology and the structural method influenced further developments and applications of J.P.B. de Josselin de Jong's model.

The development of Steinmetz's ideas

Nineteenth-century evolutionists used the comparative method to apply knowledge of what were known as 'savages' to reconstruct the origins and earlier stages of development of the institutions of present-day 'civilized' societies. Deductive reasoning led to the conclusion that these 'primitive' institutions would have been the exact opposite of the bourgeois norms of Western European and North American elites. Applying this reasoning to Indonesian data, G.A. Wilken (1847–91), professor of the ethnology of the Dutch East Indies at Leiden, combined disparate ethnographic facts from many parts of the archipelago into a unified framework (Jaarsma and de Wolf 1991). Steinmetz, who had studied law at Leiden, picked up Wilken's suggestion that the study of primitive law would be valuable for comparative jurisprudence. He chose the origins and early development of legal punishment as the topic for his research and published the result in two separate volumes (Steinmetz 1894). Steinmetz sought the origins of legal punishment in private vengeance between equals, which he conceived as an impulsive act, rooted in self-interest and performed without constraints. This was a direct contrast to civilized peoples, among whom legal punishment presupposes recognition of a common authority that stands above the parties concerned, while the penalty itself takes into account the general interest and is intended to be adequate and useful.

Steinmetz early on conceived of the aim of ethnology as the explanation of the ways of life of 'primitive' peoples and the discovery of the laws (the descriptive regularities) that pertain to the incidence, spatial diffusion and development in time of these ways of life. Such laws were empirical generalizations that could be reduced to physiological, psychophysical or psychological laws or enduring universals (Steinmetz 1894, I: xxii). Steinmetz wanted to improve the methods of ethnology. He emphasized the importance of considering counter-examples and of stating the argument as precisely as possible by counting positive and negative cases. Although he acknowledged the value of Tylor's article 'On a method of investigating the development of institutions' (1889) as a step in the right direction, he regretted Tylor's failure to supply the

data on which his numerical presentation was based or to consider other explanations (Steinmetz 1894, I: xxxi–xxxii).

Steinmetz's theory of the origin of punishment in vengeance identified
cruelty as the psychological condition that caused vengeance. He thought it
unnecessary to prove that 'savages' were cruel; the examples simply abounded
(Steinmetz 1894, I: 300). He only found it necessary to investigate whether
cruelty could be sufficiently enduring to motivate vengeance. He found fifty
cases in which it appeared to, against twenty cases in which it did not (ibid.:
306, 309). The original motive for vengeance, he concluded, was the cult of the
dead, and as punishment is universal among 'savages', so must the cult of the
dead – and more particularly the fear of the dead – be universal. (Steinmetz's
speculations may appear bizarre, but they had their empirical base in reports on
headhunting among the Dayaks of Borneo [Pleyte 1891; Wilken 1889; cf.
Rosaldo 1980]). A large part of Volume I was devoted to an exhaustive demonstration of this argument (Steinmetz 1894, I: 141–296). Steinmetz then
considered the evolution of vengeance as blood feud and the development of
compensatory payments. In Volume II, he dealt with duelling and the position
of women, punishments within the family and the domination of men over
women, which he saw as leading eventually to punishment by the state. He
concluded his work with an overview of beliefs about divine punishments on
earth and in the hereafter.

In the years following his 1894 study on punishment Steinmetz elaborated
and revised his ideas on classification. In a long article published in the *Année
Sociologique* in 1900 (Steinmetz 1930: 96–210) he argued that the widespread
reluctance to consider alternative social types was based on a conservative
tendency to consider one's own social and legal forms eternal, unchangeable
and normal. If one seeks to justify one's own social situation, one need not
explore social types that do not represent its evolutionary stages. But Steinmetz
maintained that different human groups must have experienced different types
of development, resulting in widely different types of cultures that coexist in
time (ibid.: 104–5).

The need for social classification arises, according to Steinmetz, when we
become aware of enough peoples who are sufficiently different from ourselves
that we recognize their variety – and who are too numerous to be dealt with
individually. To see their apparent similarities, however, one must know them
so well that it becomes difficult not to feel that each case is unique. We have
become sensitive to their underlying resemblances only because anthroposoci-
ology, comparative ethnology and political economy have shown how social
structure, biological characteristics and ways of gaining a livelihood influence
all social manifestations. In ethnology scientific analysis had to precede and
prepare the way for classification (Steinmetz 1930: 117–18), unlike the field of
natural history, in which classification came before thorough studies of
morphology and physiology.

Nieboer's work on slavery

Steinmetz's article on classification ties in with the work on slavery undertaken by H.J. Nieboer (1873–1920), who studied law at Utrecht University and began his PhD research in 1896 under Steinmetz's supervision. (Steinmetz had been granted the status of honorary lecturer [*privaatdocent*] at Utrecht in 1895.) Published in English in 1900, and in an enlarged and somewhat revised edition in 1910, *Slavery as an Industrial System* is comparative in quite a different sense than nineteenth-century evolutionary studies, including Steinmetz's on legal punishment. Nieboer aimed to investigate the conditions that caused slavery to be successful as an industrial system and the conditions under which slavery eventually had to give way to free labour. Although he limited his research to 'savage' tribes, he was not interested in reconstructing the early history of mankind: 'It is sociological laws that we want in the first place' (Nieboer 1910: xvi). Ethnology is key to learning the circumstances on which these social phenomena depend because '[a]mong savages social life is much simpler than among civilised men; the factors which govern it are comparatively few, and so the effect of each of them can be traced without much difficulty' (ibid.).

Nieboer wrote (1910: 8) that, following Puchta, 'we may define the slave as *a man who is the property or possession of another man, and forced to work for him*' (emphasis in original), which he then simplified as '*slavery is the fact that one man is the property or possession of another*' (ibid.: 9; emphasis in original). Having defined slavery in this manner Nieboer considered phenomena that resemble slavery and are often called slavery, but do not come under his definition: however abject their position, wives are not slaves, and children, although subject to the authority of the father, occupy a quite different place in the social system than slaves do. In fact, slavery can only be said to exist outside the boundaries of the family (ibid.: 30).

Nieboer tried to make a comprehensive list of all 'savage' peoples, indicating whether or not they were reported to have slavery. In his 1900 edition he recorded 176 positive and 164 negative cases; in 1910 he included 210 tribes with slavery and 181 without. Had a good scientific classification been available, he would have liked to divide the tribes according to their general level of culture and investigate at which stages of culture slavery is found. Instead, Nieboer took 'one prominent side of social life, that may reasonably be supposed to have much influence on the social structure: ... the economic side of life' (Nieboer 1910: 171).

Nieboer distinguished five modes of subsistence production: hunting and fishing, pastoral nomadism, and three stages of agriculture. The demarcation is not clear-cut, and the classification implies no given evolutionary sequence. Peoples who depend to a large extent on hunting, fishing and gathering wild vegetable foods are one form of agriculturalists; the other two groups are (a) people who rely to a considerable extent on agriculture but not to the exclusion of hunting, fishing and gathering; and (b) agriculturalists for whom hunting, fishing and gathering are of negligible importance. Even using secondary criteria in this subsistence classification, Nieboer was unable to include all tribes that offered cases of the absence or presence of slavery (Nieboer 1910: 174–9).

How, then, can the presence or absence of slavery among peoples with the same mode of subsistence be explained? Starting with slavery among hunting and fishing peoples, Nieboer came to the provisional conclusion that 'slavery can only exist when subsistence is easy to procure without the aid of capital' (Nieboer 1910: 258; emphasis in original). When a combination of capital and skilled labour is necessary – as with the Eskimos, who need boats and sledges with dogs – there is no room for slavery. When unskilled labour combined with capital is so productive that it creates a surplus beyond the subsistence of the labourer, and the demand for labour exceeds the supply of labour, slavery is at least a theoretical possibility, although among the cases considered no such instance was found. When subsistence requires much skill but no capital, slavery is useless because slaves cannot be compelled to perform their work well. Only when the produce of an unskilled labourer can exceed the primary wants of the labourer and all members of society can provide for themselves, because no capital is needed, does slavery become the only means to get others to work for one. Even then, however, slavery does not always exist (ibid.: 256–8).

Clearly, secondary factors increase or diminish the occurrence of slavery. Important among them are the status of women and the accumulation of stored foods and other forms of wealth. Where most of the productive and domestic tasks are allocated to women, slaves are not needed. Where food is preserved in large quantities, there is much demand for unskilled labour, which can be provided by slaves; moreover, this stored food makes possible large permanent settlements, which may be more easily organized to prevent the escape of slaves. In societies where trade and craft production are important occupations, extra labour is needed to supply the primary needs of the traders and craftspeople and certain commercial commodities require unskilled labour that can be supplied by slaves. Finally, increased wealth stimulates a demand for luxuries, and to the extent that people's wants exceed their primary needs there is more room for slave labour (Nieboer 1910: 258–61). Many of these factors are present among the Indians of the Northwest Coast, which may explain why fifteen of the eighteen cases where slavery is present among hunters and fishers belong to this group (ibid.: 201–7).

Pastoral tribes, in which there tend to be sufficient numbers of men without animals to act as servants of animal owners, have little use for slave labour (Nieboer 1910: 288–91). At the 'lowest' stage of agriculture, in Nieboer's terminology, where hunting is still an important activity, slavery is much less common than at his 'higher' stages. The cases in which slavery does occur will have to be accounted for by secondary causes, but Nieboer does not investigate these in detail (ibid.: 293–6). Instead, he turns his attention to the factor he has identified as the main cause of slavery: the easy procurement of subsistence without the aid of capital. As it turns out, this general rule requires an important qualification. When all cultivable land has been appropriated, a landless person must apply to a landowner for work as a tenant or labourer, and the availability of such free labour makes slavery unnecessary (ibid.: 302–3). This hypothesis is tested by an examination of the situation in Oceania, excluding New Guinea.

Combining his earlier findings on the absence of slavery where subsistence is dependent on capital with the outcome of his research on the role of landed property, Nieboer proposed a general rule: '[S]lavery, as an industrial system, is not likely to exist where subsistence depends on material resources which are present in limited quantity' (Nieboer 1910: 384; original emphasis). He then proposed to divide all peoples on earth, whatever their means of subsistence, into 'peoples with open resources and peoples with closed resources' (original emphasis), contending that 'only among peoples with open resources can slavery or serfdom exist, whereas free labourers dependent on wages are only found among peoples with closed resources' (ibid.: 385). He acknowledged, however, that there are exceptions due to secondary causes, and stressed that open resources do not necessarily lead to slavery or serfdom. In many simple societies everyone, or nearly everyone, works for his own needs and there are no labouring as opposed to ruling classes.

Most later writers on slavery refer to Nieboer's study, either rejecting or modifying its thesis (e.g. Baks et al. 1966; Kloosterboer 1960; MacLeod 1929; Siegel 1945), and renewed attention on the part of contemporary historians and anthropologists to the phenomenon of slavery also revived interest in the substantive issues he raised (e.g. Domar 1970; Engerman 1973; Hoetink 1973; Miers and Kopytoff 1977; Patterson 1977; Watson 1980). His pioneering work cannot be ignored. 'In reviewing the literature on slavery I have found myself returning, again and again, to the seminal work of H.J. Nieboer', writes Watson (1980: 7), and Kopytoff (1982: 217) grudgingly admits his influence: 'Whatever the reason, the ghost of Nieboer rather than of any other anthropological fore-father rises up whenever a search for theories of slavery begins.' Vincent (1990: 9) recently named Slavery as an Industrial System a landmark in the history of political anthropology, together with such classics as African Political Systems and Political Systems of Highland Burma.

Nieboer's study of slavery, which differentiated economic regimes not as stages in an evolutionary development but as types of possible combinations of factors of production, is important for having overcome the evolutionary bias of the comparative method. Although his definition of slavery was ethnocentric, formulated in terms derived from current thinking in political economy, Nieboer was able to make universally valid propositions that help us understand slavery as an outcome of rational choice, rather than as an expression of funda-mentally different views on the value of human life and dignity. Nieboer confronts us with the undeniable fact that slavery is first and foremost the exploitation of human labour by means of direct compulsion. Where slavery does not exist it is because the specific combination of factors of production and regulation of ownership and access to these factors makes such direct compulsion an irrational way of controlling the labour supply – and not because of any more advanced stage of moral development.

Other comparative studies instigated by Steinmetz

In 1907 Steinmetz had been appointed professor at the University of Amsterdam, where his primary duty was teaching geography to secondary school teachers. Steinmetz emphasized the autonomy of social life, and in his courses the descriptive sociology of industrialized societies became as much a part of the subject as ethnology. In 1921, Geography was officially recognized as a field for an academic degree and graduates could engage in research for PhD theses. Many of Steinmetz's students who chose to work in the Netherlands wrote community studies that were partly based on fieldwork, others wrote ethnological dissertations based on library research and continued Steinmetz's and Nieboer's tradition of comparative research.

Although Steinmetz recognized the value of Nieboer's comparative studies of different types of simple society, he wanted to retain the methodological principle that contemporary 'primitive' cultures were representative of earlier stages of the development of the most 'advanced' societies. In an article published in 1912 (Steinmetz 1930: 404–38), he admitted that the old evolutionary schemes that showed an automatic progression from simple to complex were probably no better than classificatory devices and did not necessarily reflect temporal developments. Nevertheless, he believed that it would be possible to classify peoples according to their general level of development, at least in the case of 'higher cultures' as exemplified by the north-western European culture area. Here, according to Steinmetz, one could see how peoples with the most advanced mental development and at the highest stage of economic life were also superior in terms of social organization, pursuit of truth, altruism and estimation of individual worth. Why should this correlation between technical development and advanced economic organization, on the one hand, and moral, political, artistic and religious progress, on the other, be absent among 'lower peoples'? After all, the same psychological characteristics responsible for material progress also caused moral and intellectual advancement. Of course, it was possible to find exceptions, but whether these were only superficial or were fundamental enough to invalidate the entire argument only future research would tell. In any case, it was certainly more plausible than Wilhelm Schmidt's idea that the Pygmies (who, according to Schmidt, had retained the earliest forms of human culture) were characterized by pure religion in its monotheistic form (Steinmetz 1930: 412–16).

In 1927 J.J. Fahrenfort defended the first ethnological dissertation completed under Steinmetz at the University of Amsterdam, a critique of Schmidt's ideas on the original form of religion and the attempts by him and his students to prove its existence (Fahrenfort 1927). J.H. Ronhaar, another student of Steinmetz, looked critically at the concept of 'matriarchal culture' as used especially by Schmidt and Graebner (Ronhaar 1931). Ronhaar's voluminous study gave exhaustive listings of negative and positive examples but did not formulate any generalizations, no doubt partly because the examples were not related to a classificatory typology.

Two other dissertations, concerning topics with which Steinmetz himself had dealt earlier, reached more positive results. T. van der Bij, in his 1929 study on '*Ontstaan en eerste ontwikkeling van den oorlog*' ('The origin and first development of war'), concluded that at the 'lowest' stage of cultural development, where foraging is dominant, fighting between groups is very unusual and aggressive warfare absent. At the next higher stage, that of primitive agriculturalists, pastoralists and probably hunters, fighting between groups is frequent, but courageous behaviour is notably lacking. The most important motive for violence is fear of the dead, who demand blood revenge (van der Bij 1929: 262–3) – an argument taken directly from Steinmetz's study on the origins of legal punishment. Steinmetz, however, disagreed with van der Bij's conclusion that people at the lowest stage of cultural development were essentially peaceful and lacked courage and aggressiveness and wrote a lengthy article presenting detailed evidence to the contrary (Steinmetz 1935: 352–415).

J. Wisse, in his thesis on '*Selbstmord und Todesfurcht bei den Naturvölkern*' ('Suicide and the fear of death among primitive peoples') (1933), assessed the frequency of suicides among *Naturvölkern* (ibid.: 460–70), categorized motives and discussed the relative importance of sociological and psychological explanations (ibid.: 479–501), paying special attention to the fear of death as a factor that could inhibit suicide. When life is harsh and miserable, Wisse concluded, people have an indifferent attitude towards death (ibid.: 502–8). Although his data were by no means comprehensive, Wisse believed that they contained those peoples who differed most in race, habitat and cultural development and were sufficient in number to present a representative picture of 'savage' society. (Steinmetz and his students placed great emphasis on counting negative and positive instances among as many peoples as possible, but had no systematic sampling procedures, did not use correlation measures and made no assessments of statistical probability. In this respect, they totally ignored Tylor's pathbreaking article of 1889.)

Steinmetz's study on legal punishment was an original attempt to apply the then-current evolutionary theory to a field other than the development of kinship, marriage and religion. But although Nieboer had provided an excellent example of the advantages of a theoretically inspired typology of societies without evolutionary implications, Steinmetz did not explore its possibilities. Perhaps his commitment to a Social Darwinist ideology with regard to contemporary social issues made him reluctant to renounce an evolutionary perspective (cf. Köbben 1992). (Nieboer's distinguished career as a civil servant took quite a different turn, concerned mainly with national public health and social housing policies. Nieboer was also active in the pragmatic and reformist Dutch Labour Party [de Wolf 1994: 123–6].) By the time the first graduates in Geography started to write PhD theses for Steinmetz, his evolutionary ideas had become distinctly old-fashioned, and although there was some merit in the critique of Schmidt's diffusionism, alternative explanations were not forthcoming.

A.J.F. Köbben and the statistical method

In 1952 the *Journal of the Royal Anthropological Institute* published a prize-winning essay by A.J.F. Köbben, a recently graduated Dutch anthropologist. Köbben had been a student of J.J. Fahrenfort, Steinmetz's successor at Amsterdam, and had conducted fieldwork in the Ivory Coast on peasant cash-crop production and its consequences. He succeeded Fahrenfort in 1955 (cf. Köbben 1955a). A revision of an earlier Dutch version (1951), his 1952 article reviewed G.P. Murdock's *Social Structure* (1949) and some related studies using similar methods.

Köbben's evaluation is preceded by a critical review of earlier work in this field, especially by Dutch authors. Following G. Gonggrijp, he calls their approach *hologeistic*: interested in studying one culture trait or group of traits among as many peoples as possible across the globe in order to discover regularities that cannot be attributed to historical contact and geographical location, and emphasizing the inductive-statistical method. Köbben, however, rightly points out that this so-called method is a mere technique and rejects the claim that it guarantees the truth of the results, as different scientists may come to opposing conclusions (Köbben 1951: 321–6). Köbben objects that one cannot be sure that similar cases are really independent and not based on historical influence, and that the cultural context to which the analysed phenomena belong are not taken into account. In extreme examples we only get 'laundry lists' (ibid.: 329). As was demonstrated by Driver and Kroeber (1932), however, these criticisms apply not to the technique itself, but to the use scholars have made of it.

Köbben turned next to Murdock's *Social Structure*. He admires the strict argumentation used in some chapters, but criticizes general statements that are unsupported by systematic treatment of empirical data. He also objects to the constitution of Murdock's sample, which seems to be limited by the quality of the sources rather than considerations of representativeness. Although Murdock did take into account historical connections, it was only to show that changes due to the impact of one kinship system on another will be restricted in scope. The only functional relation he considered is the correlation between kinship relations and kinship terminology, ignoring such factors as technical development, modes of subsistence, property relations, political organization and demography. In certain cases such contextualization would have been impossible due to lack of information; in others its absence leads to serious mistakes (Köbben 1951: 333–9).

Köbben maintained that the hologeistic method would show its greatest usefulness only when combined with functional analyses: analysing a few examples in depth to explain widespread regularities discovered with statistical means, or discovering if characteristics typical of one society might also occur elsewhere (Köbben 1951: 340). The latter possibility was explored by Köbben in his inaugural lecture of 1955, which he later revised and expanded (1964: 21–37), using an example of conflicts he observed among the matrilineal Agni of the Ivory Coast. Here, sons live and work with their father but cannot inherit from him. However, a father may give his son gifts during his lifetime, provided his matrilineal relatives agree and the wealth was acquired by the father himself. The inheritance is passed on to a full brother, or, if there is none, to the eldest sister's son; at this point, sons are able to move away from their father's home. Conflicts arise from this constellation, and they have been exacerbated by the introduction of coffee and cacao, crops that require much hard labour to establish.

Köbben raises a number of questions: are these types of conflict unique for the Agni, or do they occur among other, perhaps even all, matrilineal societies? Or do institutions exist among other matrilineal peoples that mitigate such conflicts? Looking at the dynamics of the problem, Köbben asks, are these conflicts the result of Westernization or did they exist before, at least latently? If they are recent, are economic factors more important than the influence of missions, education and government policies (1964: 24–8)?

Reviewing data from seven other matrilineal societies, Köbben concluded that Western influences, especially economic changes, had heightened an already existing conflict of interests between son and sister's son and that, where this did not occur, mitigating circumstances could be identified (ibid.: 28–36). Köbben's later research among the Djuka (Surinamese Bush Negroes) yielded a truly negative case, but this could be explained by the fact that here an inheritance was divided among as many people as possible and matrilineal descendants would hardly profit if sons received no share at all (ibid.: 36–7). In my view, this raises the question of whether the real problem is not the organization of the transfer of property to the next generation, which may also be a source of tension and quarrels in *patrilineal* societies (cf. Fischer 1956).

Köbben added in 1971 that he used the term 'functional' in a broad sense: that when comparing phenomena one should consider as similar those with the same or comparable effects (i.e. function), even if the forms may show great differences. He did not mean a functionalism that implies integration, adaptation and self-regulating systems (Köbben 1971: 225). Reflecting on his initial statement that in matrilineal societies tensions exist between Ego, his maternal uncle and his maternal uncle's son, Köbben wrote that this could give the impression that two isolated traits are being compared. On the contrary, it should be understood that he also referred to the economic, juridical, political, supernatural (witchcraft and sorcery) and moral connotations of these tensions. Moreover, the various peoples under review were very much aware of these tensions and discussed this aspect of their societies in much the same manner (Köbben 1970: 591–2).

At a time when fieldwork was not yet part of the university curriculum for anthropologists in the Netherlands, comparative studies in which hypotheses were tested quantitatively with the aid of library research were considered suitable for master's dissertations at the University of Amsterdam. Some of these studies formed the basis for articles in anthropological journals. In a broad sense, most of these publications can be called functional. They are concerned with the effects of institutions: matrilateral cross-cousin marriage and social cohesion (Berting and Philipsen 1960), fraternal interest groups and the use of violence in conflict solving (Thoden van Velzen and van Wetering 1960), the advantages of matrilocality when status is inherited matrilineally (Kloos 1963), social stratification and open resources and the use a society may have for slavery (Baks et al. 1966). In some of these studies statistical measures are not calculated, but only Berting and Philipsen (1960) mention the doubtful value of applying statistical tests of significance when a sample is not random. However, these studies problematize not probability but exceptions to general rules (cf. Köbben 1966), and one way to confront exceptions is to emphasise the problem of operationalizing theoretically relevant factors – a special case of the more general issue of errors of observation. This was done in studies by Thoden van Velzen and van Wetering (1960) and by Baks et al. (1966).

Köbben and his students were quite successful in terms of publications and international recognition, particularly among US followers of Murdock (cf. Naroll and Cohen 1970), but none of Köbben's students considered here pursued this type of research. Most of them went on to do field research on which they wrote PhD theses, and their later careers were characterized by other intensive field studies, often supplemented by historical investigations. Köbben himself resigned in 1976 to take up a position as director of a research institute associated with Leiden University that undertook studies of the position of ethnic minorities in the Netherlands.

It is probably the work of H.J.M. Claessen on the early state that remained closest to the programmatic intentions of Köbben's inaugural lecture of 1955. Claessen's dissertation (supervised by Köbben and completed in 1970) was a comparative study of the administrative and political organization of five different states as they were at the time of their discovery: Inca, Tahiti, Tonga, Dahomey and Buganda. Many aspects are presented in tabular form and given numerical values indicating the frequency and/or intensity of their occurrence. On the basis of these tables, a number of general characteristics are identified and it becomes possible to express differences and similarities quantitatively. The study, however, is essentially descriptive and there is no explicit theory from which hypotheses are derived and then tested. Measures of association and statistical significance are absent (Claessen 1970).

Later Claessen widened this comparative approach and framed it in terms of evolutionary theory, first in collaboration with P. Skalnik. Together, they proposed that the early state was a stage of political development between chiefdom and state and emphasized common criteria applicable to all early states. But evolutionism was also only a stage in the development of Claessen's ideas, and he went on to evolve a complex interaction model to explain structural change within the early state. Because the relationships between various elements are not specified in a quantifiable way, however, the work's useful and interesting interdisciplinary links are with historians and archaeologists, not with statistically minded political scientists and sociologists (cf. Oosten and van de Velde 1994).

Murdock's project left a deep impression on Dutch anthropology, not least because of the tremendous expense involved in establishing the Human Relations Area Files (HRAF). It was another example of US superiority, and no university or foundation in the Netherlands could even afford to buy a copy. In the other social and behavioural sciences in the Netherlands one also turned to the USA in the 1950s and 1960s for inspiration (cf. Koenis and Plantenga 1986), and many Dutch scientists and scholars were proud of having spent a year at a US university or research institute. In the field of anthropology the only serious competitor to the USA was Great Britain. British functionalism was represented at the University of Amsterdam by S. Hofstra (1898–1983), professor of sociology from 1949 until 1968. He had been a research fellow of the International African Institute and was trained by Malinowski at the London School of Economics in the 1930s. (Initially, Lévi-Strauss's appeal was limited to specialists in the field of Indonesian and Australian kinship.)

The 1960s and 1970s saw a great increase in the number of university students in the Netherlands. Anthropology graduates could easily get teaching jobs, which were made attractive by generous leaves of absence for field research, or they became research fellows funded directly by national government-sponsored foundations. Many PhD theses were written; a hundred were submitted between 1970 and 1980 alone. Most were based on first-hand field research, but even dissertations that used mainly or only secondary literature concentrated on one society or culture or took as their focus the analysis of a theoretical orientation (cf. Kloos 1981). The statistical-functional approach seemed no longer relevant, due in part to the realization that cultures and societies had become interrelated to such an extent that explanations that focused on internal 'functional' correlations alone, without taking into account external connections, no longer could provide a realistic picture. Such considerations were especially important if one wanted to do research that could somehow be applied and yield practical results benefitting the subjects of that research. Apart from that, by 1970 many students and staff considered positivism and empiricism to be tainted legitimizations of imperialist aggression, capitalist exploitation and racist discrimination.

The Leiden tradition of regional–structural comparison

When the first chair of ethnology in the Netherlands was established at Leiden in 1877, its scope was limited to the Dutch East Indies and its main function was to provide trainees for the colonial civil service with some basic knowledge of Indonesian ethnology. The region remained the focus of teaching and research until Indonesia gained its independence in 1949, but even after that date a strong interest in this area was retained at Leiden. The study of native customary law (*adat*) was established as an entirely different subject area, dominated after 1900 by C. van Vollenhove (1874–1933), who distinguished no fewer than nineteen different regions in Indonesia, each with its own *adat* system. Descriptions made use of a unified system of categories, which facilitated comparison (van Vollenhove 1928; cf. Koentjaraningrat 1975: 88–93). Attempts to link this *adat* to the social life of which it was a part were rare, although the best examples are still considered to be valuable ethnographic descriptions (cf. for instance Vergouwen 1964).

Interest in sociological aspects was especially apparent in the work of the lawyer F.D.E. van Ossenbruggen (1869–1950), as can be seen in his application of Durkheim and Mauss's insights on primitive classification (Durkheim and Mauss 1903; cf. Koentjaraningrat 1975: 94–101). His article on Javanese village structure dating from 1916 (van Ossenbruggen 1977) was used in turn by W.H. Rassers in his dissertation on the stories of Pandji. These narratives form an important part of traditional Indonesian literature and are used as scripts for a specific genre of the famous puppet performances of the Javanese theatre (Rassers 1922: 5–7). In a discussion of the diffusionist Schmidt's interpretation of mythical parallels to a major plot in the Pandji stories, Rassers argues that certain anomalies become understandable if we accept that these myths originated in societies characterized by exogamous groups, which were also the basis for a cosmological classification similar to those of Australian and North American tribes (ibid.: 215–19). Van Ossenbruggen had hypothesized that the ancient Javanese classificatory system originated in a society similar to that of the Australian aborigines, which Rassers believed to have proved with the aid of data derived from the Pandji stories. He concluded that the Pandji myth belonged to a totemistic environment and that consequently the origin of Javanese theatre could be traced back to totemistic ritual (ibid.: 323).

Philologists, archaeologists and some anthropologists – Schmidt among them – were sceptical of Rassers's treatment of the Pandji stories. Schmidt rejected Rassers's criticism, preferring his own type of culture history explanation, based on a reconstruction of the diffusion of two cultural complexes. The oldest complex, he maintained, had entered Indonesia from the west and the youngest from the east, having originated in New Guinea. On the island of Sulawesi these two complexes mixed (cf. Koentjaraningrat 1975: 117–18). Rassers opened the way for a new perspective, which emphasized the enduring influence of a very ancient, perhaps even original, form of social organization, of which traces could still be found in myth and ritual. Rassers also showed that this archaic culture could explain certain peculiarities of the ways in which, on Java, Buddhism and Sivaism were related to each other, as was apparent from old manuscripts and ancient monuments (Rassers 1982: 65–91).

In his scholarly work Rassers cooperated closely with his colleague J.P.B. de Josselin de Jong. Like Rassers, de Josselin de Jong was curator at the Ethnological Museum at Leiden and, since 1922, part-time professor of general ethnology at Leiden University. He had done linguistic and ethnographic field-work among Blackfoot Indians and archaeological research on the Dutch Antilles. It is generally assumed that de Josselin de Jong's interest in Durkheim and Mauss was stimulated by Rassers, as the first evidence of their influence appears in his work after Rassers's 1922 publication.

In 1926 J.Ph. Duyvendak submitted his dissertation on the Kakean Society of the Eastern Indonesian island of Ceram, a work that shows the unmistakable influence of his supervisor J.P.B. de Josselin de Jong in the more theoretical and comparative sections (Locher 1988: 57–8). Duyvendak concluded that there had been in Ceram two exogamous moieties consisting of subgroups linked by matrilateral cross-cousin marriage and that this social organization formed the basis for a system of classification that was still present in certain popular games (Duyvendak 1926: 119–38). He also assumed that totemism linked with initiation rituals had formerly existed (ibid.: 173–8; cf. Koentjaraningrat 1975: 147–8).

By 1930 J.P.B. de Josselin de Jong had become interested in the inherently double unilineal aspect of Australian systems of marriage classes (Locher 1988: 61). In F.A.E. van Wouden's dissertation (1935), which he also supervised, this double unilineality was connected with prescribed matrilateral cross-cousin marriage and circulating connubium. Although van Wouden was able to work this out as a model, there was no evidence at the time (or today) that the different parts occurred together in any particular instance (cf. Koentjaraningrat 1975: 150–2).

When in 1935 J.P.B. de Josselin de Jong gave his inaugural lecture as professor *ordinarius* of Indonesian ethnology, he tried to demonstrate that the phenomena dealt with by Rassers, Duyvendak and van Wouden were not separate ethnographic curiosities, but formed an integrated whole or system. He identified a structural core that was present in numerous ancient Indonesian cultures in many parts of the Archipelago: a typical tribe consisted of exogamous clans linked through fixed connubial relationships, with each clan connected to two other clans. As a junior partner, a clan would receive brides from a senior partner, but at the same time it would be senior partner to a third clan to which it would give brides. Appropriate 'male' and 'female' gifts would accompany these exchanges. Each clan was also divided into two exogamous moieties. The number of clans within a tribe had to be even – at least four – if each clan were to have both a junior and a senior partner. These clans and moieties were both patrilineal and matrilineal; the system was in fact double unilineal. The social divisions were connected with an all-embracing totemic classificatory system. The world view underlying the system included a belief in mythical ancestors, and the system's dualism was also present in the world of the gods, particularly in the mythical couple of the benefactor and the trickster. Following Rassers's analysis of the Javanese shadow theatre, de Josselin de Jong also saw initiation as part of the ancient structural core (J.P.B. de Josselin de Jong 1977: 168–79; cf. Koentjaraningrat 1975: 142–5). Methodologically this model was linked to the concept of the 'field of ethnological study', which was defined as

> certain areas of the earth's surface with a population whose culture appears to be sufficiently homogeneous and unique to form a separate object of ethnological study, and which at the same time apparently reveals sufficient local shades of differences to make comparative research worth while.
>
> (J.P.B. de Josselin de Jong 1977: 167–8)

For many years to come the notions of 'structural core' and 'field of ethnological [anthropological] study' were important guidelines for the research of many of the best Dutch anthropologists, particularly of those trained by J.P.B. de Josselin de Jong. However, there was also much discussion about the definition and application of these concepts. P.E. de Josselin de Jong (1984a: 2) identified four elements that constitute a structural core: circulating connubium, double unilineality, dual symbolic classification and resilience in the face of foreign cultural influences. The fourth element refers to processes of Hinduization and Islamization to which J.P.B. de Josselin de Jong devoted the second part of his inaugural lecture (1977: 174–81). No consensus has developed about whether or not a 'structural core' exists when one or more of the core elements appear to be absent (P.E. de Josselin de Jong 1984b: 244).

There is also a question of how to delimit the 'field of ethnological study'. J.P.B. de Josselin de Jong dealt with the Malay Archipelago without defining its boundaries; in practice it meant the Dutch East Indies, without Western New Guinea. Yet G.J. Held applied the model of the 'structural core' to Papuans of the north-west coast of New Guinea (Held 1947: 7; cf. Koentjaraningrat 1975: 155), and P.E. de Josselin de Jong extended the field to the Mnong Gar of central Vietnam (1965). More recently, in line with the 'linguistic turn' in anthropology, others have stressed the linguistic unity of a 'field of ethnological study' (cf. Fox 1980). This would be in accordance with what J.P.B. de Josselin de Jong 'almost certainly had in mind': 'a comparative study of societies which are *genetically* related to each other – the presumption being based on the proved genetic relationship of the languages spoken by the members of these societies' (P.E. de Josselin de Jong 1984b: 257).

The structural–regional comparative approach developed at Leiden in the 1930s can be explained in terms of the colonial focus of anthropology as taught at that university. It also provided a theoretical alternative to the outmoded evolutionism that still characterized *adat* law studies. J.P.B. de Josselin de Jong expanded Durkheim and Mauss's scheme of social organization and innovatively included matrilateral cross-cousin marriage in his model of archaic Indonesian social organization, demonstrating that its structural consequences were the same whether patrilineality or matrilineality was emphasized. (In fact, both lines were present and could be used as a principle of recruitment for unilineal descent groups or categories.) J.P.B. de Josselin de Jong found Mauss and Durkheim's model attractive because it corresponded to his own conviction that culture was like language – a systematic whole based on underlying principles.

The structural–regional model enabled J.P.B. de Josselin de Jong's students to make sense of often disparate ethnographic data of varying quality and to fill gaps in knowledge by recourse to information from other societies, based on the supposition that they had all shared the same ancient structural core. This assumption was important because these students were using available ethnographic sources for their secondary analyses, but it also supported J.P.B. de Josselin de Jong's moral and political commitments. Josselin de Jong and many of his contemporaries, including the historian Huizinga, experienced and interpreted the rise of modern society as a loss of social cohesion and demise of humanistic values. By contrast, Indonesian tribal societies were seen to represent the very opposite of the negative aspects of modern society. J.P.B. de Josselin de Jong advised his Indonesian students to cherish the ancient values of their indigenous communities, which might be the only guide left to them in a chaotic world (cf. Prager 1999: 346–8).

Lévi-Strauss and the Leiden school

Héran, in his 1998 review of the historical connections between Lévi-Strauss and 1930s Leiden structuralism, discounts the Leiden School's influence by way of M. Granet, although Lévi-Strauss himself mentioned Granet's early recognition of the importance of cross-cousin marriages for systems of restricted and generalized exchange. Lévi-Strauss added that one should not overestimate Granet's originality, however, as both T.C. Hodson and G.J. Held had already touched on the problem and its solution (Héran 1998: 5–6). J.P.B. de Josselin de Jong had pointed out correspondences between Lévi-Strauss's book and van Wouden's earlier thesis, and in the 1967 edition of *Les Structures élémentaires* Lévi-Strauss acknowledged his ignorance of van Wouden's work and claimed that there was no doubt that Granet was influenced by van Wouden (Héran 1998: 6, 310). But a close analysis of van Wouden, Granet and Lévi-Strauss shows that the similarities between Granet and Lévi-Strauss are much greater than those between van Wouden and Granet (ibid.: 311–12, 313).

However, Héran does emphasize the importance for Lévi-Strauss of another of J.P.B. de Josselin de Jong's students, G.J. Held. Among the several diagrams that Held used in his 1935 thesis on the Mahabharata, two were a direct inspiration for those presented by Lévi-Strauss in the *Elementary Structures*.

Moreover, Held had pointed out that exclusive matrilateral cross-cousin marriage that allowed for the unlimited expansion of the number of groups linked by those marriages was quite common, extending from India to Siberia and from Eastern Indonesia to Australia. This, Héran notes, was to be exactly the thesis of Lévi-Strauss himself (1998: 317–18).

In 1951 P.E. de Josselin de Jong, a nephew of J.P.B. de Josselin de Jong, submitted his thesis on Minangkabau, a people living in west-central Sumatra, and Negri Sembilan, a community with a similar culture located on the Malaccan Peninsula. P.E. de Josselin de Jong identified double unilineality and asymmetric connubium as the principles of Minangkabau social organization. Held (1953b) granted that this model agreed with the facts, but pointed out that its validity appeared to be only partial – a difficulty that de Josselin de Jong countered by positing that it was an ideal pattern, a standard for perfection. Held disagreed, considering the model a timeless conceptualization of certain logical possibilities, which ceases to be perfect as soon as it is found as a cultural reality (cf. Koentjaraningrat 1975: 159).

P.E. de Josselin de Jong put more emphasis than Held on the importance of comparison, holding that elements that appear inexplicable within the framework of a single culture may be quite comprehensible in another culture where they are elements in a system. Within a field of ethnological study, then, one could construct a structural core or basic pattern that would be valid for the entire field (P.E. de Josselin de Jong 1977: 234; cf. Koentjaraningrat 1975: 159). Whereas Rassers and J.P.B. de Josselin de Jong seemed to believe in the historical reality of the structural core of archaic Indonesian culture, P.E. de Josselin de Jong was more cautious, acknowledging that it was quite possible that at no time in the past did reality completely agree with such a reconstruction. He compared the structural core with the asterisked forms in historical linguistic research: purely theoretical and never observed forms that represent the most acceptable reconstruction from the available data and the best suited to explain present-day facts (P.E. de Josselin de Jong 1951: 6, cited in 1980: 322).

Around 1955 the emphasis of Dutch ethnological studies shifted, according to David Moyer, a Canadian anthropologist who took his PhD at Leiden in 1975. Before 1955 there was a focus on the formal analysis of the various properties of social systems and the demonstration that correspondences existed between formal properties of different systems within a field of ethnological study. Maximal correspondences were of special interest. Later, attention shifted from maximal correspondences to the total range of correspondences, involving a more thorough analysis of the social manifestations of the formal properties of the systems under consideration. Moyer identifies an additional differentiation between 'rule principles' and 'idea principles' (Moyer 1981: 65–6), a distinction also made by Held, although his contribution is not acknowledged.

The shift from maximal correspondences to the total range of correspondences was facilitated by the concept of transformation, which Lévi-Strauss used to tackle the study of American myths. At the very least it gave researchers a reason to stop looking for (imperfect) resemblances and instead to consider oppositions as parts of the same set. P.E. de Josselin de Jong admitted that although the Leiden structuralists, himself included, had achieved useful results by applying the structural core as a tool for uncovering the frequently hidden framework of Indonesian social systems, no systematic programme of comparison had yet been carried out within the field of ethnological study in which differences played as important a role as resemblances: individual cultures had not been investigated as variants (linked together by transformations rather than imperfect resemblances) on a common theme (P.E. de Josselin de Jong 1980: 321–2). He pointed out, however, that work inspired by the concept of transformation could not be subjected to the laws of logic as Lévi-Strauss had advocated (P.E. de Josselin de Jong 1984a: 7–8) and warned that uncritical application of the concept could make almost everything into a transformation of everything else (P.E. de Josselin de Jong 1984b: 254). A lack of agreement on what constitutes a structural core and uncertainty about the boundaries of a field of ethnological study threatened to reduce the structural–regional comparative approach to the minimal format of a 'mutual interpretativeness' of cultures (P.E. de Josselin de Jong 1980: 319).

The post-war Dutch government gave a boost to comparative ethnology by commissioning several anthropological studies and stimulating fieldwork by independent academics in Western New Guinea. Indonesia had become independent in 1949, but Western New Guinea (Irian Barat) remained under Dutch rule until 1962. No longer a remote outpost of a colonial empire centred on the island of Java, it became a colony in its own right, to be governed according to UN standards for trusteeship areas. The colonial government needed information on the native population, and a first result of this official interest was J. Pouwer's 1955 PhD thesis on the Mimika, an ethnic group in the south of Western New Guinea, completed under the supervision of J.P.B. de Josselin de Jong. Pouwer was less concerned with applying elements of the structural core identified by his supervisor than was his colleague A.C. van der Leeden, who also completed a PhD thesis under J.P.B. de Josselin de Jong on the social structure of some small groups in the northern part of Western New Guinea (van der Leeden 1956, 1960; cf. Pouwer 1960). The two scholars shared an interest in regional comparison, although van der Leeden was more inclined to take the ideas of Lévi-Strauss as a starting point for his analysis. Pouwer emphasized the influence of the physical environment and a low level of technology in group formation and social integration and saw sufficient commonality in the region to propose New Guinea as a 'separate field of ethnological study', characterized by, among other things, a strong emphasis on reciprocity (Pouwer 1961).

In 1962 Pouwer became the second professor of cultural anthropology at the University of Amsterdam. In his inaugural lecture, he criticized Lévi-Strauss for his neglect of individuals in specific situations – including their physical environment and economic conditions – although he agreed with him that one should look for ordering principles not within but behind the empirical reality

(Pouwer 1962: 13, 17). He also referred to Köbben's comparative functional method, which he considered more acceptable but still too concerned with generalizable regularities of human action. He also criticized the method for its inability to deal with the typical configuration of elements that provided each culture with cohesion and a specific orientation (ibid.: 18–19). Pouwer opted for a method that would concentrate on individual choice, identify cultural themes on the basis of realized options and consider the configuration of these themes in the different cultures within a field of ethnological study. Only then could the comparative functional method usefully be applied.

If we regard structure as ultimately rooted in the human mind, we are able not only to observe that a combination of elements occurs, which is what functionalism does, but also to explain the position these elements occupy relative to each other (Pouwer 1966: 138–9). By reducing supposedly relevant phenomena arising over a wide front to gradually rising levels of abstraction, one may ultimately reach the structuring principles rooted in the human mind. In this regard, Pouwer acknowledged his debt to Lévi-Strauss's *Anthropologie structurale* (ibid.: 139). Köbben, some of whose studies were cited as examples of the functionalist approach, responded. Objecting to the structuralists' claim that they could characterize a structure by a restricted number of 'fundamental principles', he argued that structuralists call fundamental what they *believe* to be fundamental and that their beliefs are seldom founded on objective grounds (Köbben 1966: 148–9).

The regional–comparative approach developed by J.P.B. de Josselin de Jong was based on the analysis of existing literature on specific ethnic groups in Indonesia, which often did not provide complete information. When funds became available for fieldwork, these gaps could have been filled empirically, but unfortunately Indonesia remained closed to Dutch researchers for many years. Even after diplomatic relations between Indonesia and the Netherlands were restored, local conditions might prevent fruitful research – as was the case when P.E. de Josselin de Jong and other anthropologists from Leiden University started a project among the Minangkabau in 1973. In 1975 the Dutch and Indonesian governments came to a formal agreement on a programme of social and cultural research and matters improved (Vermeulen 1987: 32–3), but anthropology was only one part of the programme and the comparative–structural perspective was by no means the only approach adopted. International developments in anthropology also led in different directions. For Indonesian research James Fox (1980) advocated a focus on metaphors, rather than on abstract, analytical models, and David Parkin (1987: 60) claimed that regional structural comparison could survive as a method only if the concepts making up 'underlying structures' were recast in terms of what they meant (their ontological and metaphysical status) to the peoples who actually use them.

P.E. de Josselin de Jong was obviously the heir to the research tradition of his uncle, and he emphasized its importance by frequent references to the common roots of Leiden structuralism and the anthropology of Lévi-Strauss. Lévi-Strauss was also invoked by Pouwer when he tried to incorporate Köbben's empiricism into an '*ordre des ordres*'. The application of the programmatic principles to which they referred remained embryonic, however, and did not result in major comparative studies.

Conclusion

In the nineteenth century the comparative method meant a reconstruction of earlier stages of cultural development by means of data derived from contemporary 'savages'. Steinmetz's comparative study on the origins and early development of legal punishment was comparable to similar work being done on kinship and marriage and on religion. Steinmetz emphasized the importance of considering systematically all the available evidence. To do this, it was necessary to develop a classification scheme to reduce the number of cases to manageable proportions, and this in turn could open the way for an analysis that no longer assumed evolutionary stages – as in Nieboer's work on slavery. Steinmetz and Nieboer were searching for laws; they did not make use of statistical correlations and did not frame their statements in terms of probabilities. What makes their work interesting is that they wanted to explain exceptions, which led Nieboer to a detailed functional analysis of the multiple determination of concrete ethnographic cases. A drawback of their approach, however, was their neglect of those differences that had no place in their system of categorization. Nieboer reduced slavery to its economic aspects, framed in terms of a supposedly universally valid economic theory that also allowed him to explain why slavery is absent in modern, industrialized societies.

Later studies that followed the methodological example of Steinmetz and Nieboer remained much more committed to evolutionism and to exoticizing the 'savage'. Often merely descriptive, they lacked explanatory theoretical sophistication. It is little wonder that Köbben, an anthropologist of the next generation, was amazed at the reinvention of this comparative wheel by Murdock and could mercilessly expose its weak points, many of which were shared by the earlier studies supervised by Steinmetz. Köbben hoped that the drawbacks of this approach could be amended fairly easily by taking into consideration functional relationships, and he remained committed to the discovery of laws and the priority given to universally valid categories which this implied.

After 1970 Köbben himself, along with most of his students, abandoned the functional–comparative approach. Köbben turned his attention to the study of conflicts in Dutch society, and his students became immersed in analyses of their fieldwork, often expanded into or supplemented with historical studies. The functional–comparative approach lingered on at Leiden in studies of the early state, but after a while the study of the interaction of many different elements in actual historical developments became more important.

The emphasis of early Dutch anthropology on the Dutch East Indies almost automatically implied a regional comparative approach. For Wilken, the

Indonesian material provided illustrations for evolutionary stages of development. Other approaches fragmented Indonesia into many different culture areas or explained variety in terms of the sequencing and differential impact of successive waves of migrants into the region. The cultural core of Indonesia as a field of ethnological studies stressed the unity within Indonesian cultural diversity and explained it in terms of historical continuity. After 1955 the search for maximal resemblances and the explanation of imperfect realizations made way for a description based on the potential transformations of a structuralist, i.e. timeless, model. When funds for field research became available, however, Indonesia was no longer willing to admit Dutch anthropologists, and as soon as the Indonesian government extended its authority over Western New Guinea as well, the promising start of Dutch anthropological research came to an end in this remnant of the former colonial empire. Most of the non-Dutch anthropologists who did research in Indonesia (including Irian Jaya) during those years were not at all committed to the type of structuralism that had become the hallmark of Leiden anthropology.

Comparative research depends primarily on secondary sources of information, which inevitably means a reliance on the research of others. Evolutionary theory in anthropology required comparative studies, but the focus on comparison has waned. Since at least the time of Malinowski, anthropologists have given precedence to fieldwork conducted by their professional peers. And for each individual researcher, the specific society studied as participant–observer has become the centre of the analytic universe. Comparison has often served only to emphasize the unique character of that one society. Even the library-based Leiden dissertations completed under J.P.B. de Josselin de Jong usually concentrated on a detailed analysis of one particular society or a few closely related societies. The model of the structural core of archaic Indonesian societies was used more as an heuristic device for investigating new cases than in an attempt at formulating abstract laws. In turn, this orientation easily accommodated to the scientific ambitions of the structuralist theory of Lévi-Strauss.

Both Nieboer and J.P.B. de Josselin de Jong were creative and original thinkers who developed their path-breaking ideas without reference to any other great contemporary anthropologists. They also had in common that after formulating their key intellectual contributions they became political radicals – Nieboer as an active member of the Dutch Labour Party (de Wolf 1994: 123) and J.P.B. de Josselin de Jong as president of an association favouring Indonesian independence (de Wolf 1999; Prager 1999). In both cases we see a parallel between original theoretical thought and strong morally coloured political convictions that put the two men into minority political positions. The parallel is not purely contingent, and the substantive issues with which the two were concerned – exploitation of labour for Nieboer, cultural authenticity for J.P.B. de Josselin de Jong – can be found in their anthropological analyses as well as in their ethical beliefs and political choices.

Such connections between anthropological theory and political practice seem to be absent among later representatives of the two traditions considered here. Both Köbben and P.E. de Josselin de Jong deftly modified some aspects of the orientations of earlier comparative studies, but they were restrained by the examples of Murdock and Lévi-Strauss, respectively. Although they were not uncritical, they were only too happy to partake in the international discourses originating from the Human Relations Area Files at Yale or the Laboratory of Social Anthropology in Paris. This primacy of internationally acknowledged frameworks may explain why the contributions of Köbben and P.E. de Josselin de Jong were not related to any definite ethical concerns and were not reflected in political action. P.E. de Josselin de Jong's politics remained private, while Köbben, although known to have a preference for the Dutch Labour Party, distinguished carefully between objective social research and subjectively held values that determined the goals of policy choices. When Köbben turned more explicitly to the study of social problems in the Netherlands, he always defined these in terms of a broad consensus based on universal values.

The nexus of theoretical innovation, ethical conviction and public political commitment discerned in the cases of Nieboer and J.P.B. de Josselin de Jong was by no means absent in Dutch anthropology at the time the two were active. Both J. van Baal and W.F. Wertheim, whose careers are part of a different story than the one told here about Dutch comparative traditions, wrote memoirs in which they demonstrated the link between their own works and lives. Van Baal and Wertheim were also much less inclined than P.E. de Josselin de Jong and Köbben to refer to important non-Dutch anthropologists when they developed their theoretical vision (van Baal 1986, 1989; Wertheim and Wertheim-Gijse Weenink 1991).

Specific historical constellations influenced the conditions under which comparison in Dutch anthropology contributed to new developments in the discipline at large. Nieboer began his work on slavery at a time when the basic suppositions of evolutionism turned into questions for which there were no easy answers. J.P.B. de Josselin de Jong formulated his research programme after evolutionism and diffusionism had failed to show what was authentic in Indonesian cultures and how these cultures constituted integrated wholes. Their research problems provided new orientations to data that had been collected with other purposes in mind. These perspectives could be tested empirically, and the theoretical insights confirmed or modified accordingly.

Although Nieboer was highly influential in the field of slavery studies, his approach failed to establish itself in other domains. Second-generation studies completed under Steinmetz reverted to a simple-minded and atheoretical evolutionism that was more concerned with speculation about early stages of development than with processes of change. Köbben's attempt to supplement Murdock with British functionalism may have given the students who applied his method a greater sensitivity to tracing relations between institutions when they started their fieldwork, but it failed to provide a compelling theoretical framework for that research. The approach was not sufficiently holistic, did not take into account subjective meanings or emic peculiarities and lacked awareness of the importance of historical processes.

Lévi-Strauss's analysis of elementary forms of kinship clearly owes a debt to the ideas current among J.P.B. de Josselin de Jong and his students in the 1930s, but its significance is difficult to estimate. The contribution of J.P.B. de Josselin de Jong and his students, including Needham, to the popularizing of Lévi-Strauss's ideas in the early 1950s is beyond doubt, however, and is rooted in the shared heritage of Durkheim and especially Mauss. Still, the importance of Leiden structuralism for guiding empirical research remained rather limited. Global political developments prevented Dutch anthropologists from putting the paradigm to the test of intensive anthropological fieldwork in a sufficient number of different sites in Indonesia, and its most important modifications were due mainly to a more thorough-going acceptance of Lévi-Straussian notions. By the time research in Indonesia became feasible again, post-structural and postmodern criticisms had pre-empted the need for empirical confirmation.

Perhaps the most significant aspect of these two Dutch comparative traditions is the innovative potential demonstrated by both Nieboer and J.P.B. de Josselin de Jong in the connection between positive awareness of pressing public issues that call for practical action and the treatment of basic aspects of these same issues in their comparative projects. The connection is also present in more recent attempts at explicit comparison in British social anthropology, particularly the work of Mary Douglas and Marilyn Strathern. Douglas analyses contemporary social problems with the aid of a theory of the relationship between social relations and forms of classification and thinking derived from the anthropological comparison of different 'tribal' societies, and she is able to do so because she herself is morally committed to combining comparative research with a broader public mission, a viewpoint that allows her to evaluate and criticize the seeming naturalness of other positions (cf. Fardon 1999). Strathern acknowledges explicitly that an important source of inspiration for her unique combination of postmodern reflexivity with a regional comparative approach to the problems of gender analysis in Melanesia has been her own feminist commitments (1988: 3–40). The originality of her insights is far from being exhausted, and recently her findings have been shown to be applicable also to interregional comparison (Strathern and Lambek 1998).

The history of anthropology, not unlike the discipline itself, balances uneasily between an immersion in the thoughts and actions of 'others', which seem more fascinating the stranger and more incomprehensible they appear, and a confrontation with issues that are felt to be relevant to present-day predicaments, be they of a disciplinary or a more general social character. The present chapter attempts to give a meaningful description of thought patterns from a rather obscure past and to provide enough information on the context to help us understand why these ways of thinking took the form they did.

However, this chapter must also be understood in terms of contemporary efforts, at least in my own country, to subject scholarly creativity to quantitative forms of appraisal that purport to measure international impact. The examples of Nieboer and J.P.B. de Josselin de Jong make it clear that their original contributions to the development of the anthropological discipline were rooted in uniquely local discourses and owed much of their creativity to allowing anthropological facts to reflect and address their own moral convictions. Even if their methods of comparison are no longer relevant, the conditions under which they were able to develop them may still teach us some valuable lessons.

Bibliography

Baks, C., Breman, J.C. and Nooij, A.T.J. (1966) 'Slavery as system of production in tribal society', *Bijdragen tot de Taal-, Land-en Volkenkunde* 122: 90–109.

Berting, J. and Philipsen, H. (1960) 'Solidarity, stratification and sentiments', *Bijdragen tot de Taal-, Land-en Volkenkunde* 116: 55–80.

Claessen, H.J.M. (1970) *Van vorsten en volken: Een beschrijvende en functioneel-vergelijkende studie van de staatsorganisatie van vijf schriftloze vorstendommen*, Amsterdam: JOKO.

Domar, E.D. (1970) 'The causes of slavery or serfdom: a hypothesis', *Journal of Economic History* 30: 18–32.

Driver, H.E. and Kroeber, A.L. (1932) *Quantitative Expression of Cultural Relationships*, University of California Publications in American Archeology and Ethnology, 31: 211–56.

Durkheim, É. and Mauss, M. (1903) 'De quelques formes primitives de classification', *Année Sociologique* 6: 1–72.

Duyvendak, J.Ph. (1926) *Het Kakean genootschap van Seran*, Almelo: Hilarius.

Engerman, S.L. (1973) 'Some considerations relating to property rights in man', *Journal of Economic History* 33: 43–65.

Fahrenfort, J.J. (1927) *Het hoogste wezen der primitieven. Studie over het 'oermonotheïsme' bij enkele der laagste volken*, Groningen and Den Haag: Wolters.

Fardon, R. (1999) *Mary Douglas: An Intellectual Biography*, London: Routledge.

Fay, B. (1996) *Contemporary Philosophy of Social Science*, Oxford: Blackwell.

Fischer, H. Th. (1956) 'Dr. A.J.F. Köbben, *De vergelijkend-functionele methode in de volkenkunde*', Rede, Amsterdam [Book Review], *Mens en Maatschappij* 31: 117–19.

Fox, J.J. (1980) 'Models and metaphors: comparative research in Eastern Indonesia', in J.J. Fox (ed.) *The Flow of Life: Essays on Eastern Indonesia*, Cambridge, MA: Harvard University Press, pp. 327–33.

Held, G.J. (1935) *The Mahâbhârata: An Ethnological Study*, London: Kegan Paul and Amsterdam: Uitgeversmaatschappij Holland.

—— (1947) *Papoea's van Waropen*, Leiden: Brill.

—— (1953a) 'Applied anthropology in government: the Netherlands', in A.L. Kroeber (ed.) *Anthropology Today*, Chicago: Chicago University Press, pp. 866–79.

—— (1953b) 'Boekbespreking [Book Review]. P.E. de Josselin de Jong *Minangkabau and Negri Sembilan; sociopolitical structure in Indonesia*, dissertation Leiden 1951', *Bijdragen tot de Taal-, Land- en Volkenkunde* 89: 180–90.

Héran, F. (1998) 'De Granet à Lévi-Strauss', *Social Anthropology* 6: 1–60, 169–202, 309–30.

Hoetink, H. (1973) *Slavery and Race Relations in the Americas: Comparative Notes on Their Nature and Nexus*, New York: Harper and Row.

Holy, L. (1987) 'Introduction: description, generalization and comparison: two paradigms', in L. Holy (ed.) *Comparative Anthropology*, Oxford: Blackwell, pp. 1–21.

Jaarsma, S.R. and de Wolf, J.J. (1991) 'Wilken, George Alexander', in C. Winters (ed.) *International Dictionary of Anthropologists*, New York: Garland, pp. 759–60.

Josselin de Jong, J.P.B. de (1952) *Lévi-Strauss's Theory on Kinship and Marriage*, Leiden: Brill.

—— (1977) 'The Malay Archipelago as a field of ethnological study,' in P.E. de Josselin de Jong (ed.) *Structural Anthropology in the Netherlands: A Reader*, The Hague: Nijhoff, pp. 164–82.

Josselin de Jong, P.E. de (1951) *Minangkabau and Negri-Sembilan: Socio-Political Structure in Indonesia*, Leiden: IJdo.

—— (1965) 'An interpretation of agricultural rites in Southeast Asia', *Journal of Asian Studies* 24: 283–91.

—— (1977) 'The participants' view of their culture', in P.E. de Josselin de Jong (ed.) *Structural Anthropology in the Netherlands: A Reader*, The Hague: Nijhoff, pp. 231–52.

—— (1980) 'The concept of the field of ethnological study', in J.J. Fox (ed.) *The Flow of Life: Essays on Eastern Indonesia*, Cambridge, MA: Harvard University Press, pp. 317–26.

—— (1984a) 'A field of anthropological study in transformation', in P.E. de Josselin de Jong (ed.) *Unity in Diversity: Indonesia as a Field of Anthropological Study*, Dordrecht: Foris, pp. 1–10.

—— (1984b) 'Summary and conclusions', in P.E. de Josselin de Jong (ed.) *Unity in Diversity: Indonesia as a Field of Anthropological Study*, Dordrecht: Foris, pp. 234–66.

Kloos, P. (1963) 'Matrilocal residence and local endogamy, environmental knowledge or leadership', *American Anthropologist* 65: 854–62.

—— (1981) 'Themes of the seventies: anthropology in the Netherlands 1970–1980', in P. Kloos and H.J.M. Claessen (eds) *Current Issues in Anthropology: The Netherlands*, Rotterdam: Nederlandse Sociologische en Antropologische Vereniging, Afdeling Culturele antropologie/sociologie der niet-westerse volken, pp. 9–35.

Kloosterboer, W. (1960) *Involuntary Labour since the Abolition of Slavery*, Leiden: Brill.

Köbben, A.J.F. (1951) 'De nieuwe uitwerking van een oude gedachte: Over de statistische methode in de volkenkunde', *Mens en Maatschappij* 26: 321–40.

—— (1952) 'New ways of presenting an old idea: the statistical method in social anthropology', *Journal of the Royal Anthropological Institute* 82: 129–46.

—— (1955a) *Zwarte Planters: Proeve ener Facet-Ethnografie*, 's Gravenhage: Excelsior.

—— (1955b) *De vergelijkend-functionele methode in de volkenkunde*, Groningen and Djakarta: Wolters.

—— (1964) *Van primitieven tot medeburgers*, Assen: Van Gorcum.

—— (1966) 'Structuralism versus comparative functionalism; some comments', *Bijdragen tot de Taal-, Land- en Volkenkunde* 122: 145–50.

—— (1970) 'Comparativists and non-comparativists in anthropology', in R. Naroll and R. Cohen (eds) *A Handbook of Method in Cultural Anthropology*, New York: Columbia University Press, pp. 581–96.

—— (1971) *Van primitieven tot medeburgers, tweede gewijzigde en uitgebreide druk*, Assen: Van Gorcum.

—— (1992) 'Sebald Rudolf Steinmetz (1862–1940); een hartstochtelijke geleerde', in J.C.H. Blom *et al.* (eds) *Een brandpunt van geleerdheid in de hoofdstad*, Hilversum: Verloren, pp. 314–40.

Koenis, S., and Plantenga, J. (eds) (1986) *Amerika en de sociale wetenschappen in Nederland*, Utrecht: Stichting Grafiet.

Koentjaraningrat (1975) *Anthropology in Indonesia: A Bibliographical Review*. Koninklijk Instituut voor Taal-, Land- en Volkenkunde, Biographical Series 8, 's Gravenhage: Martinus Nijhoff.

Kopytoff, I. (1982) 'Slavery', *Annual Review of Anthropology* 11: 207–30.

Lévi-Strauss, C. (1949) *Les Structures élémentaires de la parenté*, Paris: Presses Universitaires de France.

Locher, G.W. (1988) 'J.P.B. de Josselin de Jong en het Leidse structuralisme', *Antropologische Verkenningen* 7, 1–2: 51–74.

Macleod, W.C. (1929) 'The origin of servile labor groups', *American Anthropologist* 31: 89–113.

Miers, S. and Kopytoff, I. (eds) (1977) *Slavery in Africa: Historical and Anthropological Perspectives*, Madison, WI: University of Wisconsin Press.

Moyer, D.S. (1981) 'Fifty years of W.D.O.: the growth of the idea of the "idea"', in G.A. Moyer, D.S. Moyer and P.E. de Josselin de Jong (eds) *The Nature of Structure*, Leiden: Institute of Cultural and Social Studies, Leiden University, pp. 55–73.

Murdock, G.P. (1949) *Social Structure*, New York: Macmillan.

Naroll, R. and Cohen, R. (eds) (1970) *A Handbook of Method in Cultural Anthropology*, New York: Columbia University Press.

Nieboer, H.J. (1900) *Slavery as an Industrial System: Ethnological Researches*, 's Gravenhage: Nijhoff.

—— (1910) *Slavery as an Industrial System: Ethnological Researches*, 2nd rev. edn, 's Gravenhage: Nijhoff.

Oosten, J.G. and van de Velde, P. (1994) 'Constructing the early state: the rise of a research programme', in M. van Bakel, R. Hagesteijn and P. van de Velde (eds), *Pivot Politics: Changing Cultural Identities in Early State Formation Processes*, Amsterdam: Het Spinhuis, pp. 1–21.

Parkin, D. (1987) 'Comparison as the search for continuity', in L. Holy (ed.) *Comparative Anthropology*, Oxford: Blackwell, pp. 52–69.

Patterson, O. (1977) 'The structural origins of slavery: a critique of the Nieboer-Domar hypothesis from a comparative perspective', *Annals of the New York Academy of Sciences* 292: 21–33.

Pleyte, C.M. Wzn. (1891) 'De geographische verbreiding van het koppensnellen in den Oost Indischen Archipel', *Tijdschrift van het Koninklijk Nederlandsch Aardrijkskundig Genootschap*, 2nd series, number 8: 908–46.

Pouwer, J. (1955) *Enkele aspecten van de Mimika-cultuur*, Den Haag: Staatsdrukkerij.

—— (1960) ' "Loosely structured societies" in Netherlands New Guinea', *Bijdragen tot de Taal-, Land- en Volkenkunde* 116: 109–18.

—— (1961) 'New Guinea as a field for ethnological study', *Bijdragen tot de Taal-, Land- en Volkenkunde* 117: 1–24.

—— (1962) *Het individu in samenleving en cultuur: Enkele methodologische beschouwingen*, Wolters: Groningen.

—— (1966) 'The structural and functional approach in cultural anthropology: theoretical reflections with reference to research in western New Guinea', *Bijdragen tot de Taal-, Land- en Volkenkunde* 122: 129–44.

Prager, M. (1999) 'Crossing borders, healing wounds: Leiden anthropology and the colonial encounter 1917–1949', in J. van Bremen and A. Shimizu (eds) *Anthropology and Colonialism in Asia and Oceania*, Richmond, Surrey: Curzon Press, pp. 326–61.

Ras, J.J. (1973) 'De Panji romance and W.H. Rassers' analysis of its theme', *Bijdragen tot de Taal-, Land- en Volkenkunde* 129: 411–56.

Rassers, W.H. (1922) *De Pandji-roman*, Antwerpen: De Vos–Van Kleef.

—— (1982) *Pañji, the Culture Hero: A Structural Study of Religion in Java*, 2nd edn, The Hague: Nijhoff.

Ronhaar, J.H. (1931) *Woman in Primitive Motherright Societies*, Groningen: Wolters.

Rosaldo, M. (1980) *Knowledge and Passion: Ilongot Notions of Self and Social Life*, Cambridge: Cambridge University Press.

Siegel, B.J. (1945) 'Some methodological considerations for a comparative study of slavery', *American Anthropologist* 47: 357–92.

Steinmetz, S.R. (1894) *Ethnologische Studien zur ersten Entwicklung der Strafe, nebst einer psychologischen Abhandlung über Grausamkeit und Rachsucht*, two volumes, Leiden: Van Doesburgh and Leipzig: Harrassowitz.

—— (1930) *Gesammelte kleinere Schriften zur Ethnologie und Soziologie*, II, Groningen: Noordhoff.

—— (1935) *Gesammelte kleinere Schriften zur Ethnologie und Soziologie*, III, Groningen: Noordhoff.

Strathern, M. (1988) *The Gender of the Gift: Problems with Women and Problems with Society in Melanesia*, Berkeley, CA: University of California Press.

Strathern, M. and Lambek, A. (1998) 'Introduction. Embodying sociality: Africanist–Melanesianist comparisons', in A. Lambek and M. Strathern (eds) *Bodies and Persons: Comparative Perspectives from Africa and Melanesia*, Cambridge: Cambridge University Press, pp. 1–28.

Thoden van Velzen, H.U.E. and van Wetering, W. (1960) 'Residence, power-groups and intra-societal aggression: an inquiry into the conditions leading to peacefulness within non-stratified societies', *International Archives of Ethnography* 49: 169–200.

Tylor, E.B. (1889) 'On a method of investigating the development of institutions', *Journal of the Royal Anthropological Institute of Great Britain and Ireland* 18: 245–72.

van Baal, J. (1986) *Ongelipt verleden I, Tot 1947: Indisch betuursambtenaar in vrede en oorlog*, Franeker: Wever.

—— (1989) *Ongelipt verleden II, Leven in verandering*, Franeker: Van Wijnen.

van der Bij, T.S. (1929) *Ontstaan en eerste ontwikkeling van den oorlog*, Groningen and Den Haag: Wolters.

van der Leeden, A.C. (1956) *Hoofdtrekken der sociale structuur in het westelijk binnenland van Sarm*, Leiden: IJdo.

—— (1960) 'Social structure in New Guinea', *Bijdragen tot de Taal-, Land- en Volkenkunde* 116: 119–49.

van Ossenbruggen, F.D.E. (1977) 'Java's *monca-pat*: origins of a primitive classification system', in P.E. de Josselin de Jong (ed.) *Structural Anthropology in the Netherlands*, The Hague: Nijhoff, pp. 32–60.

van Vollenhove, C. (1928) *De ontdekking van het adatrecht*, Leiden: Brill.

van Wouden, F.A.E. (1935) *Sociale structuurtypen in de Groote Oost*, Leiden: Ginsberg. (Translated by R. Needham (1967)), *Types of Social Structure in Eastern Indonesia*, The Hague: Nijhoff.

Vergouwen, J.C. (1964) *The Social Organization and Customary Law of the Toba-Batak of North Sumatra*, The Hague: Nijhoff.

Vermeulen, H.F. (1987) 'P.E. de Josselin de Jong and the Leiden tradition: a short history', in R. de Ridder and J.A.J. Karremans (eds) *The Leiden Tradition in Cultural Anthropology: Essays in Honour of P.E. de Josselin de Jong*, Leiden: Brill, pp. 4–84.

Vincent, J. (1990) *Anthropology and Politics: Visions, Traditions and Trends*, Tucson: University of Arizona Press.

Watson, J.L. (1980) 'Introduction. Slavery as an institution: open and closed systems', in J.L. Watson (ed.) *Asian and African Systems of Slavery*, Berkeley, CA: University of California Press, .pp. 1–15.

Wertheim, W.F. and Wertheim-Gijse Weenink, A.H. (1991) *Veir wending in ons bestaan, Indië verloren, Indonesië geboren*, Breda: De Geus.

Wilken, G.A. (1889) 'Iets over de schedelverering bij de volken van den Indischen archipel', *Bijdragen tot de Taal-, Land- en Volkenkunde van Nederlandsch-Indië*, 5th series, no. 4: 89–129.

Wisse, J. (1933) *Selbstmord und Todesfurcht bei den Naturvölkern*, Zutphen: Thieme.

Wolf, J.J. de (1994) 'Beyond evolutionism: the work of H.J. Nieboer on slavery, 1900–1910', in H.F. Vermeulen and A.A. Roldán (eds) *Fieldwork and Footnotes: Studies in the History of European Anthropology*, London: Routledge, pp. 113–28.

—— (1999) 'Colonial ideologies and ethnological discourses: a comparison of the United Faculties at Leiden and Utrecht', in J. van Bremen and A. Shimizu (eds) *Anthropology and Colonialism in Asia and Oceania*, Richmond, Surrey: Curzon Press, pp. 307–25.

Chapter 5

Some current kinship paradigms in the light of true Crow Indian ethnography

Emmanuel Désveaux

> D. Rivers is therefore more sanguine than accurate when he states ... that not only the general character but every detail of systems of relationship has been demonstrated as determined by social conditions. The parts of systems that correlate with social conditions have indeed been correlated by him: but those parts that do not correlate have for the most part not even been considered.
>
> (A.L. Kroeber 1917)

In 1925, Leslie Spier proposed the first comprehensive typology of kinship terminology for Native North America. His work proceeded, of course, by comparison, since he took into consideration the whole body of information on kinship terms available at the time, data on more than 170 tribes. His study produced the following typology: Omaha, Crow, Salish, Acoma, Yuma, MacKenzie Basin, Iroquois and Eskimo. Although one might find a certain similarity between Spier's division and Kroeber's earlier reflections on the basic 'principles or categories of relationships' that would frame any given kin terminology (Kroeber 1909) – both lists contain eight items, and it appears that each of Spier's types is inspired by one of Kroeber's more abstract principles – it is clear that Spier's typology aimed only at a better overview of North American ethnography and had no universal pretensions (Spier 1925).

In subsequent years, Spier's North American typology was to be transformed, and it became the standard typology of kin terminologies worldwide (Désveaux 2002). In the process, an important shift occurred: only the relationship of Ego with the persons belonging to his own generation is preserved as a criterion of distinction.[1] This allowed for a drastic trimming of the original typology. Only the Eskimo, the Hawaiian (Spier's Salish type) and the Iroquois types remained. A Sudanese type was later introduced by Murdock (1949). However, the bases of this universal typology are not perfectly coherent. A place has to be preserved for what I will term 'skewedness'. Skewedness is an aspect of kin terminology in which some positions in each generation are designated by terms belonging primarily to adjacent generations. In Murdock's view, skewedness expressed itself in the Crow-Omaha subtypes of the Iroquois types (Héritier

1981: 20). As a corollary, the extension of a typology of kinship terminology to the whole world implies a general exercise of comparison, but a poor one indeed, since it will necessarily produce distortions and simplifications. As soon as an ethnographer 'discovered' a new terminology, he or she looked at what is happening at the generation of Ego (Is there crossness? Are brothers and sisters differentiated from cousins, and so forth?); then he or she rapidly checked if there was any trace of skewedness in his or her data in order to be able to put a label on his or her findings. However, in many cases, the ethnographer ignored most of the complexity of the object.

In a certain way, Lévi-Strauss's *Les Structures élémentaires de la parenté* (1st edn 1947, 2nd edn 1967), followed by Dumont's *Dravidiens et Kariera, l'alliance de mariage dans l'Inde du Sud et en Australie* (1974), played a challenging role by focusing the discussion on alliance and reasserting Rivers's lesson ([1913] 1968) that somehow the feature of a terminology depended on the form marriage takes. Crossness (which characterizes Iroquois-type relationship terminology) was said to be motivated by a given form of prescriptive marriage of which the Dravidian people offer the best example but which, considering the paradigmatical dimension of Rivers's argument, may occur in any society. We have recently contested this view, showing that the so-called Dravidian terminology of North (and probably South) American Indians is not necessarily linked to cross-cousin marriage (Désveaux and Selz 1998).

The connection between the Iroquois (or Dravidian) type of kin terminology and elementary structures of matrimonial exchange remains quite loose, for, although Lévi-Strauss clearly opposed two forms of elementary exchange – restricted and generalized – he failed to associate each form systematically with a given type of kinship terminology.

It may be that this partial failure explains the strategy Lévi-Strauss pursued in the introduction to the second edition of *Les Structures élémentaires de la parenté* (1967). Here, borrowing the language of finance, we can say that he made a 'take-over bid' on the Crow-Omaha type, assigning it to his '*structures semi-complexes de l'alliance*'. He defined these structures as occurring in societies in which marriage is neither prescribed, as in the elementary structures, nor largely authorized, as in complex structures (such as our Western societies) in which only a small set of persons close to Ego is excluded by the incest prohibition. What allows Lévi-Strauss to take this position is the observation, made by many ethnographers, that extensive marriage prohibitions exist in societies supposed to belong to Crow-Omaha types. These prohibitions seem to concern all the 'clans' to which Ego or his close kin are linked either by consanguinity or affinity. Lévi-Strauss's idea is that, considering the relatively small scale of these societies, these large prohibitions designate the '*zone*' in which Ego is expected to marry. The work of Héritier (1981) on the Samo is dedicated to an empirical confirmation of this hypothesis. But one must remember that a crucial prelude to Lévi-Strauss's hypothesis is Radcliffe-Brown's (1942) interpretation of so-called Crow-Omaha societies, which, getting back to Kohler's (1897) first attempt to resolve skewedness, imposed an image of social organization governed by a strict division into 'clans'.[2] Interestingly, from Kohler to Héritier, skewedness as a terminological feature (which, in the first place, raises difficulties because it hurts our common sense) progressively came to be seen merely as a sign that a given society belongs to the supposed Crow-Omaha family and is susceptible to the appropriate analysis (which of course varies according to the author). Even researchers like Lounsbury, who was mainly preoccupied by a terminological perspective, contributed to building the 'Crow-Omaha paradigm'. As a result, in a comparative practice of anthropology that too often reduced itself to placing objects in pre-designed boxes, Crow-Omaha societies appeared to bloom around the globe, mainly in South America, Africa and Melanesia.

R.H. Barnes was one of the few authors to cast doubt on the relevance of the category 'Crow-Omaha terminologies/semi-complex societies' – as the category has been consolidated in an effective 'alliance' between the American and French traditions of kinship studies. (The alliance, by the way, is not devoid of misunderstandings; one may recall Barnes's bitter exchange with Héritier on the matter [Barnes 1976; Héritier 1981: 74–5].) Barnes (1984) has written an entire – and very convincing – book to demonstrate that the 'real' Omaha never had anything like a 'structure of alliance' in the sense Lévi-Strauss understood it, in spite of their typical Omaha terminology. He was not persuaded of the value of uncontrolled comparison, such as Héritier's between the Omaha of the Plains of North America and the Samo of West Africa.

Our scepticism about the usual far-flung comparative approach to kin terminologies increases when we contemplate Fred Eggan's ([1939] 1955) classic *Social Anthropology of North American Tribes*. Here, in a diagram that attempts to give an overview of Plains Indian terminologies, the reader discovers that the Crow do not possess a prototypical Crow terminology but a 'transitional Crow' one (ibid.: 93).[3] This seems to imply not only that the Omaha case is hardly exportable, but that the Crow Indians are not even Crow! It is true that when Kohler (1897) and Durkheim (1898) discussed the matter, they associated the characteristic skewedness with the Omahas for the patrilinear version, with the Choctaws for the matrilinear version, but with the Crows not at all. It is also true that Spier rebaptized his Choctaw type the 'Crow type' without giving much justification for it, and everyone else apparently followed suit without questioning the shift or going back to the sources (Lowie 1934; Radcliffe-Brown 1942; Murdock 1949; Lévi-Strauss [1947] 1967; Lounsbury 1964; Héritier 1981; to name but a few).

So let us consider these sources now. In light of its status as one of the major paradigms of kinship studies, the true Crow case deserves to be more closely examined. We suggest, first, to scrutinize the terminology; second, to try to decipher its underlying logic; and third, to look at the Crow culture in order to find elements or features that may correspond with or make sense in terms of this logic. We will conduct these inquiries without any preconceptions, paying, for example, no particular attention to marriage and descent rules in the analysis (though we do not intend to exclude them, either).

Crow Indian kinship terminology

The Crow Indians lived in the western Great Plains and up into the foothills of the Rockies. They shared the basic traits of Plains Indian culture: their primary subsistence depended on the bison, which (after European contact) they hunted on horseback; they lived in tepees, spread out in small groups in the wintertime and gathering in large concentrations in the summer, a period of intense cere-monial activity and warfare. At the beginning of the twentieth century, the Crows maintained a vague oral tradition about their separation from the nearby Hidatsa Indians, who lived along the Missouri River in permanent villages and practised a mixed economy of agriculture and bison hunting. This oral tradition is confirmed by anthropologists, especially Lowie, who believed the adoption of the horse led to a life-style based exclusively on bison hunting – a life-style that had been out of reach for Plains Indians before. In this case, the native and the scientific narratives for once converge to relate a very probable diachronic sequence, though one entirely undocumented otherwise. With the introduction of the horse, a segment of the Hidatsa converted entirely to the economics of mounted bison hunting, while the main body of the tribe maintained its mixed agricultural and hunting economy.

As proof of this development and of its relative recency, anthropologists point to the great similarity of the Crow and Hidatsa languages, both of which are of the Siouan family. The evidence for a close historical relationship based on a comparison between the social institutions of both tribes raises more diffi-culties, but anthropologists have tended to content themselves in this matter with the presence of 'matrilinear clans' in both tribes.

Unlike the Sioux, the Crow have not been the object of a great deal of ethnography, and documentation about them is quite poor. For our present concern, we have only two sources at our disposal: Morgan's famous tables in *Systems of Consanguinity and Affinity of the Human Family* (1871) and Lowie's ethnographic writings. Morgan's Crow data are first-hand, collected during Morgan's travels in the West, including Crow country, as early as 1862 – more than ten years before the Battle of the Little Big Horn, which resulted in General Custer's death. His informants were a Crow woman and her husband, a Scottish trader who had been adopted into the tribe (Morgan 1871: 385). One may thus assume a feminine bias in the data, but it is not so important as to invalidate the corpus. Many of the needed corrections can be done with the help of Lowie's data. By the way, Lowie was the first to praise the quality of Morgan's work. The fact that Morgan's collection was made so early has evident benefits for the quality of information, not only in regard to the extremely low level of acculturation of the Crow people, but also in regard to the 'theoretical virginity' of the fieldworker. Eventually, Lowie's much more confused contributions to the subject will help us clarify what we mean by the idea of 'theoretical virginity'.

Lowie began his fieldwork among the Crow in 1907, approximately fifty years after Morgan's visit to the tribe. Traditional knowledge was still very much alive, and Lowie produced a number of ethnographic sketches that appeared in the *Anthropological Papers of the American Museum of Natural History*. Of primary concern here, since they deal directly with kinship, are his 'Social life of the Crow Indians' (1912) and 'Notes on the social organization and customs of the Mandan, Hidatsa, and the Crow Indians' (1917). Crow kinship terminology is by no means simple to grasp, but Lowie's presentation renders the subject even more difficult. For example, Lowie is very attentive to the distinction between terminology of address (vocative) and of reference (denotative), but his entire presentation is obscured by its contamination by the question of the possessives in the Crow language. The development of anthropological theory also plays a role in Lowie's entangled description. In his first paper (1912) he missed the skewedness of Crow terminology; in the second (1917) he acknowledged it, but may well have overestimated it, seemingly overwhelmed by remorse at having committed so serious an error.

If the first version of Lowie's Crow terminology lacked skewedness, the second was more skewed even than Morgan's. Lowie's explicit motivation in returning to Crow kinship in 1917 was to answer his critics, especially Goldenweiser (1913). One suspects that Lowie was influenced in his reappraisal by the increasing debate at the time about the nature of so-called Crow-Omaha terminologies. In many instances, Lowie corrects himself and, more dubiously, Morgan, without reference to empirical data (see, e.g. Lowie 1917: 68), deducing what he thinks to be the right term based on what anthropological theory of the time understood about the logic of the skewing principle. Still, Lowie omits many kin positions that were provided by Morgan. The role of so-called clans in the shaping of kin terms also gains importance in Lowie's second text. We need to mention one last distortion in Lowie's work. Lowie was obsessed with the historical link between the Crows and the Hidatsas, and his absolute certitude that the Hidatsas preceded the Crows biased his interpretation of the Crow data. Even so, we have the impression that Lowie himself was never satisfied with his understanding of the Crow terminology. In the 1917 paper he wrote, 'My impression is that Crow usage (of kin terms) ... is not rigidly fixed – certainly less so than among the Hidatsa' (Lowie 1917: 67).

We can hear in this statement an avowal of distress, an exasperation about Crow kinship that is best expressed in Lowie's *The Crow Indians*. Published in 1935, after a short return trip to the Crows in 1931, the book is, for the most part and with few modifications, a compilation of the various articles previously published in the *Anthropological Papers of the American Museum of Natural History*. Clearly, Lowie intended to combine within a single cover all of his ethnographical materials, reflections and conclusions about the Crows. But in this volume, Lowie left out most of his data on and discussions of kinship, treating the matter very superficially, as if he were sick of the entire subject and just wanted to forget about it.

And here is the paradox: despite his struggles with Crow kinship, Lowie continued to praise the quality of Morgan's information, with the exception of the latter's poor phonetic renderings (Lowie 1935: 339). This confirms our intuition that the superiority of Morgan's data can be attributed in large part to the condition of 'theoretical virginity' in which Morgan, unlike the more theoretically experienced Lowie, gathered his information. Also key to the quality of Morgan's work was his explicitly comparative perspective and a well-defined categorical routine in his collecting procedures. This being said, we are fortunate that Lowie, in the process of revising his own work (1917: 67–74), discussed Morgan's and justified correcting his forerunner on various points. This allows us basically to follow Morgan's table and to refer to Lowie only occasionally. As far as we know, Morgan's greatest error was to have failed to record the two different terms used to designate the father, one for a man speaking (m. sp.) and the other for a woman speaking (w. sp.).[4] Lowie's ethnography made this point very clear. None of the remaining discrepancies between the two authors are so definitive.

There is, however, an enormous difference between the phoneticization of Morgan and that of Lowie, as illustrated by the following few examples: *ah-he*, 'father' (m. sp.) in Morgan becomes *axe* in Lowie; *bä-sä'-na* 'elder brother, mother's brother' (w. sp.) in Morgan appears as *basaare* in Lowie; *meeka* 'elder brother' (m. sp.) in Morgan is *bi'ika* in Lowie; *bos-me'ä-kun-is-ta* in Morgan turns to *basbi'akaricta* in Lowie, etc. Morgan derived his spelling of vowels from the English pronunciation, which is, of course, not the best solution. What is more striking is that the consonant *m* in Morgan becomes *b* in Lowie, and that Morgan's *n* tends to become Lowie's *r*. This shift raises the possibility of a rapid evolution of Crow phonetics between 1860 and 1910 and leads us to wonder if perhaps the underlying logic of the terminology had not also changed – which would explain some nonlinguistic differences between the two sources. We lack evidence, however, to decide in favour of either of these hypotheses. There is no doubt, in any case, that Lowie's transcriptions represent an improvement over Morgan's 'rustic' ones, but we nevertheless follow Morgan's tables of kinship terms because of their greater coherence, and will quote parenthetically the equivalent for any term found in Lowie.[5]

Underlying logic

The skewedness of Crow terminology first eluded Lowie for the simple reason that the phenomenon is not at all obvious. In fact, as is the case for the vast majority of kin terminologies, the generations are (aside from the sexes) the primary shaper of Crow terminology. Our presentation, then, will follow generations (G), and we shall begin with the easiest: the extreme generations G+2 and G–2. At G+2, only the sex is recorded: *me-nup-h'is-saka* (Lowie: *masa'k-isaka*) (w. sp.), meaning 'old father'; it applies to both grandfathers and to all the kin belonging to their generation. Morgan did not record the equivalent for a man speaking (remember that his main Crow informant was a woman); Lowie renders it as *axe' -isa'ke*. *Bäsäkana* (Lowie: *masa'k-ka'are*) applies to both grandmothers and to all the women of their generation. The members of G–2 are all called *bus-bä'-pe-ta* (Lowie: *bacbapi'te*) ('grandchild'), with no indication of sex. It seems that these terms also fit even more extreme generations, such as G+3 and G–3. According to Morgan, however, one thing is sure: skewedness does not affect the levels of G+2 or G–2. Lowie, to the contrary, claims that the MMB[6] on one side and FZSS on the other were taken over by skewedness. This was exactly what the theories on Crow-Omaha systems predicted at the time (and still do), which raises serious suspicions about the influence of theoretical assumptions in the production of Lowie's data.

The picture of the intermediary generations is more difficult to grasp, due in part to skewedness. In an attempt to overcome this complexity, we will begin with the description of the generation of Ego (G0), where, side-by-side with skewedness, four other logical principles are mobilized: the sex of the speaker, the speaker's seniority, the dichotomy between parallel- and cross-cousins, and – not to be forgotten – the sex of the person referred to. As in any standard analysis of Crow-Omaha skewed terminologies, we begin with the observation that parallel cousins are merged with siblings (as opposed to cross-cousins, who are the 'normal' target category of skewedness).

In the category of siblings and parallel cousins, the principle of seniority dominates, combined with the sex of the speaker and of the person referred to. For a man speaking, we have the following terms: *meek'a* (Lowie: *bi'ika*), elder brother, and *moo'äka* (Lowie: *bu'aka*), his wife ('my sister-in-law'; Morgan glosses the term as 'my young woman'); *bazäkat* (Lowie: *basaka'ta*, for which he gives the etymological meaning 'little mother'), elder sister, and *mä-nä-zha*,[7] her husband ('my brother-in-law'); *bächuka* (Lowie: *matsu'ka*, 'the crazy one', in the sense of someone who is too bold, particularly a warrior), younger brother, and *bäsachete* (Lowie: *basatsi'ta*), younger sister. For a woman speaking, all the terms are different except *bächuka*, 'younger brother': *bazäna* (Lowie: *basa're*), elder brother, and *bos-me'-ä-kun-is-tä* (Lowie: *basbi'akaricta*), his wife ('my sister-in-law', which Morgan glosses as 'my younger woman'); *buswanä*,[8] elder sister, and *bächena*, her husband ('my brother-in-law'); *bäsoko* (Lowie: *basoka*) is the younger sister of a woman. For both sexes speaking, the wives and husbands of younger brothers and sisters are designated by the same terms as those of the elder brothers and sisters. Here is a pure logic of affinity as it appears in a typical pseudo-Dravidian terminology, similar to the one that we collected among the Northern Ojibwa of Big Trout Lake: seniority (or what Lounsbury called *polarity* in his 1964 analysis of Seneca Iroquois terminology) cannot interfere with it.

Terms for affines resulting from Ego's own alliance are also worth looking at. *Moo'a* (a term that seems to be the root word for *moo'ä-ka*, previously mentioned) means 'my wife' and applies also to her sisters. The brother of Ego's wife (or husband) is *mä-zhe*. A woman calls her husband *bächena*, which is the term for brother-in-law (ZH), and there is a single term, *bäkoo'a*, to designate the sister's husband. In this sequence, we observe a striking differentiation of the man's and the woman's points of view. A woman's husband is already her brother-in-law (the husband of her sister), whereas, symmetrically, a man's wife is called by a special term, as is her brother. The fact that *moo'a* applies also to the sisters of the wife and that the husband, *bächena*, is the equivalent of the brother-in-law (the sister's husband) appears to be an expression of sororal polygyny, a widely distributed institution in North America. But does this tell the whole story? We think not. There may be another point to stress here: that from the point of view of a woman, affinity is static. Marriage does not create a new category: the husband falls into an already designated category. From a male Ego's point of view, however, affinity is dynamic in the sense that marriage generates a specific new category: *moo'a*, the wife, which eventually extends to include her sisters. One may also say that this affinity comes first, since the more general term for sister-in-law (BW, but also, thanks to skewedness, the MBW of ZSW), *moo'aka*, obviously derives from *moo'a*, a fact already pointed out by Lowie. Finally, the man and the woman share a common specific term, *mä-zhe*, to designate the brother-in-law (SpB). It seems highly probable that, as in the pair *moo'a* and *moo'aka*, this term is a root word for *mä-nä-zhe* (or a contraction of it), the term for BW.

We next look at the generation below Ego (G–1). Here, the complexity increases, but it is at this level that we can except to find the key to the under-lying logic – provided we endorse the widely accepted idea that skewedness is an emanation of crossness and that we agree (which we do) with Héritier (1981: 171) and localize the core of crossness in the difference between brother's children and sister's children. For both sexes speaking, the son is *bot'sa-sä* (Lowie: *iro'oce*[9]) and the daughter, *näkmeä* (Lowie: *xu'tse*[10]). These terms extend quite smoothly to the children of both the elder brother and the cross-cousins (from both sides), again for both sexes speaking. The husband of the daughter is always *boo-sha*, but the wife of the son is either *bos-me'-ä-kun-is-tä* (m. sp.) or *mänä'ka* (w. sp.). The difference between these last two terms of affinity is that one, *mänä'ka* (w. sp.), is tied to a generation (G–1), and the other is transgenerational. *Bos-me'-ä-kun-is-tä* has already been shown to mean the BW (sister-in-law); what is unusual is that in one case, at G–1, the term is used by a man speaking, and in another, at G0, by a woman.

With this observation, we begin to uncover a sort of twist operating throughout the terminological logic by means of skewedness and the sexes. This is precisely the phenomenon that totally escaped Lowie's attention. It is even better revealed in the terminological handling of the sister's children. In this case, for both sexes speaking, the ZS is *bächuka*, i.e. younger brother. His wife is *moo'äka*, for a man speaking, and *mänäka*, for a woman. Now, *moo'äka* is also the term used to designate the sister-in-law; all of this is consistent with the fact that this ZS is assimilated with a younger brother. Now let's look very carefully at what is happening in the case of the ZD (the sister of ZS). Here, again, appel-lations diverge according to the sex of the speaker. For a woman speaking, ZD is a daughter (*nak'me-ä*), which conforms with theoretical predictions, since her own daughter and the daughter of her sister are parallel cousins. For a man speaking, ZD is *bäsoka*, which means 'younger sister', but at G0 (when it designates the *real* 'younger sister') the term is used by women and not by men, who then use *bäsachate*. We observe a similar feminization of the point of view of male Ego, when he uses the feminine term for BW (*bos-me'-ä-kun-is-tä*) to designate his own daughter-in-law (SW).

It is time to give a first overview of our reading of the terminology: everything in Crow kinship is expressed as if the succession of births – attached to a grossly defined feminine side wherein mother's and sister's attributes seem to merge – were a continuous flow, ignoring the generations but determined by Ego's position. Elder brothers and sisters are on one side, born before Ego; younger brothers and sisters are on the other side, which includes the sister's children as well. At this generational level, though, we find the feminization of the male point of view. For a woman, sister's son and daughter are like her own son: they belong to the first descending generation. For a man, they are like his younger brothers and sisters, equivalent to the sons and daughters of his mother. In order to conceptualize this equivalence, however, the man must take on a feminine perspective. We also detect a symmetrical inversion of points of view regarding affinity. If I am a man, the wife of my nephew is like a sister-in-law; if I am a woman, I deny such an equivalence and reassert the generational division of kin by using a term of so-called affinity, *mänäka*, which is restricted to this generation (G-1). In doing so, I differentiate again the masculine from the feminine points of view on affinity, at least for this first descending generation. For the man, affinity remains somewhat subordinated to the order of birth: since my younger brother is equivalent to my nephew, the wives of both are equivalent. For a woman, affinity adheres strictly to the generational frame.

Let us consider now the situation at the generation of Ego's parents (G+1) and see how it confirms our analysis. On the one hand, there are two terms for father, according to the sex of the speaker: *ah'ha* (Lowie: axe) (m. sp.) and *masaka*[11] (w. sp.). On the other hand, there is only one term for mother: *eka-ä* (Lowie: *i'ga*). The extension of these terms is quite wide. On the father's side, they apply to all uncles and aunts, making no difference between so-called consanguinity and affinity (FB = FZH, FZ = FBW). The principle of skewedness extends them to cross-cousins (and their respective spouses), but not further down generationally – where, oddly enough and contrary to current theories of Crow-Omaha systems, the children of all these people are classified as grandchildren (*bus-bä'-pe-ta*). On the mother's side, these terms apply only to the mother's sister and her husband; in other words, to the parallels, since the maternal uncle and his wife are called *bäzäna* and *moo'äka*, a set of terms that also designate the older brother and his wife, their children being assimilated with Ego's own children, just as are those of his own brother. As for skewedness, these last assimilations apparently conform better to current theoretical paradigms, which hold that the maternals 'gain' one generational level relative to Ego in societies ruled by matrilinearity, while at the same time the paternals 'lose' one.

But there is a further subtlety here. When applied to the elder brother and his wife, the terms *bäzäna* and *moo'äka* belong to women's speech; when applied to the maternal uncle and his wife, they belong to both men's and women's speech. Logically, the singular (here, one sex speaking) follows from the more general (here, two sexes speaking). One may also say that, contrary to the current kinship doctrine, it is the set of terms designating the maternal uncle and his wife for both sexes that, from the point of view of a woman, descends one generational level to designate the elder brother and his wife. Here, we find Lowie's attitude as being very symptomatic of how theory can distort facts. Lowie blamed Morgan for not having recorded the two pairs of terms (one set for each sex speaking) designating the maternal uncle and his wife, sets of terms which, in his view, are supposed to duplicate the ones used for the elder brother and his wife. Consequently, Lowie 'harmonized' the data. I am convinced that he was wrong in doing so, for the single reason that in Crow terminology there is only one term to designate the mother, not two as for the father. Now, it is clear that the brother of the mother is a sort of masculine mother; so is the elder brother, but for women *only*. To summarize this analysis of G+1, we conclude that the man clings to the generational division and the woman encompasses it. In other words, the man refers to a fixed generational order preceding him, whereas the woman defines herself as a position in a stream of engendered individuals. This stream is the essence of femininity, the significa-tion of which is carried, at least in Crow terminology, by the maternals as a whole. In that sense, there is a reversal, in the articulation between generations G0 and G+1, of the split perspective that we already observed in the articula-tion of G0 and G–1. There, we noted that the woman takes a predefined position as the pure affine, a position itself tributary to a closed generational frame, while the man enjoys a more dynamic openness demarcated only by the smooth ordering of successive births.

We must stress that Crow terminology is, above all, Ego-centred. Like a pseudo-Dravidian terminology (Désveaux and Selz 1998), it is Ego-centred, but in a more accomplished manner, since Ego's sex and positioning among his or her siblings are determinant factors. Let us use a spatial metaphor and say that Ego is like a localized body in the middle of a hillside field that represents his kin. If Ego is a man and looks uphill, he has a generational perspective, with himself as the product of a past affinity and all his paternals appearing as a consolidated group of past affines. If, now, he looks downhill, he adopts a sort of feminine perspective that considers kinship as a stream of continuous births. The femi-nization of his point of view, corollary to transgenerationality, is so radical that it continues to affect positions that we could imagine being shielded by affinity: for example, he calls his daughter-in-law by the feminine term for sister-in-law.

When Ego is a woman, the picture is turned upside down. Looking uphill, she perceives only the non-generational stream of births, but looking at her own level and downhill, her point of view is superseded by a strict generational perspective, one that is, at least for the Crows, a masculine and affinal perspective. There is a fundamental opposition behind all this. Maternity or birth-giving is a feminine prerogative and represents an active role for a woman. For a man, of course, maternity is passive; a man is born from a woman. It is, as we have seen, affinity that represents an active, dynamic relationship.

Ethnographic context

To this point, our analysis has been limited to Crow terminology and its internal logic. It is time to widen the scope to see how the rest of Crow ethnography – and we have no choice here but Lowie – matches our present conclusions. Most of the facts that are significant for us are precisely the ones that Lowie recorded, but left unexplained. The first one directly confirms the idea that affinity is a predefined fate from a woman's perspective: although Lowie (1912: 220) did not stress the point (the custom had been discontinued at the time of his fieldwork), he noted that girls were supposed to be married before their first menses. If we admit a general tendency in human cultures to see in the menarche the passage from childhood to adulthood, this would mean that for the Crow, a woman belongs, in her passive role, to affinity – and this already in childhood. One could say that she belongs to affinity from her birth. Consequently, the Crow Indians did not mark with any rituals or public manifestations the first menstruations of their young girls – except for those who were not yet married, who were cruelly mocked on this occasion.

In the same vein, we examine next the so-called parents-in-law taboo. The interdiction against having any social interaction with these kin is very strong, and stronger towards the mother-in-law than the father-in-law. At least for Lowie, however, there was something even more puzzling about it: it concerned only the men. Thanks to our analysis of the terminology, we are better able than Lowie to comprehend this apparent oddity. A woman refers to her parents-in-law with the same terms she uses for her own parents (*eka-ä* and *masaka*). If, as we have seen, she belongs to affinity as such, and this at her own generational level, we have also seen that for G+1, she defines herself according to the principle of succeeding births. In this respect, then, her parents-in-law are perceived as strictly equivalent to her own parents. In conformity with this configuration, the woman might call 'sister' her husband's sisters, and Lowie (1917: 73) noted that sometimes the mother-in-law refers to her daughter-in-law as if she were her own daughter. We have seen that this rule is entirely reversed with the son-in-law, for whom the strongest taboo is in addressing his mother-in-law. It appears also that in the event of the dissolution of a marriage, either by divorce or death of the wife, this taboo is lifted. After his wife's death, in fact, a man is considered as if he were their own son by his parents-in-law. Here, we see clearly that the determining factor regulating relations between in-laws is the capacity to give birth, a capacity that, at least semantically, all women share as long as they live. The strength of the taboo between mother-in-law and son-in-law expresses something more of that nature, using a simple principle of antinomy, than something about affinity as such.

In most ways, however, the relationship that binds a man to his parents-in-law is more likely to correspond with our classical notion of affinity. In reference – and in reference only, since he cannot address them directly – he calls them *boo-sha* and *boo-sha gä na*. The term *boo-sha* applies also, as previously seen, to the son-in-law (both sexes speaking). As for *boo-sha gä na*, it is clearly an enrichment of *boo-sha*; *gä na* means 'old woman' (Lowie 1917: 73). In other words, *boo-sha gä na* specifies not only the sex but also the age of the person to whom it refers. Since *boo-sha* applies similarly at G+1 and G–1, we may be tempted to see in it a trace of the well-known terminological device that produces cycles that assimilate, for example, grandparents and grandchildren, and that are found in North America in California and the adjacent Southwest (Kroeber 1917). However, a simpler solution inevitably comes to mind: *boo-sha* applies to the affines with whom you cannot speak. Its reciprocal characteristic reflects the fundamental reciprocity of a non-talking relationship, just as a talking relationship, *a fortiori* a joking relationship, is fundamentally reciprocal. We could call a man's affinity with his parents-in-law a *silenced* affinity, or in more radical terms a de-substantialized affinity.

The foregoing suggests the existence of various kinds of affinities from the point of view of a male Ego in connection with the logical principle of generational division. The couple formed by his own parents retains a trace of the affinity of his father toward his mother: it is a *fossilized* affinity. We could likewise say that his parents-in-law fall into a sort of *frozen* (rather than *silenced*) affinity. The affinity is there, although denied, unlike the affinity of G0, which, clearly recognized with appropriate terms for brothers-in-law and sisters-in-law, is very much alive and is the vector of the traditional joking relationship.

We have deliberately kept the delicate question of alliance out of the discussion until now, but can no longer delay it. Basically, Lowie relates two rules regarding marriage, both of which find strong correlations in the terminology – or, one might better say, high indices of compatibility with it. First, the Crows did practise sororal polygyny, which gives a man a matrimonial right to his wife's sisters. We have already shown how this rule is sustained by the terminology, which makes a 'brother-in-law' of the husband and a 'wife' of any wife's sister. Second, a woman cannot marry into her maternal or paternal clans, whereas only the maternal is forbidden for a man. Lowie (1935: 46–7) takes pains to report the rule because it contradicts his theoretical views on Crow-Omaha systems. As Barnes (1976: 386) has already pointed out, however, the transcription of his informants' statements and the few cases illustrating them leave little doubt about the rule. One must remember that extended matrimonial prohibitions belong to the core definition of Crow-Omaha systems – the underlying idea being that Ego should not renew an alliance already concluded by close kin such as his parents. These prohibitions cover *a minima* both 'clans' or lineages of Ego's parents, but frequently extend to all grandparents' clans, and sometimes beyond. In theory, of course, this principle also forbids the renewal of Ego's own marriage – in other words, sororal polygyny (Héritier 1981: 78).

Among the Crows, paradoxically, not only is sororal polygyny deeply rooted – both explicitly affirmed and terminologically embedded – but matrimonial prohibitions in general appear rather limited. The most striking fact, however, may be that men and women are, as we have seen, bound by different, asymmetrical matrimonial prohibitions.

How are we to interpret these prohibitions? The reason the mother's 'lineage' is forbidden for both sexes resembles the standard exogamy rule: one cannot marry into where one came from. The only difference among the Crow is that the mutual exclusion of the mother's clan and of the possibility of marrying into it have to do with semantic, rather than genealogical, determinants. This group is defined as an order of births in which Ego places him- or herself. For a woman, alliance – in which she acts passively – is necessarily located outside of the series of individuals, the 'clan' or 'lineage', she descended from and into which she eventually is going to inscribe new individuals by producing them. For a man, this same grouping is perceived as having as its essence an active femininity, something to which he does not belong. His own space of action allows him to exercise the prerogative of seeking affinity, and all of social space is open to him with the exception of this group. For a woman, on the contrary, it is also impossible to marry into the paternal group. Her position is one of prefixed affinity at her own generational level, a level preceded by another generation that appeared as consolidated under the preclusions of a past series of birth-givings: a wife refers to and treats her parents-in-law exactly like her own parents, and a new series of birth-giving starts with her, first through her younger brothers and sisters and then her own children. It is logically impossible for her to interfere by an alliance with this precluded order.

Having established that these two rules are fundamentally compatible with the terminology, we do not see how their mutual existence could in any way define a structure of marriage, even a semi-complex one in the sense in which Lévi-Strauss understood it, i.e. as a structure of exchange. The reason for this failure is simple: the matrimonial fields open respectively to men and to women are too heterogeneous to match. If we take them into a common notion of exchange, we are struck by two facts: due to sororal polygyny, a man 'weighs' the same as a group of sisters, potentially unbalancing the measurability of exchange, and, perhaps more important, the greater matrimonial choice offered to each man makes impossible a harmonious circulation of women between groups. Lévi-Strauss's theory of exchange relies on the assumption that the giver is in the same position as the taker towards the women who circulate between them. I give up my sister because I expect to receive another woman in return. But in a system such as the Crows', the taker enjoys a scope of marriageability virtually twice that of the giver. In other words, a woman has as little as half as much value for a taker as for a giver.[12] Whatever the nature of an eventual return path, the perpetuation of an exchange implies a balanced perspective of the partners on the value of the object of 'trade'. If we want to talk about a structure of *exchange*, and still maintain a shared meaning for a common word, a notion of balance must somewhere prevail. But if it is not present in the poten-tiality of marriage partners, where could it be? Along with the Omaha case, masterfully studied by Barnes (1984), Crow terminology and marriage practices lead one to question the Lévi-Straussian concept of semi-complex structures of matrimonial exchange, at least as an instrument useful for understanding American Indian societies.

Conclusion

Does our study of Crow terminology carry a wider lesson? We think it does. First, it shows that a phenomenon like skewedness cannot be reified to the point of being regarded as the basis for a type of kinship terminology. In the present case, skewedness cannot be understood independently of the sex of the speaker and the sex of the referred, or of their respective positions in terms of seniority within their own generation. Second, and on an even more general level, our close re-examination of the Crow terminology seriously challenges the dichotomy of consanguinity and affinity that rests at the foundation of all kinship studies since Morgan. Looking at the Crow terminology, one has to wonder whether something like consanguinity really makes sense, when, for example, a woman designates her parents and her parents-in-law by the same terms. What seems more pertinent when describing how the Crows conceive of a certain number of kin who belong to our category of consanguinity would be the notion of birth order.

From the beginning of our attempt to untangle Crow terminology, we have made frequent use of the notion of affinity. Our study has resulted in the emer-gence of various kinds of affinities: the classic one, which provides Ego with a brother-in-law; the one we have called 'frozen' affinity, which is contracted by the father of Ego; denied affinity, which applies to the parents-in-law or the son-in-law of male Ego; the affinity that is conferred on a woman at birth; and so on. This dismantling of the concept of affinity is significant. We cannot allow ourselves to have preconceptions about what affinity means for the Crows. In a way, frozen affinity is linked to the previous generation, but it is also linked to death. The marriage that your father contracts with your mother is a prelude to your own birth, but also to your father's death. Perhaps Crows see their paternal kin as potential dead people, just as the Sioux see their cross-cousins (Désveaux 1997: 135). If this is the case, we have to rethink our analytical categories, taking into consideration that kinship terminologies are primarily semantic devices and that we must decipher what they tell us instead of applying to them preconceived, sociologically framed categories. Our analysis of Crow termi-nology suggests that sexual differentiation (the sex of Ego) and temporality (the position of Ego in relation to his other kin, measured by generations or by even more accurate measures such as birth order) are more important to some cultures than the supposedly universal dichotomy between consanguines and affines.

We are convinced that, as far as kinship is concerned, we now have to study phenomena on a regional or continental scale. In their introduction to

Transformation of Kinship, co-editors Godelier, Trautmann and Tjon Sie Fat
(1998: 11) assert that there are only two possible 'paths', logically speaking, to
travel from a terminology framed on a Dravidian type of crossness to the
Iroquois type of crossness. These paths lead past either the ethnographically
attested variant of the Yafar or that of the Yuma. This would mean that to move
from the Northern Ojibwa, who possess a perfect prototypical 'Dravidian' terminology, to their neighbours the Iroquois, one has to make a side-trip to the
Highlands of New Guinea where the Yafar and the Yuma live. This is a clear
reflection of the strongly idealistic conception of kinship. If pseudo-Dravidian
crossness is connected one way or another to Iroquois crossness (and in turn to
'Crow-Omaha' skewedness), it seems more reasonable to look for the connection in a regional context.

Ever since Rivers, kinship specialists have strangely reified their subject,
lured by phenomena like crossness (and, to a lesser degree, skewedness) to
believe that whatever the cultural context, the solution must be unique.
Morgan, who was the first to see formal resemblances between Eskimo terminologies and our own, was less naïve and was never convinced of their common
origins. Our own priority now lies in understanding the characteristics of a
terminology (and not only of crossness or skewedness, which focus our attention
because they contradict our common sense) in relation to other features of
social life (including, of course, but not restricted to institutions like the rules of
marriage). At the same time, we should attempt a comparison with the terminologies of neighbouring groups and their institutions. Progressively, we may
come to develop adequate theories of American Indian kinship, African
kinship, New Guinean kinship, European kinship, and so on. Only when this is
achieved for each area of the world shall we turn with some chances of success
to the question of the common features or differences of kinship systems. Only
then shall we have the capacity and the intellectual tools to determine whether
American Indian crossness shares a common nature with that found in South
India (but we doubt that it does); whether the so-called Hawaiian pattern (a
terminology that makes no distinction among Ego's kin except between generations) is dictated by the same process among the Hawaiian people as among the
Salish, who, ever since the publication of Spier's classic North American
kinship systems typology, are depicted as possessing an 'Hawaiian' terminology;
and whether the skewedness of Samos terminology has anything to do with
what is going on in the terminology of the Omahas.

Our present analysis of the Crow case is a very modest contribution to this
vast programme. This said, the case reveals a general lesson concerning kinship
that has remained largely unnoticed by specialists preoccupied with sociological
clues. If there is a sort of neutralization of descent from the paternal side in
Crow kinship terminology, the people who belong to this side are by no means
non-existent in the life of Ego. Indeed, they play a very important role for him
as the side that provides him with a *personal* name. Among the Crow, the father
names his child or chooses a man to assume this duty. Whatever the sex of the

newborn, the name refers to a war deed, ideally accomplished by the namer himself (Lowie 1912: 215).

In such a configuration, one is tempted to say that the essence of 'kinship terms' comes from the maternal side and the essence of personal names from the paternal. This opposition has a value that transcends the Crow case, which sheds a new light on what kinship is about. We realize that all human societies possess this double system of appellation: the first is based on personal names, which are, by definition, metaphoric (in the sense that they are taken out of the original context to be applied to a specific individual); the second is based on kinship terms that are purely metonymic (in the sense that they depend only on the position of the individual within a certain given network of relationship). Given these circumstances, it is clear that we need to understand better, and for every culture, the relationship between these two inscriptions of the person into his or her immediate and more distant social surroundings. In addition to the Crow case, we can quote two examples that are very revealing of the person's semantic double bind within society. Among the Bushmen of the Kalahari, marriage depends on personal names rather than kinship category (Barnard 1992).[13] In European societies (as in many others of the Old World), each of us carries a double personal name: a patronym, to which is attached what in English is called the *first name* and in French the *forename* (*prénom*). This two-part name tells us a lot about kinship and about the nature of the underlying social organization. It tells us almost as much as do kinship terms in so-called primitive societies, in the restricted sense in which Morgan understood them. One's destiny in regard to marriage or inheritance is likely to be vastly different if one is named Leopold (von) Habsburg or Heinz Kunz, Henry de la Tour d'Auvergne or Gaston Piccard, John D. Rockefeller, Jr., or Walter B. Smith.

Notes

1 In his paper, Spier gave very little indication of the method he employed to build up his typology on North American kinship terminologies. The legend transmitted by various handbooks says that he considered only the position of the siblings v. cousins; in other words, he considered only the generation of Ego. This is not entirely true, since he could not have built his entire typology by doing so.

2 See Chapter 3 of *Structure and Function in Primitive Society* (Radcliffe-Brown 1942).

3 In Eggan's table, only the Mandans and the Hidatsas are 'typical' Crow in the area. Eggan does not explain why the Crows are 'transitional', or more precisely towards what they are transitioning.

4 Morgan did not save space in his standard table for this redoubling at G+1. For an elaboration of the standard table, see Trautmann (1987).

5 Morgan's table extends to second-degree kinship (the descendants of grandparents' siblings), and Lowie's data are restricted to first-degree kinship. On this point, we shall follow Lowie's lead. We are convinced that, if there is an underlying logic to be discovered by the study of terminologies, the clue is to be found in the first circle of kin (Désveaux and Selz 1998: 154).

6 For a key to standard kin term abbreviations, see Appendix 5A.

7 Morgan's spelling. Lowie failed to mention this term.

8 Lowie contested the existence of this particular term, saying that men and women used the same word here.
9 According to Lowie, Morgan's term is a term of reference and not of address, as his is.
10 Ditto.
11 This is Lowie's spelling; Morgan did not record the term. Lowie points out that the term may be used by both sexes to designate any man of the father's so-called clan, thus reintroducing the idea of the feminization of the notion of 'lineage' or 'clan' as a whole.
12 In building his argument about the Crow-Omaha systems, Lévi-Strauss is perfectly aware of the necessity of a balanced ratio of men and women: '*Comme la règle vaut pour les deux sexes et qu'une lignée inclue au moins un homme et une femme à chaque génération (sinon le modèle ne serait pas en équilibre)*' (1967: xxv).
13 I thank Adam Kuper for bringing this source to my attention during the Vienna conference.

Appendix 5A: Kin term abbreviations

F	father
M	mother
B	brother; B+: elder brother; B–: younger brother
Z	sister; Z+: elder sister; Z–: younger sister
S	son
D	daughter
H	husband
W	wife
Sp	spouse

Example: MFZS means mother's father's sister's son.

Appendix 5B: Crow kinship terms

The following list of kinship terms is taken from Morgan (1871) and amplified by terms from Lowie (1917) (identified with an asterisk).

*axe' -isa'ke** (m. sp.) *me-nup-h'is-saka*; (w. sp.) FF, MF, FFB, MFB
bäsäkana (m. & w. sp.) FM, MM, FMZ, MMZ
ah'ha (m. sp.) F, FB, FZH, FZS, FZDH, MZH
*Masaka** (w. sp.) F, FB, FZH, FZS, FZDH, MZH, HF
eka-ä (m. & w. sp.) M, MZ, FZ, FBW, FZD, FZSW; (w. sp.) HM
meek'a (m. sp.) B+, FBS+, MZS+
bazäna (m. & w. sp.) MB; (w. sp.) B+, FBS+, MZS+
bazäkat (m. sp.) Z+, FBD+, MZD+
buswanä (w. sp.) Z+, FBD+, MZD+
bächuka (m. & w. sp.) B–, FBS–, MZS–, ZS; (m. sp.) FBDS, MBDS
bäsachete (m. sp.) Z–, FBD–, MZD–; FBDD, MBDD

bäsoka (w. sp.) Z–, FBD–, MZD–; (m. sp.) ZD
moo'äka (m. & w. sp.) MBW; (m. sp.) BW, FBSW, MZSW
bos-me'-ä-kun-is-tä (w. sp.) BW, FBSW, MZSW, MBSW; (m. sp.) SW
mä-nä-zha (m. sp.) H, ZH, FBDH, MZDH
bächena (w. sp.) ZH, FBDH, MZDH
mä-zhe (m. sp.) WB; (w. sp.) HB
moo'a (m. sp.) W, WZ
bäkoo'a (w. sp.) HZ
boo'sha (m. & w. sp.) DH, BDH, ZDH, FBSDH, MZSDH, MZDDH, MBDH;
(m. sp.) WF
boo'sha gäna (m. sp.) WM
mänäka (w. sp.) SW, ZSW
bot'sa-sä (m. & w. sp.) S, BS, FBS, MZSS, MBS; (w. sp.) FBDS, MBDS
nak'me-ä (m. & w. sp.) D, BD, FBSD, MZSD; MBD; (w. sp.) ZD, FBDD, MZDD
bus-bä'-pe-ta (m. & w. sp.) grandchild and all persons belonging to G–2
bot-ze'no-pä-che (w. sp.) HBW; HF, HM; (m. sp.) WBW, 'comrade'
me-nä-pä'che (m. sp.) SWF, DHF
ha'-nä (w. sp) SWM, DHM

Bibliography

Barnard, A. (1992) *Hunters and Herders of Southern Africa*, Cambridge: Cambridge University Press.
Barnes, R.H. (1976) 'Dispersed alliance and the prohibition of marriage: reconsideration of McKinley's explanation of Crow-Omaha terminologies', *Man* 11, 3: 384–99.
—— (1984) *Two Crow Denied It: A History of Controversy in Omaha Sociology*, Lincoln: University of Nebraska Press.
Désveaux, E. (1997) 'Parenté, rituel, organisation sociale: le cas des Sioux', *Journal de la Société des Américanistes* 83: 111–40.
—— (2002) 'Critique de la raison parentaire', *L'Homme* 167, January–March.
Désveaux, E. and Selz, M. (1998) 'Dravidian nomenclature as an expression of ego-centered dualism', in M. Godelier, T. Trautmann and F.E. Tjon Sie Fat (eds) *Transformations of Kinship*, Washington, DC: Smithsonian Institution Press, pp. 150–67.
Dumont, L. (1974) *Dravidiens et Kariera, l'alliance de mariage dans l'Inde du Sud et en Australie*, La Haye and Paris: Mouton.
Durkheim, É. (1898) 'Zur Urgeschichte der Ehe, Prof. J. Kohler', *Année Sociologique* 1: 306–19.
Eggan, F. ([1939] 1955) *Social Anthropology of North American Tribes*, Chicago: University of Chicago Press.
Godelier, M., Trautmann, T. and Tjon Sie Fat, F.E. (eds) *Transformations of Kinship*, Washington, DC: Smithsonian Institution Press, pp. 150–67.
Goldenweiser, A.A. (1913) 'Remarks on the social organization of the Crow Indians', *American Anthropologist* (n.s.) 15: 281–97.
Héritier, F. (1981) *L'Exercice de la parenté*, Paris: EHESS.

Kohler, J. (1897) 'Zur Urgeschichte der Ehe. Totemismus, Gruppenrecht, Mutterrecht', *Zeitschrift für Vergeleichende Rechtswissenschaft*, vol. 11.

Kroeber, A.L. (1909) 'Classificatory systems of relationship', *Journal of the Royal Anthropological Institute* 39: 77–84.

—— (1917) *California Kinship Systems*, Berkeley, CA: University of California Publications in American Archaeology and Ethnology, 12, 9: 339–96.

Lévi-Strauss, C. ([1947] 1967) *Les Structures élémentaires de la parenté*, Paris: Mouton.

Lounsbury, F.G. (1964) 'The structural analysis of kinship semantics', in H.G. Lunt (ed.) *Proceedings of the Ninth International Congress of Linguistics*, The Hague: Mouton, pp. 1073–93.

Lowie, R.H. (1912) 'Social life of the Crow Indians', *Anthropological Papers of the American Museum of Natural History* IX: 179–248.

—— (1917) 'Notes on the social organization and customs of the Mandan, Hidatsa, and Crow Indians', *Anthropological Papers of the American Museum of Natural History* XXI: 53–99.

—— (1934) 'The Omaha and the Crow Kinship Terminologies', in *Verhandlungen des XXIV. Internationalen Amerikanisten-Kongresses*, 7–13 September 1930, pp. 103–8, Hamburg.

—— (1935) *The Crow Indians*, New York: Rinehart.

Murdock, G.P. (1949) *Social Structure*, New York: Macmillan.

Morgan, L.H. (1871) *Systems of Consanguinity and Affinity of the Human Family*, Smithsonian Contributions to Knowledge 17, Washington, DC: Smithsonian Institution.

Radcliffe-Brown, A.R. (1942) *Structure and Function in Primitive Society*, London: Oxford University Press.

Rivers, W.H.R. ([1913] 1968) *Kinship and Social Organisation*, London: Athlone Press.

Spier, L. (1925) *The Distribution of Kinship Systems in North America*, Washington, DC: University of Washington Publications in Anthropology 1, 2: 69–88.

Trautmann, T.R. (1987) *Lewis Henry Morgan and the Invention of Kinship*, Berkeley, CA: University of California Press.

Chapter 6

Comparison and contextualization
Reflections on South Africa

Adam Kuper

> Without systematic comparative studies anthropology will become only
> historiography and ethnography.
>
> (A.R. Radcliffe-Brown, 1951)

Not very long ago, an orthodox account of social anthropology would have situated it unhesitatingly within the social sciences. As a social science, three
distinctive features were said to mark its special character and to guarantee its
value. First, in pride of place, was its charter method: participant observation, as
patented by Malinowski. Second, the ethnographer's field of operation was
usually exotic, and often very far away. (Some argued that these two features must
be connected. Perhaps fieldwork by participant observation became increasingly
reliable the further one got from home.) Third, the information yielded by participant observation in exotic or marginal communities mattered because it
provided the stuff for comparison. This was perhaps the crucial justification for
anthropology, the most persuasive that remained in the postcolonial world.
Social anthropology universalized a social science discourse that was otherwise
limited to observations of contemporary, industrial, Western societies and to
forms of analysis that were restricted to taken-for-granted Western categories.

These claims are now muted. Today the very character of the social sciences
is in question. Disciplines have polarized between a natural science wing and an
opposing tendency that would prefer to be counted in with philosophy and
literary theory, or that would be content to merge into cultural studies. As to
the particular claims that used to be made for the identity of social or cultural
anthropology, all these are now widely regarded as problematic. From one flank,
participant observation is attacked for its subjectivity. From another, it is
denounced for dehumanizing its subjects, making them into objects. Claims
about the value of exoticism are also suspect. The difference between what
Sahlins called the West and the Rest is now illusory, according to one school of
thought, globalization the one super-narrative of the age. Alternatively,
according to a slightly different story, globalization has set off cosmic culture
wars so ferocious that only those untainted by the privileges of the West can be
trusted to study the Rest, and then only for a political purpose. Finally, the very

possibility of comparison has been placed in question. If there is no generalizing social science, if objectivity is an illusion, then comparison must be abandoned as a relic of an obsolete positivism.

No doubt this dismal picture is overdrawn. In Europe, at any rate, although cultural studies has established its beachheads, social anthropologists are by and large still accustomed to turn for analytical inspiration to the social sciences, and particularly to the anthropological tradition of theorizing. Malinowski, Mauss and Lévi-Strauss remain potent figures in their work. To be sure, there are few obvious successors. Bourdieu and Gellner may be claimed for the anthropologists, but on the whole there has been a retreat from the concerns of grand theory.

But if theory is in the doldrums, empiricism flourishes. Ethnography is now the core business of social anthropology, and long-term immersion in ethnographic research is increasingly common. Standards are high. There is no room for the insouciant invention of ethnographic fictions. The challenge is to add value to the dauntingly large body of ethnographic and historical reports available on almost any region. Ethnographers operate within a multidisciplinary and international community of regional specialists, so that their work is subject to expert appraisal and their findings routinely checked against those of other researchers in other fields. They feel that this guarantees them against accusations of bias, and they are content to aim at the delivery of reliable and sensitive ethnographic studies.

But there is a price to pay. Investing in empirical research while discounting theory has made most social anthropologists essentially into regional specialists. Few any longer attempt essays in cross-cultural comparison or generalization. Yet while regional specialization is perfectly respectable and has many advantages, there is a real danger that a regional field of research tends to become closed off from outside influences, crystallizing into a tradition with its distinctive preoccupations (see Fardon 1990). Absorbed in local issues, ethnographers will be tempted to neglect general issues of social science. In the end, they may find that they have little to say to other regional specialists, including the great bulk of social scientists whose primary interest is the modern West.

But in any case, I will suggest that the comfortable sense of security lent by this immersion in local scholarship is illusory. Regional studies cannot escape from all the epistemological problems that haunt cross-cultural comparison and ambitious theory building. And ethnographic research itself, the centre of our comfort zone, is prey to many of the same dangers as regional comparison.

Modalities of comparison

Comparative approaches in anthropology are conventionally classified along two dimensions. First, for all sorts of good historical and logical reasons, a distinction is made between studies that are restricted to a region (defined culturally, or ethnically, or historically, or on ecological grounds, or indeed in several or all of these ways), and on the other hand the much riskier business of making cross-cultural comparisons that range across the world. This is not a watertight opposition. The *Kulturkreis* school combined a culture area approach with a cross-cultural perspective, identifying local cultural types and then arranging them in a developmental series. This is in fact a recurrent temptation of culture area studies, challenged as they always are by more universalist projects.[1] Nevertheless, there are many evident differences between the methods and preoccupations of genuinely cross-cultural research and culture area studies. Most obviously, cross-cultural studies require the definition of ethnographic objects in culturally neutral terms, while regional comparisons often borrow local cultural conceptions.

Second, a distinction is often made between approaches that are intended to recover historical or genetic relationships and synchronic comparisons. Again, this distinction should not be insisted upon too strongly. For example, the cross-cultural comparative exercises of the structural-functionalists often simply recapitulated the studies of the evolutionists, while discarding their historical framework. To cite a famous instance, the categories used by Fortes and Evans-Pritchard in *African Political Systems* (1940, editorial introduction) were taken over directly from Morgan and Maine. In a similar fashion, the culture area studies of the diffusionists mutated easily into structural accounts of particular regional systems. These often took up the same issues, within the same cultural boundaries. Boas's diffusionist account of myths on the Northwest Coast provided the inspiration and even the model for Lévi-Strauss's *Mythologiques* (1969–81), although Boas's historical mechanism of diffusion was replaced by Lévi-Strauss's notion of transformation. These simple contrasts are summarized in Table 6.1.

Whatever their differences, however, all the modalities of the comparative method share certain fundamental problems. To begin with, the unit of comparison – the culture or society – is always difficult to isolate. How are boundaries to be drawn? Are the South African Bushmen one ethnographic case or several? Second, in what sense are the units that are constructed strictly comparable? Can the Bushmen reasonably be treated as a 'case' alongside 'the Bedouin', let alone Ming China? Much the same difficulties arise when it comes to defining an ethnographic object for purposes of comparison. Is 'sacrifice' among the Nuer really a distinctive, separable thing? And in what sense is it like 'sacrifice' among the ancient Israelites, or in classical Greece or among the Aztecs? Can one take a local, complex notion like *tabu*, or *mana*, or *caste*, and abstract some

Table 6.1 A classification of comparative methods

	Diachronic	*Synchronic*
Cross-cultural	Evolutionist Globalization/world system	Functionalist Structuralist
Culture area	Diffusionist Historical	Regional comparison Ecological

culture-free essence that will serve for purposes of comparison? Is the category 'Melanesian cargo cult' an artificial, colonial construct that ruptures the integrity of a broader system of beliefs and practices? Is it the same sort of thing as the Ghost Dance of North America, the nineteenth-century Xhosa cattle-killing, the eighteenth-century Jewish messianic movement associated with Shabbatai Zvi and Christian millenarian movements through the ages?

There is another problem – in a way, the opposite problem – which is that apparently independent societies and ethnographic objects may have a common origin. The statistician Francis Galton presided over the meeting at which Tylor presented his pioneering exercise in statistical cross-cultural comparison, 'On a method of investigating the development of institutions'. In the discussion period he pointed out that Tylor had no way of controlling for the historical relationships between the cases in his sample (Tylor 1889). The 'Galton problem' has haunted cross-cultural comparisons ever since. So, for example, it may be that many early twentieth-century millenarian movements, including cargo cults in Melanesia, were triggered by contact with evangelical Christian missionaries preaching the coming of the Apocalypse. In discussions of Murdock's sample of world cultures, the possibility was raised repeatedly that societies treated as independent cases were in fact historically related. Murdock tried to counter this line of criticism by introducing shadow culture areas in an attempt to ensure that his worldwide sample of societies was properly represen-tative, but it has been pointed out that the best correlations thrown up by Murdock's sample were regional rather than universal (e.g. Driver 1973).

Summing up, the methodological difficulties with comparative research have to do, first, with problems of commensurability, and second, and more funda-mentally, with problems of defining the units for comparison. These considerations have made cross-cultural studies unfashionable. However, although culture area studies have by and large been spared parallel method-ological critiques, they present (still more insidiously) equally fundamental and often very similar problems. These methodological difficulties do not arise only when comparisons are in question. They infiltrate even the most apparently routine ethnographic enquiry. There is a false security that comes from concen-trating on the empirical description of a particular people, especially if they already enjoy a sort of ethnographic identity, enshrined in generations of schol-arly research. But in every ethnographic report, in every regional study, compromises will be made between native categories and the established cate-gories of ethnographic reportage. And the fieldworker must still wrestle with the intractable problem of defining the ethnographic field.

Common ancestry was traditionally the usual basis for identifying an ethno-graphic unit. Evans-Pritchard's Nuer were defined as a single people because they claimed common descent. They were then situated as members of a broader Nilo-Hamitic family of peoples because scholars had determined (on racial or linguistic criteria) that they shared a common origin with some other groups of a similar kind. To be sure, not all tribes or peoples or culture areas were defined on genetic grounds. Boas rejected this sort of logic, constituting his geographical areas on the basis of contacts and interchanges between local populations. The Indonesian culture area posited by the Leiden school presupposed a common baseline, a shared heritage of cultural formulae, deposited by interchanges over a long period, which might be expressed in a variety of different media and languages (de Josselin de Jong 1984: 10). Edmund Leach (1954) isolated the set of political systems of Highland Burma as a system of structural transformations that shared a common symbolic foundation. Louis Dumont's India is defined with reference to a common religious tradition (Dumont 1974). Yet while these scholars did not rely on a myth of common ancestry to define their culture areas, they also ended up with units that have their own particular taken-for-granted quality. This is because they all correspond to political units established by colonial rule and legitimized by modern nationalist movements. These political conditions in turn often generated regional schools of scholarship, which only seldom and reluctantly crossed political borders.

'Blood' and 'soil' are, of course, the established modern grounds for defining a *Volk* or a nation. It is hardly to be wondered at that these same criteria underpin the definition of ethnographic fields. Ethnographers are accustomed to imagine a universe of ethnic groups (thought of in terms of common descent) that operate within nations or empires. The ethnic group, a community of blood and culture, is where we do ethnographic fieldwork. The boundaries of the nation or empire prescribe the framework for regional comparison. These underlying assumptions are seldom made explicit, and once they are brought into the open, some of the difficulties become immediately apparent. There is no necessary reason to suppose that people everywhere define their community in terms of blood and soil. Nor is it necessarily the case that all significant fields of social and cultural relations will be bounded by modern political borders. Indeed, contemporary anthropologists generally take the view that ethnic or social or cultural boundaries are porous, situational, negotiated, always liable to be contested. They very properly question conventional ethnic classifications and pay attention to the way in which these are generated by political discourses.

There is a further, methodological, problem in defining the field of ethnographic research. The classical ethnographers set out unselfconsciously to describe what they thought of as tribal cultures. However, the empiricism of the Malinowskians introduced a new source of tension. Ethnographic research is actually conducted in a small community, or as Radcliffe-Brown famously defined it, 'any convenient locality of a suitable size' (1953: 193). But this research field was then normally treated as the microcosm of a larger entity (the culture, the society, the tribe), which was named 'the Bemba' or 'the Balinese'. This was obviously a risky procedure. We end up not knowing, for example, whether Mead's Samoa corresponds ethnographically and historically with Freeman's – one perhaps getting things right, while the other got them wrong – or whether each report generalized from very different ethnographic observations that might represent a reliable picture of life in particular times and places but did not apply to an undifferentiated 'Samoa' (see Freeman 1983; Holmes 1987; Mead 1928). Some ethnographers accordingly refuse to move beyond the handful of people they have studied intensively at first hand, though it is difficult to see why we should take an interest in an arbitrary little network of friends or informants unless we can learn something of more general relevance (but see Barth 1992).

In practice, ethnographic reports do not usually confine themselves to the small sample of people who were the immediate subject of study in the field. But as soon as neighbouring villages are brought into the picture, on the basis of short excursions beyond the ethnographer's base camp or by drawing on the reports of other scholars, another troubling question arises. Why stop at some convenient or conventional boundary? Why not carry on, consult the work of other ethnographers and draw the boundaries of the study more liberally? On what grounds did Evans-Pritchard choose to write about all the peoples he designated the Nuer, occasionally noting regional variations, while excluding the people he called the Dinka, even where they constituted distinctive minorities in Nuer communities? To put it another way, it is not always easy to see at what point ethnographic generalization about a specific population – or small region – gives way to culture area syntheses.[2]

Comparison in Southern African ethnography

This is all perhaps too abstract. Like a good anthropologist, I will now try to probe these problems in the field, by considering the practice of ethnography and comparison in Southern Africa and in particular by examining the way in which ethnographic objects have been constituted.

Venturing along the East African coast from the late fifteenth century, Portuguese seafarers picked up ideas about the interior that were current among the coastal Islamic traders. They took over the term for the inland peoples that was used by Moslems: *kafirs*, or unbelievers. When the Dutch established the first colonial station in the Cape, in the middle of the seventeenth century, the Cape itself was sometimes referred to as Kaffraria. Dapper's account of the Cape, published in 1668, was entitled *Kaffraria or Land of the Kafirs, also Named Hottentots*.

The eighteenth century was the age of Linnaeus, and classification was the central concern of the natural sciences. By 1719 Kolb was complaining, 'Some confound the *Hottentots* with the *Caffres* or *Keffres*, and call them by that Name. But the *Caffres*, who inhabit the Monomotapa, tho' encompaf's'd in a Manner by the *Hottentot* Nations, are a very different kind of People' (Kolb 1968: 28). Soon it was taken for granted that the indigenous population of Southern Africa should be divided into two groups. The first, the 'Hottentots', occupied the Western Cape, the site of the original white colony, and was made up of small bands of pastoralists, hunters and foragers. The people to the east of the colony were called 'Kaffirs', perhaps because they were similar in appearance to peoples encountered earlier in East Africa, and were, like them, farmers. Pastoralists and horticulturalists, with an elaborate iron technology absent in the west, they were organized into often formidable chiefdoms.

In the spirit of Linnaeus, each of these major categories was again, in time, divided into two sections. In the Western Cape, 'Bushmen' came to be distinguished from 'Hottentots'. It was generally assumed that they were related – all were small, yellowish in colour, with peppercorn hair and so on – and that their languages had a common origin, since they were full of click consonants. The difference between them was economic. The Bushmen were hunters, the Hottentots pastoralists. At the same time, the term Kaffirs came to be restricted to the chiefdoms on the eastern littoral. A new term, Bechuana, introduced at the end of the eighteenth century, was applied to the newly contacted peoples of the highveld. The difference between 'Kaffirs' and 'Bechuanas' was established by a mixture of criteria, including dress, customs and language. The linguistic criterion became particularly significant in the nineteenth century, as philology became increasingly influential, and studies showed that the 'Caffre' and 'Bechuana' languages belonged to two (closely related) families.

In the course of the nineteenth century, home-grown racial criteria were used to define the main political categories in South Africa: 'white' or 'European' and 'native' (Ross 1993, II). Later, neo-Darwinian ideas on racial identity gradually infiltrated the South African scientific discourse (Dubow 1995). Racial criteria now became the main basis for distinguishing 'Khoisan' and 'Bantu', and race was added to the economic, linguistic and broadly cultural terms in which earlier classifications were formulated, sometimes introducing modifications. In 1928, for example, a German physical anthropologist, Schultze, introduced the term 'Khoisan' to describe what he took to be the common racial stock of the Bushmen and Hottentots, and in 1930 Schapera adopted this coinage for his ethnographic survey, which he entitled *The Khoisan Peoples of South Africa: Bushmen and Hottentots*. The linguistic term 'Bantu' or 'Southern Bantu' was applied to the other congeries of native peoples, and it was itself subdivided into two major categories, Nguni and Sotho, while marginal outliers were called Venda and Thonga or Tsonga. These were also primarily linguistic labels, but from the turn of the century there was a persistent assumption that the linguistic subdivisions corresponded to distinctive and enduring racial and cultural units, each of which had migrated separately into Southern Africa (see e.g. Stow 1905; Theal 1910). In short, broad racial and linguistic families were defined, on the same lines as in the Indo-European model, and these were divided into ethnic categories, called *Volke* in Afrikaans (see Figure 6.1).

'Tribes' were distinguished within these broad categories, but their definition immediately raised a problem. Was a tribe made up of a chief's subjects, who might be of diverse origins, or was it a descent group of some kind, even though it might not constitute a political community? In practice, by the early twentieth

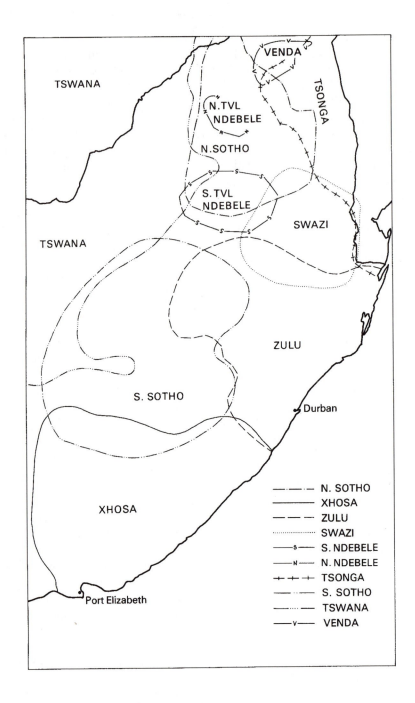

Figure 6.1 Languages of the Southeastern Bantu
Source: Van Warmelo (1952) (Extract from Ethnological Publication, reproduced under Copyright Authority 7666 of 15.5.81 of the Government Printer of the Republic of South Africa)

century a tribe was defined as a political community, although the political communities that were picked out for study had often been formed – and trans-formed – by relations with white administrators and missionaries.

The missionary anthropologist Henri Junod defined 'the Thonga tribe', living on both sides of the Mozambique/Transvaal border, with a population he estimated at three-quarters of a million, divided into six main clusters and a great number of chiefdoms (Junod 1912, I: 13–19). He conceded that the term 'Thonga' was not used by the people themselves, but was applied to them by their neighbours.[3] He also admitted that the various parts of 'the Thonga tribe' had no tradition of common identity, that there was no indigenous name for the whole grouping, and that the various clans, or major divisions, had different traditions of origin, but he argued that they all spoke dialects of a common language and shared some cultural features that set them off from the Zulu-speakers to the south, to whom they were otherwise obviously related. It has been plausibly argued, however, that Junod's classification was based on the field of operations of his missionary society, the Swiss Romande Mission. The missionaries standardized the language and fostered assumptions of linguistic and cultural unity. Wittingly or not, they were in the business of nation building (Harries 1989: 85–90; Comaroff and Comaroff 1991).

More commonly, colonial boundaries shaped ethnographic classification. Schapera pioneered a series of now-classic ethnographic studies in the Malinowskian mould, which appeared between 1930 and 1950. These were designed to provide a generalized description of a common tradition. Each ethnic or cultural group was assumed to be broadly uniform in its social institu-tions, language and culture. It was also geographically bounded. However, the decisive feature in these ethnic classifications was in practice their administra-tive status. Where individual chiefdoms were picked out for study, as was the case for the Zulu, the Swazi and the Basotho, each corresponded to a colonial administrative state or province. Their ethnographers confined their attention to the Zulu, Swazi or Basotho who lived within the boundaries of Zululand, Swaziland or Basutoland.[4] Schapera's own most extensive and detailed field-work was conducted among the Kgatla of the Bechuanaland Protectorate, but his writings generally deal with the history and customs of the set of Tswana tribes living in that country (now Botswana) and exclude the Tswana of South Africa, although they share a language and traditions of common origin. State boundaries were equally decisive in broader culture area studies. *The Bantu-Speaking Tribes of South Africa*, edited by Schapera and published in 1937, dealt only with Bantu-speaking populations within the borders of South Africa and the three British protectorates and excluded the substantial Nguni and Sotho offshoots in Zimbabwe and Zambia and the Tsonga of Mozambique.

Another perspective emerged in the 1920s, offering an alternative context for thinking about ethnographic reports. This was the one-society thesis of the radical historian W.M. Macmillan. Dismissing conventional ethnography as antiquarian, and complaining that it drew attention away from the actualities of

South African life, he pointed out that as early as 1915 'barely half the natives of the Union appeared to have homes except on land owned ... by Europeans' (Macmillan 1929: 312). The Reserves were in any case grossly inadequate even for their residual populations, and the traditional institutions of rural Africans had been shattered. Radcliffe-Brown, South Africa's first professor of social anthropology, agreed that traditional social organization had been radically undermined, and he insisted that the organization even of a Transkeian tribe could be understood only in the context of the national state and economy (see 'South African anthropology: an inside job' in Kuper 1999). This was the view that shaped the classic ethnography of a Transkeian people, tellingly entitled *Reaction to Conquest: Effects of Contact with Europeans on the Pondo of South Africa* (Monica Hunter [Wilson] 1936).

In 1934 Schapera edited a book entitled *Western Civilization and the Natives of South Africa: Studies in Culture Contact*. It opened with a chapter entitled 'The Old Bantu Culture', but then moved on to the description of culture change, land shortages, labour migration, Christianity and urbanization, with little reference to local cultural variations or traditional forces. In 1937, Schapera summed up the situation in this way:

> Of the Bantu as a whole it can be said that they have now been drawn permanently into the orbit of Western civilization. They do not, and probably will not, carry on that civilization in its purely European manifestations. It is more likely that in certain directions at least they will develop their own local variations. But these variations will be within the framework of a common South African civilization, shared in by both Black and White, and presenting certain peculiarities based directly upon the fact of their juxtaposition. Already such a civilization is developing, a civilization in which the Europeans at present occupy the position of a race-proud and privileged aristocracy, while the Natives, although economically indispensable, are confined to a menial status from which few of them are able to emerge with success ... But despite all this, the Bantu are being drawn more and more into the common cultural life of South Africa.
>
> (Schapera 1937b: 386–7)

It is this single-society orientation that became the orthodoxy in the next generation in the English-language universities in South Africa. In the 1970s a new wave of studies was inaugurated which interpreted this single society in Marxist terms. The most influential writers were historians (see Saunders 1988), who introduced a three-stage model. Traditionally the African people had lived in small chiefdoms recruited by descent and organized into lineages. Then, in the late seventeenth or early eighteenth centuries, there was a general transition to a state system. Finally, all these independent political units were conquered by whites and absorbed into the colonial state, and their peoples were reduced to a uniform status of landless peasantries and labour migrants, distinguished not by culture but by a racially defined socio-legal status, or, in some formulations, by their position within a particular kind of capitalist economy, one dominated by the demands of the gold industry.

The Marxist perspective that became current in the English-speaking universities had no place for tradition, ethnicity and culture; or rather, these appeared only as mystifications in the service of a politics of divide and rule. The new ethnographic studies were designed to demonstrate the effects of apartheid. The distinctive ethnographic object became the urban Africanist church, the migrants' hostels and associations, the rituals and songs associated with labour migration, the impact of migration on the rural domestic group, and the displaced peoples deposited by resettlement schemes or deprived of their squatter rights on white farms. All this, of course, was against the background of an ideology that insisted upon the importance of cultural differences, not only between white and black but within the black population, and a policy that was constructing pseudo-traditional tribal governments, and trying – brutally, but ultimately unsuccessfully – to reverse the flow of people into the urban areas. It was left to the ethnologists in the Afrikaans-language universities, who accepted the objectives of apartheid policies, to collect traditions and codify tribal law.[5]

The single-society thesis reinforced the tendency of South African anthropologists to limit their ethnographic curiosity to the boundaries of the state. This concentration was buttressed by the international cultural boycott of the 1970s and 1980s, during which South African scholars turned in upon themselves. Comparisons were rarely made with countries to the north, including even Botswana and Zimbabwe. However, the model also discouraged comparisons within South Africa itself. It was assumed that the single society was divided vertically into classes or racial castes, but not horizontally into ethnic groups. Any concern with cultural differences was suspect, as potentially serving the interests of apartheid. All the oppressed were in the same boat, and ethnic identities were the creation of white initiatives (see e.g. Vail 1989).

Khoisan studies

The classic modern South African ethnographies, published in the 1930s and 1940s, dealt with Bantu-speaking rural populations. Only one comparable study was devoted to a Hottentot or Khoi group, the Nama.[6] However, following a further study of the Nama in the 1960s (Carstens 1966), anthropologists from the University of Cape Town began to make ethnographic studies in the Cape and in Namibia of 'Hottentot' or 'Coloured' groups.

Following the same course as other branches of South African ethnography, 'tribal' studies were abandoned. The designation of the subjects of these studies was now a sensitive matter. Legally, they were members of a specific caste within the apartheid system, termed 'Coloureds'. Intellectuals preferred the ironic self-designation 'so-called Coloureds', but the grounds for any categorization were a matter of bitter dispute. Where did these people belong? In whose eyes? Hottentot origins were played down by all concerned, as were slave antecedents. On the other hand, there were evident cultural links with the Afrikaners, whose language and religion (and family names) they shared, but from whom they were segregated socially and politically. In general, the preferred strategy among both political activists and social scientists was to represent them as 'black South Africans', on the argument that their consciousness and the conditions of their lives were shaped by apartheid in the same way as the rest of the disenfranchised proletariat. The effect of this orientation is illustrated by the story of a South African anthropologist who wrote a structural account of a northern Cape Nama community for a Cambridge PhD in the early 1970s, but returned to South Africa and repudiated the work, never publishing any part of it, on the grounds that it might provide indirect support for the supposition that ethnic identities were significant.

The trajectory followed by Bushman studies was very different. This was because the field fell outside the scope of South African anthropology as it had come to be defined. Research was concentrated in Botswana, with outliers in Namibia, and it was therefore not constrained by the academic boycott. Following Lorna Marshall's pioneering study of the !Kung in the 1950s, a new wave of foreign ethnographers began to work in Botswana. South African–based scholars showed no interest in the revival of Bushman studies, which seemed irrelevant to their new concerns.[7] The research was defined by the very different agendas of (mainly) US anthropology.

The great theoretical debate that came to shape Bushman studies focused on the !Kung. Richard Lee's famous study was carried out in the White/Steward tradition, yielding an ecologically driven account of the adaptation of hunter-gatherers to a desert environment. Lee presented his findings as a contribution to the reconstruction of the transition to the upper Palaeolithic in Africa, and his !Kung study gained currency as a result of the endorsement of two of the leading anthropologists in the USA, the physical anthropologist Sherwood Washburn and the archaeologist Desmond Clarke. In consequence, the !Kung served for a generation as the ethnographic exemplars of a universal stage of human evolution (see Lee and DeVore 1968; Lee 1979).

This view of the !Kung was later challenged by a revisionist school, represented most powerfully by Edwin Wilmsen, who argued that all the Bushmen had been subjugated and incorporated for centuries by pastoralist peoples, black and white. They were not the last African representatives of an ancient hunter-gatherer way of life, but rather dispossessed people, the underclass of a complex, wider social system (Wilmsen 1989). Within Botswana they came to be represented by development workers as part of a broader category of 'remote peoples', defined by poverty and political weakness.

Although this was the dominant debate (see Barnard 1992b), there was another research trajectory, as well. Linguists had reclassified the Khoisan languages, drawing attention to the fact that linguistic boundaries did not coincide with the traditional Hottentot/Bushman division. The US historian Richard Elphick (1977, 1985) pointed out that, at least in some areas, pre-conquest Bushman and Hottentot groups cycled between pastoralist and hunter-gatherer ways of life. Alan Barnard, a Bushman ethnographer, produced a comparative account of kinship systems, patterns of settlement and religious ideas that demonstrated the existence of certain shared structural principles throughout the Khoisan region. (He also paid exemplary attention to the theoretical underpinnings of his project of regional comparison; Barnard 1992a.) Mathias Guenther (1986) showed that traditional ideas and forms of domestic organization persisted even among people who had been working for generations on white farms.

To sum up, in South Africa the context of ethnographic research has been dictated very largely by local political conditions and debates, and the definition of a culture area was itself shaped by political boundaries. When the culture area perspective gave way to a single-society framework, at least within the English-language universities, this was in response to a particular view of the modern political history of the country. The South African situation was treated as unique, and the peculiar history of the country was taken to explain local social and cultural processes. In consequence, comparisons were seldom encouraged. This willed provincialism was reinforced by the political boycott that insulated South African scholars from the 1970s, reinforcing their natural concern with developments at home and drying up the flow of foreign scholars who might have introduced different theoretical perspectives, as they did in Botswana.

The contrast with the course of Bushman studies in Botswana is instructive. Although local political influences were by no means absent, from the 1960s onwards Bushman studies developed largely within the framework of a cosmopolitan anthropological discourse. There is nevertheless a common thread between the single-society thesis in South Africa and the revisionist thesis on the Bushmen, which insisted that the Bushmen be situated in history and that their development was shaped decisively by external political and economic pressures. There is also an interesting difference of emphasis. For South African scholars, it seemed obvious that the structuring forces are exerted by the state, or by the highly corporate and centralized capitalist mining system, which was in turn closely associated with the state. For the largely US-based revisionists working in Botswana and Namibia, the state was ignored, and power to influence local communities was attributed instead to the vague global forces of imperialism and capitalism that play such a central role in the modern demonology of the American left. Working also from a Botswana perspective, John and Jean Comaroff (1991) constructed a thesis on intellectual imperialism, in which the missionaries played a central role.

The new orthodoxy both in South African and in Bushman ethnography converged on a common question. This concerned the relationship between an ethnic group, on the one hand, and the state or empire on the other. An old issue, it was given a new twist because it was assumed that the ethnic group was invented by the state for its own nefarious purposes, or by the imperial discourse or the capitalist system. The researcher then had to constitute new subjects of research – the underclass of Botswana, the victims of apartheid – which were once more defined in relation to the state, but were now identified as the real products of political and economic exploitation. This strategy has its advantages. Certainly, it goes to the heart of the political discourse in the region. However, it leads away from comparison and from a whole range of alternative routes of anthropological enquiry. Indeed, one of its purposes is to deny that cultural entities can be defined except in relation to the state, which constitutes them.

Structural transformations

South African anthropology is a special case, but its concerns were not unique, and its course illustrates some very general problems. Comparison depends on the drawing of boundaries. The establishment of boundaries is also a crucial part of the business of constructing an ethnographic account. Since ethnic boundaries are typically in question, these are often highly politicized matters.

The English tradition of social anthropology in South Africa abandoned ethnic categories and came to define its social field as the state, or rather as the impact of the state on local social processes. Certainly the South African state was a powerful centre of social engineering. Nevertheless, there are good reasons to doubt that even in South Africa the life of every community is determined in all significant respects by the power of the state or the logic of the economic system. Moreover, there may be interesting continuities or parallels between the life of local groups in one society and processes beyond the boundaries of the state. In other words, there is room for other kinds of questions, which may not always be answered simply by invoking the political and economic institutions of the state. And, of course, there are elements within the anthropological tradition that to some degree worked against the purely political definition of the context of enquiry, though without necessarily essentializing tribes or perpetuating the functionalist illusion that societies – closed, integrated social systems – could still be identified in some isolated region within the colonial state.

Perhaps it is no coincidence that as a long-time expatriate, I was one of the few anthropologists to attempt comparative research in Southern Africa in these troubled years. In any case, whatever may account for the fact, my project may serve as an illustration of an alternative anthropological strategy of comparison, common enough elsewhere in the 1960s and 1970s, if not later, but unusual at the time in South Africa. Influenced by Lévi-Strauss and Leach, I tried to describe the pre-industrial systems of kinship and marriage in Southern Africa as variations on a common theme, local (or temporary) realizations of recurrent structuring principles, which, I suggested, also influenced adaptations to the conditions of industrialization (Kuper 1982).

Marriage in this region was based traditionally on elaborate cattle–bridewealth accounts. The fundamental transaction, of cattle for wives, was (among other things) a way of balancing investment in pastoralism with investment in agriculture, agriculture being essentially women's work. The relative importance of agriculture and pastoralism in a particular region was therefore critical to the demand for wives, and so to the level of bridewealth. Cross-cutting this calculation was a second structural determinant, the preferential marriage rules. There were various forms of cousin marriage, each of which inflected the timescale that regulated the chain of exchanges of wives for cattle. There was also a series of hierarchical exchanges, cattle passing down the system from patron to client, wives passing up, in an exchange that elided bridewealth, patronage and tribute transactions. Finally, within the inner circles of the chiefly families, marriage was the currency of factional attachments, the goal being to see your sister's son installed as a chief. All these systems could be treated as transformations of each other, sharing a common structuring grammar.

This account of the traditional system had its relevance for contemporary social processes. Migrant labour was in many ways a functional equivalent to the traditional male activity of cattle keeping, sustaining a similar dual economy based on male and female labour respectively, men investing some of the proceeds of their work in wives, who would maintain their farms back home. This logic worked itself out in various ways, in response to regional ecological and economic differences. In Botswana, for instance, a dominantly pastoral region with marginal agriculture, the proceeds of migrant labour were invested in livestock; men married late, and many women remained unmarried; illegitimacy became virtually the norm; and bridewealth, if paid at all, was a small and purely symbolic transaction.

The situation was very different in Lesotho, although the two countries had a similar precolonial and colonial heritage. (Both became British Protectorates within the sphere of influence of the South African state and economy.) In Lesotho, white conquest had resulted in the loss of traditional pastures. Consequently, the main domestic field of economic activity was agriculture. Since pastoralism was of marginal importance, the incidence of male migrant labour was much higher than in Botswana. And precisely because domestic investment had to be in farming rather than in pastoralism, these labour migrants married young and made high bridewealth payments, mostly in the form of cash. Marriages were stable (Kuper 1987: Chapter 10). Reports suggested that there were areas in the Transvaal, where neither agriculture nor pastoralism were any longer viable, where marriage had become marginal, and the crucial kinship bond was between brother, sister and sisters' children (Niehaus 1994).

My book had very little impact on South African studies, partly no doubt because it did not address the great political issues of the day or the related academic debates, partly because most of the book had to do with rules of preferential marriage and bridewealth systems, at a time when few anthropologists were still interested in kinship.[8] Nevertheless, one aspect of my research did have a considerable and quite unexpected impact. This had to do with the layout of the homestead. In the course of writing about the social organization of the domestic group I had become intrigued by the physical layout of its home base, influenced by Lévi-Strauss's accounts of the symbolic structure of village settlements and by the recent anthropological discussions on the 'house' (once more inspired by Lévi-Strauss). The comparison of a large number of descriptions recorded over the past 150 years revealed that beneath the temporal and local variations there was a single fundamental structure. The same symbolic values were being deployed throughout the region (Kuper 1982: Chapter 10).

The traditional homestead is circular in plan. The main symbolic oppositions are between the upper section and the lower section, which correspond to the western and eastern orientations; between the centre and the sides; and between the right side and the left side. The central axis, passing from the great hut through the cattle byre, is associated with the agnatic family and its ancestors. The great hut, belonging to the chief wife of the homestead head, or to his mother, is placed at the apex of the settlement, which is also usually both the highest and the westernmost point. At the centre of the homestead is the cattle byre. This is the men's assembly place and the focus of homestead rituals. Senior male ancestors are buried here, and grain pits are often sunk beneath the byre to store sorghum for the ceremonial beer of the men. Women cannot enter the byre except on some ceremonial occasions. The other huts are arranged in a horseshoe around the cattle byre and are associated with in-marrying wives or with bachelors. The huts are grouped into two or three sections: a right, left, and perhaps a central section. The right is of higher status than the left. Units

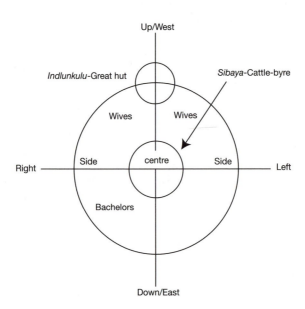

Figure 6.2 The symbolic dimensions of the Swazi homestead

nearer the apex have a higher status than those placed below them. The lower entry to the homestead is associated with visitors. Each hut is itself organized on similar principles, the entry facing east, a hearth in the centre around which the family gathers, the sacred spot to the rear. The right side is associated with the higher status members of the household (Figure 6.2).

Transformations of these structures are sometimes deliberately deployed by healers and prophets. Other transformations marked ethnic boundaries. The Zulu, for instance, determined the right and left sides of the homestead by facing outwards from the great hut, while the Swazi reversed the perspective. A more significant transformation marked the Sotho–Nguni boundary. Among the Sotho, many homesteads typically clustered together to form a dense settlement, and they tended to be organized again in a rough circle, the most senior to the west and at the highest part of the settlement, the other groups organized into right and left divisions, with a men's assembly place at the centre.

South Africa's leading iron-age archaeologist, Thomas N. Huffman, picked up on this model to define what he called the Southern Bantu Culture System, or the Bantu Cattle Culture, emphasizing the fact that its symbolic core was the relationship between men and cattle (Huffman 1982). As he explained, this settlement pattern had not been previously noted because archaeologists had been concerned with the recovery of ceramics rather than with settlement layout. Moreover, they had been interested in human habitations and neglected the importance of the central cattle byre. Re-examining the sites, however, it was soon apparent that the basic layout had been constant for a thousand years. Huffman predicted that examples of the structure would be found even earlier, as old sites were re-examined with the model in mind, a prediction that was confirmed by a study of Broederstroom, a site dating between AD 350 and 600 and representing the first phase of iron-age occupation in the Transvaal (Huffman 1990). Huffman also recast the opposition between Sotho, Venda and Nguni settlements in a developmental framework, suggesting that as chiefs became more powerful so settlements became larger and the central cattle byre was replaced by a dedicated men's assembly place. Finally, he adapted the model to explain the symbolic structure of the most famous archaeological site in South-Central Africa, the Zimbabwe ruins.

The predictable lines of criticism have developed, pointing to local variations that may or may not constitute transformations, and arguing for more specific local historical causes of settlement layout, including ecological determinants (e.g. Hall 1984; Lane 1994–5). Notwithstanding, the model of the Central Cattle Pattern has come to dominate South African iron-age archaeology. It also influenced a few studies of modern settlements by geographers, architects and town planners. However, it had little impact on ethnographic or historical research, despite the obvious implications, such as Huffman's suggestion that variations in settlement structure were markers of political centralization. I have recently been working on a related development of the model, which concerns the homestead of the ruling family of a chiefdom, a line of research that picks up on studies published in the 1940s by an associate of the Leiden structuralist school, J.F. Holleman (Holleman 1940, 1941).

The great places of major chiefs are blown-up versions of the basic homestead. Moreover, the administrative structure of the chiefdom is typically based on the process of the division of an aristocratic household, each of the 'sides', right and left, splitting off to form independent households, and then dividing again in time into right and left sections. This framework is typically imposed on the whole chiefdom, which is organized into districts with reference to the dispersed segments of the chiefly household, and, in the case of the Swazi, the opposition between the headman's part of the homestead and that of his mother (Kuper 1993). One conclusion suggested by this line of research is that there was not in fact a great structural transformation of Southern Bantu political systems in the late eighteenth century, but that even the largest pre-conquest chiefdoms were organized in a similar way to the homesteads. This suggested long-term continuities rather than radical change in political structure. Another conclusion was that all the pre-conquest Southern Bantu social systems were organized on a similar basis and shared a common symbolic code. This, in turn, raised new questions about the internal dynamics of social and cultural change in the twentieth century.

But there was obviously another direction in which these questions could be pursued: not back in time, but outwards in space, beyond the region. The ethnography on the Shona is rich, but despite the similarities it has never been conceptualized with reference to the Southern Bantu ethnography. The parallels between the interlacustrine East African chiefdoms and the Southern African chiefdoms are striking – in rituals, settlement structure and kinship rules – yet they have hardly ever been systematically compared (an inspiring exception is Luc de Heusch's comparison of Rwanda and Swazi [1982: Chapter 7]).

But these are not the only options. Several more particular themes could be followed up. For example, the Southern African association of pastoralism and agriculture with cattle bridewealth payments and patrilocal residence on marriage is repeated among the Shona, but it is not found to the north and west, in the so-called matrilineal belt. This belt is not only matrilineal; it is also without cattle. Could one develop a causal connection between the absence of cattle, the absence of bridewealth payments and matrilineal relations? And, if so, what would one make of the fact that this is also a tsetse fly belt?

Among the Southern Bantu there was traditionally a relationship between patrilocal residence, bridewealth payments made in cattle and an economy based on a combination of pastoralism and agriculture. I argued that there was an economic logic at work here, so that when a man paid bridewealth in cattle for a wife, he was investing resources from his stock of pastoral capital in agricultural production, since his wife would work his land. This was not to suggest that the system was simply economically determined: after all, the division of labour between men (pastoralists) and women (agriculturalists) on which it rested was clearly culturally specific. Nevertheless, it is striking that of the seventy-six societies represented in the *Ethnographic Atlas* that combine substantial reliance on pastoralism and agriculture with patrilocal residence at marriage, 82 per cent have substantial bridewealth payments. These societies account for only 17 per cent of the total sample, but for 42 per cent of the societies in which bridewealth is paid (Kuper 1982: 168–70).

A common humanity

The different forms of comparison that I distinguished at the beginning of this argument are not necessarily mutually exclusive, as I hope my example has suggested. Every ethnography is implicitly comparative, ethnographic studies shading into regional analyses, regional analysis into cross-cultural comparison. Synchronic comparisons raise historical questions, and these may in turn suggest further topics for ethnographic investigation. Ethnography, comparison and theoretical argument should be constantly interacting elements in a single process of research. Together, they make up the conversation that anthropologists carry on among themselves, exchanging notes, talking about what they think they know. The conversation has been flagging recently, not so much because we lack information but because we are losing the thread, becoming uncertain about the relevance of what we know.

Begin with problems, not periods, said the philosopher and archaeologist Collingwood. Study problems, Malinowski said, not peoples. If we begin with a problem, a question, an intuition, then the next step is contextualization. An alternative way of thinking about comparison is as the business of contextualizing information in order to address a question. The ethnic groups of conventional comparative research need not be our exclusive points of reference. Each question, emanating at once from a particular discourse and a set of observations, will suggest its own contexts for investigation, through both fieldwork and comparison. Each contextualization will raise fresh questions, suggest references to other observations and reports, and stimulate doubts about the underlying assumptions of the discourse within which it is set.

In his first great monograph, published in 1922, Malinowski studied the *kula*, an inter-island system of exchanges. This was not a practice specific to the Trobrianders, but rather part of a system of external relationships. In his conclusion, Malinowski remarked that the most important contribution of *Argonauts of the Western Pacific* was precisely that it created a new object of ethnographic study, which might prove to be related to similar institutions elsewhere. This suggestion was followed through by Mauss, who published his essay on the gift two years later (Mauss [1924] 1954). Eight years further on, Malinowski took up Mauss's conclusion that the underlying idea that lay behind the *kula* was a principle of reciprocity, and in *Crime and Custom in Savage Society* (1932) he analysed the process of social control in the Trobriands as a product of the same principle of reciprocity.

To be sure, the course of comparative research is not straightforward. I have flagged many of the evident difficulties raised by the various comparative methods, suggesting, incidentally, that similar problems may confront even the most empiricist ethnography. We must be careful, learn our lessons. It is necessary to historicize comparison, to put in question the processes by which categories are constructed. But I remain convinced that methodological difficulties are the least of our problems. There are enough good examples to show that comparison remains possible. The real source of our current troubles is to be found not so much in our methods of ethnographic fieldwork or comparison, but more in the poverty of current theoretical discourse. We lack questions rather than the means to answer them. What we need in order to revive the comparative enterprise is not new methods but new ideas, or perhaps simply fresh problems.

But much contemporary theory leads away from comparative research, even denying its possibility on theoretical grounds. The extreme relativism of some recent US cultural anthropology has persuaded many that all meaning is subjective, all practices incommensurate. James Clifford spurns what he calls 'vapid humanism', but even he recognizes that the extreme relativism of some contemporary anthropology leaves a problem. 'To stress ... the paradoxical nature of ethnographic knowledge', he admits, 'does mean questioning any stable or essential grounds of human similarity' (Clifford 1988: 145). This is, of course, a familiar dilemma within the counter-Enlightenment tradition. The more strongly the claim is made that each culture has its own take on reality, the less there is to say about humanity as a whole. There is no common ground.

But perhaps we can turn this around. Recognizing the grounds of human similarity, we may take heart when we try to understand others, and to make comparisons, comparisons that implicate ourselves but without arrogating to ourselves a privileged status, as the ultimate point of reference. Whatever its difficulties, cross-cultural comparison remains necessary. If we abandon broader comparisons, we stop asking the fundamental question in anthropology: what do different peoples, different societies, have in common? In other words, comparison, whatever its methodological difficulties, is required by one of the basic theoretical programmes of anthropology. The premise on which the comparative exercise ultimately rests is the assertion of our common humanity, although we must be ready also to test its limits.

Notes

1   Lévi-Strauss (1969) could be read as a similar sort of exercise. He defined Australian, South Indian and Chinese structures, and then represented these as strata of a putatively universal, unidirectional historical development. Sahlins (1958, 1963) worked out a series of political types for Melanesia, and then suggested that these represented stages in a more general, even universal, evolution. One can also find examples of genre mixtures that go in the contrary direction, in which an arbitrary geographical area is treated as a microcosm of the variety of primitive societies in the world. This is the unexamined premise behind I. Schapera's *Government and Politics in Tribal Societies* (1956) and Lucy Mair's *Primitive Government* (1962).

2   The problem is similar to that of the linguist who puzzles over whether a dialectical variant should be treated as a separate language. Linguistic classifications often provide the basis for the delimitation of the ethnographic unit, even though we are surely aware that definitions of dialect and language have as much to do with polit-ical history as with purely linguistic criteria. (If a language is a dialect with an army, the same could be said of a nation as opposed to an ethnic group.)

3   The term 'Thonga' was commonly used for low-status neighbours of the Shona who were traditionally without cattle – usually because they had been dispossessed by Shona overlords.

4   A partial exception was J.H. Soga, son of an early Xhosa convert and an amateur ethnographer and historian. However, he described the Xhosa peoples as a congeries of people who had traditions of common origin and spoke essentially the same language; but the key factor in his classification was that they occupied the adminis-trative districts of the Transkei and Ciskei, which had emerged in the course of colonial conquest (Soga 1931).

5   This is a very generalized picture, and an obvious exception is W.D. Hammond-Tooke (ed.) 1974, *The Bantu-Speaking Peoples of Southern Africa*. An attempt to bring Schapera's two edited volumes on the Bantu-speaking peoples up to date, the result was an awkward compromise between two halves, the first about 'tradition', the second entitled 'incorporation into the wider society'. This volume was criticized by historians for its ahistorical approach, and by social scientists for its neglect of the state and the political economy; see Adam Kuper (1976), 'Culture area or political system?'. For a general review of South African anthropology, see W.D. Hammond-Tooke (1997), *Imperfect Interpreters: South Africa's Anthropologists 1920–1990*.

6   This research, carried out by Agnes Winifred Hoernlé, a close associate of Radcliffe-Brown, was published in the form of essays rather than in the conventional monograph, but her papers were edited and republished in book form by Peter Carstens (Hoernlé 1985) as *The Social Organization of the Nama and Other Essays*.

7   The only South African ethnographer involved was George Silberbauer, an adminis-trative officer in the Bechualand Protectorate.

8   Within South Africa the only anthropologist working on similar lines was W.D. Hammond-Tooke, professor of social anthropology at the University of the Witwatersrand. Although he was the senior figure among the English-speaking anthropologists and a productive scholar, he became increasingly isolated among his colleagues. A *Festschrift* to Hammond-Tooke has recently appeared, *Culture and the Commonplace*, edited by P. McAllister (1997). It is a good reflection of much current anthropology in South Africa, but the bulk of the contributions have little to do with the central interests that shaped his own work. See also Hammond-Tooke's own account of the development of social anthropology in South Africa, *Imperfect Interpreters: South Africa's Anthropologists 1920–1990* (1997).

Bibliography

Barnard, A. (1992a) *Hunters and Herders of Southern Africa: A Comparative Ethnography of the Khoisan Peoples*, Cambridge: Cambridge University Press.

—— (1992b) *The Kalahari Debate: A Bibliographic Essay*, Edinburgh: Centre of African Studies, Edinburgh University, Occasional Papers 35.

Barth, F. (1992) 'Towards greater naturalism in conceptualizing societies', in A. Kuper (ed.) *Conceptualizing Society*, London: Routledge.

Carstens, P. (1966) *The Social Structure of a Cape Coloured Reserve*, Cape Town: Oxford University Press.

Clifford, J. (1988) *The Predicament of Culture: Twentieth-Century Ethnography, Literature and Art*, Cambridge, MA: Harvard University Press.

Comaroff, J. and Comaroff, J. (1991) *Of Revelation and Revolution: Christianity, Colonialism, and Consciousness in South Africa*, Chicago: University of Chicago Press.

Dapper, O. ([1688] 1933) *Kaffrarie, of lant der Hottentots* [*Kaffraria, or Land of the Hottentots*], translated by I. Schapera, in I. Schapera (ed.) *The Early Cape Hottentots*, Cape Town: The Van Riebeeck Society, vol. 14, pp. 6–77.

Driver, H. (1973) 'Cross-cultural studies', in J. Honigmann (ed.) *Handbook of Social and Cultural Anthropology*, Chicago: Chicago University Press.

Dubow, S. (1995) *Illicit Union: Scientific Racism in Modern South Africa*, Johannesburg: Witwatersrand University Press.

Elphick, R. (1977) *Kraal and Castle: Khoikhoi and the Founding of White South Africa*, New Haven, CT: Yale University Press.

—— (1985) *Khoikhoi and the Founding of White South Africa* (rev. edn of Elphick 1977), Johannesburg: Ravan Press.

Fardon, R. (ed.) (1990) *Localizing Strategies: Regional Traditions of Ethnographic Writing*, Edinburgh: Scottish Academic Press.

Fortes, M. and Evans-Pritchard, E.E. (eds) (1940) *African Political Systems*, London: Oxford University Press.

Freeman, D. (1983) *Margaret Mead and Samoa: The Making and Unmaking of an Anthropological Myth*, Cambridge, MA: Harvard University Press.

Guenther, M.G. (1986) *The Nharo Bushmen of Botswana: Tradition and Change*, Hamburg: Helmut Buske.

Hall, M. (1984) 'The myth of the Zulu homestead: archaeology and ethnography', *Africa* 54: 65–79.

Hammond-Tooke, W.D. (ed.) (1974) *The Bantu-Speaking Peoples of Southern Africa*, London: Routledge and Kegan Paul.

—— (1997) *Imperfect Interpreters: South Africa's Anthropologists 1920–1990*, Johannesburg: Witwatersrand University Press.

Harries, P. (1989) 'Exclusion, classification and internal colonialism: the emergence of ethnicity among the Tsonga-speakers of South Africa', in L. Vail (ed.) *The Creation of Tribalism in Southern Africa*, London: James Currey.

Heusch, L. de (1982) *Rois Nés d'un Cœur de Vache*, Paris: Gallimard.

Hoernlé, A.W. (1985) *The Social Organization of the Nama and Other Essays*, P. Carstens (ed.) Johannesburg: Witwatersrand University Press.

Holleman, J.F. (1940) 'Die twee-eenheidsbeginsel in die sosiale en politieke samelewing van did Zulu', *Bantu Studies* 14: 31–75.

—— (1941) 'Die Zulu isigodi', *Bantu Studies* 15: 91–118, 245–76.

Holmes, L.D. (1987) *Quest for the Real Samoa*, South Hadley, MA: Bergin and Harvey.

Huffman, T.N. (1982) 'Archaeology and ethnohistory of the African iron age', *Annual Review of Anthropology* 11: 133–50.

—— (1990) 'Broederstroom and the origins of cattle-keeping in Southern Africa', *African Studies* 49, 2: 1–12.

Hunter, M. (1936) *Reaction to Conquest: Effects of Contact with Europeans on the Pondo of South Africa*, London: Oxford University Press.

Josselin de Jong, P.E. de (ed.) (1984) *Unity in Diversity: Indonesia as a Field of Anthropological Study*, Dordrecht: Foris.

Junod, H.A. (1912) *The Life of a South African Tribe*, 2 volumes, Neuchatel: Imprimerie Attinger.

Kolb, P. (1968) *The Present State of the Cape of Good-Hope* (first German edition 1719; English translation 1731), New York: Johnson Reprint Corporation.

Kuper, A. (1976) 'Culture area or political system?', *Africa* 46, 3: 291–4.

—— (1982) *Wives for Cattle: Bridewealth and Marriage in Southern Africa*, London: Routledge.

—— (1987) *South Africa and the Anthropologist*, London: Routledge.

—— (1993) 'The "house" and Zulu political structure in the nineteenth century', *Journal of African History* 34: 469–87.

—— (1999) *Among the Anthropologists*, London: Athlone Press.

Lane, P. (1994–5) 'The use and abuse of ethnography in the study of the Southern African Iron Age', *Azania* XXIX–XXX: 51–64.

Leach, E.R. (1954) *Political Systems of Highland Burma: A Study of Kachin Social Structure*, foreword by Raymond Firth, London: London School of Economics and Political Science.

Lee, R.B. (1979) *The !Kung San: Men, Women, and Work in a Foraging Society*, Cambridge: Cambridge University Press.

Lee, R.B. and DeVore, I. (eds) (1968) *Man the Hunter*, Chicago: Aldine.

Lévi-Strauss, C. ([1949] 1969) *Elementary Structures of Kinship*, London: Eyre and Spottiswoode.

—— ([1964] 1969–[1968] 1981) *Mythologies*, 3 volumes, London: Cape.

McAllister, P. (ed.) (1997) *Culture and the Commonplace*, Johannesburg: Witwatersrand University Press.

Macmillan, W.M. (1929) *Bantu, Boer, and Briton: The Making of the South African Native Problem*, London: Faber and Gwyer.

Mair, L. (1962) *Primitive Government*, Harmondsworth: Penguin Books.

Malinowski, B. (1922) *Argonauts of the Western Pacific*, London: Kegan Paul.

—— (1932) *Crime and Custom in Savage Society*, London: Kegan Paul.

Mauss, M. ([1924] 1954) *The Gift: Forms and Functions of Exchange in Archaic Societies*, London: Cohen and West.

Mead, M. (1928) *Coming of Age in Samoa*, New York: Morrow.

Niehaus, I. (1994) 'Disharmonious spouses and harmonious siblings', *African Studies* 53, 1: 115–35.

Radcliffe-Brown, A.R. (1951) 'The comparative method in social anthropology', *Journal of the Royal Anthropological Institute* 18: 15–22.

—— (1953) 'On social structure', in *Structure and Function in Primitive Society*, London: Cohen and West, pp. 118–204.

Ross, R. (1993) *Beyond the Pale: Essays on the History of Colonial South Africa*, Hanover: Wesleyan University Press.

Sahlins, M. (1958) *Social Stratification in Polynesia*, Ann Arbor, MI: University of Michigan Press.

—— (1963) 'Poor Man, Rich Man, Big-Man, Chief: political types in Melanesia and Polynesia', *Comparative Studies in History and Society* 5: 285–303.

Saunders, C. (1988) *The Making of the South African Past: Major Historians on Race and Class*, Cape Town: David Philip.

Schapera, I. (1930) *The Khoisan Peoples of South Africa: Bushmen and Hottentots*, London: George Routledge.

—— (ed.) (1934) *Western Civilization and the Natives of South Africa: Studies in Culture Contact*, London: George Routledge and Sons.

—— (1937a) 'Cultural changes in tribal life', in I. Schapera (ed.) *The Bantu-Speaking Tribes of South Africa: An Ethnographical Survey*, London: George Routledge.

—— (1937b) *The Bantu-Speaking Tribes of South Africa: An Ethnographical Survey*, London: George Routledge and Sons.

—— (1956) *Government and Politics in Tribal Societies*, London: Watts.

Schultze, L. (1907) *Aus Namaland und Kalahari*, Jena: Custyav Fischer.

Soga, J.H. (1931) *The Ama-Xosa: Life and Customs*, London: Kegan Paul.

Stow, G.W. (1905) *The Native Races of South Africa*, London: Swan Sonnenschein.

Theal, G.M. (1910) *Ethnography and Condition of South Africa Before A.D. 1505*, London: Allen and Unwin.

Tylor, E.B. (1889) 'On a method of investigating the development of institutions; applied to laws of marriage and descent', *Journal of the Anthropological Institute* 18: 245–72.

Vail, L. (ed.) (1989) *The Creation of Tribalism in Southern Africa*, London: James Currey.

van Warmelo, N.J. (1952) 'Language map of South Africa', Pretoria: Government Printer.

Wilmsen, E.N. (1989) *Land Filled with Flies: A Political Economy of the Kalahari*, Chicago: University of Chicago Press.

Chapter 7

The study of historical transformation in American anthropology

Richard G. Fox

From the time of Franz Boas, many anthropologists in the United States have been quite sceptical of the comparative method used by nineteenth-century evolutionists.[1] They were equally wary of the cross-cultural comparisons later pursued in the name of science by Radcliffe-Brown and his followers.[2] Many American anthropologists feared that the comparative method and cross-cultural comparison too often sacrificed history and historical process in the pursuit of trite, superficial general laws.

Instead of cross-cultural comparison of this sort, American anthropologists have pursued a quite different method of comparison, namely, the study of what I shall call 'historical transformation'. This method focuses on the histories by which cultures have come to vary from an anterior state – that is, the histories through which they have become transformed. The study of historical transformation aims to understand the interplay of (historical) event and (cultural) structure that leads to variant outcomes. Rather than identifying general laws, it hopes to illuminate historical processes. Rather than comparing traits, institutions, beliefs, or other cultural 'facts', it compares the divergent outcomes of similar historical processes. Historical transformation defines a comparative anthropology as the study of variation over time.

In this chapter I briefly trace the history of the methodology of historical transformation in American anthropology, beginning with Boas and his critique of the comparative method. The most forthright theoretical statement of the methodology came from Fred Eggan, who tried to find a way to bring together British functional analysis of social structure and American historical anthropology. Aside from Eggan's own use of the method for the Western Pueblos, good examples of this methodology can be found in the Pawnee research by Alexander Lesser and the comparison of 'irrigation civilizations' by Julian Steward. Eric Wolf, in his concern for the 'lifelines' of cultures, has carried out this research programme further than anyone else. Other American scholars – for example, Clifford Geertz, Sidney Mintz and Marshall Sahlins – have also made studies using, in effect, the methodology of historical transformation. This methodology therefore crosses supposedly major theoretical differences in American anthropology and appears to develop out of an early and deep commitment to the study of historical process.

Franz Boas and the historical method

In 1896 Franz Boas strongly attacked the ahistorical assumptions built into the comparative method. The comparative method, Boas argued, assumed that whenever comparable cultural phenomena were found to exist at present, they must have had a common origin in the past. In opposition to this assumption, Boas gave several examples in which a current similarity in culture arose from separate – and therefore, non-comparable – histories. Totemic clans, Boas said, were widely distributed, but in some places they arose from the break-up of existing clans, whereas in others they came about from the combination of such kinship groups (Boas [1896] 1940: 273). Any comparison of totemic clans based on their present-day similarities, Boas contended, would impute a historical connection that did not necessarily exist.

Masks, found in many cultures, represented for Boas another instance of the comparative method's failings. In some cultures, masks were worn to scare off hostile spirits; in others, to disguise persons; in still others, to personify spirits. Some cultures used masks to commemorate a dead person, some used them to impersonate a god, some employed them as part of secular theatrical performances (ibid.: 274). How could any insightful comparison be made of masks with such different historically derived functions?

Boas sharply distinguished this illegitimate comparative method from the 'historical method' that he championed, of which he wrote:

> The object of our investigation is to find the *processes* by which certain stages of culture have developed. The customs and beliefs themselves are not the ultimate objects of research ... we wish to discover the history of their development.
>
> (Boas [1986] 1940: 276)

He also stipulated that initially, at least, this method must be employed on a regional level, for example, within a single culture area. By making comparisons over too wide a compass, Boas warned, one risks falling into the major error of the comparative method, namely, taking present-day similarities in cultural phenomena as evidence of their derivation from a common historical process. Boas thus initiated American anthropology into a distrust of comparisons that ignore history and that favour breadth of generalization over depth of context.

Alexander Lesser and 'careers in time'

Alexander Lesser, a student of Boas, took Boas's distaste for the comparative method and developed an alternative methodology, a methodology of historical transformation, in his 1933 study of Pawnee hand games (Lesser [1933] 1978). In the hand game played by the Pawnee Indians of the Great Plains, as Lesser describes it, several players on one team hid counters in their hands and tried to confuse their opponents so that they incorrectly guessed which hands held them. This description greatly simplifies a very complex game of chance, which Lesser discusses in loving detail (ibid.: 124–59). Lesser (ibid.: 334) analyses what he calls the 'career in time' of these hand games, a term that bears a remarkable resemblance to Eric Wolf's later concept of 'lifeline' (which I shall discuss shortly). By 'career in time', Lesser means that a cultural institution such as the hand game has a core that persists over time, but that other features associated with this institution can be transformed. In the case of the hand games, the persistent core is the actual play of the game; the context in which the game was played and the significance of the game in Pawnee society, however, underwent major transformation.

Before 1890, Lesser tells us, Pawnee hand games were simply recreational – they were merry occasions for gambling. By the end of the nineteenth century, however, as the consequences of white domination took hold, the Pawnees had come to what Lesser terms a 'cultural impasse'. The US government pursued a policy of assimilation that stripped the Pawnees of their social, political and religious institutions and destroyed the pre-contact tribal economy in favour of individual land allotments (Lesser [1933] 1978: 105). Pawnee life in 1892 was 'barren' and 'empty of cultural value', according to Lesser (ibid.: 328), and by then, even the hand games had fallen into desuetude. In that year, however, the Ghost Dance religion, a revivalist movement that swept across Native American populations at this time, came to the Pawnees from further west. The Ghost Dance revived the persistent core of the hand games – that is, the *way* they were played – at the same time that it transformed the context in which the core set of relationships existed. The hand games became ritual performances, not occasions for gambling, and were incorporated into the Ghost Dance religion.

The subsequent 'career in time' of the Pawnee hand games shows further transformations. After the Ghost Dance died down among the Pawnees and Christianity reasserted itself, the Protestant Church took over sponsorship of the games. The connection with religion and ritual forged in the Ghost Dance days thus persisted, but in a new religious context. The final transformation of the games was under way when Lesser did his ethnography in the 1930s. By this time, the games had moved out of the churches and into homes – there to be played as a Pawnee alternative to standard Euro-American parlour games such as bridge, rummy or canasta. This last transformation reflected the Americanized domesticity that had come to rule Pawnee life.

In his Pawnee research, Lesser put into practice what Boas took to be the defining element of the historical method: namely, the study of historical process. Through concepts like 'career in time' and 'core' sets of relationships, Lesser refined the methodology of what I have labelled 'historical transformation'. He writes:

> When we understand one basic form and follow it through a series of transformations, we have a foundation for statements of the character of

processes of change, and what these indicate as to the identity of the institution or complex considered through its changing phases.

(Lesser [1933] 1978: 330)

Starting with a single cultural form or trait, Lesser took the appearance of variations or varieties over time as central to his method. His objective was to explain the historical processes through which X trait or institution becomes transformed into X^1, which in turn becomes X^2, and so on. Lesser's use of the term 'form' indicates that he was still wedded to Boasian anthropology's focus on the 'culture trait', but his recognition of sets of relationships shows that he placed culture traits within a wider context in which some relationships are more functionally integrated than others and thereby make up the core.

Lesser's historical method seems to have had little immediate influence on the discipline, as anthropology abandoned culture history in favour of studies in culture and personality just before World War II. The historical method revived only with anthropology's renewed interest in cultural evolution after the war, although even then it remained a minority orientation.

Fred Eggan and controlled comparison

Some twenty years after the publication of *The Pawnee Ghost Dance Hand Game*, the fact that Fred Eggan either did not know of Lesser's work or did not see its relevance indicates that the study of historical transformation developed as a subaltern and intermittent scholarship in American anthropology. In 1954, however, Eggan alluded to Boas's 1896 article and adopted similar misgivings about overly broad comparisons. Eggan (1954) directed his apprehension, however, at the comparative methodology then being practised by A.R. Radcliffe-Brown, who sought to discover general and widespread cross-cultural principles of social structure, such as the 'joking relations' and the 'equivalence of siblings' he associated with unilineal descent groups (Radcliffe-Brown [1952] 1963, [1951] 1970). For Eggan, such 'universal comparisons' were suspiciously large-scale, and he rejected them in favour of a method he called 'controlled comparison' (Eggan 1954: 747).

Eggan states that the methodology of controlled comparison attempts to combine Radcliffe-Brown's quest for a scientific functionalism and for cross-cultural comparison with American anthropology's emphasis on history and process. Whatever Eggan's intentions, the methodology he proposed is much closer to the 'historical method' recommended by Boas than to Radcliffe-Brown's pursuit of grand theory by means of very broad comparisons. Controlled comparison, explained Eggan, operates 'on a smaller scale' than Radcliffe-Brown's universal comparisons, and 'with as much control over the frame of comparison as it is possible to secure'. Echoing Boas, Eggan continues: 'It has seemed natural to utilize regions of relatively homogeneous culture or to work

within social or cultural types, and to further control the ecology and the historical factors so far as it is possible' (Eggan 1954: 747).

Eggan gives an example of his methodology in practice from his work on the
kinship organization of the Western Pueblos, where he noted what he calls the
'variations' in kinship types that arose from an original Puebloan kinship
system. He thus dealt with forms of descent historically by looking at the
processes underlying transformations of an original type (ibid.: 758).

The term 'controlled comparison' that Eggan proposed for his methodology
emphasized the small-scale procedure he followed in comparison to Radcliffe-
Brown's cross-cultural methodology. It is quite misleading, however, in terms of
defining the actual focus of comparison he recommends. Eggan emphasizes
comparative methodology based on a focus on history and processes over time;
it is more than just comparison within narrow ('controlled') geographical
boundaries or comparison with a limited design. We find both these aspects –
the emphasis on historical process and the requirement that comparison be
restricted in scope – in Eggan's example of the sort of question his comparative
methodology would take on. 'Why', he asked of future research based on
controlled comparison 'did tribal groups coming into the Plains from
surrounding regions, with radically different social structures, tend to develop a
similar type?' (Eggan 1954: 757).

Some later anthropologists in the US elaborated Eggan's approach by developing its controlled aspect over its engagement with historical process (see
Vogt 1994). The objective of this 'phylogenetic model' is 'the delineation of
phylogenies or historical sequences of divergence from a common ancestor'
(Kirch and Green [1987], quoted in Vogt 1994: 377). The phylogenetic model
seems to extend Eggan's notion in the wrong direction, however, because it
requires that the groups to be compared share a common physical type and
speak historically related languages. This requirement does allow a highly
controlled comparison, and within such a narrowed field any variant or divergence can be safely assumed to arise from a common historical process. The
model therefore answers the criticism Boas made of the comparative method,
but it does so at considerable intellectual cost. It greatly narrows the boundaries of comparison, and historical processes cease to be the objective of
research; instead, only the empirical varieties arising from the process of divergence are put under scrutiny.

Other American anthropologists elaborated the second aspect by which
Eggan distinguished his methodology of comparison from that of Radcliffe-
Brown. These scholars have emphasized the study of historical processes and the
cultural transformations to which they give rise, even if that has required them
to go beyond the boundaries of a single region or culture area. Indeed, they take
a shared historical process as the basis of any comparison, and the empirical
outcomes of this process may appear so unlike that their common history may
be hidden. Examples are the divergences among anthropology's so-called primitive peoples, most of them in fact the outcome of transformations brought on by

contact with European capitalism, or the divergent nationalisms thrown up by modernity (see my later discussion of Eric Wolf and Clifford Geertz).

Not all of these anthropologists come from the same theoretical school, and none of them studied historical transformation exclusively. Some employed the methodology before Eggan defined it, and still others, coming afterward, acknowledge neither Eggan, Lesser nor Boas as sources for their ideas. The approach they share seems to arise from a general predilection among American anthropologists for cultural-historical investigation – a predilection augmented by healthy doses of historicity from Weberian and Marxist sources, especially after World War II. There has been surprisingly little discussion of this shared methodology, however.

Julian Steward and the study of 'developmental regularities'

Also shortly after World War II, and before Eggan's publication on the Western Pueblos, Julian Steward made two major innovations in the historical method: he studied the historical transformation of entire societies, not just individual cultural institutions, and he looked for cross-cultural regularities in cultural evolution. At the same time that Steward greatly broadened the purview of the historical method, his search for regularities and laws moved it away from the study of actual histories and towards the comparison of evolutionary types or levels.

In 1949, Steward put forward an approach he would later call 'multilinear evolution' and called for a renewed interest in 'developmental regularities' across cultures (Steward 1949). Anthropology needed to develop causal explanations of cultural development, which, in turn, would generate scientific laws. Steward's 'trial formulation' involved the rise of early civilizations in the Near East and the New World. He compared the 'primary' cultural institutions that arose in Mesopotamia, Egypt, China, Mesoamerica and Peru in order to find the shared causal factor or developmental regularity underlying their individual patterns. Steward later refined his idea of primary cultural institutions into the concept of a 'cultural core' consisting of those functionally interrelated institutions most responsive to ecological conditions (Steward [1955b] 1972: 6). In 1949, however, he presented a sequence of eras (which he later called 'developmental eras') – Incipient Agriculture, Formative, Florescent and so forth – that each early civilization supposedly passed through (Steward 1949: 8–9). To explain this 'succession of culture types' (Steward 1955a: 3) or 'cross-cultural types' (Steward [1955b] 1972: 88), Steward took irrigation as the causal factor, asserting that the growth of irrigation agriculture as an ecological adaptation created conditions for the eventual development of civilization in each of these areas.

Steward makes very clear that his goal is the identification of scientific regularities, not the presentation of individual histories; general causal factors, not particular historical processes. He states:

The objective of multilinear evolution ... differs from that of the more strictly historical approaches in that it seeks to ascertain the causes of cultural phenomena and to formulate them as laws in a scientific, generalizing sense, whereas the latter is more interested in tracing the history ... of different cultural features.

(Steward 1955a: 1)

Steward's version of the historical method was a significant departure from a methodology of historical transformation, since he did not study the actual historical processes by which simple societies were transformed into early civilizations in each area of the world. Instead, he compared cross-cultural *types*, whose validity depended on a causal factor – irrigation – that was assumed to have similar effects across cultures. Steward's purpose, after all, was to find evolutionary convergences, not historical variations, but because he claimed an interest in divergent outcomes (in comparison to unilinear evolutionists like White and Childe), it was easy to mistake his multilinear evolution for a methodology of historical transformation. That it was not will become clear in my discussions of Sidney Mintz and Eric Wolf, Steward's students but not his acolytes.

Eric Wolf and the 'lifeline' of a civilization

Eric Wolf returned the historical method to studies of cultural variation and transformation as they take place within real historical processes. His work does not focus on evolutionary levels, as Steward's does. Instead, Wolf emphasizes the historical processes by which a core set of relationships can lead to divergent outcomes as it manifests itself in different times, places and cultures.

In the following analysis, I concentrate on the historical transformations Wolf studied in such works as *Sons of the Shaking Earth* (1959) and *Europe and the People without History* (1982) rather than the related but different procedure he follows in *Peasant Wars of the Twentieth Century* (1969) and *Envisioning Power* (1998) (among others). After I analyse Wolf's approach to the study of historical transformations, I will make clear how it differs from this other methodology, which I term 'controlled case studies'.

To understand Wolf's approach to historical transformation, I find the concepts of 'diffusion' and 'descent' useful, even though Wolf does not use these terms. By 'diffusion', I refer to Wolf's emphasis on the history through which these core sets of relationships spread from their source to take over new locales. Unlike the Boasian notion, diffusion in this sense emphasizes the power relations that allow one institution – European capitalism, for example – to spread out from its source and transform other areas of the world. I use 'descent' to characterize Wolf's approach to the reproduction or transformation of cultural institutions over time. Wolf traces genealogies of power relations in a society and how they materialize in new racial, class and ethnic identities. Neither in mapping diffusion nor in tracing descent does Wolf depend on evolutionary eras or levels, however. The regularities he finds are the core sets of relationships themselves, and what is variable is the historical process by which they take form. For Wolf, the variety of ways in which such processes play out cannot be contained within an evolutionary typology such as Steward's. Instead, like Lesser, Wolf attempts, in effect, to trace out 'careers in time', but at the level of whole societies.

As he expanded his viewpoint to account for global changes, Wolf also refined his historical methodology, becoming more concerned with tracing the human agencies and contingencies behind historical transformation. In his early work, *Sons of the Shaking Earth*, Wolf says his purpose is 'to trace the life-line of a culture' (1959: vii). To that end, he provides a sweeping cultural history of Middle America from its prehistoric beginnings up to the present. Wolf periodizes his chronicle in terms of important institutional and cultural transformations in this region. Its lifeline is punctuated by major changes in power, as, for example, when Spanish conquistadors replaced an indigenous elite. This lifeline also includes the development of new power seekers, like the *mestizo* offspring of Spaniards and Indians, and of new subalterns, the Indians, now incorporated into the emerging nations of Mexico and Guatemala.

The lifeline concept was not yet fully realized at this early point in Wolf's work. It is not clear, for example, what, if any, continuity lies behind the long narrative of Middle American cultural history – that is, what set of relationships might constitute a 'core' or a line of descent over time similar to Lesser's analysis of the 'career in time' of the Pawnee hand games. There is an implicit argument, however, that the core consists of relations of power and inequality, which, as they undergo transformation at key historical points, constitute the life course of Middle America.

Wolf makes this core institution and the historical transformation it undergoes explicit in his later work, *Europe and the People without History* (Wolf 1982). This rich narrative reveals how the West made 'the Rest' – the non-Western world that anthropologists later treated as untouched and autochthonous. The core institution behind this forceful diffusion of European culture was capitalism, initially in its mercantilist form and later transformed into an industrial variety. As it diffused to regions beyond Europe, capitalism materialized in many different ways – the fur trade among North American Indians, slave plantations in the Caribbean, bonded peasantries in India and Southeast Asia. Wolf chronicles these divergent outcomes as this core institution created new lifelines of culture across the globe – except that he does not use that trenchant phrase from his early work in this book. Instead, he speaks of 'chains of causation and consequence' that drove 'people of diverse origins and social makeup' to create an interlinked world (Wolf 1982: 385). Perhaps the new terminology highlights Wolf's greater concern for agency in this later work, and his seeming desire to ensure that the human actions making up a lifeline are remembered – and not disappeared by any reified notion of a cultural life-line. To that end, he writes:

> We can no longer think of societies as isolated and self-maintaining systems. Nor can we imagine cultures as integrated totalities ... There are only cultural sets of practices and ideas, put into play by determinate human actors under determinate circumstances. In the course of action, these cultural sets are forever assembled, dismantled, and reassembled.
>
> (Wolf 1982: 391)

I think Wolf's original notion of lifeline could easily accommodate his later emphasis on human agency; in fact, I would argue that even his early work treated a civilization's lifeline as something that emerged from human action placed in history. But by 1982, Wolf had come to reject any lingering super-organic and holistic notions of culture. The concept of lifeline, if applied to his later work, would refer to a core set of relationships such as capitalism, not to an entire civilization, as it had in his early writings. Wolf now recognizes that there are multiple lifelines, which represent the divergent paths taken by the core institution as it, a cultural practice, is put into new contexts of play. On a much larger scale than Lesser but in a similar manner, Wolf shows the historical processes by which the capitalist mode of production manifests itself as it encounters new worlds and peoples. The result is an array of historical outcomes – production based on slaves here, on peasants there, on Indians left 'primitive' still elsewhere – that indicate the historical transformations, the divergent contexts, in which this core institution operates.

Wolf uses a somewhat different methodology in such works as *Peasant Wars of the Twentieth Century* (1969) and his last volume, *Envisioning Power* (1998). In these studies, he makes it clear that there is no necessary historical connec-tion among the cases under examination. In *Envisioning Power*, for example, he compares the sixteenth-century Aztecs, the nineteenth-century Kwakiutl and the twentieth-century Nazis; in *Europe and the People without History*, by contrast, he analyses only those societies overcome by and harnessed to European capitalism. When Wolf compares historically unconnected cases, his objective is precisely to discover any cross-cultural regularities that might exist, as, for example, Did the middle-peasant class instigate agrarian upheavals in twentieth-century peasant wars? In his studies of historical transformation, however, Wolf begins with a core set of relationships, such as capitalism, that affects all of his historical cases and leads to variant outcomes under different historical conditions. Comparing historically disconnected cases, Wolf ends up with a set of relationships shared in spite of the different times and societies. In this volume, Andre Gingrich employs this latter method, what I wish to call 'controlled case studies', to find the similarities underlying several different cases of 'dethroned majorities'.

Sidney Mintz and the return to 'careers in time'

To this point I have traced an intellectual line of descent from Boas through Lesser to Wolf, with Steward and Eggan positioned in somewhat collateral relationships to this lineage. The actual links were much more complex, of course, and there was never a single line of descent or a single method of analysis. For example, even though I have argued that Wolf shares more with Lesser than he does with Steward, the fact is that Wolf was a student of Steward and did not know Lesser's work until quite late. Although having no direct contact with Eggan, Wolf was introduced to his concept of controlled comparison while still a student, and thought well of it (Wolf 1999).[3] Sidney Mintz, by comparison, studied as an undergraduate with Lesser and did graduate work with Steward, but he uses Lesser's methodology only in his later work, and Steward's hardly at all.

In his illuminating study of sugar as comestible, commodity and cultural trait, Mintz (1985) comes closest among contemporary anthropologists to Lesser's methodology, but he applies it on a much vaster scale. Although he does not explicitly use the concepts Lesser developed, Mintz has long admired Lesser's work, and its influence on *Sweetness and Power* is clear. Mintz starts with a core institution, 'sugar', and its fundamental cultural characteristics: that it pleases the human palate, that it is processed from sugar cane (mainly), that human labour must be harnessed for its production and that access to it demands economic and political arrangements that usually involve inequality. Mintz then traces out the 'career in time' of sugar by chronicling the cultural beliefs and practices that have attached to it over a long history as the modern world system emerged. For example, he shows sugar's development from being a scarce medicine for the wealthy in precapitalist Europe to becoming a plentiful source of cheap calories for the burgeoning European working class in the nineteenth century. Coincident with these transformations in cultural usage go alterations in the conditions for the production of sugar: among them, the growth of European sugar colonies in the Caribbean, dependent on the transportation of African slave labour and the subsequent importation of indentured East Indians.

Lesser chronicled the history by which the Pawnee hand games transformed from entertainment to religious rituals to (parlour) games once again. Mintz similarly shows the changing roles that sugar played as it, a core institution, became embedded in different cultural contexts: from being a potent and scarce medicine, it became a powerful and cheap food that directed major alterations in the world economy and population. Today, sugar has become an additive that is taken for granted, rarely even noticed, but is nevertheless a significant component in almost all prepared foods.

I now want to move laterally across this intellectual genealogy and discuss the historical methodologies of Clifford Geertz and Marshall Sahlins. Both Sahlins and Geertz are contemporaries of Wolf and Mintz, but they come from very different intellectual orientations: modernization theory defined Geertz's approach at the time in his career I will discuss; Sahlins, once strongly inclined towards Steward's ideas, abandoned them for a modified French structuralism. My aim is to show how despite this, their viewpoints are sibling to Lesser's and Wolf's historical methodology. No doubt Boas would be pleased to learn that scholars like Geertz and Sahlins, so different in their theoretical allegiances, could end up – in terms of historical methodology – close to Wolf and Lesser. It would confirm in the world of scholarship the convergent evolution that Boas believed quite common in the real world of culture – his major argument against the comparative method, as we have seen. For me, it confirms that the methodology of historical transformation develops out of a general, albeit subaltern, orientation towards the study of cultural history in American anthropology. This orientation leads to similar approaches by scholars who may not have known each others' work, who did not study historical transformations exclusively and who therefore might reject any suggestion of intellectual connection. The subaltern status of this orientation probably interfered with the elaboration of its methodology, as, for example, in the work of Wolf and Mintz, where it is employed but not explicitly theorized. For the same reason, it has proved difficult for scholars with different theoretical perspectives to recognize the methodology they in fact shared. In evidence, I take up briefly some selected works by Geertz and Sahlins that represent studies in historical transformation.

Clifford Geertz, Marshall Sahlins and doing history backward

In *Islam Observed* (1968), Clifford Geertz compares the historical transformation of religious faith in Morocco and in Indonesia, focusing on the actions of charismatic individuals in both societies to explain why they institutionalized different forms of Islam. Kalidjaga, whom Geertz treats as an exemplary religious innovator in Indonesia, fused existing Hindu elements, especially asceticism, with the Islam he celebrated. Lyushi, Kalidjaga's Moroccan counterpart, brought forth an Islam that depended on force of character and the superior sanctity it conferred upon certain people – saints – and their descendants.

Geertz then investigates a general crisis in faith – akin to Weber's notion of 'disenchantment' – that came to Indonesia and Morocco as they attempted to become modern nations. This crisis created very different accommodations in the two societies, as they responded in terms of their respective Islams. In Morocco, the nation was embodied and led by a sultan with routinized charisma; in Indonesia, a leader had to prove his worthiness to lead by continual symbolic acts that would construct a national community. Geertz chronicles a complex history of what we might call two core sets of relationship – first Islam, then modernity – and the ways they affected widely separated parts of the world. As Islam constructed faith in very different ways in Morocco and Indonesia, it also set the terms for the reaction of these societies to the loss of faith that modernization would later bring.

Geertz calls his methodology 'doing history backward', but it bears a very strong resemblance to Wolf's lifelines. Geertz allows that a core set of relationships can materialize quite differently as a result of specific historical processes; he also devalues cultural determinism in favour of individual agency.[4] In addition, Geertz is more explicit about his historical methodology than anyone other than Eggan. Geertz writes:

> What we want to know is ... by what mechanisms and from what causes these extraordinary transformations have taken place. And for this we need to train our attention ... on processes, on the way in which things stop being what they are and become instead something else.
> ... [T]o pose the problem as I have ... is to do history backward. Knowing ... the outcome, we look for how, out of a certain sort of situation obtaining in the past, that outcome was produced. ... [I]t is all too easy to reverse the reasoning and to assume that given the past situation the present was bound to arise. This is, in fact, the mistake ... that the social evolutionists ... and all varieties of historical determinists make ... From the shape of things in Kalidjaga's or Lyushi's time thousands of futures were accessible. The fact that only one was reached proves not that the present was implicit in the past but that in history events are possibilities before they happen and certainties after .... Life ... is lived forward but understood backward.
>
> (Geertz 1968: 59–60)

In his studies of changes in Hawaiian society after the arrival of the Europeans, Marshall Sahlins approaches Geertz's history-backward question – Why did Hawaiian society change in the way it did, and not in some other way? – by presenting, in effect, Hawaii's lifeline. He demonstrates that Hawaiian commoners and chiefs, or men and women, attempted to reproduce their pre-contact cultural understandings but within a framework already altered by European intervention. The result was that the more the Hawaiians acted to maintain cultural meanings and relationships, the more they altered them. For Sahlins, acting culturally always puts cultural understandings at the risk of revaluation, and any one structural relationship deformed by such action pressures and reconfigures other relationships. Sahlins shows, for example, how Hawaiian notables transformed the indigenous concept of *mana* into the conspicuous consumption of foreign goods: the elect status formerly enjoyed by chiefs was now to be ratified by the latest fashions from the mainland; the spiritual awe the chiefs once elicited was now to be inspired by their sporting the latest mode (Sahlins 1985: 138–51).

Sahlins says less than Wolf or Geertz about possible divergent outcomes, but this may be because he presents the Hawaiian lifeline alone, whereas Geertz contrasts Morocco and Indonesia and Wolf presents multiple contingent outcomes. Alternatively, it may be because Sahlins believes that the pre-existing culture severely limits historical possibilities for transformation at any moment in time. Sahlins also differs from Wolf and Geertz in that his analysis does not focus on a core set of relationships such as capitalism or Islam and the historical manifestations that core set assumes. Instead, he places Hawaiian culture itself at the centre of the historical transformations he analyses. In this respect, Sahlins's analysis is most akin to Wolf's treatment of the lifelines of Middle American culture.

Sikh culture in the making

To conclude this chapter, I give two examples of the way I have used the methodology of historical transformation. One involves an anticolonial movement in British India based on Sikh identity; the other analyses the transformation of Gandhian protest methods in the United States. In both cases, I hope to show how this methodology can be further elaborated and, in particular, to show how historical contingency and social agency are necessary ingredients of it.

In the case of the Sikhs, the question was, Why was it a Sikh identity and not a Hindu one that mobilized mass protest against colonialism in Punjab during the 1920s (Fox 1985)? My starting point in this analysis was Wolf's core institution of capitalism as it diffused from Europe to India under the aegis of British colonialism. I then followed capitalism's lifeline or career in time in northern India by describing the transformations British colonialism induced in the Punjab. Rule by Britain reduced rural cultivators to debt bondage, which colonial authorities used as a means to impose the cultivation of market crops like wheat and sugar cane. In order to supplement the family income, many cultivators sent sons off to the British Indian army, where their service as mercenaries permitted them to remit money home. In cities, colonialism subsidized the growth of an English-educated Indian professional class: bureaucrats, lawyers, teachers and others who could staff the British administration more cheaply or provide it with services more economically than could professionals brought from England.

By the early twentieth century, the urban educated elite in the Punjab had created two reformist cultural associations, one based on a renovated notion of Hinduism (the Arya Samaj), the other formulated in pursuit of a renewed Sikh orthodoxy (Singh Sabha). At the time, it was equally probable that an anticolonial mass movement would collect around either of these organizations and the Hindu or Sikh identity each championed – both movements, after all, promoted nativist Indian sentiment against the British. In the event, an attempted Hindu protest in 1907 failed, whereas shortly after World War I, a mass movement based on Sikh identity threatened British rule fundamentally and for several years. The rebellion was only put down by violent state repression and back-door liaisons between the government and certain Sikh leaders, and, even then, the British had to offer the Sikhs many concessions.

The Sikh anticolonial protest provides an excellent example of why doing history backward is necessary. We know what happened in history, but we also know that it did not have to happen in only that way: therefore, we must explain why a Sikh protest succeeded and a Hindu movement failed. The salient fact is that the orthodox Sikh identity put forward by urban reformers mobilized rural cultivators who had failed to respond to an earlier protest based on Hinduism. The ethnic boundary separating rural Sikhs from Hindus at the time was very fuzzy; Sikhs and Hindus intermarried freely, their religious practices overlapped and many Sikhs considered themselves only a sect within Hinduism. But the cultivators had been primed to accept orthodox Sikh identity by their experience of British military recruitment, which supposed that Sikhs were a martial race and enforced an equivalent orthodoxy on those inducted into the army. As the British military sharply marked the Hindu/Sikh ethnic boundary by its recruitment strategies, it also laid the basis for the appeal of the urban reformers in the rural areas. Once the movement turned overtly anticolonial, the now rebellious Sikhs' British military experience also provided the mass protest with martial discipline, organization and courage.

The Sikh case shows historical transformation is always contingent; in other words, the historical processes surrounding a core set of relationships are complex and can potentially lead to many different manifestations. Only by tracing the processes that create a particular manifestation is it possible to answer the question of why one outcome prevails over others.

Transformations of Gandhian protest

My research on the use of Gandhian non-violence in social movements in the United States elaborates Lesser's notion of a core institution that has a career in time. Gandhi developed non-violent resistance (*satyagraha*) in South Africa and India. By about 1920, he had established a pattern of social protest, *satyagraha*'s institutional core, on the basis of several elements: a moral commitment to non-violence, mass protest and civil disobedience. Gandhi himself believed that other elements were just as essential to his non-violence, such as spinning, vegetarianism, teetotalism, celibacy, boycotts and penitential fasting (Fox 1989).

The question is, What happened to Gandhi's protest method when it took passage to America? How was it transformed as activists in the US developed versions that added or subtracted elements from the original formulation? Wolf suggests the general notion that 'cultural sets of practices and ideas, put into play by determinate human actors under determinate circumstances ... are assembled, dismantled, and reassembled' (Wolf 1982: 391), and in the US Gandhian protest is precisely dismantled and reassembled. It undergoes an historical process of what I have called cultural 'dis-integration', and then reintegration in novel forms (Fox 1995). This history consists of the ways in which different elements of Gandhian protest were subtracted, augmented or put together in new combinations. By emphasizing a 'dis-integrated' view of culture, we can explain cultural innovation as the product of putting existing cultural forms into new combinations.

Gandhian protest methods did not take passage easily from India to the Americas. Activists in the United States initially mistranslated non-violent resistance either as being akin to Christian non-resistance and pacifism, and therefore nothing new ('over-likeness'), or as being so dependent on Indian culture that it would never work in America ('hyper-difference') (Fox 1997). To overcome mistranslating Gandhian protest by 'hyper-difference', US leaders of the non-violence movement consciously or unconsciously eliminated certain aspects of Gandhian non-violence, such as vegetarianism, celibacy, spinning and (initially) penitential fasting. To surmount mistranslating it by 'over-likeness', other elements, such as boycott, mass marches and civil disobedience – and, later, property destruction and 'blockading' – became central.

By the 1940s, Gandhian protest had been more properly translated to the US, mainly in mass marches, real or threatened (such as A. Philip Randolph's March on Washington Movement), and in small-scale civil disobedience (by the Congress of Racial Equality (CORE) and James Farmer). After Martin Luther King, Jr.'s use of non-violent resistance in Montgomery, Alabama, in 1955 (in the form of boycott), non-violent resistance burgeoned – and went through additional transformations. By the 1960s and 1970s, several varieties coexisted: Cesar Chavez reintroduced penitential fasting and joined it with boycotts and mass marches; anti-Vietnam protesters began to practise mass civil disobedience. The Berrigan brothers added two more elements in the 1970s: property destruction (of draft records) and avoidance of legal punishment for civil disobedience (by hiding out). In the 1980s and 1990s, we have seen further transformations: Greenpeace and Operation Rescue have introduced blockades, forcibly preventing access in a way Gandhi never did in India but still claiming to be non-violent. Some animal-rights activists release animals and destroy research facilities, all the while insisting that they are votaries of non-violence. Captain Paul Mitchell and his Sea Shepherds ram and sink whaling ships – non-violently, they say, because they make every attempt to spare the ships' crews. By late in the twentieth century, then, Gandhian non-violence has been transformed into many new forms and operates in novel contexts, just as the Pawnee hand games started out as games, then became rituals and ended up as games again.

Conclusion

In 1961, when E.R. Leach decried British structural–functionalism as 'butterfly collecting', his dislike included much more than just the legacy of Radcliffe-Brown. Leach (1961) attacked any comparative anthropology that depended on creating abstract categories or types from empirical cases and then comparing these derived types to discover correlations, associations and universal laws. Radcliffe-Brown's cross-cultural comparison was only an early and rather undeveloped version of this methodology. Leach undoubtedly would have said even worse about today's 'holocultural studies', which, although mainly North American, continue Radcliffe-Brown's search for general laws through cross-cultural comparison in a much more sophisticated (and numerate) way (Levinson and Malone 1980; Naroll *et al.* 1976). What troubled Leach about these methodologies – and what troubles many anthropologists today, as, for example, Thomas Fillitz in this volume – is their high cost in terms of empirical richness and their resultant inability to deal with actual cultural or institutional change over time. How, for example, could history be brought to bear on Radcliffe-Brown's principle of the equivalence of siblings, which claims a universal and timeless correlation with societies having clans and lineages?

Instead of examining historical processes, these comparative methodologies require categorizing, in the case of Radcliffe-Brown's studies, or coding, in the case of holocultural correlation analyses. Coding and classifying, which is what Leach meant by butterfly collecting, necessarily sacrifices cultural particulars in the quest for defining general types. Finding, for example, that certain forms of religious belief correlate with certain levels of social stratification comes at too high a cost for many anthropologists, just as Radcliffe-Brown dissatisfied Leach when he generalized about the correlation between joking relations and unilineal descent groups. If the trade-off of empirical richness and historical depth for general statements is not acceptable, the question then becomes, What sort of comparative methodology will pay off for anthropologists?

In this chapter, I have discussed one such comparative methodology, based on the analysis of historical transformation. A comparative methodology that rests on the study of controlled comparisons, lifelines, and careers in time and on doing history backward commits to a fundamental historicity. It is rich in phenomena, but eschews general laws. It makes comparisons, but only within historically determined lines of descent, some of which, however, like Wolf's studies of the capitalist world system, are global in breadth. Its focus is on the study of historical process; specifically, the process of transformation by which core cultural practices and beliefs – what I have called sets of relationships – take variant forms as they move through time, diffuse to new locales and operate in new social contexts.

These historical processes define the lines of descent within which comparison is made, and they can encompass a range from the diffusion of European capitalism, at the widest, to, much more narrowly, the spread of Gandhian protest methods from India to North America. This range corresponds roughly to the difference between Wolf's concept of lifelines and Lesser's notion of careers in time, which differ mostly in the scale of the historical process under study. Although its basic principles have never been formally elaborated in full, this methodology has nevertheless informed American anthropology's actual practice over a long period. It is the way many American anthropologists have accommodated their distaste for the comparative method or for cross-cultural comparison to their felt need that some kind of comparative understanding was necessary. To that end, many anthropologists in the USA have practised comparison as the study of historical variation. The outcome has been an anthropology well suited to understanding how historical contingencies can come to transform cultural structures or institutions in variant ways.

Notes

1 Throughout this chapter, I use the label 'comparative method' to refer to the particular methodology of comparison championed by nineteenth-century evolutionists.
2 I want to thank Andre Gingrich, Thomas Fillitz and other members of the September 1998 Vienna conference, 'Comparative methods in social and cultural anthropology', for their comments on this chapter. I also received valuable comments from Rayna Rapp. My greatest debt, however, is to Eric Wolf, who clarified many of the historical issues raised in the chapter and also gently prodded me to correct its original lazy use of terms. It was our last conversation – in Cape Town in January of 1999. In it, Wolf helped me immeasurably with this chapter in particular, and, as in all our conversations, with my ideas in general.
3 Wolf learned of Eggan when he used course notes from Eggan's University of Chicago classes on American Indians to study for his Columbia University prelims. In using these notes – which Wolf had borrowed from John Murra, a Chicago PhD, because Columbia did not offer such a course – Wolf became acquainted with the notion of controlled comparison (E.R. Wolf, personal communication 1999).
4 Geertz's concern with agency leads him to emphasize the role of charismatic individuals, whereas Wolf locates agency in groups thrown into conflict by relations of inequality. Here I minimize this commonly recognized difference in order to draw out the similarities between Geertz and Wolf, which are rarely acknowledged.

Bibliography

Boas, F. ([1896] 1940) 'The limitations of the comparative method of anthropology', in F. Boas (ed.) *Race, Language and Culture*, New York: Macmillan, pp. 270–80.

Eggan, F. (1950) *Social Organization of the Western Pueblos*, Chicago: University of Chicago Press.

—— (1954) 'Social anthropology and the method of controlled comparison', *American Anthropologist* 56: 743–63.

Fox, R.G. (1985) *Lions of the Punjab: Culture in the Making*, Berkeley, CA: University of California Press.

—— (1989) *Gandhian Utopia: Experiments with Culture*, Boston: Beacon Press.

—— (1995) 'Dis-integrating culture and the invention of new peace-fares', in R. Rapp and J. Schneider (eds) *Articulating Hidden Histories*, Berkeley, CA: University of California Press, pp. 275–87.

—— (1997) 'Passage from India', in R.G. Fox and O. Starn (eds) *Between Resistance and Revolution*, New Brunswick: Rutgers University Press, pp. 65–82.

Geertz, C. (1968) *Islam Observed*, Chicago: University of Chicago Press.

Leach, E.R. (1961) *Rethinking Anthropology*, London: Athlone.

Lesser, A. ([1933] 1978) *The Pawnee Ghost Dance Hand Game*, Madison, WI: University of Wisconsin Press.

Kirch, P.V. and Green, R.C. (1987) 'History, phylogeny and evolution in Polynesia', *Current Anthropology* 28: 431–56.

Levinson, D. and Malone, M.J. (1980) *Toward Explaining Human Culture*, New Haven, CT: HRAF Press.

Mintz, S.W. (1985) *Sweetness and Power*, New York: Penguin.

Naroll, R. *et al.* (1976) *Worldwide Theory Testing*, New Haven, CT: HRAF Press.

Radcliffe-Brown, A.R. ([1951] 1970) 'A case for the comparative method', in A. Etzioni and F.L. Dubow (eds) *Comparative Perspectives*, Boston: Little, Brown, pp. 17–24.

—— ([1952] 1963) *Structure and Function in Primitive Society*, London: Cohen and West.

Sahlins, M. (1985) *Islands of History*, Chicago: University of Chicago Press.

Steward, J. (1949) 'Cultural causality and law: a trial formulation of the development of early civilizations', *American Anthropologist* 51: 1–27.

—— (1955a) 'Introduction', in J. Steward (ed.) *Irrigation Civilizations: A Symposium*, Washington, DC: Pan American Union, pp. 1–5.

—— ([1955b] 1972) *Theory of Culture Change*, Urbana, IL: University of Illinois Press.

Vogt, E.Z. (1994) 'On the application of the phylogenetic model to the Maya', in R.J. DeMaillie and A. Ortiz (eds) *North American Indian Anthropology*, Norman, OK: University of Oklahoma Press, pp. 377–414.

Wolf, E.R. (1959) *Sons of the Shaking Earth*, Chicago: University of Chicago Press.

—— (1969) *Peasant Wars of the Twentieth Century*, New York: Harper & Row.

—— (1982) *Europe and the People without History*, Berkeley, CA: University of California Press.

—— (1998) *Envisioning Power: Ideologies of Dominance and Crisis*, Berkeley, CA: University of California Press.

Part III

New methods of comparison

Chapter 8

Comparison and ontogeny

Christina Toren

We all of us intuitively know, as people who have parents, children, siblings, friends, neighbours, teachers, colleagues and so on, that comparison is fundamental to our daily lives. We're engaged in comparison all the time. It's part of how we get on in the world and, willy-nilly, we're doing it, consciously or unconsciously, in every single one of our engagements with others in the world. We look at and listen to each one of the others whom we encounter and each one of them looks back at and listens to us. Comparison is implicit in that mutual looking and listening; it informs all our ideas of the peopled world.

Were valid comparison impossible, as is maintained in certain postmodernist perspectives, there would be, so far as I can see, little or no reason to continue working as an anthropologist. As 'the whole science of human being', anthropology necessarily entails comparison; the problem has been how, precisely, it is to be accomplished.

All our models of comparison rest on an idea of what it is to be human and on an entailed idea of mind. Comparison is *intrinsic* to the processes that constitute mind, but to understand this requires an understanding of how mind functions to bring ideas into being and, in so doing, changes them. The present chapter is a version of the introduction to my 1999 book, *Mind, Materiality and History*, in which I argue that *mind is a function of the whole person constituted over time in intersubjective relations with others in the environing world.* This model is the outcome of a theoretical synthesis, described below, that at once justifies comparison in anthropology and suggests a new method by which it may be sensibly accomplished. The justification resides in showing how the transformation of ideas occurs, and how comparison is intrinsic to the transformational process. The method entails investigations of the microhistory of how, exactly, children constitute anew the practices and concepts of the adults alongside whom they live their lives. In brief, the developmental process is one in which children make meaning over time out of meanings that others have already made, and in so doing at once maintain and transform them. The investigation of this process is the methodological corollary of the view that the task of anthropology is to understand how we become who we are. It does not rule out other methods of comparison; indeed, as will become plain, the idea of human being that it entails justifies certain existing comparative methods; for example, the comparative analysis of structural transformation in kinship practices and terminologies or in a mythological corpus – two of the remarkable contributions to anthropology made by the genius of Lévi-Strauss.[1]

Becoming who we are

I pointed out above that comparing ourselves to others is something we do all the time. In doing so we are acknowledging not so much our sameness to others or our difference, but rather the commonality that resides in our difference. In other words, because each one of us is at once remarkably similar to, and remarkably different from, all other humans, it makes little sense to think of comparison in terms of a list of absolute similarities and a list of absolute differences. Rather, in respect of all other humans, we find similarities in the ways we are different from one another and differences in the ways we are the same. That we are able to do this is a function of the genuinely historical process that is human ontogeny, that is to say, of the process through which each of us embodies the history of our own making.

We embody the history of our own making because, like other living systems, we are autopoietic: self-creating or self-producing (see Maturana and Varela [1972] 1980, 1988). Each of us begins as a single-celled being: the zygote that is given by the union of a female ovum and a male spermatozoa; thereafter foetal development is a function of structural transformations occurring within this entity – itself an autonomous living system – from zygote to embryo to foetus to newborn infant. Thus, while the conditions lived by a pregnant woman are important for foetal development, it is the newly developing system itself that governs what structural changes occur and specifies what constitute viable environing conditions and what happens when they are upset. Once out of the womb, the newborn infant continues the process of its self-production, but this process itself depends on other humans, on those who feed and care for the newborn child. Indeed, being human, even in the abstract, necessarily implies relations with other humans, for we cannot conceive of humans *as human* outside social relations. Thus human autopoiesis is an inherently social process – one that resides in a fundamental intersubjectivity.

Intersubjectivity is a primary condition of human being. Humans are biologically social beings and, because they are, they cannot help but engage others in the process of becoming themselves. Throughout infancy others are necessary if a child is to remain alive; nevertheless, these others cannot entirely determine what happens to a child, nor do they have absolute control over the relations between themselves and the child. Because even in infancy, even as a newborn, a child's responses to those others who care for it are a function of its own being, and as such they contribute to the precise nature of the intersubjective relations in which that child engages (see, e.g. Trevarthen 1987).

This is precisely *not* an argument for a radical individualism. The process of becoming oneself can cease only with death, but this does not mean that we are independently the authors of our own being. We do not control the conditions of our own existence. What I am arguing for here is merely the inevitable autonomy of each and every human being that is given by the process of autopoiesis.

Once out of the womb the newborn child is immediately engaged in relations with others; one can argue that even before birth it is positioned *vis-à-vis* those others, in the sense that they have certain expectations of it. The ideas about newborn babies held by parents and other carers structure the conditions of a child's early life: how often it is fed and when and how it is weaned; whether or not it is picked up as soon as it cries; whether or not it is talked to; the kind of language used to and around it; the way it is clothed; where it is taken and how it is carried about; and so on. And as a child grows older, becomes a toddler, learns to talk, continues to grow and develop, undergoes the changes induced by puberty, arrives at sexual maturity and adulthood – throughout all its existence, it encounters and is inducted into manifold kinds of relations with others. The ideas held by those others and the practices with which they are associated inform, and over the whole course of life continue to inform, the process of any given person's being in the world.

This process is one in which being and becoming are aspects of one another; it *cannot* correctly be characterized as 'socialization' or as 'social construction' (i.e. it is not about 'individuals' who engage in 'social interaction' with other 'individuals' in a world whose characteristics are 'objectively given'). I am arguing here for a process of human autopoiesis in which we engage others in the processes of our own becoming. So, for example, in bringing you into the world, your parents quite literally constituted themselves as such, as your parents, even as you constituted yourself their child – and a particular child at that, for even if you have an identical twin you cannot help but be uniquely yourself. This uniqueness is a function of human autopoiesis, for even if you are one of genetically identical twins, your understanding of the peopled world as you grow up has to be brought into being by you. However close you are, your twin cannot do this for you, and the specificity of your experience, the sheer fact that it is *yours*, constitutes the difference between you and your twin.

So if, as I am arguing, we were not 'socialized', how did we become who we are? The process is complex, but it can, in essence, be stated quite simply. In the course of growing up we cannot help but enter into manifold relations with others and, in so doing, we make meaning (or what might also be called knowledge) out of our experience in the world. It follows that my idea of who and what I am, for all that it has to be brought into being by me, is a function of my relations to all those others alongside whom I live the environing world.

This process of making meaning is the psychological aspect of human autopoiesis. The constituting process is not willed by you, you do not have to be explicitly conscious of it and nor can you escape it: it is a function of being human. Like the process of physical development, the meaning- or knowledge-making process should be understood as giving rise to psychological structures that are at once dynamic and stable over time. These psychological structures are usually referred to as 'schemas' or 'schemes'. This term has come to be used with some frequency in contemporary social and developmental psychology and certain subdisciplinary areas of anthropology and sociology, so I have to emphasize that Piaget's idea of the scheme is my referent here. This brilliant and essentially simple idea is the core of Piaget's work. Just how very clever it is, is rarely acknowledged.

Piaget's cognitive scheme is 'a self-regulating transformational system'; in other words, it is autopoietic. Originally a biologist, Piaget argued that 'only self-regulating transformational systems are structures' (Piaget [1968] 1971: 113) and that, because the character of structured wholes depends on their laws of composition, these laws must in their nature be structuring.[2] This assumption gives rise to the dual attributes of structured wholes – that is, that they are simultaneously structured and structuring. If a structured whole has stable boundaries and conserves adaptation, these features themselves presuppose that structures are self-regulating or, to use Maturana and Varela's term, autopoietic. Piaget argued moreover that 'the idea of *structure* as a system of transformations [is] continuous with that of *construction* as continual formation' ([1968] 1971: 34). He demonstrated his argument via his studies of children's cognitive construction of fundamental categories of quantity, space, time, number and so on.

In Piaget's theory of cognitive development, the newborn child starts off with only a few 'reflex-like' behaviours at its disposal, for example, sucking, swallowing, crying, grasping, etc. The primitive psychological structures that govern these behaviours become differentiated through functioning. So, for example, the scheme for grasping rapidly becomes differentiated via the baby's experience of grasping different objects: a finger, a dummy, a piece of cloth. The baby assimilates the feel, as it were, of each new object to its grasping scheme and in so doing accommodates to the feel-aspect of that particular object. And when the baby grasps the dummy and gets it into its mouth, the assimilation schemes of grasping and sucking are assimilated to one another in such a way as to produce a qualitatively different, more highly differentiated, scheme that provides for a new and more complex accommodation to the world.

So, for Piaget, all behaviour has innate roots, but becomes differentiated through functioning; and all behaviour contains the same functional factors and the same structural elements. The functional factors are assimilation, accommodation and equilibration. Psychologically, assimilation is a process whereby a function, once exercised, presses towards repetition; in assimilation an action is actively reproduced and comes to incorporate new objects into itself (e.g. sucking incorporates the thumb, the nipple, the teat of a bottle, a piece of cloth, a dummy, someone's finger, a spoon and so on): this is an assimilation scheme. In accommodation, schemes of assimilation become modified in being applied to a diversity of objects. Equilibration is the process by which assimilation schemes become mutually coordinated in such a way as to produce an 'equilibrated structure' that yields a necessity that is a non-temporal, because reversible, law. An example might be the scheme that is constituted via the cross-modal matching of the sound of people's voices and what they look like; the particular sound of mother's voice is very rapidly associated with the particular configuration of her face, such that the perception of either necessarily suggests its complement.[3]

The structural elements in behaviour are order relations, e.g. the order of movements in an habitual act; subordination schemes, e.g. when an infant gets hold of your finger and pulls it towards its mouth, grasping is subordinate to pulling; and correspondences, or what Piaget calls 'recognitory assimilation', e.g. the kind of motor recognition a baby evinces when its physical movements mimic those of the person to whom it is attending.

> So assimilation, the process or activity common to all forms of life, is the source of that continual relating, setting up of correspondences, establishing of functional connections, and so on, which characterizes the early stages of intelligence. And it is assimilation, again, which finally gives rise to those general schemata we called structures. But assimilation *itself* is not a structure. Assimilation is the functional aspect of structure-formation, intervening in each particular case of constructive activity, but sooner or later leading to the mutual assimilation of structures to one another, and so establishing ever more intimate inter-structural connections.
>
> (Piaget 1971: 71; emphasis in original)

It is clear from the foregoing that comparison – i.e. comparison considered as an explicit concept and as a *conscious* process – has its source in assimilation as an aspect of autopoiesis.

Autopoiesis entails that structure and process be recognized as aspects of one another. Thus, to say that a cognitive scheme becomes differentiated through functioning suggests at once an increasing fineness and subtlety in the differentiating process and increasing stability in structure. Perhaps it is useful to point out here that it is because structure and process are aspects of one another that if we concentrate on the processual aspect to the exclusion of the structural, it appears as if all is transformation – and if we ignore process, it seems that what is structural is also static. That structure and process are inextricable and mutually defining means that the process that Piaget called 'genetic epistemology', while it produces stable and mutually confirming sets of ideas about the peopled world, is never in principle finished but always open to further elaboration. So, meaning is always emergent, never fixed. And this would be true even if each of us acted directly on the world and made meaning in isolation from other persons – as Piaget so often seems to suggest. When we incorporate intersubjectivity into his model, it becomes plain that the meanings we make of the peopled world are themselves constituted in an encounter with the meanings already made, and still being made, by others. So, for example, when as anthropologists we discuss comparison and how best to go about it, the idea of comparison that each of us brings to the discussion is going to be informed by and to differ from the others as a function of the microhistory of our intellectual development as particular anthropologists living in particular times in particular places.

The idea of the scheme as a self-regulating transformational system in which structure and process are aspects of one another has not, so far as I can see, been widely understood. It follows that its theoretical usefulness has not been recognized. As used by researchers other than Piaget himself, the term 'scheme' usually denotes a mental representation of experience. The formation, continuity over time and transformation of these so-called schemes (also referred to by cognitive anthropologists as 'cultural models') are treated as separable aspects; moreover, the structure and transformation of any given scheme are by and large taken to be a function of pressures from an environment that can itself be objectively specified because it is held to be separable from the person in whose head the representation is supposed to be stored. This peculiarly static idea of the scheme has long militated against the development of a model of embodied mind that is phenomenologically sound.[4]

The answer one gets to any question is a function of the terms in which the question is stated, so any scientific hypothesis contains a more or less explicit theory that structures the terms in which it can be answered. An artefact of our disciplinary distinctions between biology, psychology, sociology and anthropology is that biological questions are held to be more basic than 'higher-level' psychological questions, which, in their turn, are said to be at a less inclusive level than sociological questions. So disciplinary distinctions structure the kinds of questions that researchers ask, and so-called interdisciplinary research tends to produce ever more specialized subdisciplines, such as cognitive anthropology, social psychology, psychological anthropology and evolutionary psychology.

Irrespective, however, of their disciplinary or subdisciplinary identification, theorists of cognition continue to take for granted as their starting point the universal epistemic subject, the ahistorical individual. It follows that for cognitivists of all persuasions (including connectionists, who, not unreasonably, like to distinguish themselves as followers of a new paradigm, and evolutionary psychologists, whose similar claim remains unconvincing), it seems obvious that 'culture' or 'society' is a variable.[5] So they cannot help but find attractive the idea that there has to be a substrate, at the very least, of innately given, domain-specific, cognitive universals that taken together define the mind of the universal epistemic subject. The trick, then, is to find them.

A series of wonderfully ingenious and interesting experiments suggests that neonates and very young babies have abilities at their disposal that might have surprised Piaget (see Mehler and Dupoux 1994). It seems that babies are born with a body scheme, a scheme for human voices, and a scheme for human faces – all of which seems reasonable enough, given that sociality or intersubjectivity must, in some minimal sense, be given, if its particular forms are to be achieved.

Indeed, one might say the same for infants' abilities at four months to conceive of objects in the world as solid and stable across time, and at six to eight months to detect intermodal correspondences in numerosity between sounds and sights (see Smith *et al.* 1988). But given the extraordinary complexity of the human nervous system, the infant's immersion in a world of highly differentiated sensation and the rapid growth of interneuronal connections, these few months are surely ample time for the autopoietic development of these abilities out of much more primitive beginnings.[6] Moreover, as a 'self-regulating transformational system', a Piagetian scheme, even in its early stages, is going to 'look like' what cognitive psychologists call a module.

But let's say one accepts the thesis of innate modularity: that is, that we are born with certain minimally defined cognitive modules at our disposal – a language acquisition device, for instance, and modules for the perception of colour, or depth, or other living kinds, or humans or solid objects. We have still, given the autopoietic nature of human being and the infant's orientational bias towards other humans, to conceive of these structures of mind as self-regulating transformational systems that are elaborated, if not constituted, in and through intersubjectivity. Proponents of massive modularity cannot accept such a view because it threatens the vaunted objectivity of their model with its own historical specificity. So the massive modularity thesis entails that cognition about people (so-called social cognition) can be axiomatically separated from other kinds of cognition (e.g. ideas about number, space, time and so on), such that sociality and the history that is its artefact cannot be held to have contaminated the logic that justifies as objectively given the modularity theorists' own perspective.[7]

Mind and intersubjectivity

I noted above that the theoretical synthesis I propose can be expressed in the following formulation: *Mind is a function of the whole person constituted over time in intersubjective relations with others in the environing world.*[8] This radically phenomenological perspective on mind is derived in part from my reading of the work of Merleau-Ponty.

Merleau-Ponty's view that '[t]he body is our general medium for having a world' ([1945] 1962: 146) accords with Piaget's insistence on sensorimotor or practical intelligence as the foundation for the subsequent development of logical categories. Piaget's driving interest was to understand how the necessity that seems to be given in our categories of space, time, number and so on, could be the outcome of a process of cognitive construction, rather than an innate function of mind as Kant had argued – a project that is at least related to Merleau-Ponty's inheritance of Husserl's concern to render human science phenomenologically sound.[9] Piaget, however, appears to have been, at least initially, untroubled by any awareness that history might constitute a problem for the human sciences; thus Piaget's subject is the universal epistemic subject who acts on a world whose material properties can be directly apprehended. By contrast, for Merleau-Ponty subjectivity presupposes intersubjectivity and the self has to be understood as the always emergent product of the history of its becoming: 'I am installed on a pyramid of time which has been me' (Merleau-Ponty [1960] 1964: 14).

A crucial aspect of this process is that Merleau-Ponty's subject is for itself an 'other'. In other words, the self-conscious awareness of oneself as the subject of one's being in the world (for example, I-the-writer-of-this-essay or you-the-reader) entails a conscious awareness of one's otherness or, to give a simple example, a consciousness of the distance that enables any one of us to ask ourselves questions such as, Why did I do that? Or, why do I have this quality and not that one? Or, why can't I be more …? The problem here for any one of us is that even while we embody our particular past, we do not have access to it except from the perspective of who we are now. We can, for example, remember the details of our childhood more or less well; what we cannot do is again be in the world *as that child*. It follows that we cannot have access to how we came to know what we know. This opaqueness of our own past – and its density – are further intensified by our having lived the peopled world, and ourselves as given in it, in manifold and ever more complex ways hour-by-hour, day-by-day, for a good twelve months or so before we speak our first word and, in so doing, for the first time indicate something in language.

A key element in Merleau-Ponty's analysis of the fundamentals of human perception is his idea of intentionality. This has two components: (1) that all consciousness is consciousness of something, and (2) that 'the unity of the world – before being posited by knowledge in a specific act of identification – is "lived" as readymade or already there' (Merleau-Ponty [1945] 1962: xvii). Merleau-Ponty's idea of intentionality is important, too, for the theoretical synthesis I am proposing here because it asserts both that consciousness is a material phenomenon and that what we take for granted as given in the very stuff of the world (what others might call a 'belief system' or a 'cultural model') is brought into being by ourselves as a function of our lived experience of the peopled world and of ourselves as given in it. So, for example, for some years before I begin consciously to posit my own existence *as an object of knowledge* – Who am I? Where did I come from? What am I doing here? – I have already embodied a sense of the spatio-temporal dimensions of the world I live. I come to consciousness of myself and other people and all the manifold objects of the world by virtue of the motility of my body, whose movements bring the object-laden world into direct contact with me and bring me into consciousness of myself, and I embody particular spaces in so far as I am able, as it were, to command them. So it makes sense that a park that is unimaginably large to a 4 year old is more-or-less average-sized in the view of the child's 7-year-old sibling. Likewise, rather than being in time, I am myself the embodiment of the time I have lived. It then follows, for instance, that a year is experientially longer for a 7 year old than for a 14 year old because it constitutes one-seventh of his or her life rather than one-fourteenth.

I come into awareness of myself in a world I take for granted as including myself and as being, quite simply, the way the world is. It is perhaps a world where attending the university nursery is what we pre-school children do from nine till four Monday to Friday, where shopping with mother or playing or watching TV or reading a story with Daddy is what we do in the evening after nursery, where going to the supermarket and playing in the park is what we do on Saturday, and where on Sunday grown-ups with children around my age come to lunch, where by and large I get to choose the food I want to eat and the clothes I want to put on. We live in a house with a big back garden and three bedrooms where I have a room all to myself. While I'm at nursery Mummy is reading books and talking to other people somewhere else in the university and Daddy is at work. Like all the other kids I know, I watch lots of cartoon shows on TV, have lots of brightly coloured toys and games, go out to eat at fast-food restaurants with my parents, go on holiday in the summer and so on. I have lived this world and have developed a complex and highly differentiated embodied knowledge of it as the way the world *is* before, as a 4 year old, I begin to ask, Why?[10]

Thus for Merleau-Ponty intentionality denotes a mode of being-in-the-world that, in the case of humans, is in its nature historical because human being-in-the-world entails a consciousness that not only lives the world, but explicitly reflects on itself and the world. My ability explicitly to posit the world and to question it and my own existence is, at any given time, a function of the depth and complexity of my explicit knowledge at that time – i.e. the knowledge I can articulate. But however profound that knowledge, however subtle and penetrating my gaze, however incisive or sceptical my questions, I can neither access nor do away with the lived, embodied consciousness of myself in the world that I knew as an inarticulate infant and young child – it is the initial radius of the knowledge from which my understanding continues to spiral outwards, and as such it is always with me. Of course, all knowledge, including explicit knowledge, is embodied; here I am referring however to that visceral, felt knowledge that itself becomes ever more highly differentiated with increasing experience but cannot be easily justified in language.[11]

The embodied but inarticulate structures of consciousness that constitute the lived knowledge of the infant and young child continue inevitably to assimilate new experiences. In so doing, they arrive at new accommodations to the world that are shaped by those earliest experiences. Because they are and will always continue to be, quite literally, inaccessible in language, and because the sheer fact of living renders them ever more complex, these embodied but inarticulate structures of consciousness may be likened to, or perhaps even equated with, the 'unconscious' of psychoanalysis. I cannot here explore the implications of this observation, but only suggest, in passing, that Merleau-Ponty's idea of intentionality does not rule out a psychodynamic perspective on development.

In the preface to the *Phenomenology of Perception*, Merleau-Ponty ([1945] 1962: xvi–xvii) observes that '[t]he world is not what I think but what I live through. I am open to the world, I have no doubt that I am in communication with it, but I do not possess it; it is inexhaustible'. It is because the world is 'what we live through' that we are able both to assert with confidence the reality of our own particular experience and to assume that others are bound to experience the world as we do ourselves. This latter assumption is of course problematic (though we may live our lives in such a way that we never find it out, or if we do, put it down to the other's ignorance), but it is not unjustified.

The challenge, then, is to try to understand how it is that humans are able at one and the same time to have the world in common and to live it as a function of their own particular histories. And we can do this by complementing our studies of what adults have to say about the world with a contemporaneous study of how, exactly, children are constituting over time the concepts and practices their elders are using. And here, method becomes an important issue.

The language aspect of becoming who we are

Participant observation remains the primary method of anthropology because it provides for the possibility that the researcher has neglected crucial questions – not out of stupidity or laziness, but because he or she did not know they were there to be asked. By contrast, psychologists set out to test definite hypotheses or to answer definite questions. Studies of cognitive development tend therefore to focus on children in convenient settings where it is possible to film their responses to certain stimuli or to a play task that bears on the research question; the filmed behaviour then becomes the focus of study. If, however, the researcher has been influenced by the work of the Russian psychologist Vygotsky, the filmed sequence may include the child's mother, teacher or other adult. This difference in the conditions of the experimental situation reflects a difference in developmental theory; in the latter case, the researcher may be interested in understanding what Vygotsky ([1934] 1986: 187–9) called 'the zone of proximal development'. This developmental domain is created by the way that, at any given time, adult interventions explicitly or implicitly address the gap between a child's present knowledge and its potential knowledge. Via observation, the child internalizes what an adult is saying and/or doing and in the process arrives at a greater depth of understanding. This idea has obvious implications for any study of how people become who they are, but it is just as obvious from an anthropological perspective that this same study demands participant observation as its primary method, a matter I return to below.

Vygotsky's contribution to our understanding of how people become who they are lies primarily in his insistence that language, considered as the symbolic form *par excellence*, is rooted in historically specific material relations between people.[12] His observations concerning the functional implications of speech in infants and young children led him, in 1934, to argue that:

> Words and other signs are those means that direct our mental operations, control their course, and channel them toward the solution of the problem confronting us ... Real concepts are impossible without words, and thinking in concepts does not exist beyond verbal thinking. That is why the central moment in concept formation, and its generative cause, is a specific use of words as functional 'tools'.
>
> (Vygotsky [1934] 1986: 106–7)

Vygotsky made considerable use of a distinction between what is 'natural' or 'biological' and what is 'sociohistorical' or 'cultural'; thus he believed that because the child's initial use of language is directed towards communication with another, it is language that transforms the child from a natural into a cultural being.

> Every function in the child's cultural development appears twice: first, on the social level, and later, on the individual level: first, *between* people (*interpsychological*), and then *inside* the child (*intrapsychological*). This applies equally to voluntary attention, to logical memory, and to the formation of concepts. All the higher functions originate as actual relations between human individuals. ... The internalization of cultural forms of behaviour involves the reconstruction of psychological activity on the basis of sign operations.
>
> (ibid.: 57; emphasis in original)

Internalization is not, however, a matter of 'received meaning'; rather, Vygotsky maintained that 'it goes without saying that internalization transforms the process itself and changes its structure and functions' (Vygotsky 1981: 163, quoted in Wertsch and Stone 1985). Moreover, he observed that during the early years of the child's use of its native language, 'The child's and the adult's meanings of a word often "meet", as it were, in the same concrete object, and this suffices to ensure mutual understanding' (Vygotsky [1934] 1986: 111).[13] From an anthropological perspective, this is an immensely useful insight because, of course, it can apply just as much to communicative exchanges between adults as it does to those between children and adults – especially when those adults have significantly different histories: for example, an Australian and a Fijian or, within a particular language group, a man and a woman or people of different class and/or regional backgrounds. No doubt we have none of us to think very hard to remember numerous experiences of the way that agreement on reference to objects, processes and visceral experiences such as hunger, anger or jealousy can be mistaken for agreement on meaning.

From my point of view 'internalization' is not a useful term because it too easily implies (contra Vygotsky's own view) that knowledge or meaning is received. Because every child has itself to make meanings anew, and because meanings are transformed in the very process of being conserved, I prefer to talk of constituting meaning or of making sense. The key point here, however, is that if as anthropologists we can show in what respects the child's meanings differ from the adult's, and chart the transformations through which the child arrives eventually at a complexly nuanced understanding of what adults mean by what they say, this analysis will have profound implications for our own understanding of how history informs the processes in and through which the manifold forms of human intentionality are constituted. Or, in other words, it will enable us to show how the process of constituting meaning over time itself produces, for any one of us, an abiding sense that the world conforms to our understanding of it.

The phenomenology of learning

Participant observation will have to be the primary method for such studies because, given that it is adults who structure the conditions in which children live, the researcher must also be gathering data on relations between adults and the world as they live it. As I pointed out above, adults cannot have access to how they came to know what they know. And given that what they are able to articulate is founded in what is taken-for-granted, the meaning of what adults say goes well beyond what they can make explicit. So, for example, a study of white, middle-class US-American children's ideas of personhood and social relations would require not only a long period of participant observation in suitable settings such as pre-school and elementary school (where teachers and auxiliary staff as well as children would be the object of study), but a lot of contact with their parents, a lot of television viewing, a lot of hanging out in people's houses, a lot of eating in fast-food restaurants and so on. In other words, in order to understand the conditions lived by the children, the researcher would have to gather extensive data on adults' practices and their ideas of the person and relations between people. As good ethnography demonstrates over and over again, the interview method is not adequate for this purpose.

Extended participant observation is essential even if I-the-researcher am a white, middle-class US-American, because only systematic participant observation, and the discipline of writing field notes that it entails, is capable of revealing to me what I myself take for granted. In such a case, to be able to lay bare what is taken-for-granted and to ground one's analysis there requires, for example, *systematic* data on the way that relations between people are projected into the spatio-temporal dimensions of their lives and made concrete in the rhythm of the day as this is lived in one's own house and the houses of one's friends and neighbours, in the streets along which we drive, in the classrooms and gym and playground of the children's schools, in the shopping malls, the church and so on. The embodied understanding of a certain spatio-temporal dimension as given in the conditions of existence is an aspect of the taken-forgranted that is fundamental to ideas of person and collectivity. How, exactly, it is constituted over time – and in the process informs our ideas of the world, ourselves, other people and human relations – requires, for example, that one map the layout of these different spaces and the objects in them and, throughout the period of participant observation, record how they are used by children and adults and what they have to say, in passing, about what they're doing and the spaces where they are. One has also to pay careful attention to the ritualized behaviour that characterizes day-to-day life: greetings and politeness; the conduct of meals; hospitality of various kinds; birthday parties; the conduct of staff and children at school and the etiquette appropriate to relations between them, between peers of various ages, and between children of different ages; Halloween, Christmas Day, Thanksgiving and so on.

Towards the end of a year or so of participant observation, these accumulated data will enable the researcher to begin to see what should be the focus of diagnostic tasks with a balanced sample of children of different ages (from, say, 3 to 12 years old) and of interviews with their parents and teachers. Note, however, that these diagnostic tasks and interviews are not designed with an hypothesis in mind; they are designed in the hope that they will reveal aspects of children's and adults' ideas and the process of their understanding that have not, previously, been obvious to the researcher.

Interviews with adults will be largely unstructured and open-ended; a researcher might propose, for example, a topic such as what interviewees like and dislike about their neighbourhood, or how they think children should be reared and educated, their views on abortion and/or assisted conception, or why it's important to observe Christmas and other holidays. A content analysis of these interviews will not only reveal a particular idea of person, sociality and kinship, but may also bring to light, for example, a perspective on political economy that conflicts with the same interviewees' overt opinions on democracy. Children might be asked, for example, to 'draw where you live' and subsequently asked to 'tell me about your drawing', or, if they are literate, to label their drawing or write a story about what it depicts. (Note that children's drawing is not a useful research tool unless it is supplemented by the children's own accounts of the various features of what they have drawn.) A content analysis of these drawings and the children's commentary on them is likely to reveal not only how children's ideas of 'where I live' are transformed over time, but also how they implicate ideas of the person and social relations. I have to emphasize here that there is little point in obtaining data from children haphazardly; whatever means is used to find out the content of children's understandings, the data must be obtained from a balanced sample of girls and boys of all ages up to 12, at least. Only by analysing data that has been systematically obtained can the researcher find out what kinds of transformations children are effecting in the concepts adults use to describe the world.

In this imaginary case, a year to fifteen-months' research should produce richly complex and varied data from long and careful participant observation, systematic interviews with adults and older children on various topics and the systematic use with younger children of a number of different diagnostic tasks that bear on ideas of the person and social relations. The resulting ethnographic analysis of these data should be able to lay bare the concrete logic of adults' and children's ideas of person and sociality and show how exactly it is made material in the spatio-temporal dimensions of their day-to-day lives – there to be continually constituted anew by each succeeding generation, and in the process at once maintained and transformed. It should show in what respects the children's ideas differ from each other and from those of adults; these differences may well be unforeseen and, if they follow a particular pattern, are likely to make a significant difference to the analysis. It should reveal any reliable features of the constituting process – particular stages for instance, or gender – and how it is that the oldest children in the sample (i.e. those around 12) have come to hold ideas that are closer to those of adults' than to those of 5 year olds. In sum, it should be able to reveal what ideas of person, kinship and collectivity are held by a certain population of middle-class white Americans and how these ideas come to be taken for granted as, by and large, given in the nature of human being.

Only this kind of study is capable, I would argue, of revealing the microhistory of how people come to be who they are, how they come to embody the ideas and practices of which they appear to be the product (see e.g. Toren 1990). The empirical validity of such research rests not on assertions of its objectivity, but in its capacity to reveal in any given case the complexity of the constituting process and how it produces the taken-for-granted. So, in the imaginary case of research into middle-class white Americans' ideas of the person, kinship and collectivity, the study is likely to have profound implications for the development of theory in the human sciences. Our notion that the world is objectively given to us is not peculiar to ourselves; everyone, everywhere thinks the same – the problem being, of course, that what is objectively given for a white middle-class Londoner, for example, may not be what is objectively given for a black middle-class Londoner, and this in spite of their easy agreement on reference. And both would be likely to reject as entirely unwarranted a great deal of what is objectively given to, say, a Bimin Kuskusmin or Kashinaua person.

Conclusion

This chapter has argued for a theoretical synthesis that allows us to understand that *mind is a function of the whole person that is constituted over time in intersubjective relations with others in the environing world*. This model is, I argue, good for anthropologists because it has at its core a perspective on humans as at once products and producers of history. And because transformation and continuity are intrinsic to it, this model is a good basis, too, for our attempts to understand other peoples and their different responses to, for example, the various forms of colonization. By the same token, we can use it to understand ourselves and the historical specificity of our own models of human being and how their continuity is an aspect of their transformation.

My imaginary ethnographic examples have concerned ourselves – a rhetorical device that is intended to emphasize that the model of human being we use has to be as good for understanding ourselves as it is for understanding others. My own fieldwork, however, has been carried out entirely in the chiefly *vanua* (country) of Sawaieke, on the island of Gau, central Fiji. The ethnographic questions I have explored led me, by degrees, to the point where I felt it necessary to propose the model described above (see Toren 1999). Or, to put it another way, my attempts to answer the questions that arose out of long and repeated participant observation have, over the years, brought me ever closer to understanding how it is that I and the Fijian villagers with whom I work come to be remarkably similar to one another in the ways we are different, and wonderfully different in the ways we are the same.

I pointed out at the outset that valid comparison in anthropology can take different forms; for this very reason it is important that, whatever form it takes, the comparative project should rest on a theory of mind and human being that calls into question the adequacy of any model in which our historical nature is merely one dimension of human being in the world. Moreover, an anthropology that has at its heart a model that is capable of comprehending human historicity can properly claim to be science, precisely *because* it provides a way of explaining its own project as valid without implying that it is immune from history or that those who are not scientists are inferior in understanding to ourselves. And in so far as scientific explanation is our project, we are bound to dispute the relative adequacy of our models with others who maintain that it is their project too. As one engaged in this scientific dispute, I argue that my model of ontogeny as an historical process is able at once to acknowledge all that we currently know about humans and to provide an explanation for its stunning complexity that is essentially simple to formulate and demonstrable. Which is not to say, of course, that in time my argument may not be undone.

Notes

1 For a fascinating contemporary example, see Gow (2001).
2 The description of Piaget's cognitive scheme is derived from his book *Structuralism*. First published in 1968, when he was 72, this is a succinct statement of Piaget's key ideas as they apply to mathematical and logical structures and also to 'structures … whose transformations unfold in time' (Piaget [1968] 1971: 15).
3 See Piaget ([1968] 1971: 63 and 71), from which I took the formal description given in this and the succeeding paragraphs, adding examples of my own in order to clarify the technical terms.
4 Piaget's scheme, by contrast, provides intrinsically for structure and process, continuity and transformation; nor is there any mystery about its being a function of embodied mind. Cf. the schema as 'representation' or 'cultural model' that figures in works by Holland and Quinn (1987, esp. the editors' introduction), D'Andrade (1995, especially the discussion in Chapters 6 and 7), and Shore (1996, especially Chapter 2), who gets into something of a muddle trying to distinguish between 'conventional models' and 'personal models' (as should be plain by now, the conventional and the personal are bound to be aspects of one another).

5 Contemporary connectionist models of mind do, however, attempt to make compu-
   tational theory consistent with what we know of the workings of the human nervous
   system: they employ an idea of parallel distributed processing that allows for a cognitive scheme that is always emergent, never fixed. In this narrow sense, the
   connectionist scheme is consistent with Piaget's. (For an overview of connectionist
   theory, see Clark 1990.)
6 According to Maturana and Varela (1988: 159):

> In humans, some one hundred billion interneurons connect some one million
> motorneurons that activate a few thousand muscles, with some ten million
> sensory cells distributed as receptor surfaces throughout the body. Between
> motor and sensory neurons lies the brain, like a gigantic mass of interneurons
> that interconnects them (at a ratio of 10:100,000:1) in an ever-changing
> dynamics.

7 See, for example, the papers by Sperber, Carey and Spelke, and Keil, in Hirschfeld
   and Gelman (eds) (1994). Jerry Fodor was the first, and remains the most influential,
   contemporary cognitive psychologist to propose a modularity theory (see Fodor
   1983). In a review of Plotkin (1997) and Pinker (1998), however, Fodor argues
   against the idea of massive modularity in large part because 'eventually, the mind has
   to integrate the results of all those modular computations and I don't see how there
   could be a module for doing that' (Fodor 1998: 12).
8 It will be apparent to the reader that this perspective rejects certain long-established
   analytical distinctions: individual–society, biology–culture, body–mind, subjective–
   objective, structure–process. In the model proposed here the terms in each of these
   distinctions are viewed as aspects of one another.
9 Interestingly enough, Merleau-Ponty held the chair of child psychology and pedagogy at the Sorbonne from 1949 to 1952 and was succeeded by Piaget (Johnson and
   Smith 1990: xxiv).
10 What middle-class British, Australian or American parents may take to be a natural
   stage of child development – the 'Why?' stage – is not observable in Fijian children;
   indeed, given the high value placed by middle-class Western parents on the idea of
   the intelligent child as an inquiring child, it seems likely that we actively foster this
   stage.
11 For example, the awareness that another, a stranger to oneself, is angry or upset or
   afraid or lying, etc., even when there are no overt signs to justify one's certainty that
   this is so.
12 He appears not to have read his contemporary Volosinov's brilliant *Marxism and the
   Philosophy of Language* ([1929] 1986), which argues against Saussure's distinction
   between *langue* and *parole*, and for an analysis of 'the utterance' as a social
   phenomenon.
13 For an excellent psychological discussion of this aspect of Vygotsky's work, see
   Wertsch and Stone (1985).

Bibliography

Clark, A. (1990) *Microcognition: Philosophy, Cognitive Science and Parallel Distributed
   Processing*, Cambridge, MA: MIT Press.
D'Andrade, R. (1995) *The Development of Cognitive Anthropology*, Cambridge: Cambridge
   University Press.
Fodor, J.A. (1983) *The Modularity of Mind*, Cambridge, MA: MIT Press.

—— (1998) 'The trouble with psychological Darwinism', *London Review of Books* 20, 2: 11–13.

Gow, P. (2001) *An Amazonian Myth and Its History*, Oxford: Oxford University Press.

Hirschfeld, L.A. and Gelman, S.A. (eds) (1994) *Mapping the Mind: Domain Specificity in Cognition and Culture*, Cambridge: Cambridge University Press.

Holland, D. and Quinn, N. (1987) *Cultural Models in Language and Thought*, Cambridge: Cambridge University Press.

Johnson, G.A. and Smith, M.B. (1990) *Ontology and Alterity in Merleau-Ponty*, Evanston, IL: Northwestern University Press.

Maturana , H.P. and Varela, F.J. ([1972] 1980) *Autopoiesis and Cognition: The Realisation of the Living*, Dordrecht: D. Reidel.

—— (1988) *The Tree of Knowledge*, Boston, London: New Science Library, Shambhala.

Mehler, J. and Dupoux, E. ([1990] 1994) *What Infants Know*, Cambridge: Blackwell.

Merleau-Ponty, M. ([1945] 1962) *Phenomenology of Perception*, London: Routledge and Kegan Paul.

—— ([1960] 1964) *Signs*, Evanston, IL: Northwestern University Press.

Piaget, J. ([1968] 1971) *Structuralism*, London: Routledge and Kegan Paul.

Pinker, S. (1998) *How the Mind Works*, London: Allen Lane.

Plotkin, H. (1997) *Evolution in Mind*, London: Allen Lane.

Shore, B. (1996) *Culture in Mind: Cognition, Culture and the Problem of Meaning*, Oxford: Oxford University Press.

Smith, L.B., Sera, M. and Gattuso, B. (1988) 'The development of thinking', in R.J. Sternberg and E.E. Smith (eds) *The Psychology of Human Thought*, Cambridge: Cambridge University Press.

Toren, C. (1990) *Making Sense of Hierarchy: Cognition as Social Process in Fiji*, LSE Monographs in Social Anthropology 61, London: Athlone Press.

—— (1999) *Mind, Materiality and History: Explorations in Fijian Ethnography*, London: Routledge.

Trevarthen, C. (1987) 'Universal cooperative motives: how infants begin to know the language and culture of their parents', in G. Jahoda and I.M. Lewis (eds) *Acquiring Culture: Cross-Cultural Studies in Child Development*, London: Croom Helm.

Volosinov, V.N. ([1929] 1986) *Marxism and the Philosophy of Language*, Cambridge, MA: Harvard University Press.

Vygotsky, L.S. ([1934] 1986) *Thought and Language*, Cambridge, MA: Harvard University Press

—— ([1936] 1978) *Mind in Society*, Cambridge, MA: Harvard University Press.

—— (1981) 'The genesis of higher mental functions', in J.V. Werstch (ed.) *The Concept of Activity in Soviet Psychology*, Armonk, NJ: Sharpe.

Wertsch, J.V. and Stone, C.A. (1985) 'The concept of internalization in Vygotsky's account of the genesis of higher mental functions', in J.V. Wertsch (ed.) *Culture, Communication and Cognition: Vygotskian Perspectives*, Cambridge: Cambridge University Press.

Chapter 9

The notion of art

From regional to distant comparison

Thomas Fillitz

Comparison will be considered in this chapter as the *condition par excellence* for an anthropology of art. The approach is based on three aspects that underlie the perception of non-Western art, both traditional and contemporary, and which may serve as a basis for comparison. First, scholars applied the notion of 'art' to objects that had formerly not been considered under that label, and transposed the methodology of Western art history onto the study of traditional non-Western art. Second, at the turn of the twentieth century, artists not only 'discovered' the aesthetic value of objects they could see in ethnographic museums in Paris, Munich or Dresden, but also reflected them in their own works of art. And third, as I discuss below, there is and has been a return movement of interplay with Western modern art in the contemporary art of Africa.[1]

I will discuss the complexity of comparison by analysing it in four different types of anthropological studies: (1) in cross-cultural, holocultural analyses; (2) in the context of regional studies on style; (3) in research on meaning and aesthetics; and, finally, (4) as 'distant' comparison. I argue that within the anthropology of art the usefulness of holocultural comparison is highly questionable; that comparison should not be restricted to regional, controlled comparison; and that the proper scope is a 'distant' comparison with Western art, especially given the present phenomenon of globalization. The discussion will allow me to analyse how comparison itself changes, from the point of view of the units as well as of its results.

Cross-cultural studies of art and society

In his discussion of cross-cultural, holocultural comparison, Harold Driver (1973: 375) highlights two studies on art that he considers to have produced good results: one by John Fischer (1961) and one by Alvin Wolfe (1969) (see also Naroll 1970: 1247). Fischer's analysis is based on a sample taken by Herbert Barry III (Fischer 1961: 93) and deals with the graphic arts of Andaman, Samoa, Maori, Hopi, Zuni, Navaho, Kwakiutl, Ashanti, Dahomey, Masai and so on. Linking Murdock's social classification scheme with the development of art styles, he concludes that there is a striking statistical relationship between art styles and the development of social hierarchy (Fischer 1961: 81). His conclusion is based on a presumption of a continuum between two ideal social types – the authoritarian type, in which social hierarchy is positively valued, and the egalitarian type, in which hierarchy as a principle of organization is rejected – and he relates stylistic aspects to the two types (ibid.).

Let us first examine the assumptions that led Fischer to the hypothesis that art is a reflection of social hierarchy. He assumes first:

> that, regardless of the overt content of visual art, ... there is always or nearly always at the same time the expression of some fantasized social situation which will bear a definite relation to the real and desired social situations of the artist and his society.
>
> (Fischer 1961: 80)

This assumption is problematic in itself, but Fischer proceeds directly to the assertion that the hypothesis is being tested in his study and must be related to the opposition between latent and overt (representational) content. He then transforms this latent content into the notion of the 'latent social meaning' of visual art, which refers 'primarily to people, especially to characteristic physical configurations and to characteristic gestures and motor patterns' (ibid.: 81). Next, Fischer moves beyond the relationship between art and social organization to introduce a psychological dimension to graphic arts, stating that pictorial elements in design are 'on a psychological level, abstract, mainly unconscious representations of persons in the society' (ibid.).

From these basic assumptions, Fischer (ibid.) deduces a number of hypothetical polar contrasts in art styles:

1   Design styles that repeat a number of rather simple elements relate to egalitarian society; styles that integrate a number of unlike elements are connected to hierarchical society.
2   Designs with a large amount of empty and irrelevant space are associated with egalitarian society; designs with little irrelevant or empty space belong to hierarchical society.
3   Symmetrical design (a special case of repetition) reflects egalitarian society; asymmetrical design, hierarchical society.

In explanation of these correlations Fischer introduces a further psychological component, 'security':

> Security in egalitarian societies depends on [the] number of equal comrades ego possesses. The simple repetition refers in its symbolic [meaning] to the members of society, it is easier to repeat simple than complex elements, and it corresponds to a need to de-emphasize the actual interpersonal differences.
>
> (ibid.: 82)

In egalitarian society, then, typical persons are conceived of as being relatively simple. In a hierarchical society, however, security rests on the relationships between persons of different position. Its art therefore integrates a variety of distinct elements, and the more complex the elements, the greater the possible social difference and the greater the emphasis on personal differences (ibid.).

Fischer's explanation of empty, 'irrelevant', space is also noteworthy. In egalitarian society, he asserts, other people are either comrades or nothing at all, and security is related to isolation from 'others' and close togetherness with the inside group. This societal isolation is represented as empty space around a central design. In hierarchical society, on the other hand, security is produced by integrating strangers into the social hierarchy. As a general point of view of art styles, Fischer notes the high correspondence to social conditions of various sorts as determinants of artistic fantasy and creativity (ibid.: 89).

Raoul Naroll (1970: 1247) finds:

> Fischer's results ... particularly striking. Fischer (1961) hypothesized that complexity of art styles was related to cultural evolution ... These findings strongly support the 'cultural theme' idea. Do art styles, like the overtones of a vibrating musical string, repeat in higher octaves, ... harmonically, the basic themes of social structure?

Unfortunately, I cannot join in this cross-culturalist enthusiasm. Each of Fischer's assumptions and deductions about art is highly problematic. Let us begin with his assumptions of the relationship between social stratification and art style,[2] the opposition between latent and overt (representational) content and his judgements about the 'simple' and the 'complex'. In his primary hypothesis, Fischer relates overt content to 'some fantasied social situation', which in turn reflects 'the real and *desired* social situations of the artist and his society' (ibid.: 80; my emphasis); later, he speaks of 'artistic fantasy and creativity' when there is a 'high emphasis [on] social conditions *of all sorts* as determinants' (ibid.: 89; my emphasis). But what is an artist in the context of a specific society? What realms of creativity and fantasy are available to the artist? Is it the same endeavour to produce an object for secular use as for ritual use? And why does Fischer term empty spaces 'irrelevant', if he considers them to be symbolic of societal isolation?

I would argue that what Fischer reduces to an opposition between 'latent' and 'overt' content is rather an issue of the fundamental and highly complex connection between 'representing', the 'representation' and the 'represented' (*Darstellunsgsweise, Dargestellte, Darzustellende*). Instead of opposition, a major issue is the congruity among these three conditions. To put it simply, the question concerns what needs to be represented, what visual image is chosen for the representation, and how the artist (stylistically) realizes this image. The interplay of these aspects constitutes what we call a work of art.

One could go on to interrogate Fischer's notions of 'fantasy' and 'creativity'.

If he uses these terms as part of the common discourse about Western modern art (from the nineteenth century onward), then they are ideas that should be problematized. Fischer distinguishes these modern Western artists from those in his cross-cultural sample by means of their personalization and freedom of creativity. Such notions are reintroduced for non-Western artists, without explicitly determining their specific cultural meanings. If we consider African traditional artists, we see very different social positionings at work. Daniel Biebuyck (1973: 23) locates the creativity of artistic enterprise in Lega art in the connection individual artists forge between tradition and innovation, and Daniel Crowley (1971: 327) states that Chokwe artists have creative freedom comparable to that in Western societies. In Tiv society, on the other hand, Paul Bohannan (1966: 248) has shown that the artist has an unimportant role and that only the piece itself is highly valued; and William Bascom (1973:112) found that in Yoruba figurines the freedom of creativity is concentrated on the shaping of the ear.

Fischer's results, summarized by the relationship between the related evolution of social stratification and pictorial art styles, seem extremely problematic – and not only because of the introduction of the psychological notion of 'security'. Consider the pairs 'repetition of *simple* form' and 'complex form', as well as 'empty (*irrelevant*) space' and 'complex space' (my emphasis). First, I know of no basis for assuming that 'empty' is equivalent to 'irrelevant'. Emptiness is, rather, a relational aspect of dynamics and may stand in significant relationship to essential aspects that are being expressed. Second, I would assert that repetition, even of so-called '*simple* forms', may be stylistically related to rhythm, and that the frequency and way in which a form is repeated may have meaning for the people viewing it. In any formalist analysis of design, the question of 'complex form' would have to be further de-constructed into the relationships between the various parts, how they are placed in space and whether they are more linear (haptic) or more painterly (optic). Fischer treats these elements as if they were a constant throughout all the works of art in a given society, and thereby connects each type of society to a specific style of art. As we shall see below, this stylistic consistency for a long time was a general assumption in the analysis of art styles in African societies.

Finally, I would contest not only Fischer's findings and theses, but also what I consider the dangerous ideological implications of his argument. Consider his correlation of the 'simple' form with the 'egalitarian' type. When, at the beginning of the twentieth century, Western artists 'borrowed' stylistic elements from traditional African art, they were impressed by these 'simple' traditional solutions (which for them were rather rigorous). Later, they were heavily criticized by anthropologists for relating these formal solutions to early evolutionary stages of society. But what Western viewers considered simple was in fact considered by the artists to be the result of a high level of sensitivity and a reductionist cognitive act working together. The artists placed a high value on this artistic process, but because they connected it to the concept of 'primitive society' (see Kuper 1991), they assumed that 'primitive men' were obviously less polluted than are we, in our complex society. From this, the artists concluded that such acts had to be more fundamental than ours. Such a conclusion need not imply that these formal solutions are easy or simple – the implication one is tempted to assume in following Fischer's argument. Fischer reproduces such archaisms and primordialities, which appear ideologically most dangerous; interestingly, from Fischer's perspective one cannot explain the open reception of traditional art by European artists at the beginning of the twentieth century.

I chose Fischer's analysis of indigenous art as an example of the drawbacks of holocultural comparison precisely because it has been mentioned by other holo-cultural researchers as a model for the quality and possible results of cross-cultural studies. But if we reflect on its theoretical assumptions and methodology, we must recognize that cross-cultural, holocultural comparison of art is deeply mingled with theories and methodologies drawn from the Western study of art. To summarize, Fischer first links art with society and in doing so, he connects diverse pieces of art without discriminating among them within a specific society. He then introduces Murdock's (1957) classifications of those societies, which take as a given a primary social, hierarchical classification that also determines the stylistic specificities of art works within those societies. Next, he applies extremely problematic methodologies and theories of art to identify stylistic characteristics, which, finally, he uses to re-typologize specific types of society.

Regional comparison in the anthropology of art

The cross-cultural holocultural approach has been severely criticized before. Isaac Schapera (1969: 55–8) concentrates his objections on the principles that govern the selection of the societies to be compared – the problem of the unit of comparison – and on the problem of the literature on which the comparisons are based – both the quantity that need to be digested and the fact that for the most part only Anglophone literature is reflected. Edmund Leach (1963: 2) saw in this sort of comparison just a mode of classification, of arranging things according to their types and subtypes, and F.S.C. Northrop (1964: 194–222) discussed the ambiguity of language. Ladislav Holy critiques, among other things, the criteria selected in cross-cultural studies to the exclusion of others (1987: 16), the eschewing of the epistemological problems of data gathering (ibid.: 4) and the function of such comparisons for theory testing (ibid.: 8). Fred Eggan (1954: 743–63) proposed an alternative method of comparison – 'controlled regional comparison' – in which British structural–functionalism combines with the North American concept of process and history (Eggan 1954: 759; see also Holy 1987). Schapera (1969: 61) explains 'controlled regional comparison' as a three-level study: (1) the intensive study of a region, followed by (2) careful comparison of the forms a particular phenomenon takes

among the peoples of that region and concluding with (3) an attempt at formulating generalizations about one or more basic types into which these various
forms can be classified. According to Schapera, these basic 'types' could then be
used as the units in wider comparative studies 'of a continental or even
universal scope' (ibid.: 62). An example of controlled, regional comparison is
Siegfried Nadel's well-known article on witchcraft in four African societies
(Nadel 1952: 18–29), in which he first compares the phenomenon in the neighbouring societies of Nupe and Gwari, then of Korongo and Mesakin, and finally
connects both comparisons.

Up until the late 1960s, the major comparative works in the study of indigenous art were concerned with the analysis of styles. The units examined in these
studies were not cultural bodies of art, in general, but rather types of pieces,
such as comparisons between figurines only, or between masks. These studies
were often further delimited according to the materials used – wood, clay, ivory,
bronze, etc. – and even more narrowly according to specific groups of figurines.
Areal coverage might be restricted to one society, to a specific area covered by
that society, to a village or even to one artist, but could also be broadened to
larger regions, as in comparisons of the art of two or more societies. The goals
for such studies were many. Researchers may have attempted to establish style
regions (not to be confused with cultural regions), to delimit zones of influence,
to distinguish variations within one geographical area or among a certain type
of figurines or to attribute works of art to regions, to ateliers, even to artists.
Some studies sought to identify seriation, the change of styles through time,
although we generally lack sufficient numbers of art works from any one area to
establish historical depth.

It soon became obvious that we need certain tools in order to accomplish
studies of style, particularly if the desired end is cultural comparison. Jan
Vansina (1995: 84) cites Frans Olbrechts (1959) as the first scholar of African
traditional art to develop such tools, including the categories of position in
space, proportion, sculptural detail and added and decorative detail. Position in
space refers to how parts are linked in a sculpture; proportions concerns the
canons of sculpture; sculptural detail relates to 'conventions'; and added and
decorative detail helps to localize objects regionally through their resemblance
to the actual ornaments worn by people in particular regions.

A prominent study that applied these criteria is Louis Perrois's (1972) analysis of the reliquary figurines (bieri) of the Fang of Northern Gabon. The study
was regionally concentrated, and highly controlled through its delimitation to
bieri figurines. The sheer number of figurines analysed – several hundred – lent
the study significance.

As a central criterion of analysis, Perrois chose proportion, which he established by measuring the different parts of the pieces. He turned next to position
in space, relating the head shapes and volumes to one another. Finally, Perrois
compared the details: the types of eyes, noses, ears, breasts, etc. He also sought
to link stylistic variation with geographical distribution throughout the region.

In the course of his study, Perrois refined his criteria. In examining proportion, he analysed the relationship between torso and the total height of the figure, compared the head to the legs, and the length of the neck also to the legs. Position in space was defined by such criteria as the form of the head, its frontal and lateral proportions, the positions of the arms in relation to the torso and the position of the legs. He was able to detect four distinct types of figurines, which he termed hyperlongiform (head to torso), longiform (torso), equiform (head to torso) and breviform (short torsos). He succeeded both in subsuming all figurines into these four established types and in ordering the stylistic variations according to areal substyles and a few centres.

Although Perrois was successful in analysing the *bieri* figurines according to the above-mentioned criteria, it would be misleading to apply these types generally to all traditional African figurines. It would be even more misleading to apply them to masks. For stylistic analysis to be meaningful, very careful selection must be made of the pieces to be compared. Each piece must then be intensively analysed, and the pieces compared in order to sort out those elements that may be unique to one work from those that constitute the 'canon'. Obviously, larger comparative studies, taking into account a number of geographical areas, would face such problems as how to delineate the criteria for comparison and how to avoid overgeneralizations.

Jeremy Coote and Anthony Shelton state that such an art-historical stylistic study constitutes an 'end in itself', but for anthropologists working in the field of art it is only 'a means *to* an end'. Their statement relates to the larger differentiation between 'the classic art-historic concern with spatio-temporal provenance and the anthropological concern with socio-cultural context' (Coote and Shelton 1992: 6).

At least in the African context, however, such studies do not only constitute an end in themselves. Still current in some circles today, and quite prominent until some decades ago, especially among art gallery operators, museum curators and the general public, are persistent assumptions such as the existence in each society of a specific, uniform art style. Perrois's study presents quite a different perspective, and Bascom (1973: 98–119) has shown that one must take into consideration much more subtle conceptualizations of style, which should be broken down into local substyles, multiple substyles that differ from each other, regional styles and individual styles.

Another incorrect assumption has been the anonymity of traditional artists, which amounts to an erasure of their individual existence. Studies in style that examine areas of influence and centres of production and even attribute works to specific carvers, smiths or ateliers contribute to the dismantling of such ideas. Intensive studies may also demonstrate that traditional art in Africa was not a simple matter of reproduction of already existing pieces and may even make explicit how artistic creativity is materialized.

When we consider these two results – that such studies provide the means by which an anthropology of art can elaborate sociocultural context, and that they convey insight into former false assumptions about the nature of traditional art – the merit of this kind of comparative work must be acknowledged. We also have to acknowledge the limits and pitfalls of such studies, however. If we look at Sub-Saharan Africa, we see that the comparison of styles based on a sound methodology leads only to clusters, patterns of style, regional distribution, the location of centres or the tracing of influences. Perrois did not begin with any primary classification; he delimited his study regionally and according to type of art pieces. His final typology, then, is the result of an analysis based on criteria that had been developed for Western art, reformulated for traditional African arts (Olbrechts 1959) and refined by him according to the specificities of the *bieri* figurines. The more general studies (e.g. Leuzinger 1962) are also, necessarily, less systematic, and they can only broadly delimit the units studied, e.g. figurines or masks, works of wood or bronze, and order them according to extremely generalized criteria. Finally, it should be mentioned that these sorts of style comparisons do not entail any evolutionary concepts; rather, society is important only as a means of selecting the unit under consideration and enters exclusively as a geographical delimitation. As a result, stylistic variations run the risk of appearing as movements of their own, of transpositions and transformations that occur without the agency of artists or anyone else. Society itself is missing and re-enters only in terms of variations or differences in art styles.

Meaning, aesthetics and comparison

Other comparative works on African arts thematic style and meaning (see Biebuyck 1973; d'Azevedo 1989; Fraser 1955; Jopling 1971; Szalay 1990), but all build on what Coote and Shelton termed style as a 'means to an end' for the anthropologist. In their contributions to these collections, most of the authors deal with art as it expresses meaning, using symbols and form to visualize the meaning. Their studies are based on the notion of aesthetics, which is considered to be synonymous with 'beauty', a relatively recent Western concept (since the nineteenth century). An alternative position was taken by philosopher Nicolai Hartman, among others, who understood aesthetics as sensuous experience (1953: 17) and as research on values and value relations (ibid.: 329).

In all these works, comparison appears in a dimension apart from aesthetics. Each author deals with a specific case, and one must read all those related to one topic in order to experience the various discourses. An additional problem may be in the different levels of intensity of the various studies, in which the frames of analysis vary considerably. Finally, there is no overall comparison between the specific case studies, no attempt to formulate differences, similarities or any general law.

It is nevertheless noteworthy in these studies that the aspect of beauty is analysed in relation to the concepts of the peoples being studied, and the criteria of the artist, the owner or user, and the public are introduced. Interestingly, in societies like the Baule (Vogel 1997), the Lega (Biebuyck

1973), the Yoruba (Thompson 1989), the Fang (Fernandez 1971, 1989) or the Chokwe (Crowley 1989: 228), beauty is connected to 'good' (see also Vansina 1995: 132). So questioning order to determine what are the criteria for beauty, one must discover what 'good' means in each cultural context.

To James Fernandez (1971: 362–3), the most pertinent aspect of indigenous criticism (from eight informants, two of whom were carvers) in relation to the *bieri* figurines of the Fang was the finished or unfinished quality of the artefact: its smoothness, whether or not it had been completely cut out from the wood, or if there were still traces of its rougher origins. Important too was the question of balance (*bibwe*): whether or not a figurine's various quadrants balanced with each other (arms to arms, arms to legs, etc.).

> There should be balance in the figure, and the proportions of opposite members whether legs or arms or eyes or breasts should display that. Without this balance of opposite members, it was said … the figure would not be a real one … , it would have no life or vitality within it.
>
> (ibid.)

As Fernandez emphasizes, balance is a crucial notion; ideas linked directly to it include opposition, smoothness and vitality. A central opposition in balance is seen in the relation of the thorax and stomach to the head. The torso, Fernandez reports, is considered the centre of power and thought, while the head is the organ of apprehension and direction, 'enabling what fundamentally belongs to the torso willfully to be put to use' (1971: 361). Both regions of the body should work together in 'complementary fashion[,] though they [do] not always succeed in doing so' (ibid.). The opposition between age and youth is also incorporated in this concept of physical balance, as the mature man (*nyamoro*) is considered capable of maintaining a balance between power and direction: 'Youth tends to be too active, too willful; age, too deliberative, too tranquil' (ibid.: 370).

It is through their connection that the aesthetic elements derive their meaning. Opposition prevents elements from being too close together, emphasizing distance, but opposition is never absolute since balance is the central value. Seen in this way, balance is not a static concept but one in constant movement around an ideal. Smoothness, as opposed to the roughness of the raw materials, corresponds to balance, and the unworked piece of wood is associated with opposition, or inconsistency. In the balanced work we can also determine vitality, the balance between youth and age (i.e. the mature man), and the capacity to survive (Fernandez 1971: 359), symbolized in the creation of harmony. As Fernandez asserts, for the Fang there is no order without art, as art itself is associated with the carrying out or creation of order (Fernandez 1989: 217).

Robert Thompson (1989: 19–61) found that the Yoruba use a technical vocabulary for aesthetic criticism and could delineate eighteen aesthetic criteria (ibid.: 29), all of which refer to general Yoruba principles of the human condition (ibid.: 32). The most important category is the 'midpoint mimesis', expressed in conventionalized faces with aspects of individual personality (lineage scarifications and hairstyle) – although it should be in no way possible to identify figurines as known persons. This aspect of Yoruba carving is further expressed by the strict avoidance of 'hypermimesis', as the creation of an exact likeness would be dangerous. On the other hand, 'excessive abstraction' is also undesirable, and each sculpture must have recognizable human traits (ibid.: 33). A shining quality, smoothness, symmetry and the visibility of the face were other important aesthetic criteria.

The most striking aspects of Yoruba figurines are their huge heads and inexpressive faces, elements that can be related to principles found by Douglas Fraser (1955) and, later, by Roland Abiodun and colleagues (1991). A central opposition used by the Yoruba to express order is that between cool and hot (Fraser 1955: 115): cool is related to order, while hot, which interrupts it, implies disorder. Hot is also associated with excessive emotions. Beauty in a figurine, then, is associated with coolness, with the body in a state of order (ibid.: 116), which can be achieved only by inexpressiveness.

The accentuated size of the heads may be related to another concept, the idea that the head is a site of protection of the gods (Fraser 1955: 24). This is also expressed in the duality between the outer skull as representative of the personal fate and the inner part of the head as a reference to the mind and spirit (Abiodun et al. 1991: 13). The well-known *ibeji* (twin) figurines exemplify the representation of duality in Yoruba concepts. *Ibejis* are carved when a twin dies, in order to pacify or 'cool' the resulting element of disorder. *Ibejis* have extremely large heads not only because the god Shango is considered to be their protector (Fraser 1955: 118, 123), but also because twins are considered living proof of the principle of duality. The figurines themselves have always to resemble each other and are nearly identical, wearing the same ornaments, clothes, etc. Even if the twins were children when one died, they are always carved as adults.

I have presented these two accounts of aesthetic discourse about Fang and Yoruba carvings in very compressed form, focusing on the Fang and Yoruba people's own criteria. The two sets are quite different as they relate to meanings, i.e. to the discourse on values intrinsic in each of the societies. It is also clear that it is not the piece of art itself that is at the core of such aesthetic comparisons, but the values that the art expresses. Individual works of art are only the units of comparison in the realm of aesthetics; the basis of the aesthetic codes are 'abstract' notions of value: symmetry in the case of the Yoruba, balance for the Fang; duality for the Yoruba, opposition for the Fang; and smoothness and shininess for both.

Although these ideas appear at first glance quite similar, they are used in very different ways to express intended meanings. For the Fang, balance may be conceived as a movement around an ideal point. Oppositions constitute an important addition to the idea; they delimit in order to avoid being reduced to sameness, but nevertheless they must be related. For the Yoruba, duality with symmetry is the emphasis of the positive pole, but the other pole is always present; *ibejis*, for example, relate to hot situations, but they themselves are cool. *Ibejis* are clearly placed within that duality. The above-mentioned 'midpoint mimesis', then, is not a continuum but a delimited place in the relation between similarity (identity) and non-visibility. For the Fang, smoothness is a quality related to balance; for the Yoruba, it is connected to inexpressiveness.

From stylistic features, we proceeded in these analyses to the fundamental ideas of the people concerned and how they look at works of art, opening the door to insights into the meanings – of values and ideas – connected to style. But we need to go further, first scrutinizing the act of seeing, of looking at these objects, second, asking how these aesthetic criteria are interrelated in each case. We face not only a given meaning, but the *process* by which this meaning is constructed via the distinctive interrelatedness of the criteria within a society. By this means we analyse not only the cultural value itself, but also – and foremost – the process by which it is established. Not only the symbolic content in the figurines of the Fang and the Yoruba differs, but also the techniques of achieving that content is specific to each culture and is embodied in different styles.

If we accept the above approach, comparison becomes the acknowledgement of diversity. Its aim is no longer the formulation of generalizations, of so-called laws, it can no longer help to predict because it lacks the general, it can no longer engage in theory testing cross-culturally and can no longer serve to the reconstruct systems of cultural evolution (an aim of holocultural studies; see Naroll 1970: 1228). According to Holy (1987: 11), 'this kind of comparison cannot achieve anything else than to posit difference; it has an heuristic rather than an explanatory value'.

To clarify things, I shall analyse briefly the notion of 'seeing', mentioned above. To elicit the aesthetic criteria for the figurines, scholars had asked members of the societies to look at the objects in a certain way, as a European visitor might look at paintings in an exhibition. 'Seeing' in the context in which the Fang or Yoruba peoples have the opportunity to experience these works was not considered. Lega art, for instance, is confined to the *bwami* society and is never seen outside ritual contexts, and certain artefacts can only be seen by persons who hold a specific grade in the *bwami* society. I would suggest that the scholarly approach described above implicitly used the notion of seeing, of looking at, in the sense of the Western notion of 'contemplation', an idea developed by Kant as 'disinterested contemplation' (*desinteressiertes Wohlgefallen*) in his *Kritik der Urteilskraft* (1957). By this formulation, Kant meant the process of perception, in which the combined sensations would lead towards understanding and knowledge without the interference of the mind. The beautiful, as apprehension of the form, can prepare viewers to embrace meanings that otherwise might even be in opposition to their interests.

Georg Wilhelm Friedrich Hegel (1955), on the other hand, used contempla-tion in order to attain knowledge of the Absolute Mind, which he later expressed as God. 'Shine' was the appearance of truth through the work of art. It is clear that Hegel held two concepts of beauty: first, beauty as apprehension of the form, a means of attracting via perception; and, more important, the shine or lustre of beauty, the essence of reality. 'Seeing' as contemplation therefore was the sensuous experience of beauty, its apprehension (through disinterested contemplation) and the perception of the essence.

Recently, Susan Vogel (1997) has identified four different notions of 'seeing' in reference to works of art among the Baule: *nian*, to look or to watch, an intentional watching that is also used for television viewing; *nyin*, a 'stare' directed at objects without sacred meaning (spoons, fans, chairs, etc.); *kanngle*, an evil look from the corner of the eye related to sacred objects and shrines; and, finally, *nian-klekle*, to look at clandestinely (ibid.: 91). Even looking at masks during ceremonies occurs in a discreet way, according to Vogel (ibid.: 92). Among the Baule, works of art should not be seen by everyone, and even owners of pieces look at them in darkness.

'Seeing', then, implies a specific relationship between the work of art and the viewer. In traditional Western aesthetics, the relationship is one of contemplation, the acting of the work on the viewer's senses and mind. In the case of the Baule, seeing is closely related to avoidance, and the four types of seeing are connected to the judgement accompanying the act: the way one looks at a piece of art could in itself be harmful. Moreover, the context in which one looks at art may be significant of what the act of 'seeing' is intended for. Looking at the *bieri* figurines of the Fang, for example, implies reflection upon the events within society and how to act accordingly (Fernandez 1989: 205). Simultaneously, in the act of seeing, the people reflect upon their own problems in order to enhance their quality of life. In the case of Lega art, seeing has a mnemonic function. In general, in traditional African art, seeing is connected to action, and action is relational to both a given social situation and the values and ideas perceived in the piece of art. Seeing is not the passive contemplation of an essence; rather, seeing enhances agency.

I would now like to relate the notion of seeing as action to the relationship between traditional African art and the development of twentieth-century Western art, which reached its first climax concerning form with the cubists (see Goldwater 1986: 144). This development was much more complex than a simple stylistic 'borrowing'. After Cézanne, artists were searching for something new that could not be found in European art traditions; they deliberately looked elsewhere, combining a continuity with Cézanne with a discontinuity with the other European traditions and an introduction of new, non-European forms. One can see in these works the artists' reaction against an old, spent Europe and their desire to embark on a new beginning. Picasso is quite explicit that this shift was not grounded on pure formalism. Although he certainly did not understand in their own context the African pieces of art he had seen in the Musée de l'Homme and is full of mystifications about them, he did derive from them a new perspective on his being as an artist. Looking at the African masks, he understood, as he told Malraux, that art was a 'weapon'. 'What made possible the acceptance ... was [Picasso's] willingness to perceive and accept [the masks'] inherent power' (Goldwater 1986: 283). The shift that occurred in this period transformed modern Western art concepts. Dadaism, Surrealism, Duchamp's ready-mades, Actionism no longer aimed to represent an essential truth or 'the good'; instead, they aimed at breaking with current ideologies and conscious-nesses (see Marcuse 1977). As formal simplicity came to be understood as an aspect of the real sense of things, the act of seeing an artwork gained a new dimension in Western aesthetics. What the perception of these new works of art required from the viewer was no longer exclusive, pure contemplation, but active reflection. Beauty, too, lost its importance, both as meaning of the repre-sented (the essential truth) and as the sensuous apprehension of form.[3]

The idea that these early twentieth-century 'borrowings' constituted a simple appropriation of form by Western artists was a misconception. As such, it was implicitly propagated by the 1984 exhibit 'Primitivism in Western Art' at the Museum of Modern Art in New York City. The process must also be understood as the transposition of the concept of 'seeing as action' from traditional African art to modern Western art. This transposition – a radically new understanding of what art is for – helped Western avant-garde artists to position the work of art as an open discourse about reality and existence, but also as a challenge to current ideologies and beliefs. The new approach enhances perceptual and mental activities, no longer centred solely in the work of art but extending to the relationship between artist and viewer.

When we introduce aesthetics into our analysis, we open up another dimen-sion of comparison. In order to scrutinize aesthetics, one had to analyse the principles involved (symmetry, balance, shine) and then raise the question of perception (contemplation, seeing as action, etc.). Interestingly, in their studies of the aesthetics of traditional African art, Western scholars had started to posi-tion aesthetics as beauty (a concept valid only for a certain historical epoch in European aesthetic philosophy), without discriminating between the notions of beauty at stake. Beauty was linked to the good and the true, a link that led back to classical Western aesthetics. This did not affect research on aesthetic princi-ples, but it did affect the analysis of perception or seeing in the cases of traditional African and modern Western arts, the question of the represented in modern Western art, and the understanding of new concepts of art and how these had been introduced and transformed in the West.

As I have mentioned, comparison in such a case deals with basic notions and how they are interrelated in order to construct meaning in specific situations. But the problem goes deeper. If we discuss elements of the logic of meaning-construction in traditional African arts in terms of Western concepts – and for traditional African aesthetics we lack both data and historical depth – we unravel an important methodological drawback of such comparison. Ideas such as 'seeing as action' may appear similar once the meaning is constituted, but the comparative focus on the process of meaning-construction reveals how apparently similar notions involve culturally different meanings. To understand traditional African aesthetics, the Western scholar must also understand the construction of these ideas in different Western scientific theories and historical epochs. If one submits one's own theories to the concept of 'historical variation' and thereby connects them to concepts from African societies, one may transcend cultural translation and position comparison as a powerful tool for the critique of Western concepts.

'Distant' comparison

The reader may have noticed that with my last example I have left the realm of regional comparison and shifted into a 'distant' comparison between African and European discourses. In comparing Sinhalese Buddhist nationalist ideology with Australian nationalist ideology, Bruce Kapferer (1989) has argued for this kind of comparison, treating Australian nationalist ideology as a window on the cultural realities within which his own subjectivity is constituted (ibid.: 166). At the same time, Sinhalese Buddhist nationalism becomes part of his analytical reflection of Australian nationalism, and vice versa, and central to the determination of vital distinction (ibid.: 166, 167). Tom Lemaire sees anthropology as having a critical impact in our own societies by keeping the dialectic between knowledge of Western and non-Western societies permanently on the move (1991: 38).

The argument for 'distant' comparison can also be supported by recent thinking concerning the concepts of 'society' and 'culture'. We no longer consider these systems as closed or homogeneous (Barth 1989), which means that we can no longer explain cultural dynamics by focusing on internal factors only; rather, we must enrich our analyses by turning to external factors as well (Nader 1994: 86, 87). In this perspective, comparison has to be positioned and reflected within the framework of globalization, the form in which the world is currently 'united' (see also Gingrich and Peacock, this volume). If it seems obvious that a spatial (not historical) mode of analysis must be adopted, then the problem resides in the units to be compared, the concept of locality to be employed and its relation to global processes (see e.g. Appadurai 1991, 1996; Hannerz 1992, 1996; Hastrup and Olwig 1997).

In the realm of a sociology of art, Howard Becker (1984) has introduced the concept of 'art world' as a possible analytical unit. An art world may be made up of artists, their assistants, their resource providers, critics, theoreticians, curators, museum and exhibition directors, gallery directors, collectors, visitors, all kinds of art media, the art works themselves, the spaces in which these are exhibited and so on. According to Becker, all works of art within one art world bear the marks of the system that distributes them (ibid.: 94). In his view, art worlds are not confined within the boundaries of societies or nation-states.

Vogel, considering recent African art production, has attempted to classify it according to units she terms 'clusters of traits' (1991: 10). She accordingly differentiates between 'extinct art', 'traditional art', 'new functional art', 'urban art' (which is also labelled 'popular art' by others) and 'international art'. 'Extinct art' is older traditional art that can be found in museums, whereas 'traditional art' comprises pieces produced nowadays but in traditional styles. 'International art' is art that exhibits strong formal influences from contemporary Western art. Vogel's distinction between 'new functional' and 'urban' art is more ambiguous, since both are related to urban spaces (consider sign painting, for instance) and the two categories may overlap. The greater problem with this classificatory scheme, however, is that the criteria are drawn from a Western point of view. It is thus incapable of explaining the systems within which artworks circulate in local societies and why 'new functional', 'urban' and 'international' art are generally subsumed in exhibitions in Europe, the Americas or Japan under the common label of 'contemporary art of Africa'. Vogel also fails to address the question of why artworks that fit into her categories of 'functional' and 'urban' art are more appreciated in the West than is so-called international art.

The arena of interaction between the various contemporary Western and African art worlds is the global space of a 'world of art'. At the beginning of the twentieth century this world of art was determined by the modern Western art world, which positioned itself as the universal arbiter of 'art'. Recently the world of art has become open to plurality, and the processes of perception and reception have a correspondingly different dimension. The question is not whether or not the contemporary art of Africa would be 'discovered' today by the Western art world; rather, the question is how it is consciously perceived and how the contemporary African art world is constituted in the global arena of the world of art. On the one hand, contemporary African art is identified as art that appears 'African', or 'authentic', like the paintings of Chéri Samba from Congo, the sign paintings of the Nigerian artist Middle Art, the pictorial alphabet of Bruly-Bouabré from Ivory Coast or the Mercedes-Benz and airplane coffins by the Ghanaian Kane Kwei. On the other hand, works that borrow formal elements from Western avant-garde are valued if they contain intensely African symbolism and subject matter. From the viewpoint of the Western art world, then, what is included in the world of art is the so-called authentic, the typical. Moreover, there is a strong tendency on the part of Westerners to devalue any non-localized artistic interactive discourse among African artists, that is, the freedom to deal with or incorporate any art tradition – a freedom that, on the contrary, is highly valued within the Western art world.

African contemporary artists have different perceptions of both the African art world and the global world of art. Though few can make a livelihood exclusively from their art, some do define themselves primarily as artists. Like Yacouba Touré and Youssouf Bath from Ivory Coast, or Moustapha Dimé and Ousman Sow from Senegal, they consider themselves members of the world of art, rejecting any regional positioning and the very notion of 'contemporary African art'. It is as social beings, in their relationships with other local people who are not artists, that such artists consider themselves members of a localized society. But art itself is for them an encompassing concept that fuses all regional artistic traditions of the world, past and present. Their freedom to deal with any and all art traditions is for them a powerful characteristic of their own art and of their positioning within the global world of art.

Certain other artists, like Romuald Hazoumé or Georges Adéagbo from Benin, do consider themselves 'contemporary African' artists. Although they share the concept of an encompassing world of art, they feel that each tradition contributes to it by being specific and local. The Western art world, then, is but one among many, and the task of these artists is to find in their work the specific contribution a contemporary art of Africa can make to the global space. They do not reject fundamentally the idea of borrowing from non-African art worlds, but they believe that African works should be recognized as African. Their emphasis is on the quality of cultural difference in an egalitarian interaction within the world of art.

Leaving aside the question of galleries, critics, curators and so on, it is important to consider in this controversy over contemporary African art the artists and their works. I will take Youssouf Bath and Georges Adéagbo as my examples. Bath lives in Dabou, a small city 60 kilometres west of Abidjan, Ivory Coast, and secures his livelihood by teaching art in a school and maintaining some small palm-tree plantations. Adéagbo lives from his artwork in a home in Cotonou, Benin, without water or electricity. Bath was trained in Abidjan and at the Beaux Arts in Paris; Adéagbo graduated in law and political science in France and is a self-taught artist. Both have exhibited widely. Bath believes his art belongs to the 'world of art' without any regional specification, whereas Adéagbo considers his work to be 'African'.

Youssouf Bath paints with local materials, using *tapa* (bark cloth) rather than Western canvases, and making his colours from local plants and sometimes from natural medicines. The only non-local materials he uses are china ink and a specific red pigment. Though one can see the Western influence in Bath's style, his colours and the *tapa* require a technique entirely different from that of acrylic or oil painting. The symbols he uses stem from various African traditional social contexts – he employs forms found on Senufo textiles, though he is not Senufo – and he mixes them, empties them of their local meaning and combines them with symbols he finds in societies outside Africa. Bath's content, however, remains located in African society, elements from traditional society such as the topic of the younger brother or local spiritual concepts, contextualized in a setting of African modernity and pushes into a general dimension. In Bath's art the important connection is African modernity itself and the general condition of being in given social relations; though traditional values are incorporated as important for reflection, his art does not represent a return to those values.

Unlike Bath, Georges Adéagbo uses many different materials to create ephemeral installations: small paintings and tourist art figurines (which are made according to his directives), pictures from magazines, clothes, cowrie shells, objects that may relate to the sacred or the secular. Unique are the numerous small sheets of paper on which he notes his ideas in French. His ephemeral installations are extremely complex, with the major topic (African leadership, for example) subdivided into subtopics, each of which is made up of numerous elements. Adéagbo always places empty cigarette packets or matchbooks somewhere in each installation, to suggest that the viewer take a break and reflect before moving on. Interestingly, each part within the complex whole has three structural elements: what is given, what should be and what is part of the human condition. In each subtopic, these three elements flow out of a central form (a chair, a group of figurines, etc.). In his installations Adéagbo emphasizes the universal human condition, which transcends present social conditions.

Bath, who supports the notion of a non-localized, de-territorialized world of art, localizes his paintings in a transnational African space by connecting symbols of various African traditions with African modernity. His style may be characterized as a combination of Western avant-garde painting (abstract expressionism) with specific elements of traditional African art (ornamentation being smaller than symbolic forms, centrally meaningful symbols being larger than peripheral ones). Adéagbo, who locates his art as being contemporary African, breaks definitively with local tradition (in social life, as well) and de-territorializes his art. Although he uses local objects, these have meaning only in their relationship to the multitude of French texts, which deal in a non-localized way with the overall topic of the work. Adéagbo's style can be described as an elaborated narration that begins in local tradition but is structured around the connection between the modern situation and a universal humanism.

The works of both of these artists articulate a relationship between three conceptual spaces: modernity within African societies, regional traditions and ideas of cultural universals. It is noteworthy that André Magnin, director of the 'Contemporary African Art Collection', and Jacques Soullilou developed quite similar criteria – in their terminology, 'territory', 'frontier' and 'world' – as essential for the understanding of contemporary African art (Magnin and Soullilou 1996). These are conceived less as criteria for classification than as 'intensities' that express the ways in which these concepts are related to each other within each individual artwork. Works that express a stronger link towards a specific culture would be 'territory', works that emphasize the connection to transculturality would be 'world', and those works that move between the two poles of territory and world are 'frontier'. In Magnin and Soullilou's construction, both Bath and Adéagbo would belong to 'world'.

What must be scrutinized here, however, is how the articulation in the works themselves can be related to the artist's self-positioning within the realm of either a de-territorialized, global world of art (Bath) or a specific contemporary African art world as part of a global world of art (Adéagbo). Obviously, the interplay between content (the represented) and style affects that relationship. Bath's self-awareness stems from his involvement with art and his training in

Western art traditions, and it is from this perspective that he approached the African art traditions that he analysed after his return to Ivory Coast. He tackles the problems of representation in the same way, researching new stylistic expressions in his work. It is first as artist that Bath deals with problems of content and style, and only secondarily as an individual African.

Adéagbo is not concerned with such questions. Untrained in art, he produced his ephemeral installations in the courtyard where he still lives without having thought they could be considered art. It was only when a Western curator, looking for another artist, was sent to Adéagbo for information and saw an installation that his creations were perceived as 'art'. His work expresses and reflects his local experience in relation to his thoughts on humanity. His style is neither Western nor traditionally African; it is unique to him. Style for Adéagbo is not the result of a self-conscious search for new modes of representation; it is relevant only in the context of the grand narrative he develops with each topic. His words and visual ideas are those of a specific individual, and he still has difficulty conceiving of himself as a member of the global community of artists.

My discussion of the relationship between the Western and African art worlds and of the processes of contemporary art production in Africa within the global arena of a world of art would remain incomplete if approached only from the Western art world's point of view. Certainly the dominance of the Western perspective when it comes to art has to be acknowledged, but what is more important are the various ways in which African artists are positioning themselves within the global realm. When Magnin and Soullilou (1996) speak of the 'intensities' present in each work, they highlight the relational and interactive aspects of analysis, which also became obvious in our comparison of Youssouf Bath and Georges Adéagbo. It is no longer possible for the Western art world to define universal standards for inclusion within the world of art, as it did at the beginning of the twentieth century. The global framework is now an interactive space of difference. Within the contemporary art of Africa, that difference is embodied in the various ways in which artists produce their works in the spaces and connections between modernity, regional traditions and concepts of cultural universals within African societies. In staking out their positions in this process, the artists themselves articulate their active and reactive (but never passive) participation in the world of art.

In the context of globalization, comparison becomes interactive, as all societies participate in a systemic pattern of relationships among societies (Robertson 1994: 13). This type of comparison is not only a basis for the critique of Western society through the introduction of concepts from non-Western ones. Perceptual constructions are not unidirectional; they result from multidirectional modes of global participation. In the realm of art, I have tried to show that processes of perception, of inclusion or exclusion, between the Western and the African art worlds are interpenetrating and have to be placed within the global system of the world of art in order to be understood.

Conclusion

In this chapter I developed the thesis that comparison is an essential methodological tool in the anthropology of art. Through the discussion of various units within which it could be applied, comparison has emerged as a complex methodology, varying not only with its application but also with the ends for which it is used. I have rejected the usefulness of cross-cultural, holocultural comparison, as the complexity of the relationship between art and social reality does not allow a simple connection between a typology of art and a typology of societies. Regional comparison based on style is not an end in itself, but it does convey insight into concepts of creativity, regional styles and substyles and attribution of bodies of work to local centres or individual artists. More in-depth comparison, related to the meaning of pieces of art, must take basic aesthetic concepts of a society into consideration, rather than the piece itself as unit of comparison. In this context, comparison now must deal with the processes of how people construct meaning.

Such comparative studies can no longer focus on generalizations or the testing of theories. Instead, they must examine the variations of meaning-construction within different societies. It is noteworthy that these kinds of studies open up a further important dimension, what I have called 'distant' comparison. By introducing concepts from non-Western societies into Western society, such analyses can become powerful tools for the critique of our own social worlds.

Finally, if the anthropology of art does not want to confine itself to traditional art but also directs its gaze onto recent and contemporary art developments and related discourses in various regions of the world, comparison itself must be positioned within a global frame of art systems. Comparison then will have to deal with the interpenetration of different perceptions, with geographic flows of works of art and with how they are constituted in terms of their participation in the global system.

Notes

1   I thank the Fonds zur Förderung der Wissenschaftlichen Forschung (P 12391-SPR) for funding research in Ivory Coast and Benin in 1997.
2   Fischer's topic is evolution through comparison, not seriation.
3   This idea had appeared in aesthetic philosophy in the *Aesthetic of the Ugly* (*Ästhetik des Hässlichen*) developed by Rosenkranz, a student of Hegel [1853] 1990).

Bibliography

Abiodun, R., Drewal, H.J. and Pemberton, J. III (eds) (1991) *The Yoruba Artist: New Theoretical Perspectives on African Arts*, Washington, DC and London: Smithsonian Institution Press.

Appadurai, A. (1991) 'Global ethnoscapes: notes and queries for a transnational anthropology', in R. Fox (ed.) *Recapturing Anthropology: Working in the Present*, Santa Fe: School of American Research Press, pp. 191–210.

—— (1996) *Modernity at Large: Cultural Dimensions of Globalization*, Public Worlds 1, Minneapolis and London: University of Minnesota Press.

Barth, F. (1989) 'The analysis of culture in complex societies', *Ethnos*, 54, 3–4: 120–42.

Bascom, W. (1973) 'Creativity and style in African art', in D.P. Biebuyck (ed.) *Tradition and Creativity in Tribal Art*, Berkeley, Los Angeles and London: University of California Press, pp. 98–119.

Becker, H.S. ([1982] 1984) *Art Worlds*, Berkeley, Los Angeles and London: University of California Press.

Biebuyck, D.P. (ed.) (1973) *Tradition and Creativity in Tribal Art*, Berkeley, Los Angeles and London: University of California Press.

Bohannan, P. (1966) 'Artist and critic in an African society', in D. Fraser (ed.) *The Many Faces of Primitive Art*, Englewood Cliffs, NJ: Prentice-Hall, pp. 246–54.

Coote, J. and Shelton, A. (1992) 'Introduction', in J. Coote and A. Shelton (eds) *Anthropology, Art, and Aesthetics*, Oxford: Clarendon, pp. 40–63.

Crowley, D.J. (1971) 'An African aesthetic', in C.F. Jopling (ed.) *Art and Aesthetics in Primitive Society*, New York: E.P. Dutton, pp. 315–27.

—— (1989) 'Aesthetic value and professionalism in African art: three cases from Katanga Chokwe', in W. d'Azevedo (ed.) *The Traditional Artist in African Societies*, Bloomington and Indianapolis: Indiana University Press, pp. 221–49.

d'Azevedo, W.L. (ed.) (1989) *The Traditional Artist in African Societies*, Bloomington and Indianapolis: Indiana University Press.

Driver, H.E. (1973) 'Cross-cultural studies', in J.J. Honigman (ed.) *Handbook of Social and Cultural Anthropology*, Chicago: Rand McNally, pp. 327–68.

Eggan, F. (1954) 'Social anthropology and the method of controlled comparison', *American Anthropologist* 56: 743–63.

Fernandez, J.W. (1971) 'Aesthetics in traditional Africa', in C.F. Jopling (ed.) *Art and Aesthetics in Primitive Society*, New York: E.P. Dutton, pp. 356–73.

—— (1989) 'The exposition and imposition of order: artistic expression in Fang culture', in W. d'Azevedo (ed.) *The Traditional Artist in African Societies*, Bloomington and Indianapolis: Indiana University Press, pp. 194–220.

Fischer, J.L. (1961) 'Art styles as cultural cognitive maps', *American Anthropologist* 63: 79–93.

Fraser, D. (ed.) (1955) *African Art as Philosophy*, New York: Interbook.

Goldwater, R. (1986) *Primitivism in Modern Art*, Cambridge, MA and London: The Belknap Press of Harvard University Press.

Hannerz, U. (1992) *Cultural Complexity: Studies in the Social Organization of Meaning*, New York: Columbia University Press.

—— (1996) *Transnational Connections: Culture, People, Places*, London and New York: Routledge.

Hartmann, N. (1953) *Ästhetik*, Berlin: de Gryuter.

Hastrup, K. and Olwig, K.F. (1997) 'Introduction', in K.F. Olwig and K. Hastrup (eds) *Siting Culture: The Shifting Anthropological Object*, New York: Routledge, pp. 1–14.

Hegel, G.W.F. (1955) *Ästhetik*, F. Bassenge (ed.) Berlin: Aufbau.

Holy, L. (1987) 'Introduction – description, generalization and comparison: two paradigms', in L. Holy (ed.) *Comparative Anthropology*, Oxford: Blackwell, pp. 1–21.

Jopling, C.F. (ed.) (1971) *Art and Aesthetics in Primitive Society*, New York: E.P. Dutton.

Kant, I. (1957) *Kritik der Urteilskraft und Schriften zur Naturphilosophie*, Wiesbaden: Insel-Verlag.

Kapferer, B. (1989) 'Nationalist ideology and a comparative anthropology', *Ethnos* 54, 3–4: 161–99.

Kuper, A. (1991) *The Invention of Primitive Society*, London and New York: Routledge.

Leach, E. (1963) *Rethinking Anthropology*, London School of Economics Monographs on Social Anthropology 22, London: University of London, The Athlone Press.

Lemaire, T. (1991) 'Anthropological doubt', in L. Nencel and P. Pels (eds) *Constructing Knowledge: Authority and Critique in Social Science*, London, Newbury Park and New Delhi: Sage, pp. 22–39.

Leuzinger, E. (1962) *Afrique: L'art des peuples noirs*, Paris: Albin Michel.

Magnin, A. with Soulillou, J. (eds) (1996) *Contemporary Art of Africa*, New York: Harry N. Abrams.

Marcuse, H. (1977) *Die Permanenz der Kunst: Wider eine bestimmte marxistische Ästhetik*, Vienna and Munich: Carl Hanser.

Murdock, G.P. (1957) 'World ethnographic sample', *American Anthropologist* 59: 664–87.

Nadel, S.F. (1952) 'Witchcraft in four African societies: an essay in comparison', *American Anthropologist* 54: 18–29.

Nader, L. (1994) 'Comparative consciousness', in R. Borofsky (ed.) *Assessing Cultural Anthropology*, New York: McGraw-Hill, pp. 84–94.

Naroll, R. (1970) 'What have we learned from cross-cultural surveys?', *American Anthropologist* 72: 1227–88.

Northrop, F.S.C. (1964) 'Toward a deductively formulated and operationally verifiable comparative cultural anthropology', in F.S.C. Northrop and H.H. Livingston (eds) *Cross-Cultural Understanding: Epistemology in Anthropology*, New York, Evanston and London: Harper and Row, pp. 194–222.

Olbrechts, F. (1959) *Les arts plastiques du Congo Belge*, Brussels: Standaard.

Perrois, L. (1972) *La statuaire Fang*, Paris: ORSTOM.

Robertson, R. (1994) *Globalization: Social Theory and Global Culture*, London, Newbury Park and New Delhi: Sage.

Rosenkranz, K. ([1853] 1990) *Ästhetik des Hässlichen*, Leipzig: Reclam.

Schapera, I. ([1967] 1969) 'Some comments on comparative method in social anthropology', in C.S. Ford (ed.) *Cross-Cultural Approaches: Readings in Comparative Research*, New Haven, CT: HRAF Press, pp. 55–64.

Szalay, M. (ed.) (1990) *Der Sinn des Schönen: Ästhetik, Soziologie und Geschichte der afrikanischen Kunst*, Ethnologische Schriften Zürich 10, Munich: Trickster.

Thompson, R.F. (1989) 'Yoruba artistic criticism', in W. d'Azevedo (ed.) *The Traditional Artist in African Societies*, Bloomington and Indianapolis: Indiana University Press, pp. 19–61.

Vansina, J. (1995) *Art History in Africa*, London and New York: Longman.

Vogel, S. (ed.) (1991) *Africa Explores: 20th Century African Art*, New York and Munich: Prestel.

—— (1997) *Baule: African Art, Western Eyes*, New Haven and London: Yale University Press.

Wolfe, A. (1969) 'Social structural bases of art', *Current Anthropology* 10, 1: 3–44.

Chapter 10

When ethnic majorities are 'dethroned'

Towards a methodology of self-reflexive, controlled macrocomparison

Andre Gingrich

To the memory of Eric Wolf:
Teacher, friend, compatriot

In this chapter I consider anthropology's present potential for comparison.[1] I believe the current phase of globalization requires such an exploration, as – continually and, it would seem, permanently – globalization brings together local conditions from vastly different areas, conditions that appear, at first sight, to have little in common.

How might an anthropological perspective on past and present phases of globalization improve our understanding of comparison in anthropology? In this context, I am interested, in particular, in exploring the methodological potential of 'distant' or 'macro-' comparison, which I will apply to two sets of case examples that involve specific variants of radical nationalism among what I term 'dethroned' ethnic majorities.[2]

When an anthropologist considers comparison, he or she is, of course, acting within specific contexts. My own spatial and social proximity to some of the cases compared in this chapter has certainly influenced my choice, as have contexts of my background and education and my Middle Eastern regional specialization in anthropology. Similarly, anthropology's tormented relationship with comparison influences my methodological discussion. To begin, however, it may be useful to reflect briefly on the ways in which a European cultural background influences my approach to comparison. In fact, the literature and folklore of Europe display a startling variety of opinions about comparison, among which caution and even scepticism seem to prevail.

In Roman times, for instance, Publius Vergilius Maro compared, in the fourth song of his *Georgica* (37–30 BC), the Cyclops's relentless work of forging iron with the industrious activities of the bees. In the same verse, however, Virgil warns his readers about the limits of such a comparison: '*si parva licet componere magnis*'; that is, 'if it is acceptable to compare the small with the large'. Virgil, like Horatius in his *Epistle*, argues for comparison to be conducted with balanced caution. By the early fifteenth century, however, European attitudes about comparison seem to have shifted towards a more openly sceptical perspective. John Lydgate writes, in

The Fall of Princes, 'Comparison done oft' great grievance'. And a few decades later, William Shakespeare makes a similar remark in *Much Ado about Nothing*: 'Comparisons,' says Dogberry, 'are odorous'. In the same vein, one of the most popular proverbial expressions in the German language states, '*Jeder Vergleich hinkt*', that is, there is a hitch in every comparison.

Occasionally, however, such established sceptical wisdom is contrasted by rare instances of enthusiasm about the richness of comparison. 'Shall I compare thee to a summer's day?' asks Shakespeare in his Sonnet 18. 'Thou art more lovely and more temperate'.

Perhaps a combination of the less negative attitudes about comparison from these various European traditions can serve as a useful aesthetic and philosophical guide to our exploration of the topic in the following three sections of this chapter. In the first section, 'Situating comparison in a present-day world', I relate anthropological comparison to current global conditions and then assemble and rearrange some elements from earlier methods of comparison into an updated inventory for contemporary purposes. In the second section, 'Comparing "dethroned" majorities in the collapse processes of two empires', I present case studies of 'dethroned' ethnic majorities as examples of the type of comparative analysis that I have in mind. Finally, in the 'Conclusion', I outline the Yugoslav case of the 1990s as a current field of potential application of macrocomparison and suggest some methodological conclusions.

Situating comparison in a present-day world

Any research method is to some extent a child of its time. In this volume, our discussions of the relevance of comparison for social and cultural anthropology take place in the context of a present-day world that is frequently characterized by the term 'globalization'. It is true that in many instances this term is little more than a fashionable catchword (Bourdieu 1998), a slogan that is wielded either for threat and intimidation or as an appeal for motivation and mobilization – mostly at the service of dominant social or political orders. As used in public speech or in television ads, the term's ideological and emotional connotations frequently outweigh its heuristic and analytical value. Most scholars will also agree that the world has experienced globalization of some sort not only since the end of the Cold War in 1989, but for much longer than that. For this reason, I prefer to speak of the present context as a specific phase, or the latest era, of globalization.

In spite of shortcomings and abuses, I do think there is value in a critical conceptualization of the term 'globalization' by social and cultural anthropology. Such a critical social science usage might also help us to focus on a number of processes that have an immediate impact on the issue of comparison in anthropology. For a social science understanding of today's globalization, I find the works of Ulrich Beck (1986, 1997; Beck and Beck-Gernsheim 1994), in addition to insights by Charles Taylor (1999), Anthony Giddens (1995) and

Ulf Hannerz (1992), as useful as Arjun Appadurai's admittedly fascinating analyses (1996). Beck stands in a line of thought that criticizes those ideas that hold that 'modernity' is over and done with, a thing of the past. In contrast to such naïve opinions, Beck, Taylor, and others identify today's processes of globalization as preparing the ground for new, second or alternative modernities. These processes comprise all economic, financial, political, military, media-related, ecological, social and human rights – related developments that today, with unprecedented force, speed and scope, transcend the boundaries of national states. In this perspective, the main arenas for these developments lie inside and beneath, as well as outside and beyond, national boundaries: in local, regional, international and transnational arenas and on various global levels. Taking place primarily outside and beyond the reach of national states, these processes lack any systematic form of democratic control and legitimacy. If democratic control is exerted at all, it is to a limited extent, and within the arenas of a very small number of national states.

When compared with earlier phases of globalization and modernity, these developments and contradictions represent a certain rupture. At the same time, they can be seen as leading up to two intermediate results. First, they presage the break-up of the historical alliance between capitalism, democracy and the welfare state. Although this alliance was constitutive for the rise of a first modernity in most industrialized countries of the West, it is now collapsing: capitalist globalization is less and less democratically controlled and it is less and less in need of the welfare state, which it treats as an obstacle to its own expansion. Second, the collapse of this alliance leads to an increasing shift of social burden away from welfare institutions and onto private and local networks. This shift places the burden primarily upon individuals, whose fate and future become overtaxed with risks of all kinds – professional, financial, health, safety, ecological and human rights.[3] Individualization of risk and globalization beyond the reach of democratic control are thus interrelated aspects of the same process.

If we accept this understanding of globalization and its intermediate results, a number of consequences immediately follow for anthropology. I will outline three major consequences here. First, for anthropology's analytical and research fields, national and state-related topics become less important while individual and local, as well as wider regional and global, issues gain in significance. The 'glocal' factor, as Beck (1997) calls these intertwined aspects of one and the same process, is therefore on the rise. At the same time, the significance of states as national 'containers' is diminishing, a fact that partially underlies some of the radical counterreactions in several endangered state societies: ex-Yugoslavia in the 1990s or Austria of early 2000 are only two cases in point.

Second, these globalizing relations of power only gradually bring forth their own counterforces of resistance, something like what labour movements and democratic parties were to nation-states and local capital in a first modernity. At present, global flows and relations of power largely lack their own democratic counterparts of resistance, and a reluctance to accept critical inspection and legitimate control still prevails on the global level. Citizenship is defined for the most part within national state forms, but, as Ralph Dahrendorf (1994) and others have emphasized, it is gradually being transformed: global citizenship networks such as Amnesty International, Greenpeace, Médecins sans Frontières, the international movement for a UN Declaration on the Rights of Indigenous Peoples, and a number of other human rights groups and international NGOs are part and parcel of this new, necessary and unavoidable transition towards global citizenship. So, too, I would argue, is anthropology's own current development. The Vienna meeting in September of 1998 that generated this volume, during which dozens of students and professors from at least twelve different countries worked together from morning to night for an entire week, represents an element of anthropology's transformation into a cosmopolitan intellectual branch of global citizenship.

Finally, the recognition of a dominant process of 'glocalization' has consequences for micro-anthropology and, more importantly, for a new emphasis on macro-anthropology. On the micro-anthropological level, these consequences are by now fairly familiar for students of anthropology: there is hardly any individual person or local group on the globe that is not to some degree influenced by the international flows of market forces and of the new media. Profound postcolonial upheavals of expulsion and migration connect many local groups today, through their personal relations, with other groups elsewhere on the globe. This is where Appadurai's notion of 'ethnoscapes' comes usefully into play (Appadurai 1996). On the 'micro' – the local and personal – level, the individualization of risk also results in all kinds of commodification of the body. Furthermore, it entails a new cognitive and emotional emphasis on an unpredictable and dangerous future in which anticipation and intuition become ever more important.

More significant, however, are the consequences of globalization for macro-anthropology. After all, increasing global interconnectedness relates human beings with each other in new and complex ways. Whether the anthropological mainstream recognizes it or not, this growing interrelatedness renews scholarly interest in the fundamental questions raised by anthropology since its emergence as a discipline, but too often forgotten since then – questions like, What do humans have in common? and, How do they differ?

At the same time, 'glocalization' necessitates a renewed emphasis on macro-anthropological analysis of the universal production of old and of new global phenomena such as mass hunger, mass poverty, migration or large-scale human rights violations – analyses of the sort conducted by Kirsten Hastrup and Jim Peacock in this volume. In this sense, glocalization itself demands an additional agenda of comparison, namely, the comparison of how various local societies and networks of individuals around the globe deal and interact with these processes.

Globalization thus is bringing about a renewed interest in two kinds of macrocomparative questions: a more general one about the human condition, and a more specific one about human interactions in a globalizing world. In this chapter, I am concerned with the second type of question and with its methodological challenges. Such challenges can be pursued more implicitly or more explicitly. For my part, I have come increasingly to appreciate, in recent years, the growing number of anthropological studies that focus on distant or macrocomparison displaying some explicit methodological sensitivity. The remarkable series of macrocomparative anthropological works published during the past decade or so may indeed signal a renewed relevance of macrocomparison within the discipline and beyond – a relevance that in no way negates the continuing significance of micro-anthropological comparison, of course.[4] In fact, some of the new macrocomparative work in anthropology builds directly on well-established regional (i.e. micro-) comparison. See, for example, recent inquiries into the similarities and differences between local societies in Amazonia and Papua New Guinea (Lambek and Strathern 1998).

A somewhat different type of macrocomparison in recent anthropological work is represented by the innovative approach of what might be called the macrocomparison of distant case studies. To explore similarities in the organization of cultural creativity in modern urban centres, for example, Ulf Hannerz has compared Calcutta in the mid-nineteenth century with Vienna around the turn from the nineteenth to the twentieth century, and with San Francisco of the 1950s (Hannerz 1992). By dealing with specific aspects of globalization, this type of macrocomparison is problem-oriented rather than simply interregional, an emphasis shared with most recent comparative work in feminist anthropology. Inspired by feminist anthropology's self-reflexive interest in wider parallels and variations in the human condition, these studies reflect a new and stimulating impetus for anthropological macrocomparison. Consider, for example, Margaret Lock's comparative work on concepts of menopause, suffering and death in Japan and North America (Lock 1995, 1997). This self-reflexive, critical element is one of the most important methodological contributions to comparison from feminist anthropology and has had an impact on other works as well, such as the macrocomparative anthropological analyses of nationalism. Exemplary macrocomparative studies of nationalism have been done by Bruce Kapferer in his 'Nationalist ideology and a comparative anthropology' (1989) and by Benedict Anderson in *The Spectre of Comparisons* (1998), his interdisciplinary volume on Southeast Asia's relations with the rest of the world.

All of these recent macrocomparative studies are moving beyond regional comparison, and most of them are clearly theory-inspired and problem-oriented in their focus on globalization, on female lives or on nationalism. Furthermore, some of them include a strong element of methodological self-reflexivity. I would argue that these characteristics indicate the emergence of a whole new series of macrocomparative studies in the field. Certainly the list is far from complete, but one additional work must be mentioned to give an indication of the qualitative standards and wealth of research questions explored within this new realm of macrocomparative approaches. This is Eric Wolf's last work, *Envisioning Power*, which was published shortly before his death (1999). In his emphasis on the dialectic between international influence and local or regional violence in three truly 'distant' cases (nineteenth- and twentieth-century Kwakiutl, fifteenth- and sixteenth-century Aztecs, and Nazi Germany), Wolf adds profound substance to the new macrocomparative agenda outlined above. As Richard Fox points out in this volume, however, a methodology of comparing similarities in historically and regionally distant cases was inherent in some of Wolf's earlier work, as well. In this case as in many others, then, a current trend can be seen to be building on elements from the past that to this point have represented relatively marginalized sidelines. As a working hypothesis, one may conclude that the emergence of new macrocomparative work in international anthropology represents a creative interaction with various issues of contemporary globalization. At the same time, it not only denotes a distinctive, qualitative rupture with earlier mainstream conventions about comparison in anthropology, but also retains and elaborates various earlier – but neglected – sidelines in the field.

With this working hypothesis in mind, I will now examine briefly some of the earlier conventions of comparison in anthropology in order to situate the new range of macrocomparative work in anthropology, and my own approach within it, in more explicit methodological terms. Such a recapitulation of past methods of comparison should also help us better to understand how current methods contrast against them.

For a Viennese anthropologist, discussing the old diffusionist schools of the German-speaking countries is an obvious starting point. Centred in Frankfurt around Leo Frobenius and his disciples, and in Vienna around Father Wilhelm Schmidt and his so-called Vienna school of German priests, on the one hand, and – more importantly – around Robert Heine-Geldern, on the other, these schools emphasized the comparative study of cultures worldwide and the cultural 'flows' of diffusion expressed in formal similarities between them. Apart from Heine-Geldern, most representatives of these old diffusionist schools followed extremely conservative and ideologically loaded political and research programmes. This prominent aspect of their work and influence kept a later generation of local anthropologists busy in efforts to overcome that legacy. Members of this later generation were our academic predecessors and teachers in Vienna. Their success in breaking with the old 'schools' gave my generation the liberty to occupy ourselves with radically different forms of anthropology, namely with Western European and North American critical methods and theories. Like our Scandinavian colleagues before us, we used this liberty with pragmatic flexibility to manoeuvre out of an intellectual periphery. One might argue, of course, that the old diffusionist theories and methods could still inform us – at least in bits and pieces – about the new 'diffusionist' flows of the present. Basically, however, I consider the old diffusionist methods of comparison to be obsolete (Dostal and Gingrich 1996: 265; Gingrich 1999: 160).

Turning to other, more widely appreciated, early methods of macro-anthropological comparison, we see an odd tendency in current assessments. Key publications of recent years that have dealt with anthropology's comparative legacy have restricted themselves to the local traditions of their respective editors, while largely ignoring the rest. For instance, the Blackwell *Dictionary of Anthropology*, with its embarrassingly exclusive focus on US traditions, fails even to mention comparative methods as anything other than 'a basis for constructing an evolutionary typology' (Barfield 1997: 78). I do not claim that evolutionism is as 'dead' within sociocultural anthropology as are the old diffusionist schools, but evolutionism's current comatose condition seems more closely tied to its own serious theoretical deficiencies than to the disadvantages and potentials of comparative methods in their own right.

The French *Dictionnaire de l'ethnologie et de l'anthropologie* (Bonte and Izard 1991), on the other hand, positions most other macro-anthropological methods as forerunners of Lévi-Straussian structural comparison, which is presented as the climax of anthropology's comparative record. One may well appreciate the universal, qualitative comparison of basic similarities and differences in cosmologies and kinship systems as a major advance in the discipline. I am puzzled, nevertheless, by the curious omission, in this French discussion of regional historical comparison in a Boasian tradition, of controlled comparison and, last but not least, of Louis Dumont's comparative approach to ideological systems (Gingrich 1998a).

The Routledge *Encyclopedia of Social and Cultural Anthropology* (Barnard and Spencer 1996) offers the most comprehensive discussion of the comparative method, and in this regard is of a similar quality to Ladislav Holy's (1987) reflections. Both of these publications place a particularly favourable emphasis on diverse forms of regional comparison, while sceptically reviewing sampled and complete-universe statistical comparison, including the various offspring of G.P. Murdock's work, such as the *Ethnographic Atlas* (Murdock 1967) or the Human Relations Area Files (HRAF).

This very brief overview of some recent texts and dictionary entries yields meagre and somewhat disappointing results, but does help clarify that the major trajectories in anthropology's past have all included, to varying extents, an element of comparative work. The overview also reveals the narrow cultural, linguistic and national boundaries of these recent discussions of comparison. Finally, it demonstrates that most of the conventional, formerly mainstream methods of comparative macrocomparison have to be discussed as largely obsolete remnants of an earlier time: the bygone era of anthropology's own first modernity.

Despite this generally negative assessment of previous conventions of comparative methods in macro-anthropology, I believe that a number of valuable elements from anthropology's past may be singled out and re-contextualized for the present-day purposes of anthropology's second modernity. Here, I will try to assemble and rearrange only three such neglected sidelines.

I turn first to Dumont's insistence (1994: viii) – a position supported by Laura Nader (1994) and others – that anthropologists, like any other human beings, always compare, whether they like it or not. At the very least, they compare the networks and contexts of the peoples they study with their own intellectual, social, political and cultural backgrounds (if these two do not coincide). This insight need not lead us into a dizzying hermeneutic spiral; rather, it can be incorporated into an explicit, self-reflexive and constructive application of macrocomparative methods.

Second, I would reclaim an important methodological element from anthropology's past known, since Tylor's day, as 'Galton's problem': that valid statistical comparison requires that the units compared have no mutual influence between them, no shared historical connection. This requirement means that statistical comparison of sociocultural 'units' becomes less and less possible in a world of increasingly global networks and of expanding mutual influences and flows on all levels. For today's sociocultural analysis, Galton's problem is but one of several factors that place an ever-stronger emphasis on qualitative, rather than quantitative, approaches. These are accompanied by a new awareness of the sliding scales and fuzzy boundaries that are characteristic of complex open systems (McNeill and Freiberger 1993).

Third, this renewed emphasis on qualitative comparison, which self-reflexively should include elements from one's own local society, leads me to a critical reassessment of 'controlled comparison'. In 1952, in a quite respectable attempt to reconcile the better elements of comparison in British and US anthropology, Fred Eggan presented this methodological concept for anthropology (Eggan 1954). Eggan's approach was a combination of regional, historical and macrocomparative methods. Richard Fox (this volume) interprets this synthesis primarily in terms of its application to historical and regional variation. For my part, I view Eggan's notion with a stronger emphasis on its 'controlled' and macro-anthropological dimensions. Its 'controlled' aspect refers to the careful selection of a specific and limited set of cases to be compared under identified conditions. Its macro-anthropological dimension, on the other hand, is not restricted to the sampling methods fashionable in the 1950s, but extends to the wider (but not universal) qualitative exercises of British social anthropology. My own reassessment of Eggan's concept thus leads to a methodological emphasis on selected, distant cases of controlled comparison within a medium-range perspective.

It is true that, on the whole, Eggan's presentation focused more closely on methods of micro-anthropological, historical and regional comparison than on the issues I emphasize here. A more serious shortcoming is that Eggan treated comparative methods with almost no reference to their relation with theory and epistemology. Despite these shortcomings and deficiencies, however, I think that the controlled and medium-range elements of Eggan's approach are still valuable, if rearranged and recontextualized.

It is these three elements, then, chosen from anthropology's first modernity, that I want to retain and rearrange: (1) an explicit inclusion of methodological self-reflexivity; (2) a preference for qualitative over quantitative methods; and (3) a selective, medium-range orientation of controlled macrocomparison. Taken together, and inspired by a theoretical assessment of current globalization, these form the core of an up-dated inventory that I call a methodology of *self-reflexive, controlled macrocomparison* in anthropology.

Comparing 'dethroned majorities' in the collapse processes of two empires

In the preceding section, I identified the core of a methodological approach that is inherent to several recent works in anthropological comparison, including those by Wolf, Hannerz, Lock, Kapferer and Anderson. In this section, I will attempt to demonstrate how self-reflexive, controlled macrocomparison may be applied to another set of ethnographic cases: with a comparison of the nationalist violence that occurred during the final phases and the aftermath of the decay processes of the Ottoman and Habsburg empires.[5] In 1995, Peter Schweitzer and I began to compare the decay and collapse processes of three semi-industrialized, multi-ethnic empires in the early twentieth century. Our study of the Austro-Hungarian monarchy's fall and its aftermath represents the self-reflexive element of the work: Schweitzer and I were both raised and trained in Austria, one of the successor states to that empire. At the same time, our joint comparative study includes the empires relevant to our own respective fields of regional specialization: the Ottoman (Gingrich) and the czarist (Schweitzer) empires, and their successor states. The idea of comparing these three processes is not entirely new; only recently, in fact, historians have tried to delineate what they see as parallel processes 'after empire' (Barkey and von Hagen 1997). To my knowledge, however, we are undertaking such a comparison within anthropology for the first time, and our results are likely to differ from those of historians in several ways.

This, then, is a macro-anthropological project comparing the decay of three empires in eastern, south-eastern and east Central Europe. Within this limited set of comparative cases, we investigate political and cultural processes among established ethnic majorities,[6] new proto-nations and endangered ethnic and religious minorities. Our hypothesis, inspired by recent discussions of ethnicity and nationalism in anthropology, holds that nationalism is a political and ideological process that may become especially violent under such conditions of decay and collapse. As I have stated, we embark on this comparison with the idea that globalization did not begin in 1989, but was already at work in 1914, at a time when the entire globe was, in fact, divided up into the territories of independent states and dependent colonies.

In the present chapter, I take as my focus a narrower aspect of our joint research, namely, the question of what specific political and cultural tendencies may emerge among established ethnic majorities during such processes of decay.

Without detailing the main steps of the research procedure, I will point out some intermediate results of this comparison, singling out in particular the main developments among dominant ethnic majorities during the collapse processes of the Ottoman and Habsburg empires and in their aftermaths.[7]

Before I begin, and in view of what has been argued in the first section of this chapter, I want to make a methodological remark on the interrelation of these two empires' collapse processes. Temporally and spatially, the units of this comparison display a relatively indirect and loose relationship. But the two empires were in fact related to each other throughout a long and intertwined history (Gingrich 1998b) and, specifically, through their joint participation on the losers' side of World War I. In addition, until shortly before 1914 sections of their borders met in the Balkans, and their joint territories reached from west Central Europe to the Red Sea and the Arab/Persian Gulf. This specific comparison thus comprises too large a scale of regional reference for the conventional methods of small-scale regional analysis of commonalities and variation. For statistical sampling methods, by contrast, it includes units that are too closely interrelated with each other. But for a self-reflexive controlled macrocomparison in the context of global conflict, it is perfectly reasonable to compare these collapse processes and to focus on contesting political tendencies within them.

Comparison always deals with differences as much as with parallels or similarities. In this specific comparison, it is necessary to clarify from the outset that on

Table 10.1   Primary differences in the decay and collapse processes of two multi-ethnic and semi-industrialized empires, 1916 to 1919

Primary differences	Ottoman empire	Habsburg empire
State religion	Sunni Islam	Christian Catholic
Degree of incipient industrialization	Small, very few centres	Larger, wider distribution
Labour movement	Peripheral; integrated politically into nationalist movement	Strong, well organized, independent
Political parties	Illegal or tolerated	Legal, democratic representation
Composition of other national and ethnic groups	Largely homogeneous (Arabs and Kurds) plus small minorities (e.g. Assyrians)	Largely heterogeneous (Poles, Czechs, Slovenes, Croats, Italians, etc.)
Foreign troops in core territories at the end of WWI	Large-scale interventions and fighting	Minor troop movements, no serious fighting
Domestic massacres against local minorities	Large-scale massacres against Christians in Anatolia	Attempts to mobilize (against local Slovenes) instantly prevented
Main form of previous rulers' downfall	'Young Turks' reform and Kemalist revolution	Voluntary resignation after other nations' breakaway
Orientation of majority pan-nationalism	Pan-Turkism with new Turkey as centre	Pan-Germanism with dissolution of new Austria into Germany

most levels, the differences between the two cases (within a time-span from 1915 until the late 1930s) prevail over their similarities. I outline some of these basic and structural differences in Table 10.1, where – because of the prevalence of dissimilarities – I call them 'primary differences'. They include such important factors as different degrees of incipient industrialization in the Ottoman and Habsburg empires; the absence or presence of a political labour movement and of civil institutions; a relatively heterogeneous or a more homogeneous colonial-territorial domain; a more peaceful or a more revolutionary downfall of the old leadership; the extent of foreign troop presence in local territories at the end of World War I and so on. All of these primary differences are more important than the 'secondary similarities' that also may be identified in these collapse processes. This, however, does not mean that one should not examine such secondary similarities, given a necessary degree of caution and level of abstraction.

A closer examination of these secondary similarities in fact yields remarkable results, which I list in Table 10.2. Here we see displayed a number of processual factors that were effective, with differing weight and result, in both processes of imperial decay and collapse.

Having identified and isolated these secondary factors of similarity, we may now examine their mutual and processual relation with one another, outlined in

Table 10.2   Secondary parallels in conditions and political tendencies of two 'dethroned' majorities, 1916 to 1919

Ottoman and Habsburg empires	Abstraction of secondary parallels
Majority attitudes during later phase of WWI	Increasing weariness of war while facing pressures from allied Germany and in view of growing likelihood of defeat
Empires' other nations' attitudes at end of WWI	National ('secessionist') break-away movements, supported by war opponents
Previous rulers	Lose their legitimacy also among the majority during the war; downfall towards end of WWI
Formerly dominant ethnic majority in the empire	Loses ethnic/national privileges, becomes confined to its own core territories, where some lands also are contested or taken over
Victorious former WWI opponents	Promote external interventions in core territories of majority: southern Tyrol and southern Carinthia; eastern and western Anatolia
Political rule in remainder of territory	Strong contests about new power vacuum after empire's collapse
Fighting over remainder territory's frontier	Favour radical nationalists among 'dethroned' majority
Main orientation of local nationalists	Strengthening majority 'roots'; defending core territory's 'frontiers'; reaching out for 'pan-nationalist' allies; fighting local minorities as 'collaborators' with WWI opponents, with a tendency towards mass violence against them

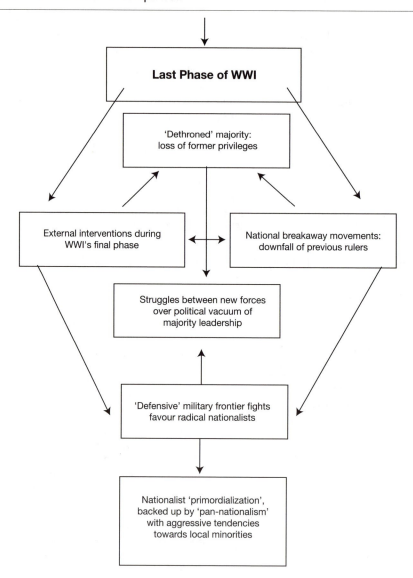

Figure 10.1 Secondary parallel factors among 'dethroned' majorities during the end phase and aftermath of World War I (the collapse of the Ottoman and Habsburg empires)

the flow diagram of Figure 10.1. This tabular and processual outcome may then be modelled into a middle-range hypothesis that deals with political and ideological tendencies among what we call 'dethroned', formerly dominant ethnic majorities' during and after the collapse of multi-ethnic, semi-industrialized empires under the conditions of global conflict.

The hypothesis can be formulated as follows: In the final phases of such imperial disintegration, and among all those heterogeneous forces that compete for power in this transitory and unstable political constellation, frontier conflicts along the remaining territory's borders tend to favour radical nationalists. The appeal made by radical nationalists to 'save the remaining parts of the homeland', including its 'cradles' of identity, becomes a powerful mobilizing force under such conditions, particularly if there is no early intervention by groups that provide an alternative to a continued war effort. In the absence of such a force or movement, a mutually reinforcing circle can arise as a dominant political and ideological force: radical nationalism favours the pursuit of frontier conflicts, and the persistence of these conflicts promotes the spread of radical nationalism. Out of this circle, the militant defence of one's alleged territorial roots, a reinvigorated cult of soldierly virility and the mobilization of hatred against the 'enemy' and its alleged local allies become successful battle cries. Another important element of ideological zeal derives from a related development: in secessionist movements, the majorities' previous ethnic and national subjects and 'underlings' are breaking away and trying to form their own political entities. Radical dethroned nationalism reacts against this conspicuous process of secession and internal decay of imperial territory with an appeal to collective feelings of humiliation among the dethroned majority, resulting in a collectively held vision of being disempowered. In reaction to this ideological sense of betrayal and disempowerment, radical nationalism seeks new allies, who are almost invariably conceived in pan-nationalist or pan-religious terms.

In this last feature, a dethroned majority's nationalism differs somewhat from other forms of nationalism. In imperial disintegration processes, radical nationalists of the ex-majorities seem to have a greater tendency to reach out for wider, allegedly natural allies, a tendency that is formulated in the terms of one or another 'pan'-ideology, but usually in those of pan-nationalism: pan-Germanism among the dethroned Austrian majority, pan-Turkism in the Ottoman decay process and pan-Slavism and Christian pan-Orthodoxism in other, more recent, cases.

In sum, the key elements of this hypothesis include the following interrelated factors: a politico-ideological circle of frontier fighting and radical nationalism; an ensuing ideological emphasis on defending 'roots' and core territories, on a soldierly virility cult and on hatred for international enemies and their local allies; a collective fear of being betrayed and disempowered; and a complementary search for new pan-nationalist allies. Based on this hypothesis, we may now take a second look at some of the key elements, in order to identify their variations within these two local and historical contexts.

In Table 10.1 I have already indicated that the search for new pan-nationalist allies evolved differently in these two cases. In the collapsing Ottoman empire and in the new Kemalist republic, its successor state, pan-nationalist sentiment regarded Asia Minor as the centre of its pan-Turkish vision. Other Turkic cultures (primarily in the Central Asian and Caucasian regions) were expected to join this centre. By contrast, in the collapsing Austro-Hungarian monarchy and its successor state, Austria, pan-Germanism did not take the tiny Austrian remainder state as its centre. From the outset, Austria's inclusion or *Anschluß* into a greater Germany was seen as the fulfilment of its pan-nationalist vision. This necessarily implied the dissolution of an independent Austria. In all its heterogeneous manifestations, then, pan-Germanism in Austria always was opposed to and fought against the existence of a separate Austrian state. Pan-Turkism, on the contrary, strove to strengthen a local Turkish state.

Radical nationalism became successful at different phases in each of these two post-imperial contexts. In Turkey it succeeded immediately after World War I; in Austria it succeeded immediately before World War II. After the First World War, the Versailles–St Germain peace treaties imposed an independent Austrian state on the government in Vienna and on the population of the remainder state, the majority of whom would have preferred an immediate *Anschluß*. The Versailles–St Germain treaties represented a serious practical setback to the ambitions of radical nationalism, which until then had enjoyed considerable popular support. Radical nationalists continued their propaganda, especially in Vienna and along Austria's eastern and southern borders, and were prepared to call for mass violence if the opportunity arose. Immediately after World War I, however, much of the populace preferred the political left and centre to radical nationalism, which had to postpone its ambitions. As Table 10.1 indicates, a major difference between the Habsburg and Ottoman empires was the presence (in the former) and the absence (in the latter) of a strong independent labour movement and of some form of civil society. Peter Schweitzer and I are convinced that this is a primary reason why, in Austro-Hungary, although attempts to mobilize for local nationalist mass violence existed, they failed completely in 1918 and the early post-war years.

By contrast, both Ottoman patriotism and Turkish nationalism contributed to the much weaker character of the labour movement and of democratic parties in Turkey. Local massacres had occurred in Ottoman Turkey as early as World War I, particularly in the east, where the czarist army had invaded parts of the territory between Erzurum and the border between the Ottoman and czarist empires. Local Christian minorities, who had already been used as pretexts for the exertion of international pressure against the Ottomans throughout the nineteenth century, now were accused of conspiring with the enemy. With the tacit approval of German and Austro-Hungarian military advisors in Istanbul, a first series of ethnic massacres occurred even before the imperial collapse. At the end of World War I and in its aftermath, however, massacres of the Christian minorities in Asia Minor reached a terrible and unprecedented climax. Between 1916 and 1921, radical Turkish nationalism could build on the ideological syndrome of 'danger at our immediate borders' by pointing out the allegedly causal role of local minorities in that danger. Mass-scale slaughter, carried out to some extent by Ottoman (Turkish, Kurdish, Arabic) and Kemalist republican soldiers, but also by civilians (Turkish in the west, Kurdish in the east of Asia Minor), was the awful consequence. Particularly in western Anatolia before and during the Anglo-Greek invasion, there was, in fact, some obvious local Greek minority sympathy and collaboration with the invading forces. A cruel wave of 'ethnic cleansing' and, later, the so-called population exchange between Greece and Turkey followed.

As I have pointed out, nothing of that kind happened at first in the Austrian remainder state. Radical nationalism was kept at bay on an international level by the Versailles–St Germain treaties and locally by labour and other civil forces among the dethroned, German-speaking and largely Catholic population of Austria. After all, the Austrian parts of the former empire had the strongest democratic and labour traditions, and as a result radical nationalism remained weak, but angry. (This had to do not only with defeat in the war and with the empire's integration; it was also related to the fact that through the peace treaties, Austria lost to Italy the southern Tyrol, as much a 'cradle of identity' for Austria – though not for Germany – as Kosovo is for Serbia.) With an eye on this nationalist anger, democratic parties in Austria, including the Socialists, continued to uphold and propagate some kind of Anschluß idea themselves until the early 1930s. In 1934, a coup d'état and an ensuing civil war were launched by Austrian Catholic fascist groups (modelled after Franco's and Mussolini's movements), which crushed and banned all democratic institutions and labour organizations. Political apathy and resignation became the dominant mood and attitude of the general populace, which had been intoxicated by local pan-Germanism for at least two decades and was now ready to abandon support for any local state leadership whatsoever.

And so an invigorated pan-Germanism began to succeed in Austria, especially after 1933/34, when the Nazi variant of pan-Germanism came to power in Berlin under the Austrian Adolf Hitler. At the centre of its explicit political programme, Hitler's pan-Germanism actively appealed for revenge for the alleged humiliations of World War I, an appeal that took on quite different meanings in the relatively recently unified German state and in the Viennese remainder state of the Habsburg empire, respectively. In Austria, the appeal for revenge for the 'humiliation of 1918' reactivated a collective emotion of having been 'dethroned' from ethnic superiority, and local 'cosmopolitan' minorities existed who could be blamed for having 'caused' that fragmentation and amputation. No memory of such a 'dethroned' ethnic majority existed in Germany, but Austria had plenty of such memories: at the time of Austria's Anschluß to Germany in March 1938, everyone thirty years old or older had lived through the end of World War I and its aftermath. Nazi pan-Germanism, with its cult of nationalist virility and its seductive appeal for retaliation for past humiliations, fell on particularly fertile ground in Austria, where it had been invented.

This comparison of secondary similarities between the two former empires may lead us, then, towards a more profound understanding of the events in Vienna of March and November 1938. In March, hundreds of thousands of Viennese enthusiastically greeted the German invasion army in the streets of the capital city. In November, mass riots against the local Jewish population exploded with more violence than anywhere else in the Nazi territories of the time.

Vienna is actually one of the twentieth-century's 'reddest' cities of Europe, with socialist voting majorities in almost every democratic election throughout the century. But paradoxically, perhaps, Vienna was also the site of one of the most sinister mass pogroms carried out under the Nazi regime. Elsewhere in the Third Reich the November pogrom of 1938 – the so-called *Reichskristallnacht* – was instigated and supervised from above by the Nazi leadership. In Vienna this attack on the Jewish population, then one of the largest in the world, was carried out so viciously and aggressively from below that local Nazi leaders themselves were stunned and even had to hold back the mob.

With these observations I do not intend to make a causal or comparative statement about the singular and unique, thus *incomparable*, crime against humanity, the Holocaust. I do want, however, to point out some of the background to one of the key events preparing the grounds for it, namely, the local massacres, raids and outbreaks of mass violence in Vienna of November 1938. Writing in the same city almost exactly sixty years after these events, I regard them here in terms of their secondary parallels to the atrocities against Armenians and Assyrians in eastern Anatolia between 1917 and 1921.

In both cases of imperial decay, radical nationalism, supported by a wider pan-nationalist ideology, won over general political opinion and the ideological mainstream within the deposed and dethroned ethnic majorities. Such a constellation of militant 'dethroned' nationalism that reaches out for pan-nationalist allies and defends alleged 'roots' and 'cradles of identity' can easily turn into an enactment of mass violence against local minorities. I call the flow of events resulting from this kind of constellation a process of nationalist 'primordialization'. During the inevitable contests for power within a fragmented state, nationalist cults of militancy, virility and revenge are turned against local minorities of different religious and linguistic affiliations, who are portrayed as 'inner enemies', conspiring with the rest of the world against the (pan-)nation. In the end, the energy generated by the sense of humiliation, by the lust for revenge and by ethnic hatred exploded into widespread massacres against local minorities in both these cases of nationalist primordialization.

Conclusion

In the first part of this chapter, I presented the argument that the present phase of globalization requires a reconsideration of comparison in anthropology. After a critical review of comparative approaches from anthropology's first modernity, I proceeded to identify the core elements of a methodology of self-reflexive, controlled macrocomparison. I then applied this method, inspired by current research in anthropology, to two historical cases from an earlier period of globalization. This comparison of the decay processes of the Habsburg and Ottoman empires and their aftermath led to a discussion of the secondary parallels among these processes.

Finally, out of these parallels, I formulated a middle-range hypothesis about the decay and collapse processes of semi-industrialized, multi-ethnic empires that runs like this: in the absence or failure of clear alternatives, and particularly if frontier issues of the remainder territory are at stake, then sooner or later during these processes, the 'dethroned' ethnic majorities will become susceptible to radical nationalism and to pan-nationalist ideologies. Combining racist nationalism with cults of militant virility and violent appeals for revenge against the alleged perpetrators of previous humiliations and betrayals, these forces will tend to mobilize for mass violence against local ethnic, religious or linguistic minorities as so-called inner enemies in order – and this is the point – to stabilize their own, new and still fragile leadership.

In conclusion, I want to examine how this hypothesis may be tested out for the decay process of former Yugoslavia and explore what we could learn for anthropology's comparative methods from this exercise.[8]

The case of ex-Yugoslavia may indeed be analysed along similar lines as another instance of a semi-industrialized, multi-ethnic empire, but with even more caution and reservation than was needed for our first set of cases. Let us briefly consider some of the main differences. In the early twentieth century, the Habsburg and Ottoman empires were monarchies with their own long colonial histories. In the late twentieth century, Yugoslavia was formally a federal republic of a post-Titoist socialist orientation. Having emerged only fairly recently in the Balkans out of the ruins of the Habsburg and Ottoman empires, Yugoslavia had no external colonial record whatsoever. Internally, however, it displayed a certain amount of ethnic and religious heterogeneity, combined with a dominant Serbian influence in army, politics and administration. In terms of industrialization and democratic institutions, Yugoslavia also exhibits more differences than commonalities when contrasted against the Habsburg and Ottoman empires. Certainly, Yugoslavia of the late twentieth century was far more industrialized than the German-speaking parts of the Habsburg empire had been before 1918, and officially, at least, the labour movement was in power in the form of post-Titoist communism. Politically, a restricted amount of democracy was combined with central bureaucratic control throughout the federation. Finally, the disintegration of the Yugoslav state and the secession (or independence) of Slovenia, Croatia, Macedonia and Bosnia were not accompanied by the simultaneous collapse of the regime in Belgrade, unlike the cases of the old empires' disintegration, in which the previous Habsburg and Ottoman leadership was brought down as well.

Even this brief overview will indicate that in its historic foundations, its political and economic organization and its regional position, the case of ex-Yugoslavia represents far more differences than commonalities with our first two cases. Even more important is the distinctive international element that complements these 'primary differences'. Yugoslavia had played an explicit, and vital, non-aligned role in the bipolar world of the Cold War, and it owed at least some of its previous internal coherence to this international dynamic.

Any comprehensive macrocomparison that includes ex-Yugoslavia will of course have to go into much greater detail than I am able to do here. It nevertheless seems fairly safe to suggest one likely outcome of such a comparison, under the methodological premises adopted in this chapter. That outcome, while emphasizing and confirming many 'primary differences' between ex-Yugoslavia's collapse and the disintegration of the Habsburg and Ottoman empires, would still illuminate a number of secondary (or even 'tertiary', for that matter) parallels.

As I have indicated, in the aftermath of the Cold War ex-Yugoslavia lost much of the internal cohesion which had been partly owed to that global constellation. In a matter of years, Slovenia, Croatia and Macedonia seceded from Yugoslavia and declared their independence, supported from the beginning by diplomatic efforts of some EU countries, including Germany and Austria. Only much later did other Western countries such as France and the USA join in (not without some initial hesitation) with their own support for secessionist independence. In this context, the Yugoslav remainder state certainly appeared to be territorially amputated, at least to those interested in its maintenance. Inside ex-Yugoslavia, the former Serbian majority had become a 'deposed' and 'dethroned' majority, some of whose former allies and dependent nations (Slovenia, Macedonia, Croatia) had broken away. Outside the borders of the remainder state, in Croatia and Bosnia, the Serbian population was no longer part of an unchallenged, dominant ethnic majority; instead, Serbs found themselves in a new minority position ringed by unstable and contested borders.

Under the conditions of primary, concrete and specific differences, therefore, main elements of our comparative hypothesis seem to apply to the case of Yugoslavia's collapse and disintegration. Among the many groups competing for power in Belgrade, those forces were successful who mobilized a 'deposed' and 'dethroned' ethnic majority's latent radical nationalism and primordialization. Appeals for revenge and retaliation channelled mass feelings of anger about the 'ingratitude' of seceding subjects and about alleged humiliations suffered at their hands. A cult of militant virility helped to focus these energies on a defence of one's 'own' borders. In the escalating violence, it was this Serbian cult of militant border virility that led to a wholesale onslaught of dishonouring and raping Muslim (Bosnian, Albanian) women. Violence, warfare and massacres against the 'inner enemies' – the non-Serbian minorities along the new and contested borders – combined with elements of 'pan'-ideologies: in this case, pan-Serbianism, pan-Slavism (towards Russia) and pan-Orthodoxism (towards Russia and Greece). In an only slightly altered form, therefore, all the key elements of our comparative hypothesis are conspicuously present in this case, as well.

One major difference on this more abstract level of comparison relates to the context in which foreign military intervention occurred in the Yugoslav case. In the Habsburg and Ottoman collapse processes, victorious powers of the 'hot' war – World War I – invaded imperial territories at the end of the war. National secession of these (Polish, Czechoslovakian ...) territories was favoured at the same time, as part of the winners' war effort. In the Yugoslav case, the winners of the Cold War only gradually became supportive of territorial secession from Yugoslavia, and then only in an effort to further deconstruct the remains of post-Titoist communism. Similarly, major Western military powers only became active locally against Serbian forces after Serbian troops and militias had turned to extreme acts of ethnic cleansing, first in Bosnia and (to a much lesser extent) in Croatia, and later on in Kosovo.

Even with regard to the effects of foreign military intervention, however, there are some remarkable parallels between Turkey at the end of World War I and Yugoslavia at the end of the Cold War. In both cases, the 'deposed' majority was seduced into resorting to 'ethnic cleansing' in its border areas. In both cases, international military intervention took place under the declared purpose of stopping such ethnic cleansing. Similarly, it would seem that in both cases these international military operations were quite futile in this regard, and actually became counter-productive in so far as they promoted and accelerated local nationalist violence.

To sum up this exploratory comparison, the Yugoslav disintegration process seems largely to confirm our hypothesis on 'dethroned' majorities in collapsing, semi-industrialized and multi-ethnic empires: whenever radical nationalism is successful and frontier issues are at stake, these majorities tend to resort to pan-ideological constructions, to be easily manipulated by nationalist appeals for retaliation against alleged conspiracy and humiliation, and to channel these manipulated feelings, through cults of virility, into hatred of local minorities against whom mass violence is directed.

Of course, such processes are interactive, whereas this comparison has focused primarily on one element in the interactive process, namely the mobilized nationalist forces among dethroned ethnic majorities. To consider other forces in such interactive processes, Peter Schweitzer and I have suggested that it would be important to differentiate the groups that, under these conditions, become the targets of a deposed majority's ethnic cleansing. Smaller and more dispersed minorities such as the Jews of Vienna or the Assyrians of eastern Anatolia, for instance, are rarely in a position to strive for local autonomy or secession. This both imposes and opens up different strategies for dealing with such situations, to a specific range of urban and rural 'weapons of the weak' (Scott 1985). Larger and territorially more coherent minorities, on the other hand, such as the Armenian and Greek populations of Turkey at the end of World War I or the Albanians of Kosovo at the end of the Cold War, tend to develop their own variants of territorial nationalism. This spectrum of new 'large minority nationalism' is frequently supported by neighbouring 'mother-lands' (Armenia, Greece and Albania in these cases). In these situations, factions within such large minority nationalisms may easily become as intolerant and violent as the enemy's 'dethroned majority' primordialization.

The intermediate results of an ongoing research process thus support a number of empirically grounded concepts that have the potential to enrich anthropology's theories of nationalism and ethnicity. These concepts relate specifically to the middle-range context of semi-industrialized, multi-ethnic empires and their processes of collapse and disintegration. If these processes take certain identifiable political and military turns, then considerable portions of the population will become susceptible to the seductions of radical nationalism. Gradually, the 'dethroned' ethnic majority may embrace a variant of pan-ideological, militant primordialization, with a particularly aggressive potential against local minorities. Some of these minorities, in turn, may develop 'large minority nationalism' with the backing of a 'motherland', while the more dispersed among such minorities might have to resort to using some form of the weapons of the weak.

This macrocomparison therefore results in the identification of the following three basic concepts:

1   'Dethroned' or deposed ethnic majorities' radical and pan-ideological, nationalist 'primordialization'.
2   'Large minority nationalism' with motherland back-up.
3   Dispersed minorities' weapons of the weak.

These conclusions lead us back full circle to the methodological issues raised in the first section of this chapter. The methodology of self-reflexive, controlled macrocomparison is conceived here as informing flexible, qualitative and open research processes. At its best, the result of applying it is the formulation of medium-range concepts with a twofold potential: empirical and theoretical.

As regards their theoretical potential, the concepts resulting from macro-comparison must be assessed in terms of their contribution to the existing theoretical inventory. This contribution may be supplementary or critical. In anthropology, the existing theoretical inventory has largely focused on nationalism in Western Europe and North America and, to a much lesser degree, on nationalism in selected postcolonial societies of Asia, Africa and Latin America. Until now, however, anthropological theory has hardly considered some of the most violent instances of nationalism in the twentieth century, which are situated in Europe's semi-industrialized periphery. In theoretical terms, therefore, the concepts resulting from the present comparison are designed to be both supplementary *and* critical, to help bridge a serious theoretical gap.

As far as their empirical potential is concerned, such medium-range concepts have to be assessed in terms of their 'complementary' explanatory power. By 'complementary', I here mean 'in addition to particular' (ethnographic, historical, etc.) analyses. Empirically, the value of such comparative concepts lies in their potential to identify and explain other dimensions of specific local-global processes and to situate specific local-global processes in wider contexts more effectively than 'thick' or 'finely textured' descriptions and analyses alone were able to carry out.

Far-reaching consequences are implied, whether an anthropological analysis limits itself to considering only specific and particular factors, or whether it is capable of moving beyond such limits. It does make a difference to our understanding of the processes when an ethnographic analysis brings the wider potentials of 'dethroned majorities' into the picture, whether analysing the Kosovo conflict, the 1938 Vienna pogroms or, for that matter, the emergence of the Ku Klux Klan in the southern USA after the Civil War.

Most importantly, such comparative concepts help to minimize the danger that ethnographic analysis itself might follow the same logic that nationalism constantly propagates and reiterates: the logic of essentializing. In these as in any other ethnographic contexts, the 'substance' and 'essence' of the particular local–global process are not everything (Gingrich 1998a). There are wider tendencies and deeper logics at work here than those observable at the empirical surface, however lovingly the ethnographer might try to comprehend that surface. It is precisely out of this epistemological perspective that qualitative anthropological macrocomparisons, like most other comparative efforts, must first of all acknowledge and respect empirical variation and primary differences before moving on to explore processual and structural parallels or differences behind the scenes.

The anthropological methodology of self-reflexive, controlled macrocomparison is a flexible, qualitative, open research process with the goal of developing concepts for middle-range contexts. Empirically and theoretically, this methodology has the potential to enrich anthropology's critical inventory and to create better explanations of the upheavals and paradoxes in a globalizing world.

Notes

1 For discussions of first drafts of this chapter or some of its sections, I thank Richard Fox (New York), Jürg Helbling (Zurich), Joan O'Donnell (Santa Fe), Peter Schweitzer (Fairbanks, Alaska) and Ulrike Sulikowski (Vienna). The second part of this chapter is based on a joint research project by Peter Schweitzer and myself (see note 5). We both gratefully acknowledge the valuable advice and support which the late Eric Wolf gave us in 1996 discussions of our presentation of this work, when he encouraged us to move on with our comparative anthropological analysis of collapsing empires. I dedicate this chapter to the memory of Eric Wolf.

2 For my qualification of the term 'ethnic majority', see note 6, below.

3 Beck's notion of 'risk' (1986) was criticized by some North American and Western European critics, who ironically labelled it as being derived from a particularly Germanic attitude towards safety, order and control. My own local background, of course, is Viennese society, which has developed a substantial reputation – or notoriety – for being much more disorderly and far less punctual than German society. Nevertheless, I do wonder if Beck's critics were not somewhat too enthusiastic in their obvious support of Reaganist and Thatcherist risk standards. It can hardly be denied that today, *new* risks are continually being placed on the individual: these range from the threats of forest fires in Indonesia to the high rates of crime in East Los Angeles, from losing entirely or profiting hugely from one's London or Sydney

investments, from a local worker's job security in Berlin or Palermo to a local citizen's chances of staying alive in Kinshasa, Rangoon or Soweto, and on to the risks of being – or not being – arrested, tortured, raped or killed in Pristina, Baghdad or Asunción. The individualization of risks, in my view, is not the manifestation of an aberrant Germanic obsession but a disturbingly global phenomenon.

4   On the contrary, various new approaches such as studying historical variation or regional commonalities and differences remain an elementary part of anthropology's comparative tool-kit (see Fox, Desveaux and Kuper, this volume). I hope to have contributed to these approaches by studying, for instance, state relations with local social groups in northern Yemen between the seventeenth and early twentieth centuries (Gingrich 1993).

5   This elaborates one specific aspect of a joint research project by Peter Schweitzer (University of Alaska, Fairbanks) and myself. Peter Schweitzer and I began work on this project in March 1995, when he visited at the School of American Research (SAR) in Santa Fe, New Mexico, where I was a Weatherhead Resident Scholar in 1994/95. During the same academic year, we continued our joint research on the subject when I visited for a week in Fairbanks. Both of us gratefully acknowledge the support from SAR. That first essential phase of work resulted, in September 1995, in a presentation at the biannual meeting of the German-speaking anthropological societies in Vienna (Gingrich and Schweitzer 1995). In 1996, we discussed the text of our Vienna presentation with Eric Wolf (see note 1). In August 1998 we met again in Vienna to elaborate this research through a step-by-step analysis that is summarized in Tables 10.1–10.2 and Figure 10.1 of this chapter.

6   I use the term 'ethnic majority' here in a sense opposite to the frequently referenced 'ethnic minority', i.e. as a shorthand for those linguistic and cultural groups in polyethnic empires whose representatives largely control the state and its legal, administrative, financial, military and educational institutions. By 'majority', therefore, I mean in this chapter a hegemonic position and relationship of power and not necessarily a demographic quantification.

7   The following summaries of the two decay processes build on a variety of historical and ethnohistorical studies. For the collapse of the Austro-Hungarian monarchy and its aftermath, I rely primarily on Galántai (1979), Rauchensteiner (1994), Schorske (1981), Talos et al. (1988) and Wheatcroft (1996). For the decay of the Ottoman empire and related issues, I refer to Fromkin (1989), Inalcik (1994), Karpat (1973), Kayali (1997), Landau (1995), McCarthy (1983) and Poulton (1997).

8   For the following section, I rely primarily on Bringa (1995), Calic (1995), Hagen (1999), Little and Silber (1995) and Malcolm (1996).

Bibliography

Anderson, B. (1998) *The Spectre of Comparisons: Nationalism, Southeast Asia and the World*, London and New York: Verso.

Appadurai, A. (1996) *Modernity at Large: Cultural Dimensions of Globalization*, Minneapolis: University of Minnesota Press.

Barfield, T. (ed.) (1997) *The Dictionary of Anthropology*, Oxford: Blackwell.

Barkey, K. and Von Hagen, M. (1997) *After Empire: Multi-Ethnic Societies and Nation-Building: The Soviet Union and the Russian, Ottoman and Habsburg Empires*, Boulder, CO: Westview Press.

Barnard, A. and J. Spencer (eds) (1996) *Encyclopedia of Social and Cultural Anthropology*, London and New York: Routledge.

Beck, U. (1986) *Risikogesellschaft: Auf dem Weg in eine andere Moderne*, Frankfurt a.M.: Suhrkamp.

—— (1997) *Was ist Globalisierung? Irrtümer des Globalismus–Antworten auf Globalisierung*, Frankfurt a.M.: Suhrkamp.

Beck, U. and Beck-Gernsheim, E. (eds) (1994) *Riskante Freiheiten*, Frankfurt a.M.: Suhrkamp.

Bonte, P. and Izard, M. (eds) (1991) *Dictionnaire de l'ethnologie et de l'anthropologie*, Paris: Presses Universitaires de France.

Bourdieu, P. (1998) *Acts of Resistance: Against the Tyranny of the Market*, New York: The New Press.

Bringa, T. (1995) *Being Muslim the Bosnian Way: Identity and Community in a Central Bosnian Village*, Princeton, NJ: Princeton University Press.

Calic, M.-J. (1995) *Der Krieg in Bosnien-Herzegowina: Ursachen-Konfliktstrukturen-Internationale Lösungsversuche*, Frankfurt a.M.: EVA.

Dahrendorf, R. (1994) 'Das Zerbrechen der Ligaturen und die Utopie der Weltgesellschaft', in U. Beck and E. Beck-Gernsheim (eds) *Riskante Freiheiten*, Frankfurt a.M.: Suhrkamp.

Dostal, W. and Gingrich, A. (1996) 'German and Austrian anthropology', in A. Barnard and J. Spencer (eds) *Encyclopedia of Social and Cultural Anthropology*, London and New York: Routledge.

Dumont, L. (1994) *German Ideology: From France to Germany and Back*, Chicago: University of Chicago Press.

Eggan, F. (1954) 'Social anthropology and the method of controlled comparison', *American Anthropologist* 56: 743–63.

Fromkin, D. (1989) *A Peace to End all Peace: Creating the Modern Middle East, 1914–1922*, London: Andre Deutsch.

Galántai, J. (1979) *Die Österreichisch-Ungarische Monarchie und der Weltkrieg*, Budapest: Corvina.

Giddens, A. (1995) *Die Konsequenzen der Moderne*, Frankfurt a.M.: Suhrkamp.

Gingrich, A. (1993) 'Tribes and rulers in northern Yemen', in A. Gingrich, S. Haas, G. Paleczek and T. Fillitz (eds), *Studies in Oriental Culture and History: Festschrift for Walter Dostal*, Frankfurt, New York and Paris: Peter Lang.

—— (1998a) 'Towards an anthropology of Germany: a culture of moralist self-education?', *Current Anthropology* 39, 4: 567–72.

—— (1998b) 'Frontier myths of orientalism: the Muslim world in public and popular cultures of central Europe', in B. Baskar and B. Brumen (eds) *Ljubljana: MESS, Mediterranean Ethnological Summer School*, vol. II: 99–127.

—— (1999) *Erkundungen: Themen der ethnologischen Forschung*, Vienna: Böhlau.

Gingrich, A. and Schweitzer, P. (1995) 'Ethnizität und Nationalismus als Prozesse: zu Zerfall und Nachfolgekämpfen poly-ethnischer Grossreiche', paper presented at Vortrag auf der Tagung der deutschsprachigen Ethnologinnen und Ethnologen, Vienna, 25–9 September.

Hagen, W. (1999) 'The Balkans' lethal nationalisms', *Foreign Affairs* 78, 4: 52–64.

Hannerz, U. (1992) *Cultural Complexity: Studies in the Social Organization of Meaning*, New York: Columbia University Press.

Holy, L. (ed.) (1987) *Comparative Anthropology*, Oxford: Basil Blackwell.

Inalcik, H. with Quataert,D. (ed.) (1994) *An Economic and Social History of the Ottoman Empire, 1300–1914*, Cambridge: Cambridge University Press.

Kapferer, B. (1989) 'Nationalist ideology and a comparative anthropology', *Ethnos* 54, III–IV: 161–89.

Karpat, K.H. (1973) *An Inquiry into the Social Foundations of Nationalism in the Ottoman State: From Social Estates to Classes, from Millets to Nations*, Princeton, NJ: Princeton University Press.

Kayali, H. (1997) *Arabs and Young Turks. Ottomanism, Arabism and Islamism in the Ottoman Empire, 1908–1918*, Berkeley, CA: University of California Press.

Lambek, M. and Strathern, A. (eds) (1998) *Bodies and Persons: Comparative Perspectives from Africa and Melanesia*, New York: Cambridge University Press.

Landau, J.M. (1995) *Pan-Turkism: From Irredentism to Cooperation*, Bloomington and London: Indiana University Press.

Little, A. and Silber, L. (1995) *Bruderkrieg: Der Kampf um Titos Erbe*, Graz, Vienna and Cologne: Böhlau.

Lock, M. (1995) *Encounters with Aging: Mythologies of Menopause in Japan and North America*, Berkeley, CA: University of California Press.

—— (1997) 'Displacing suffering: the reconstruction of death in North America and Japan', in A. Kleinman, V. Das and M. Lock (eds) *Social Suffering*, Berkeley, Los Angeles and London: University of California Press.

McCarthy, J. (1983) *Muslims and Minorities: The Population of Ottoman Anatolia and the End of the Empire*, New York and London: New York University Press.

McNeill, D. and Freiberger, P. (1993) *Fuzzy Logic: The Revolutionary Computer Technology that Is Changing our World*, New York: Touchstone.

Malcolm, N. (1996) *Bosnia: A Short History*, London: Chaptermac.

Murdock, G.P. (1967) 'Ethnographic Atlas: a summary', *Ethnography* 6: 110–11.

Nader, L. (1994) 'Comparative consciousness', in R. Borofsky (ed.) *Assessing Cultural Anthropology*, New York: McGraw-Hill.

Poulton, H. (1997) *Top Hat, Grey Wolf and Crescent: Turkish Nationalism and the Turkish Republic*, New York and London: New York University Press.

Rauchensteiner, M. (1994) *Der Tod des Doppeladlers: Österreich-Ungarn und der Erste Weltkrieg*, Graz, Vienna and Cologne: Styria.

Schorske, C.E. (1981) *Fin-de-Siècle Vienna: Politics and Culture*, New York: Vintage.

Scott, J.C. (1985) *Weapons of the Weak: Everyday Forms of Peasant Resistance*, Princeton, NJ: Yale University Press.

Tálos, E., Hanisch, E. and Neugebauer, W. (eds) (1988) *NS-Herrschaft in Österreich 1938–1945*, Vienna: Verlag für Gesellschaftskritik.

Taylor, C. (1999) 'Two theories of modernity', *Public Culture* 11, 1: 153–74.

Wheatcroft, N. (1996) *The Habsburgs: Embodying Empire*, London: Penguin.

Wolf, E.R. (1999) *Envisioning Power: Ideologies of Dominance and Crisis*, Berkeley, CA: University of California Press.

Index